DEPARTMENT OF ECONOMIC AND SOCIAL AFFAIRS

WORLD ECONOMIC AND SOCIAL SURVEY 2001

TRENDS AND POLICIES IN THE WORLD ECONOMY

UNITED NATIONS • NEW YORK, 2001

Note

Symbols of United Nations documents are composed of capital letters combined with figures.

E/2001/50/Rev.1

ST/ESA/276

ISBN 92-1-109137-3

PREFACE

Events in the last year have shown how quickly the pace of economic growth can turn around in a few countries and then, through trade and financial linkages, affect the economic prospects of large parts of the world economy.

The economic slowdown in the United States since early 2001 has been much more pronounced and widespread than most analysts expected. And it has radiated out to a large number of countries, both developed and developing, in particular those that rely heavily on the export of high-technology products.

Indeed, the **World Economic and Social Survey 2001** *shows that just as the benefits of globalization can be spread widely and quickly when the business cycle is on the upswing, so the transmission of adverse shocks can be very rapid, dramatically altering, in a very short time, the outlook for sustainable growth throughout the world economy.*

Part II of the **Survey** *examines the question of vulnerability. Some countries feel that their economic fortunes are hostage to the interplay of impersonal market forces. Some are frequent victims of natural disasters, such as floods and earthquakes. Many others, such as landlocked nations or countries with economies in transition, face more specific obstacles to full engagement in world financial and trade relations. But whatever the reason for their vulnerability, the danger is all too real that their development efforts will be significantly set back.*

The poor and vulnerable of our world must not be relegated to the margins or made to suffer from the risk-taking of others. The United Nations and its specialized agencies are continuing their efforts to ensure that globalization works for all people. The **World Economic and Social Survey 2001** *suggests that this and other important development goals will be met only with greater global solidarity. I heartily endorse that conclusion and commend to the widest possible readership the analysis and information presented in this volume.*

KOFI A. ANNAN

Secretary-General

FOREWORD

Part one of the present edition of the ***World Economic and Social Survey*** chronicles how the very positive developments in output and international trade, with reasonably buoyant levels of international finance for emerging markets for the first half of 2000, turned into retrenchment. The ongoing downturn in the business cycle in developed countries has been unusual in a number of respects, when contrasted with previous downturns in the post-war period. It has arrived at a time of a protracted upturn with, towards the end, still sizeable productivity gains with low inflation and low levels of unemployment particularly in North America and to some degree in Western Europe as well. The substantial slowdown in levels of economic activity in the world's major economies, which threatens to continue well into the second part of 2001, has been dragging growth prospects of many developing countries and economies in transition.

The slowdown in the pace of economic activity in major developed economies, largely on account of excess investments and product inventories in manufacturing, has shrunk their import demand, thus compressing the opportunities for export from developing countries and economies in transition. The pace of growth in world trade in 2001 is expected to be less than half that recorded in 2000, with at best a slight improvement anticipated for 2002.

The initial downturn has been concentrated in information and communication technologies (ICT) product-related sectors, gradually spreading into user sectors as well. This has been exerting particularly pronounced effects on developing countries with a significant presence in markets for ICT products and services. The impact on countries in East Asia is especially pronounced. The downturn has worsened conditions in financial markets, making foreign investors more cautious than they were once the recovery from the 1997-1998 crises had got under way. This has restricted the ability of many developing countries and economies in transition to finance their imports and, indeed, their broader development needs. This factor has affected a number of economies, particularly in Latin America. Most African countries are less affected by the ongoing adjustments in the world economy, though they remain vulnerable to downturns in commodity prices, which might be pronounced if the current adjustments were to take longer and spread further than currently appears on the horizon. Oil-exporting countries continue to benefit from high oil prices, though the reduction in export volumes is weakening the stimulus these countries received during the strong performances of 1999-2000. As the Western European economy weakens so does the outlook for most economies in transition.

Since early 2001, monetary policy has been loosened in virtually all developed countries, in some cases by an appreciable margin. Its impact on investment and consumption behaviour has so far been constrained, however, given the nature of the ongoing business cycle. Financial markets remain jittery and real interest rates, particularly at the longer end of the maturity spectrum, have remained high.

Looking ahead, the short-term outlook is for the present downturn to be modest, that is to say, there will be no recession in any major economy—except perhaps Japan, but for its very own adjustment circumstances. Once excess investments will have been written off and inventories worked down, a recovery is expected to get under way, perhaps towards the end of the year, going into 2002. The economic recovery should, once again, result in significant output growth, though a strong upturn in real trade volumes is likely to take somewhat longer to materialize.

However, given the imbalances in the world economy, inter alia, in trade and current accounts, and the related tasks confronting policy makers throughout the world, significant downside risks remain. The economic outlook is therefore for prudence, caution and alertness, rather than for a great deal of optimism or unwarranted pessimism.

In recent years, part two of the *Survey* has examined an aspect of globalization. This will be a major unifying theme of our Department's work in the years ahead. This year we have sought to examine the relationship between vulnerability and globalization. Many individuals in different countries are vulnerable to the effects of an economic downturn and certain countries, especially small island economies, are vulnerable to the economic disruption caused by environmental and ecological factors such as flooding, hurricanes and drought. Part two of the *Survey* looks at some examples of vulnerability in the context of globalization, with the discussions focusing on: how the liberalization of financial markets can bring benefits to individual countries, but only if a proper regulatory framework has been put in place beforehand; how trade shocks can be absorbed and whether their possibility reduces the potential gains from trade; how three small landlocked transition economies survived the shocks arising from the collapse of the centrally planned system; and how a country can cope with a recurrent and, to some extent predictable, natural disaster—flooding. The insights from these chapters should help the international community as it confronts the issues of vulnerability and globalization. I would particularly like to thank Professor Jagdish Bhagwati, who is the Department's adviser on globalization, for his intellectual guidance of this work.

Nitin Desai

Nitin Desai
Under-Secretary-General
for Economic and Social Affairs

CONTENTS

PART ONE. STATE OF THE WORLD ECONOMY

Page

ANNEX

BOXES

TABLES

FIGURES

EXPLANATORY NOTES

The following symbols have been used in the tables throughout the report:

.. **Two dots** indicate that data are not available or are not separately reported.

– **A dash** indicates that the amount is nil or negligible.

- **A hyphen (-)** indicates that the item is not applicable.

- **A minus sign (-)** indicates deficit or decrease, except as indicated.

. **A full stop (.)** is used to indicate decimals.

/ **A slash (/)** between years indicates a crop year or financial year, for example, 1990/91.

- **Use of a hyphen (-)** between years, for example, 1990-1991, signifies the full period involved, including the beginning and end years.

Reference to "tons" indicates metric tons and to "dollars" ($) United States dollars, unless otherwise stated.

Annual rates of growth or change, unless otherwise stated, refer to annual compound rates.

In most cases, the growth rate forecasts for 2001 are rounded to the nearest quarter of a percentage point.

Details and percentages in tables do not necessarily add to totals, because of rounding.

The following abbreviations have been used:

ACC	Administrative Committee on Coordination
ACIS	Advanced Cargo Information System (UNCTAD)
AIDS	acquired immunodeficiency syndrome
ASEAN	Association of Southeast Asian Nations
ASYCUDA	Automated System for Customs Data (UNCTAD)
BIS	Bank for International Settlements (Basel)
bpd	barrels per day
bps	basis points
BSEC	Black Sea Economic Cooperation
BSFF	Buffer Stock Financing Facility (IMF)

CAC	collective action clause
CAEC	Central Asian Economic Community
CCFF	Compensatory and Contingency Financing Facility (IMF)
CCL	Contingent Credit Line (IMF)
CET	common external tariff
CFA	Communauté financière africaine
CFF	Compensatory Financing Facility (IMF)
c.i.f.	cost, insurance and freight
CIS	Commonwealth of Independent States
CMEA	Council for Mutual Economic Assistance
COMTRADE	United Nations External Trade Statistics Database
CPI	consumer price index
CRED	Centre for Research on the Epidemiology of Disasters (Belgium)
DAC	Development Assistance Committee (of OECD)
DRAM	dynamic random-access memory
EAP	Enhanced Access Policy (IMF)
EBRD	European Bank for Reconstruction and Development
ECA	Economic Commission for Africa
ECB	European Central Bank
ECE	Economic Commission for Europe
ECLAC	Economic Commission for Latin America and the Caribbean
ECM	External Contingency Mechanism (IMF)
ECO	Economic Cooperation Organization
ECOWAS	Economic Community of West African States
EFF	Extended Fund Facility (IMF)
EMU	European Economic and Monetary Union
ENSO	El Niño/Southern Oscillation
EPZ	export-processing zone
ESAF	Enhanced Structural Adjustment Facility (IMF)
EU	European Union
EURIBOR	Euro Interbank Offered Rate
FAO	Food and Agriculture Organization of the United Nations
FDI	foreign direct investment
f.o.b.	free on board
FTAA	Free Trade Area of the Americas
GATT	General Agreement on Tariffs and Trade
GDP	gross domestic product

GIEWS	Global Information and Early Warning System for Food and Agriculture (FAO)
GNP	gross national product
GSP	Generalized System of Preferences
GST	goods and services tax
GUUAM	alignment of Georgia, Ukraine, Uzbekistan, Azerbaijan and Republic of Moldova
GWP	gross world product
HICP	Harmonized Index of Consumer Prices
HIPC	heavily indebted poor countries
HIV	human immunodeficiency virus
ICP	International Comparison Project
ICT	information and communication technologies
IDA	International Development Association
IEA	International Energy Agency
IFC	International Finance Corporation (World Bank)
ILO	International Labour Organization
IMF	International Monetary Fund
INTRASTAT	system of data collection for intra-EU trade
IPCC	Intergovernmental Panel on Climate Change
IPO	initial public offering
ISDR	International Strategy for Disaster Reduction
M&A	mergers and acquisitions
mdu	million dozen units
MERCOSUR	Southern Cone Common Market
MFN	most-favoured nation
NAFTA	North American Free Trade Agreement
Nasdaq	National Association of Securities Dealers Automated Quotations System
NBER	National Bureau of Economic Research (Cambridge, Massachusetts)
NCAR	National Center for Atmospheric Research (Boulder, Colorado)
NMP	net material product
NPL	non-performing loan
NTBs	non-tariff barriers to trade
ODA	official development assistance
OECD	Organisation for Economic Cooperation and Development
OFDA	Office of United States Foreign Disaster Assistance
OPEC	Organization of the Petroleum Exporting Countries
pb	per barrel
ppp	purchasing power parity
PRGF	Poverty Reduction and Growth Facility (IMF)
Project LINK	international collaborative research group for econometric modelling, coordinated jointly by the Development Policy Analysis Division of the United Nations Secretariat, and the University of Toronto
PRSCs	Poverty Reduction Support Credits (World Bank)
PRSP	Poverty Reduction Strategy Paper (IMF and World Bank)
QR	quantitative restriction
SAF	Structural Adjustment Facility (IMF)
SDRs	special drawing rights (IMF)
SEZ	special economic zone
SFF	Supplementary Financing Facility (IMF)
SITC	Standard International Trade Classification
SMEs	small and medium-sized enterprises
SOE	State-owned enterprise
SRF	Supplemental Reserve Facility (IMF)
STD	sexually transmitted disease
STF	Systemic Transformation Facility (IMF)
TNC	transnational corporation
TRACECA	Transcaucasus transportation corridor
UNCTAD	United Nations Conference on Trade and Development
UNDP	United Nations Development Programme
UN/DESA	Department of Economic and Social Affairs of the United Nations Secretariat
UNEP	United Nations Environment Programme
UNFPA	United Nations Population Fund
UNICEF	United Nations Children's Fund
UNU	United Nations University
VAT	value-added tax
VER	voluntary export restraint
WAEMU	West African Economic and Monetary Union
WFP	World Food Programme
WHO	World Health Organization
WIDER	World Institute for Development Economics Research
WMO	World Meteorological Organization

The designations employed and the presentation of the material in this publication do not imply the expression of any opinion whatsoever on the part of the United Nations Secretariat concerning the legal status of any country, territory, city or area or of its authorities, or concerning the delimitation of its frontiers or boundaries.

The term "country" as used in the text of this report also refers, as appropriate, to territories or areas.

For analytical purposes, the following country groupings and sub-groupings have been used:[a]

Developed economies (developed market economies):

Europe, excluding the European transition economies
Canada and the United States of America
Japan, Australia and New Zealand.

Major developed economies (the Group of Seven):

Canada, France, Germany, Italy, Japan, United Kingdom of Great Britain and Northern Ireland, United States of America.

European Union:

Austria, Belgium, Denmark, Finland, France, Germany, Greece, Ireland, Italy, Luxembourg, Netherlands, Portugal, Spain, Sweden, United Kingdom of Great Britain and Northern Ireland.

Economies in transition:

Central and Eastern European transition economies (CEETEs, sometimes contracted to "Eastern Europe"):

Albania, Bulgaria, Czech Republic, Hungary, Poland, Romania, Slovakia and successor States of the Socialist Federal Republic of Yugoslavia, namely, Bosnia and Herzegovina, Croatia, Slovenia, the former Yugoslav Republic of Macedonia, Yugoslavia.

Baltic States

Estonia, Latvia and Lithuania.

Commonwealth of Independent States (CIS)

Armenia, Azerbaijan, Belarus, Georgia, Kazakhstan, Kyrgyzstan, Republic of Moldova, Russian Federation, Tajikistan, Turkmenistan, Ukraine, Uzbekistan.

Developing economies:

Africa

Asia and the Pacific (excluding Japan, Australia, New Zealand and the member States of CIS in Asia)

Latin America and the Caribbean.

Sub-groupings of Asia and the Pacific:

Western Asia plus Islamic Republic of Iran (commonly contracted to "Western Asia"):

Bahrain, Cyprus, Iran (Islamic Republic of), Iraq, Israel, Jordan, Kuwait, Lebanon, Oman, Qatar, Saudi Arabia, Syrian Arab Republic, Turkey, United Arab Emirates, Yemen.

Eastern and Southern Asia:

All other developing economies in Asia and the Pacific (including China, unless listed separately). This group has in some cases been subdivided into:

China

South Asia: Bangladesh, India, Nepal, Pakistan, Sri Lanka
East Asia: all other developing economies in Asia and the Pacific.

Sub-grouping of Africa:

Sub-Saharan Africa, excluding Nigeria and South Africa (commonly contracted to "sub-Saharan Africa"):

All of Africa except Algeria, Egypt, Libyan Arab Jamahiriya, Morocco, Nigeria, South Africa, Tunisia.

For particular analyses, developing countries have been subdivided into the following groups:

Net-creditor countries:

Brunei Darussalam, Kuwait, Libyan Arab Jamahariya, Oman, Qatar, Saudi Arabia, Singapore, Taiwan Province of China, United Arab Emirates.

Net-debtor countries:

All other developing countries.

Fuel-exporting countries:

Algeria, Angola, Bahrain, Bolivia, Brunei Darussalam, Cameroon, Colombia, Congo, Ecuador, Egypt, Gabon, Indonesia, Iran (Islamic Republic of), Iraq, Kuwait, Libyan Arab Jamahiriya, Mexico, Nigeria, Oman, Qatar, Saudi Arabia, Syrian Arab Republic, Trinidad and Tobago, United Arab Emirates, Venezuela, Viet Nam.

Fuel-importing countries:

All other developing countries.

Least developed countries:

Afghanistan, Angola, Bangladesh, Benin, Bhutan, Burkina Faso, Burundi, Cambodia, Cape Verde, Central African Republic, Chad, Comoros, Democratic Republic of the Congo (formerly Zaire), Djibouti, Equatorial Guinea, Eritrea, Ethiopia, Gambia, Guinea, Guinea-Bissau, Haiti, Kiribati, Lao People's Democratic Republic, Lesotho, Liberia, Madagascar, Malawi, Maldives, Mali, Mauritania, Mozambique, Myanmar, Nepal, Niger, Rwanda, Samoa, Sao Tome and Principe, Senegal, Sierra Leone, Solomon Islands, Somalia, Sudan, Togo, Tuvalu, Uganda, United Republic of Tanzania, Vanuatu, Yemen, Zambia.

The designation of country groups in the text and the tables is intended solely for statistical or analytical convenience and does not necessarily express a judgement about the stage reached by a particular country or area in the development process.

STATE OF THE WORLD ECONOMY

I   THE WORLD ECONOMY IN 2001

With recovery from the 1997-1998 international financial crises still incomplete, the world economy is experiencing another setback in the form of a significant decline in the growth of global output and trade. While the previous global economic slowdown was set off by financial turmoil in some developing countries and economies in transition, this one started with a retrenchment in economic activity in the developed economies, particularly the United States of America, during the second half of 2000. The slowdown, which initially emerged in only a few economies, has since broadened and intensified. Although the spillover effects to and among developing countries and economies in transition have so far been less than the contagion witnessed during the 1997-1998 crises, the short-term growth of these countries, as well as their longer-term development, is already being adversely affected.

Earlier forecasts pointed to a slowdown in global economic growth for the second half of 2000, but the rapidity, breadth and depth of the declines had not been envisaged. From over 4 per cent in 2000, the growth of gross world product (GWP) is expected to slow to about 2½ per cent in 2001 (see table I.1), in contrast to the 3½ per cent that was forecast in the previous United Nations assessment of the economic situation in the world economy.[1] The expansion of international trade is also expected to decelerate, to 5½ per cent in 2001 from about 12 per cent in 2000. Only a slight improvement is anticipated for 2002, with the growth of GWP at about 3 per cent and of world trade at some 6½ per cent.

While there are a number of further downside risks, the probability of a global recession is not considered to be high. The policy responses in major developed economies since the beginning of 2001, including reductions in interest rates and fiscal stimuli, have produced cautious optimism that the slowdown in global growth will end by late 2001. Moreover, since inflation worldwide is benign, and the fiscal position in many major economies has been improved, there is room for further policy stimulus if the situation deteriorates more than anticipated. In addition to arresting the growing spillovers from the slowdown as promptly as possible, policy makers also have to address the risks posed by the large external imbalances among nations that have accumulated over the past decade. More generally, there remains a need for further reform of the global trading system and the international financial architecture in order to facilitate development by securing less volatile and more balanced world economic growth in the long run.

[1] *World Economic Situation and Prospects, 2001* (United Nations publication, Sales No. E.01.II.C.2), chap. I.

Table I.1.
GROWTH OF WORLD OUTPUT AND TRADE, 1992-2002

Annual percentage change											
	1992	1993	1994	1995	1996	1997	1998	1999	2000[a]	2001[b]	2002[b]
World output[c]	1.8	1.4	3.0	2.7	3.2	3.5	2.2	2.9	4.1	2.4	3
of which:											
Developed economies	1.7	0.9	2.8	2.3	2.7	3.0	2.5	2.8	3.6	1.9	2½
Economies in transition	-11.8	-6.7	-7.2	-0.6	-0.1	2.2	-0.7	3.0	6.1	3.6	4
Developing economies	4.8	5.2	5.6	5.0	5.7	5.4	1.6	3.5	5.7	4.1	5¼
World trade	5.7	4.6	10.5	8.6	5.5	9.2	3.3	5.2	12.3	5.5	6½
Memorandum items:											
World											
Number of countries with rising											
per capita output	74	68	100	110	122	122	104	102	123	127	..
Number of countries in sample	140	145	145	145	145	145	145	145	145	145	..
Developing economies											
Number of countries with rising											
per capita output	57	54	65	73	81	77	62	58	73	79	..
Number of countries in sample	95	95	95	95	95	95	95	95	95	95	..
World output growth with PPP-based weights[d]	2.1	1.9	3.9	3.5	3.9	4.1	2.6	3.3	4.7	3.0	..

Source: Department of Economic and Social Affairs of the United Nations Secretariat (UN/DESA).

Note: Two dots (..) indicate that data are not available.

[a] Partly estimated.
[b] Forecast, based in part on Project LINK.
[c] Calculated as a weighted average of individual country growth rates of gross domestic product (GDP), where weights are based on GDP in 1995 prices and exchange rates.
[d] Employing an alternative scheme for weighting national growth rates of GDP, based on purchasing power parity (PPP) conversions of national currency GDP into international dollars.

EVOLUTION OF THE CURRENT ECONOMIC SLOWDOWN

The current weakness of the world economy stems from several interrelated developments in the past year; these factors will also be the main determinants of global economic growth in the short term.

The cycle of monetary policy

The slowdown was triggered by escalating monetary tightening in major developed economies, particularly the United States. In the late 1990s, the economy of the United States was growing at a pace that policy makers perceived to be unsustainable, as indicated by an increasingly tight labour market, growing external deficits, negative household savings, and high levels of private sector debt. It was widely feared that, if left unattended, these pressures would result in an acceleration in inflation, followed by a rapid deceleration in growth. In mid-1999, the United States Federal Reserve began to tighten monetary policy with the aim of moderating demand in order to pre-empt a resurgence of inflation and engineer a "soft landing". Central banks in most other developed economies followed the same course and, globally, interest rates were raised by 150 to 200 basis points (bps) within a year. Monetary policy in most developed economies maintained this stance until at least the end of 2000 and in the euro zone, until May 2001.

As more signs of a sharper-than-desired slowdown emerged in the beginning of 2001, many developed countries started to ease monetary policy by reducing policy interest rates. As with the earlier tightening, the Federal Reserve led this adjustment, with five cuts in interest rates, totalling 250 bps, in the first five months of the year. The ongoing monetary easing in more and more developed economies should moderate the slowdown in the global economy. However, the lag between a reduction in interest rates and its effects on the economy is normally at least six months, suggesting that a recovery is unlikely to occur before the second half of 2001.

The collapse in global equity markets

The majority of world equity markets registered substantial losses in 2000 and during the first quarter of 2001. By March 2001, the United States National Association of Securities Dealers Automated Quotations System (Nasdaq) index, which is heavily weighted by technology shares, had fallen by more than 65 per cent from its peak a year earlier. The downturn also spread to broader United States stock indices, to most other developed country stock markets and to many smaller equity markets, with many Asian emerging market countries suffering the most.

The declining values in global equity markets had an adverse impact on consumer and investment sentiment, leading to reduced consumption and corporate investment. There had previously been fears of a large correction in equity prices and its consequences, particularly in the United States where equity prices had risen rapidly for a number of years. The nature and magnitude of the negative wealth effect on consumers and the adverse consequences for business investment since mid-2000 have been similar to earlier simulations of the consequences of a collapse of major equity markets for world economic growth.[2] The deceleration in business investment in the United States has, however, been even sharper than the magnitudes earlier simulated.

The collapse in the value of technology stocks has also reduced the availability of funding for business investment, in particular initial public offerings (IPOs) for technology companies. The supply of venture capital funds for start-up companies has contracted rapidly, in part because the decline in equity values has inhibited the recycling of funds, but also because investors have become more risk-averse.

Strains have also built up in other financial markets. Corporate borrowing tightened in the second half of 2000, as yield spreads in bond markets rose and banks raised their standards for business loans, particularly in the United States. Yield spreads for external borrowing by developing countries also widened markedly. International bond issuances by major developing countries and economies in transition faltered in the last quarter of 2000, falling to their lowest level since the 1995 crisis in Mexico. However, this was largely because

[2] See, for example, *World Economic and Social Survey, 1999* (United Nations publication, Sales No. E.99.II.C.1), box I.2.

of the economic and political turmoil in Argentina and Turkey. For other developing countries, the financial "contagion" effects have been limited, largely because many of these borrowers are perceived by lenders as being less risky than previously, having reduced their short-term external debt and expanded their foreign exchange reserves since the 1997-1998 crisis. The more flexible exchange-rate regimes adopted over the past two years by many of these economies have also made them less vulnerable to speculative attacks.

Consolidation in the technology sector

For the United States and many other developed economies, investment in the information and communication technologies (ICT) sector grew at 30-40 per cent annually in the late 1990s and was the driving force for their strong overall economic performance. Particularly through trade, it was also the major impetus for economic recovery in several developing countries and economies in transition. In the United States, the economy-wide diffusion of ICT contributed to a rise in productivity growth; in other developed economies, the effect to date has been less because their ICT-investment surge started later.

The ICT revolution appears to be in a period of consolidation. The development of new applications for existing technologies has lagged the pace of ICT capacity-building in recent years and a number of ICT-based businesses have failed to meet original high expectations. For example, many e-retailing businesses either have gone out of business, are on the brink of bankruptcy or are struggling for survival. As a result, investment spending on ICT in the United States was almost flat in late 2000 and early 2001.

However, some analysts argue that the slow development of new ICT applications, especially for consumers, and the unsatisfactory e-business results were due to inadequate investment in some dimensions of ICT: in particular, the lack of bandwidth, or speed of telecommunications over networks, has been seen as a bottleneck that is curbing new applications for consumers and businesses. The technology for broadband transmission is available, but it needs to be built into the infrastructure; this requires more investment spending than most telecommunication service providers can currently mobilize because of their debt from heavy investment spending over the past decade.

ICT will continue to be a driving force for the global economy in the medium to long run, but the duration of the current adjustment and consolidation in the ICT sector in major developed economies is unknown. The advent of the ICT-based "new economy" does not imply that the behaviour of investment in ICT differs from the pro-cyclical nature of business investment in general and therefore does not imply that the business cycle is extinct.

New features of the business cycle

For the past few decades, recessions in the United States were consistently preceded by a surge in inflation as imbalances built up during the upswing led to price pressures. The current slowdown in the United States was not preceded by a major increase in prices because inflation was muted by productivity growth, generally declining prices for most commodities other than oil, the strengthening of the dollar and the growing trade deficit.

At the same time, some analysts believe that the advent of the "new economy" has reduced the links among growth, inflation and the policy response that characterized previous business cycles. This is because the "new economy" has been fostered by the dynamics of corporate profit, the availability of credit, and investment spending, making these factors the key determinants of the new business cycle. During the boom period until the first half of 2000, corporate profits in the United States grew on average at a double-digit annual pace, investment finance was readily available on good terms and business confidence was high. A number of years of rapid growth in new technology sectors prompted a widespread belief that the trend could continue and the number of investors and the quantity of investment in these sectors grew very rapidly.

Correspondingly, the factors behind the slowdown were the interrelated decline in corporate profits, the tightening of credit conditions, and the decrease in investment spending. As a result of the excessive, or imbalanced, investment in the leading sectors, expected profits failed to materialize. The tightening of monetary policy (as a result of fears of overheating and in an effort to curb asset inflation) and the collapse in equity prices caused credit conditions to deteriorate. This combination of factors, rather than an acceleration in core inflation, caused business confidence to decline and brought the investment boom to an end, precipitating the slowdown.

The recent experience suggests that the shift from "boom" to "bust" may be much faster in the present environment than in the conventional cycle. Firms may take aggressive actions to restore profits by reducing labour inputs, trimming inventories and cutting capital spending, causing other firms and economic agents to lower their expectations about future earnings. Fragile stock markets are also likely to decline further in response to the worsening earnings' projections, causing a broader deterioration in consumer and business sentiment and tightening conditions in credit markets. The initial slowdown in manufacturing (a "supply" shock) is thus magnified and spread to both consumer and business spending, becoming a "demand" shock that exacerbates the initial slowdown.

At the same time, the prevailing tight labour market in the United States and improved inventory controls in manufacturing may cause the duration of the slowdown to be shorter than in previous cycles. Because of the costs of re-hiring, employers may opt in the first instance for reduced working hours rather than outright lay-offs if they expect the downturn to be short-lived. Similarly, with the exception of the excesses associated with the technology bubble, the application of new technologies probably means that inventories are smaller than in earlier cycles, especially in manufacturing. Both features suggest that the duration of the downturn will be shorter than usual.

Looking further ahead, however, the recovery may not be as rapid as the downturn because, once lost, business confidence may not improve as quickly as it deteriorated. This is partly because it is likely to take some time to adjust to the excess capacity that has been created by the high rate of investment in the technology sectors. On the other hand, this excess investment has been concentrated in only a few sectors and investment by "old economy" firms should continue to respond in the conventional manner.

Some analysts have questioned the effectiveness of monetary policy in these circumstances. Reductions in interest rates and the consequential easing in credit conditions are unlikely to have an impact on investment in the technology sectors until perceptions about future profits have improved, although they may have some beneficial effects on investment in other sectors and should also bolster consumption expenditure. At the same time, the consequences of lower nominal interest rates in a period of low and stable inflation may differ from the pattern followed when inflation was high and volatile. In the latter circumstances, changes in monetary policy have a direct effect on inflation and inflationary expectations and therefore on the real interest rate and the level of investment. In an environment of low and stable inflation, monetary policy is less important as a determinant of the real interest rate and may have less impact on business and consumer confidence. In either event, its effectiveness as a policy instrument would be reduced.

The virtuous circles that characterized the transmission mechanisms both within and between the real and financial sectors during the upswing phase of the "new economy" are now better understood. However, there is less clarity about these interactions—and particularly the lags involved—during a downturn. The rapid downturn is widely expected to be short-lived and followed by a commensurately speedy recovery, but the possibilities of either a more extended or a deeper slowdown or a slower recovery cannot be ruled out (see below). Moreover, just as elements of the "old economy" continue to coexist with the "new economy", so elements of the old business cycle will complement the features that characterize the new cycle. It is this intersection of the old and the new that gives rise to the unusual degree of uncertainty about short-term prospects and complicates the task of policy makers.

The role of higher oil prices

Since early 2000, prices of oil have been higher than for several years and these increased prices have been gradually feeding into the world economy by lowering consumer welfare in oil-importing countries and reducing the profits of non-oil sectors. In September 2000, the price of oil reached nearly 40 dollars per barrel (pb), its highest level in a decade. Every sharp rise in oil prices since the early 1970s (such as in 1973-1974, 1979-1980 and 1990-1991) that was sustained for a period of 6 to 12 months has triggered a significant slowdown in growth, or even a recession, in many developed economies because of the sudden downward shift in consumer and business sentiment. This may be a factor in the present slowdown and, on this occasion, may be more widespread because of the higher oil-intensity of output in developing countries and economies in transition.

Although oil prices have softened since the beginning of 2001, two cuts in production quotas by the Organization of the Petroleum Exporting Countries (OPEC) in early 2001 reduced the likelihood of a substantial fall in oil prices, something that otherwise might have provided support to global economic growth.

Deceleration in crisis-affected economies

Even without the above factors, global growth was expected to decelerate in 2001 because a moderation in growth was anticipated for many developing countries and economies in transition that were recovering from the financial crises of 1997-1998. In particular, the double-digit annual rate of growth achieved by many of the crisis-affected countries between 1999 and mid-2000 was not expected to be sustained. Reflationary policies were not expected to be continued and the strong impetus from external demand since early 1999 was forecast to diminish. Policy makers and observers hoped that the deceleration in growth could be stabilized at a sustainable rate.

The slowdown in the major developed economies since late 2000 has, however, exacerbated the slowdown in these economies. Many of them remain fragile: domestic recovery is not on firm ground, post-crisis financial restructuring has proceeded slowly, and the corporate sector is still overly indebted. Although less vulnerable to external financial shocks than a few years ago, many developing countries and economies in transition remain subject to external demand shocks when their exports have to compete in markets of major developed economies that are undergoing a substantial slowdown.

Other factors

In addition to the above, other, more regional and local, factors have exerted adverse effects on some economies. Several countries have suffered from severe earthquakes and droughts. Escalated military conflicts and political turmoil in some regions and within some countries have substantially impeded economic activity and reduced incomes for the countries involved. The outbreak at epidemic levels of bovine spongiform encephalopathy (informally known as mad cow disease) and that of foot-and-mouth disease in Western Europe have been sizeable supply-shocks for some economies and continue to pose a threat for international trade and tourism. Finally, the energy shortages that have developed in Brazil and in California, an economically important region of the United States, may have a measurable negative impact on growth in those countries.

PROSPECTS FOR THE GLOBAL ECONOMY

The short-term outlook for the global economy depends to a large extent on the path of the recovery in the developed countries, most particularly the United States. It also depends on the consequent developments in international markets and on the ability of developing countries and economies in transition to absorb the resulting negative external shocks. The vulnerability of these economies to the weaker external conditions depends not only on how closely they are linked to the major economies, but also on the robustness of their domestic economic structures and the soundness of their economic policies. Many developing countries and economies in transition adjusted their policies in the first half of 2001 to strengthen domestic demand and this should mitigate the adverse external impulses to some extent.

The international economic environment

Along with the downturn in the growth of global output, the international economic environment has deteriorated since late 2000, particularly for many developing countries and economies in transition. The main features of the worsening in international economic conditions, however, differ from those during the 1997-1998 international financial crises.

The degeneration of the international economic environment for many developing countries and economies in transition in 1997-1998 was characterized by a sudden and contagious outflow of foreign capital, placing these economies in a balance-of-payments liquidity crisis. These countries initially faced mainly an external financial shock; the other negative developments—such as slower growth of international trade, lower commodity prices, devalued currencies, and worsened terms of trade—were a fallout from the initial financial shock.

In contrast, the most important element in this slowdown has been the external shock to real demand as a result of the sharp deceleration in international trade led largely by the retrenchment in the import demand of the United States. International trade, rather than international financial flows, has been the main channel transmitting the slowdown in the United States to the rest of the world. While there has also been some impact through other international linkages, such as stagnating private capital flows, rising risk premiums on external financing for some developing countries, and softening commodity prices, the magnitude and scope of these effects have been much less than in the previous global slowdown. The highly correlated simultaneous sell-off in equity markets worldwide during 2000 and early 2001, however, was more severe than in 1997-1998.

In the near-term outlook, the growth of **international trade** is expected to decline sharply. The import demand of the United States, which had grown at a double-digit pace for the past few years and served as a driving force for the recovery of many developing countries from the 1997-1998 crises, registered a significant decline in the first quarter of 2001. As a result, many economies that have close trade connections to the United States, such as those in the Americas and South-East Asia, face a slowdown in their export demand.

Weakening world demand has led to lower prices for many *primary commodities*. Although a replay of the sharp deflation in the prices of almost all commodities during the 1997-1998 crises is not likely, the prices of many non-fuel commodities, particularly agricultural products, are still lower than before the Asian crisis. Commodity-exporting developing countries face the problems of both a downward trend in commodity prices in the long run and high volatility in the short run. Many small, low-income economies face not only the problem of mitigating the short-run volatility in international commodity markets but also the challenge of diversifying their product mix in a period of increasingly specialized global production.

In addition to the deterioration in the international trading environment, the large trade imbalances across major countries, especially the large trade and current-account deficits of the United States, pose a challenge for policy makers. Over the past decade, unbalanced growth among the world's major economies has led to a continuous increase in these external deficits, which reached about $450 billion, or 4.5 per cent of the United States gross domestic product (GDP), in 2000. Despite the decline in import demand of the United States since mid-2000, these deficits are expected to remain high. An abrupt reversal of these deficits would have major deflationary consequences for the world economy and would involve substantial changes in the exchange rates among major currencies (see the last section of the present chapter and box I.1).

Instability in **exchange rates** has increased since late 2000, with many currencies depreciating against the United States dollar. However, the scale of these devaluations has been less than during the previous round of crises. Among the major currencies, the United States dollar has once again appreciated markedly vis-à-vis the Japanese yen and the euro, in spite of the slowdown in the United States economy, its lower interest rates, and its large trade deficit. As indicated above, the short-term prospects for the world economy are critically dependent on how and when the dollar will reverse its trend of appreciation and the reduction in its external deficits will finally begin.

For many developing countries and economies in transition, the trend towards polarized exchange-rate regimes (either a fully floating rate or a fixed peg or similar arrangement, such as a currency board system) continues. Countries with intermediate regimes are facing more pressures, with Turkey as the country most recently forced to abandon its crawling peg. There is no general optimal rule for the selection of an exchange-rate regime, particularly for developing countries and economies in transition, as the trade-off between the stability and flexibility of an exchange-rate regime is always inextricably linked to other domestic policies and to the institutional framework, both of which are specific to individual economies. It remains to be seen which regime will fare better in the current global slowdown.

The global slowdown has also been accompanied by worsening **external financing** conditions for developing and transition economies. Net private capital flows to emerging markets have stagnated at levels that are lower than those prior to the Asian crisis. While foreign direct investment (FDI) flows have remained stable, they continue to be concentrated in relatively few developing economies. Meanwhile, risk premiums on funds raised in international capital markets by developing countries and economies in transition have increased since the second half of 2000, although they vary from country to country as international investors pay increasing attention to differences in economic conditions among economies. The monetary easing in major developed countries should improve conditions for external financing by developing countries and economies in transition, but external funds for these economies will remain limited in relation to their needs.

The slowdown in global economic growth

From 3.6 per cent in 2000, aggregate GDP growth for the **developed economies** is expected to decelerate to 1.9 per cent in 2001, followed by a rebound to 2½ per cent in 2002 (see table I.2). Although the slowdown in the United States has been the most pronounced within this group, a general weakening became more prominent in many other developed economies in early 2001.

A recession (that is to say, a decline in GDP for two consecutive quarters) is not expected in the United States, but growth for 2001 is forecast to be only 1.8 per cent, compared with 5 per cent in 2000, with a recovery in 2002 to 3 per cent. The deceleration in the United States in the second half of 2000 was extraordinary: growth of GDP dropped from 5.6 per cent in the second quarter

Table I.2.
DEVELOPED ECONOMIES: RATES OF GROWTH OF REAL GDP, 1998-2002

Annual percentage change[a]					
	1998	1999	2000[b]	2001[c]	2002[c]
Developed economies	2.5	2.8	3.6	1.9	2½
United States of America	4.4	4.2	5.0	1.8	3
Canada	3.6	4.5	4.7	2.8	3½
Japan	-1.1	0.8	1.7	0.7	1¼
EU-15[d]	2.8	2.4	3.3	2.6	3
EU-12[e]	2.7	2.4	3.4	2.7	3

Source: UN/DESA, based on International Monetary Fund (IMF), *International Financial Statistics.*

a   Calculated as a weighted average of individual country growth rates of gross domestic product (GDP), where weights are based on GDP in 1995 prices and exchange rates.
b   Partly estimated.
c   Forecast.
d   Member States of the European Union (EU).
e   Euro zone countries.

of that year to 1 per cent in the fourth quarter. The monetary easing since the beginning of 2001 is expected to support a rebound in late 2001, while tax reductions are expected to provide some stimulus to growth in 2002.

The Japanese economy is also having a dampening effect on the outlook for the developed economies. It grew 1.7 per cent in 2000, but indicators point to a slowdown in a broad range of economic activities since the beginning of 2001. GDP is expected to grow by less than 1 per cent in 2001, and only marginally higher in 2002. Household demand, depressed by unfavourable employment and income conditions, remains the weakest sector in the economy. The negative wealth effects of the decade-long deflation in equity and property prices have also curbed consumer spending. At the same time, structural problems (including the mounting volume of non-performing loans in the financial sector, excess capacity in the corporate sector, and the large government debt) continue to bear negatively on other components of aggregate demand.

Compared with Japan and the United States, many developed economies in **Europe** initially remained relatively resilient with respect to the slowdown, but signs of further weakening emerged as 2001 progressed. After registering 3.4 per cent in 2000, growth in the **euro zone** economies is expected to moderate to 2.7 per cent in 2001, before recovering to about 3 per cent in 2002. Weaker external demand, particularly on account of the United States slowdown, the earlier increases in oil prices and depressed equity values in these economies, continues to exert a negative impact. Tax cuts in many of these countries are expected to provide some support for economic growth and the European Central Bank (ECB) reduced its policy interest rate by 25 bps in May 2001, the first easing after the previous cycle of tightening. The extent of the deceleration in GDP growth is expected to vary considerably among countries, with the result that the convergence in growth rates and in other macroeconomic magnitudes observed over the past few years in the euro zone is likely to be reversed.

A moderation in growth is also taking place in **other European economies**, such as Denmark, Sweden and Switzerland. GDP growth for 2001 in these countries is anticipated to be significantly below the achievements of 2000 as their exports are expected to slow significantly, not only because of lower growth elsewhere but also because of the appreciation of their currencies against the euro. The impacts of the external slowdown on the United Kingdom of Great Britain and Northern Ireland and of the appreciation of its currency vis-à-vis the euro were not significant in early 2001, but a broader-based deceleration in growth over the course of 2001 is unavoidable.

There was also a slowdown in Australia and Canada and, to a lesser extent, in New Zealand in early 2001. Declining investment spending in the former two economies led the slowdown. Monetary policy in both countries was eased rapidly, and a tax reduction in Canada is expected to provide additional support for domestic demand.

The outlook for the group of **the economies in transition** points to growth's slowing from 6.1 per cent in 2000 to about 3.6 per cent in 2001 and to a figure only slightly higher in 2002 (see table I.3). Most of the driving forces behind the strength of the past year have either faded or been reversed. The weakening external environment does not bode well for many of these economies.

In 2000, the economies of the **Commonwealth of Independent States (CIS)** experienced its best collective economic performance since the beginning of the transition. For the first time in a decade, all the CIS countries registered positive growth, mainly as a result of higher prices of oil and gas and the depreciated Russian rouble. With the prices of oil expected to soften and the effects of the rouble devaluation fading, growth for the region is expected to fall from 7.9 per cent in 2000 to about 3.7 per cent in 2001. Meanwhile, structural reforms in the region remain challenging and the outcome is uncertain.

Table I.3.
ECONOMIES IN TRANSITION: RATES OF GROWTH OF REAL GDP, 1998-2002

Annual percentage change[a]					
	1998	1999	2000[b]	2001[c]	2002[c]
Economies in transition	-0.7	3.0	6.1	3.6	4
Central and Eastern Europe	2.5	1.4	4.0	3.5	3¾
Baltic States	4.6	-1.7	5.0	4.8	5¼
Commonwealth of Independent States	-3.7	4.7	7.9	3.7	4
of which: Russian Federation	-4.9	5.4	8.3	3.5	4

Source: UN/DESA and Economic Commission for Europe (ECE).

[a] Calculated as a weighted average of individual country growth rates of gross domestic product (GDP), where weights are based on GDP in 1995 prices and exchange rates.

[b] Partly estimated.

[c] Forecast, based in part on Project LINK.

The performance of the three **Baltic** economies and **Central and Eastern Europe** in 2000 was driven largely by strong external demand from the European developed economies and the Russian Federation. As external demand from Western Europe is expected to moderate, growth in these economies will need to rely more on domestic demand. GDP growth for Central and Eastern Europe is expected to be about 3½-3¾ per cent for 2001-2002 and for the Baltic countries, 5 per cent. The easing of monetary policy and progress with economic restructuring are likely to boost investment gradually.

The economic performance of many **developing economies** in 2000 was encouraging, as 73 out of 95 developing countries that are regularly monitored by the United Nations Secretariat recorded rising per capita GDP, compared with 58 in 1999 (see table I.4). As a result, the proportion of the population living in countries that experienced declining per capita output shrank to 7.4 per

Table I.4.
DEVELOPING COUNTRIES: GROWTH OF PER CAPITA GDP BY REGION, 1998-2001

	Number of countries monitored	Decline in GDP per capita				Growth of GDP per capita exceeding 3 per cent			
		1998	1999	2000[a]	2001[b]	1998	1999	2000[a]	2001[b]
Frequency of high and low growth of per capita output (number of countries)									
Developing countries	95	33	37	22	16	29	23	31	29
of which:									
Latin America	24	8	12	6	6	7	6	6	5
Africa	38	11	15	11	6	12	5	7	11
Eastern and Southern Asia	18	9	2	2	1	7	10	13	8
Western Asia	15	5	8	3	3	3	2	5	5
Memorandum items:									
Least developed countries	40	14	15	13	12	11	5	7	9
Sub-Saharan Africa	31	8	13	10	6	9	3	5	8
Percentage of population									
Developing countries	95	23.1	20.7	7.4	5.9	63.2	61.9	67.7	60.7
of which:									
Latin America	24	55.5	69.0	11.8	16.7	24.3	25.2	26.4	7.1
Africa	38	44.9	38.6	34.0	13.3	27.5	14.3	9.0	21.6
Eastern and Southern Asia	18	13.5	6.6	0.2	0.0	81.0	82.6	90.1	82.2
Western Asia	15	14.5	50.0	10.9	37.8	16.6	9.9	40.8	11.6
Memorandum items:									
Least developed countries	40	29.7	30.9	30.6	17.8	43.0	31.9	39.2	50.7
Sub-Saharan Africa	31	39.4	45.8	47.2	19.4	21.7	6.4	11.5	26.0

Source: UN/DESA, including population estimates and projections from *World Population Prospects: The 1998 Revision* vol. I, *Comprehensive Tables* (United Nations publication, Sales No. E.99.XIII.9).

a   Partly estimated.
b   Forecast, based in part on Project LINK.

cent, with a dramatic improvement in Latin America and Western Asia. In 2000, 31 countries achieved at least 3 per cent growth in per capita GDP, as compared with 23 in the previous year. Encouragingly, some sub-Saharan African least developed countries recorded a rise in per capita GDP of more than 3 per cent in 2000. Nevertheless, almost half the population in sub-Saharan Africa live in countries that suffered a fall in GDP per capita in 2000.

The outlook for many developing economies deteriorated in the first half of 2001, albeit to varying degrees. The transmission of the slowdown in developed economies to developing countries is occurring through several channels, such as reduced exports, weakening commodity prices, stagnant capital inflows and tighter credit conditions in international and local capital markets. For the developing countries as a whole, GDP growth is expected to slow from 5.7 per cent in 2000 to 4.1 per cent in 2001, followed by a rebound to 5¼ per cent in 2002 (see table I.5).

Among developing countries, aggregate GDP growth in **Africa** is expected to accelerate from just over 3 per cent in 2000 to about 4¼ per cent in 2001-2002, in spite of the adverse external environment. Even without significant further negative shocks from any of the exogenous circumstances discussed earlier, however, this growth rate will not be sufficient to reduce poverty by a significant margin in the short term, compounding the challenge for the longer term.

Table I.5.
DEVELOPING COUNTRIES: RATES OF GROWTH OF REAL GDP, 1998-2002

Annual percentage change[a]					
	1998	1999	2000[b]	2001[c]	2002[c]
Developing countries[d]	1.6	3.5	5.7	4.1	5¼
of which:					
Latin America and the Caribbean	2.0	0.4	3.8	3.1	4½
Africa	3.0	2.7	3.1	4.3	4¼
Western Asia	4.1	0.8	5.7	2.6	4
Eastern and Southern Asia	0.5	6.3	7.3	5.1	6
Region excluding China	-2.3	5.9	6.9	4.1	5½
of which:					
East Asia	-4.6	5.9	7.3	3.7	5
South Asia	5.3	5.9	5.8	5.4	6¼
China	7.8	7.1	8.0	7.3	7¼
Sub-Saharan Africa (excluding Nigeria and South Africa)	3.4	2.1	2.5	3.3	4
Least developed countries	3.8	3.5	4.4	4.4	4½

Source: UN/DESA.

[a] Calculated as a weighted average of individual country growth rates of gross domestic product (GDP), where weights are based on GDP in 1995 prices and exchange rates.
[b] Partly estimated.
[c] Forecast, based in part on Project LINK.
[d] Covering countries that account for 98 per cent of the population of all developing countries.

The economic performance of most African countries is highly dependent on two non-economic and one exogenous factor: weather conditions, political stability within a country or subregion and international prices of commodities. Growth rates have diverged significantly among countries in the region as the impact of these factors varies from country to country. Economic activity in a number of African countries was disrupted by military conflicts and political instability in 2000. There have since been renewed hopes for resolving or improving some regional conflicts, such as the war between Ethiopia and Eritrea, and the civil wars in the Democratic Republic of the Congo and Sierra Leone. The economic outlook for South Africa, the largest economy in sub-Saharan Africa, has also improved noticeably.

In 2000, the higher oil prices benefited oil-exporting economies in the region and these countries are expected to continue to sustain investment and consumption in 2001. On the other hand, the higher import bill for oil, declining prices of such agricultural commodities as coffee and cocoa, and unfavourable weather conditions, both flooding and drought, led to lower growth for many other economies in the region. With the moderate decrease in oil prices and some improvement in a number of commodity markets, economic prospects in some of the oil-importing countries should improve in 2001.

The rapid recovery of many economies in **Eastern and Southern Asia** in 1999 and most of 2000 was halted abruptly by the sudden slowdown of the United States economy. Aggregate GDP growth for this group (excluding China) is expected to decelerate from 6.9 per cent in 2000 to 4.1 per cent in 2001, followed by an improvement to 5½ per cent in 2002.

Because many economies of this region are highly integrated in the international economy, they are vulnerable to the current external demand shock, as reflected in the fall in export growth of several East Asian economies from an annual rate of over 20 per cent in the first half of 2000 to a single-digit rate in the first quarter of 2001. As a result, industrial production in these economies, particularly ICT-related production, has registered an absolute decline or no growth. Furthermore, lower stock market prices, rising unemployment in manufacturing, and weakening consumer confidence are expected to curb private consumption in many Asian economies.

The outlook for China and India is more positive. GDP growth in China is expected to be resilient, though moderating from 8 per cent in 2000 to 7.3 per cent in 2001. Strengthening domestic demand, supported by more accommodative macroeconomic policies, will offset the expected slowdown in exports. India is expected to maintain a rate of growth of around 6 per cent, as the anticipated rebound in agricultural output from the unfavourable conditions in the last growing cycle is expected to offset the slowdown in ICT-related sectors.

Elsewhere in the region, growth in 2001 is expected to moderate by 1-2 percentage points for such economies as Bangladesh, Nepal, Pakistan and Sri Lanka. The deceleration has various causes, ranging from the expected decline in exports, to dampened rural income as a result of crop failure in the previous growing year, to continued political instability.

After recovery in 2000, economic growth in **Latin America and the Caribbean** is expected to slow from 3.8 per cent in 2000 to 3.1 per cent in 2001, but to rebound to 4½ per cent in 2002. The region is facing worsening external conditions: exports to the United States provided strong support for the region's recovery in 2000, but are anticipated to slow substantially; private capital inflows are expected to decline; widening yield spreads on the region's debt are raising the cost of international borrowing; and the international prices of many commodities that the region exports are softening. Growth in a number of economies, such as Mexico and several countries in Central America and the Caribbean, is expected to decelerate sharply because of their close trade linkages with the United States. Other countries, such as Brazil, that have improved their economic fundamentals and whose exports are less dependent on the United States, are expected to be much less affected. A few economies, such as Ecuador and Venezuela, may be able to continue, or even to accelerate, their recovery. The major uncertainties and the downside risks within the region continue to be concentrated on Argentina, where market confidence is low while economic agents await policy measures to resolve the problems posed by the country's unsustainable public debt and to revive domestic private-sector demand.

Economic growth for many countries in **Western Asia** is forecast to slow after a strong performance in 2000 due to the higher oil prices. GDP is expected to increase by 2.6 per cent in 2001, down from 5.7 per cent in 2000, but to rise by 4 per cent in 2002. The surge in oil prices in 2000 was a major benefit to the oil-exporting economies in the region and led to increases in government spending, business investment, and private consumption. However, despite the cuts in production quotas by OPEC members, oil prices are expected to soften in 2001 because of the slowdown in global demand. The combination of lower prices and policies to reduce production will lead to lower oil revenues for these economies.

Growth for the oil-importing countries in the region was mediocre in 2000. The escalating conflicts in the region, especially between Israel and the Palestinian Authority, have not only caused considerable losses for the economies directly involved, but have also negatively affected neighbouring economies. The short-term outlook for Turkey has deteriorated since November 2000 because of two financial shocks; these led to severe losses in the banking sector, and forced the floating of the exchange rate, which depreciated sharply.

Benign inflation outlook

No major acceleration in inflation is forecast for 2001. The slowdown in economic growth worldwide is expected to create spare capacity and to remove some of the inflationary pressures that built up previously. Prices of non-oil commodities and high-technology goods have declined owing to the slowdown, and the loosening of labour markets is likely to curb wage growth. Inflation expectations, as measured by inflation-indexed securities in financial markets, have also moved lower. "Headline" inflation rates in many countries may, however, increase in the near term as the pass-through to other economic activities of the higher energy prices that have prevailed since 2000 is likely to continue. There may also be increases in inflation in economies that have recently experienced currency depreciation.

In many developed economies, headline inflation rates have risen since the second half of 2000. Most of these economies, except Japan, registered annual inflation rates in the range of 3 to 4 per cent in 2000, about 1 percentage point higher than in 1999; the same pace continued in the first quarter of 2001. Higher oil prices, rising food prices, and the upward drift in unit labour costs were the main causes for the rise in inflation in these countries. In addition, weakening currencies exacerbated the situation in many cases, especially where currencies depreciated against the United States dollar. The rise in "core" inflation (that is to say, excluding products with volatile prices, such as energy and food, and removing changes in taxes on goods and services from the computation) has so far been milder than the change in headline inflation. Annual inflation rates for most developed economies are expected to drop below 3 per cent by the end of 2001 as a result of weakening demand and softening oil prices. As oil prices soften, the driving force that made headline inflation diverge from core inflation will also peter out. In Japan, deflation has been a major policy concern for the past several years. Mild deflation is expected to continue for some time, despite the shift in monetary policy towards a reflationary bias.

Inflation rates in developing countries and economies in transition are likely to remain largely unchanged, but some divergent trends have come to the surface. In economies where inflation rates had been high in the past few years and where stabilization of inflation remains a key policy objective, such as a number of countries in Latin America and members of the Commonwealth of Independent States (CIS), disinflation continued during 2000 and into early 2001. On the other hand, many economies in Eastern and Southern Asia and in the Central and Eastern European and Baltic regions experienced a moderate rise in inflation rates for reasons comparable with those in many developed economies—higher oil prices and, in several cases, weaker currencies. There was also an increase in inflation in some African economies. Sounder macroeconomic management and continuation with structural reforms, aimed in particular at improving economic efficiency, are expected to reduce inflation rates further in high-inflation developing countries and economies in transition and to assist in maintaining control over inflation elsewhere.

Mixed employment situation

The global slowdown has weakened global labour markets which, in many developing countries and economies in transition, were only beginning to recover from the 1997-1998 setback. In many economies, the initial slowdown in manufacturing is transmitted to the household sector through labour markets. The response in labour markets usually lags the movement in output, but the flexibility of labour markets in many economies has improved in recent years owing to structural reforms. As a result, lay-offs in several countries have increased rapidly along with the slowdown in the growth of output, especially in manufacturing. Nevertheless, the employment situation still varies across countries and regions, depending on the flexibility of labour markets and on economic structures, and especially on the importance of exporting sectors and of manufacturing.

In the United States, the tight labour market has started to loosen with the implementation of many previously announced lay-offs and the unemployment rate is expected to rise to about 5 per cent over the course of 2001. The unemployment rate is also expected to rise in Australia and Canada. In contrast, recent improvements in Western Europe are not expected to be reversed significantly. The average unemployment rate in the European Union (EU) dropped by more than 1 percentage point in 2000 to below 9 per cent. It is expected to decline further in 2001, but at a slower pace. The growth in employment in many Western European economies has resulted not only from the strong growth of output, but also from longer-term structural improvements in labour markets enacted by several of these countries. The outlook for employment in Japan remains gloomy in the short run because of ongoing corporate restructuring and fragile overall economic growth.

The employment situation in economies in transition and developing countries varies considerably. Unemployment rates in the Russian Federation, Central and Eastern Europe and other economies in transition remain, on average, very high. However, for the first time in many years, there was a marked decline in the Russian Federation's unemployment rate in 2000. In Asia, the unemployment rate continued to fall in line with the recovery in economic growth for most of 2000. Data for subsequent quarters, however, indicate a mild reversal of that trend in a number of Asian economies, owing to weakening industrial production and exports. The unemployment rate in several economies at the centre of the 1997-1998 crises, especially Indonesia, continues to be higher than before those events. In China, the large number of lay-offs from the State sector remains a concern. Unemployment rates are high in most Latin American countries. While a few Latin American economies, such as Brazil, Chile and Venezuela, lowered their rate of unemployment slightly in the course of 2000, rates in other countries, where they were already at double-digit levels, increased. The worst situation prevails in Africa: urban unemployment rates are in the range of 15 to 20 per cent or higher, and under- and unemployment are a major cause of poverty and related problems.

Macroeconomic policy developments

Since the beginning of 2001, the stance of macroeconomic policy in many economies has become more stimulatory: led by reductions totalling 250 bps in the United States, more and more central banks have been lowering interest rates and many Governments have reduced taxes or increased expenditure. The accommodative policy environment is expected to be maintained in 2001 in an effort to secure and sustain a recovery in global economic growth.

Monetary policy makers in many economies have been very active, in the sense that they have made frequent adjustments in policy interest rates in an attempt to fine-tune the pace of economic activity. This was in part a consequence of the increasingly complicated environment for national policy-making, resulting from rapid technological and financial innovation, and intensifying global economic integration. The new cycle of policy-easing has only just begun, but avoiding unnecessary swings in policy will remain a challenge for central banks.

In the outlook, further monetary easing is expected in most developed economies, although most of the interest-rate cuts by the major central banks have probably already been made. Despite the general easing trend, the policy stance varies among major central banks, reflecting the differences in monetary policy regimes. The ECB had reduced interest rates by only 25 bps by the end of May 2001, as compared with the several cuts by other major central banks. This is mainly because the sole goal of the ECB is to keep inflation in the euro area within a range of zero to 2 per cent and the headline inflation rate in the area exceeded the upper band of this range. In contrast, the Bank of Japan has introduced some unorthodox measures, including shifting the target of monetary operations from the overnight interest rate to the Central Bank's quantity of liquid assets; using the consumer price index (CPI) as a major guideline for the duration of the new monetary easing, with the goal of reaching a stable CPI exceeding zero inflation; and increasing its outright purchases of long-term government bonds to ensure a smooth supply of liquidity.

The monetary policy stance in developing countries and economies in transition has varied. Central banks in a large number of these economies (including Chile, Hong Kong Special Administrative Region (SAR) of China, India, Poland, the Republic of Korea and Taiwan Province of China) started to ease policy as more signs pointed to weakening growth in these economies. More such action is expected if the current deceleration continues. However, interest rates are still relatively high in many of these economies, notably in Central and Eastern Europe and Latin America, because inflationary pressure, macroeconomic imbalances and the potential for devaluation limit the central banks' room for manoeuvre in reducing them. More generally, the strength of the United States dollar vis-à-vis their currencies has limited the capacity of many other developing countries and economies in transition to reduce interest rates.

Fiscal policy in most developed economies is expected to be moderately relaxed in 2001 as a result of tax reductions or increases in government spending, or both. A majority of developed economies, Japan being an exception, registered a budget surplus in 2000. Fiscal policy has since been revised so that it can play a more active role in countering the economic slowdown. Several developed economies have cut taxes or adopted tax reforms in which tax cuts are one component. Other developed countries are planning to follow suit. Fiscal surpluses are expected to diminish in most developed economies during 2001-2002: the growth of revenue will decelerate (or become negative) because of tax cuts and the slowdown in economic activity, and expenditure will rise, either because of increases in discretionary spending or as a result of automatic stabilizers, or both. Meanwhile, the large government deficit in Japan is expected to continue in 2001-2002.

Most developing countries and economies in transition have fiscal deficits, although a number reduced the shortfall in 2000, either by raising revenues, as in oil-exporting economies, or through expenditure cuts, as in several Latin American countries. The economic slowdown, however, is expected to worsen the deficits in many of these economies in 2001, leaving their policy makers only limited room for expansionary fiscal measures to counter the slowdown. Moreover, large fiscal deficits and high public debt-to-GDP ratios have been posing a threat to macroeconomic stability in several of these economies, as shown by the financial crises in Argentina and Turkey in late 2000 and early 2001.

UNCERTAINTIES AND DOWNSIDE RISKS

The outlook discussed above is based on the expectation of a "V-shaped" recovery in the United States; that is to say, in the same way that the slow-down took hold very quickly and then intensified rapidly, it is expected that there will be a correspondingly rapid acceleration in growth starting in the second half of 2002. This should allow global economic growth to return to its long-run pace of about 3 per cent in 2002. However, there are substantial uncertainties and several downside risks that might lead to a less attractive outcome.

The biggest risk for the global economic outlook is a deeper and longer slowdown than anticipated in the United States, with larger spillovers to the rest of the world through sharp adjustments in its current-account deficit. The European economies would then be unlikely to maintain the forecast degree of buoyancy. It would also be more difficult for Japan to address its lingering structural problems, thus worsening the pessimism that its economic situation and political uncertainties have been imparting to economic agents. At the same time, external constraints would confine the room for stimulating domestic demand in the majority of developing countries and economies in transition. Collectively, these events would have wider repercussions on economic growth in the near term for the world as a whole, but especially for many developing countries.

The large trade and current-account deficits of the United States continue to pose a major risk. As indicated above, these reached 4.5 per cent of GDP in 2000, aggravating concerns about their sustainability and the consequences of any drastic reversal, especially given the domestic slowdown and the shape it has taken. There is no precise indication of what level of current-account deficit is sustainable, but experience suggests two propositions. The first is that a reversal in the current account of developed economies typically starts when that external deficit reaches about 5 per cent of GDP. The second is that the nature of the reversal is a combination of slowing domestic economic growth and a significant depreciation of the exchange rate.

The sustainability of the prevailing trade and current-account deficits in the United States depends, to a large extent, on the ability of the private and public sectors to continue borrowing abroad, either through formal capital markets or by accumulating dollar revenues. The total foreign debt owed by United States agents, as measured by the country's net foreign investment position, is about 20 per cent of GDP. It therefore remains well below the ratio of 40-50 per cent, and in some cases even more, that several developed economies reached in the 1990s. However, the share of the output of the United States that is traded is only about 25 per cent of GDP and its exports of goods and services are less than 12 per cent of GDP, so that its foreign debt is about 80 per cent of its tradable GDP and about double that figure as a proportion of export earnings. These magnitudes suggest that the external deficits may not be as sustainable as other indicators suggest and may need to be compressed in the near future.

This could be accomplished either through cuts in domestic absorption, notably investment, or through a rise in domestic savings (since the current-account deficit mirrors the difference between saving and investment). The

3   Project LINK is an international collaborative research group for econometric modelling, coordinated jointly by the Development Policy Analysis Division of the United Nations Secretariat and the University of Toronto.

adjustment could be a smooth process or an abrupt reversal, involving a sharp devaluation of the dollar with respect to major currencies and a marked reduction, or even a reversal, of capital inflows.

Model simulations, utilizing the LINK modelling system,[3] were carried out to study different possibilities for reducing the deficit. Among them, a pessimistic variant assumes that the adjustment will be accomplished mainly by correcting the private sector's saving-investment imbalance through reductions in domestic absorption in the United States (see box I.1). Such a compression over the period 2001-2002 would have significant deflationary effects not only on the United States and the developed countries, but also on many developing countries. Reflecting their integration with the United States economy, the developing countries of Latin America and South and East Asia would be among those disproportionately adversely affected.

The results imply that the larger part of rebalancing the private-sector saving-investment gap in the United States would be accomplished by cutting investment and the smaller part by raising the saving rate. This is probably the worst case that most observers would consider plausible. However, even this case involves only a 15 per cent depreciation of the effective exchange rate for the dollar. A model could not adequately capture the consequences of a larger depreciation of the dollar against major currencies or of possible turmoil in financial markets, but the adverse consequences would be considerably greater.

Through international linkages, the United States adjustment would have a significant deflationary impact on the global economy. Total world trade would shrink considerably, the trade surpluses of Japan and the economies of EU would be cut sharply (in part because of the appreciation of their currencies in terms of the dollar) and the combined trade balance of developing countries would deteriorate substantially. The outcome would be a decline in global growth of about 1.7 percentage points from the baseline over two years, equivalent to a loss of output of some $600 billion. The reduction in investment that this involves not only implies a decline in domestic demand in the period concerned, but also results in a smaller capital stock for the longer run. An adjustment of this nature therefore lowers output and income growth in the long run, as well as in the short run.

Box I.1

A DOWNSIDE SCENARIO

a   For complete information on this simulation, see Pingfan Hong, "Global implications of the adjustment in the United States trade deficit", Department of Economic and Social Affairs Discussion Paper, No.17 (ST/ESA/2001/DP.17), http://www.un.org/esa/papers.htm.

The simulation of a reduction in the United States trade deficit by more than $200 billion over two years is mainly induced by compressing import demand; this declines by $224 billion as a result of a drop in consumption by 5.7 per cent and a decrease in private investment by 14 per cent (see table). The scenario implies a loss of gross domestic product (GDP) in the United States by about 4.6 per cent over two years, with a sizeable impact on the country's other macroeconomic aggregates and a pronounced deflationary effect on the global economy.[a]

World exports would be reduced by more than $300 billion, or 4 per cent, from the baseline. The trade surpluses of the European Union (EU) and Japan would be compressed by $47 billion and $31 billion, respectively. The adverse impacts on developing countries would result from a drop of $75 billion in their collective trade balance, with the largest impact being on countries in South-East Asia and Latin America. Measured relative to GDP, the cost to the global economy of this scenario would be $600 billion, or 1.7 percentage points from the baseline over two years.

MAIN RESULTS OF A SIMULATION OF A $200 BILLION REVERSAL OF THE UNITED STATES TRADE DEFICIT

	Change from the baseline over two years	
	Billions of dollars	Percentage
United States of America		
Trade balance	+206	
Imports	-224	
GDP		-4.6
Consumption		-5.7
Private investment		-14
Effective exchange rate		-15
Unemployment rate		+2[a]
Inflation rate		-2.7[a]
World trade	-307	-4
Trade balances		
Canada	-39	
European Union	-47	
Japan	-31	
Developing economies	-75	
Latin America	-30	
Eastern and Southern Asia		-25
GDP		
World		-1.7
Developed economies		-1.8
Percentage points		-1.6

a   Percentage points.

II THE INTERNATIONAL ECONOMY

The international economic environment, which has a critical bearing on the prospects of the majority of the world's economies, was shaped in 2000 and the first half of 2001 mainly by changes in real demand in the world's largest economies, rather than, as in 1997-1998, by the financial misfortunes of a small number of developing and transition economies.

International trade continued to play an important role in the recovery from the 1997-1998 financial crises for most of 2000. However, the same trade linkages are also globalizing the slowdown that began in the last part of 2000. The evolving deceleration in the economic growth and import demand of the developed economies, both led largely by the retrenchment in the United States of America, is having an adverse impact on their trading partners. These initial negative effects are being multiplied through trade to a widening circle of developing countries and economies in transition. The resulting setback will be compounded by the consequent continued weakness in the international prices of commodities that are of particular interest to many of these countries.

Net financial flows to developing countries declined in 2000, in part because less emergency financing was required to salvage countries in financial crises. On the other hand, the terms and conditions of external financing for developing countries and economies in transition seeking funding in global capital markets worsened towards the end of 2000 and into 2001 as a result of three main factors: the build-up of strains in financial markets in major developed economies, including the plunge in equity markets; the vulnerability of borrowing countries to the global economic slowdown; and persisting uncertainties regarding Argentina and Turkey, which made international investors generally more cautious and risk-averse. These factors increased the difficulties that many developing countries and economies in transition encounter in financing their development.

On the other hand, many developing countries and economies in transition have rebuilt their foreign reserves, adopted more flexible exchange-rate regimes and reduced their short-term external debt, making them better able to adjust to external real shocks and less susceptible to financial contagion. At the same time, the large imbalances in trade and current accounts across countries, especially the unsustainable deficits of the United States, continue to pose broader and largely unknown downside risks to the world economy.

Increased global economic integration and the more volatile nature of international economic activities in recent years have posed challenges for the global trading system and the international financial system. Despite progress, both require further improvements in order to reduce volatility and vulnerability in the short run and to promote the sustainable development of all countries and peoples in the longer run. In the short term, more official international financial assistance needs to be provided to developing countries and economies in transition for their development and poverty reduction efforts. The decrease in the ratio of official development assistance (ODA) to gross national product (GNP) of members of the Development Assistance Committee (DAC) of the Organization for Economic Cooperation and Development (OECD) in 2000 needs to be reversed with immediate effect. At the same time, the increased momentum gained by the Enhanced Heavily Indebted Poor Countries (Enhanced HIPC) Initiative at the end of 2000 needs to be maintained so that the initiative can be fully implemented as soon as possible.

Action should also be continued on longer-term issues. Consensus needs to be reached on launching a new round of global negotiations to further reduce trade barriers, especially those impeding exports from developing countries to developed economies. At the same time, the pace of reform of the international financial architecture needs to be sustained. In both areas, efforts at the international level can usefully be complemented by integration within regional and subregional groupings. Actions on all these fronts, as well as several others, are indispensable if the international community is to achieve the goals it set itself in the United Nations Millennium Declaration.[1]

[1] See General Assembly resolution 55/2 of 8 Septemeber 2000.

WIDE SWINGS IN GROWTH OF INTERNATIONAL TRADE

The strong momentum that international trade developed in 1999 lasted throughout much of 2000 and lifted world trade growth from 5.2 per cent in 1999 to 12.3 per cent in 2000. Growth of world trade is expected to decline sharply to 5½ per cent in 2001, with at best a slightly better performance (6½ per cent) in 2002 (see table I.1).

Increased global integration after 1990 lifted the ratio of the growth of world export volume to the growth of gross world product (GWP) to a range of 2.5-3 from an average below 2 in the 1970s and 1980s. The increased role of transnational corporations (TNCs), with their trade-intensive strategies of globally integrating production, distribution and services, contributes a large part of the explanation for this increased trade propensity of growth. However, with the source of the current slowdown being a fall in demand centred on the United States, the major home country for TNCs, the trade propensity of growth is expected to decline from about 3 in 2000 to 2.3 in 2001and 2.1 in 2002.

Strong expansion in 2000

World trade expanded briskly for 2000 as a whole, in spite of the deceleration in growth during the last quarter of the year. World exports increased by 12.1 per cent in volume and 12.3 per cent in value when measured in current dollars (see table II.1). The strong growth of global trade had three major sources. First, buoyant import demand prevailed in developed economies, par-

Table II.1.
WORLD TRADE VOLUMES, 1999-2001

Annual percentage rate of growth						
	Exports			Imports		
	1999	2000[a]	2001[b]	1999	2000[a]	2001[b]
World	5.1	12.1	5½	5.3	12.5	5½
Developed economies	4.4	10.8	5¼	6.1	11.0	4½
of which:						
North America	6.4	10.6	4	10.4	15.6	3
Western Europe	3.9	11.0	6¾	3.4	9.2	6
Japan	2.7	11.0	1	9.5	6.3	1½
Economies in transition	4.0	13.0	7	-6.0	15.0	8
Central and Eastern Europe and Baltic States	7.0	20.0	10	5.0	15.0	9
CIS	2.0	7.0	4	-28.0	14.0	7
Developing countries	7.2	15.0	5½	4.0	16.3	7¾
Latin America and the Caribbean	6.6	11.6	7	-6.9	9.3	10¾
Africa	2.1	2.5	3	1.5	5.7	4¼
Western Asia	0.6	9.7	-¾	2.3	14.5	¾
Eastern and Southern Asia	10.0	17.0	6¼	6.9	18.6	8
China	7.4	26.0	7½	18.6	33.4	9¾
Memorandum items:						
Fuel exporters	7.5	17.6	5¼	-0.4	12.0	-1½
Non fuel exporters	7.1	13.4	5¾	10.3	9.0	4¼

Source: United Nations.

a   Partly estimated.
b   Forecast, based in part on Project LINK.

ticularly the United States where double-digit import growth was powered by the strong United States dollar and robust domestic demand. Second, there was a surge in import demand in many developing countries and economies in transition as they overcame the constraints that the 1997-1998 financial crises had imposed on their import levels. Finally, import demand from oil-exporting countries increased sharply on the strength of higher oil revenues—resulting from a combination of increased oil exports, higher oil prices, and the strength of the United States dollar (in which oil prices are denominated). These impulses were the major factors behind the strength in global trade in 2000 for nearly all groups of countries.

The volume of imports, as well as that of exports, for **developed economies** rose by 11 per cent. The United States continued to lead the group with growth of 15 per cent in import demand, maintaining the annual double-digit growth of imports it had achieved for most of the past decade. That stemmed to a large extent from the differentials in gross domestic product (GDP) growth between the United States and other major economies: during 1991-2000, the United States registered an average annual rate of GDP growth of 3.3 per cent compared with the 1.3 per cent recorded by Japan and the 2 per cent recorded by the European Union (EU). During the same period, the appreciation of the

United States dollar and the rising propensity to consume by households also contributed to the strong import demand of the United States. Exports from the United States, on the other hand, grew less rapidly for most of the 1990s. In 2000, however, the volume of United States exports grew 10.6 per cent, chiefly on account of strong demand from the rapidly recovering economies in South-East Asia.

Imports by European developed economies in 2000 grew by 9.2 per cent—nearly three times the 1999 pace. This owed much to the acceleration in economic activity in major European countries. The weakness of the euro, especially against the dollar, dampened import demand for products from outside the euro area, but it bolstered the growth of export volume of the euro area by 11 per cent in 2000 (compared with growth of 3.9 per cent in 1999).

Despite fragile overall economic growth, imports into Japan grew by 6.3 per cent in 2000, driven mainly by increased demand for information and communication technologies (ICT)-related products. Japan's exports, on the other hand, rose by about 11 per cent, well above the 2.7 per cent recorded in 1999, partly owing to the strong economic recovery in other Asian economies.

Import demand from **economies in transition** rebounded strongly in 2000 too, with the volume of imports for the group increasing by 15 per cent, compared with a decline of 6 per cent in 1999. Increased revenues from higher oil prices and rising volumes of oil exports bolstered the purchasing power of the Russian Federation and of a few other economies in the Commonwealth of Independent States (CIS), enabling them to raise their import demand. The CIS volume of imports rose by 14 per cent in 2000, reversing large successive declines in 1998 and 1999 induced by the devaluations of the rouble and other CIS currencies. Exports of CIS rebounded by 7 per cent from near-stagnant levels in the previous three years.

The Central and Eastern European and Baltic economies also registered strong growth in both imports and exports. The performance of exporting sectors in many countries was particularly vigorous. Exports increased by 20 per cent in real terms, owing mainly to increased import demand from Western European economies. With the rising integration of selected sectors of these economies into the global economic strategies of TNCs, foreign-owned firms in these economies played an instrumental role in promoting these countries' trade, inter alia, through intra-industry trade.

Both imports and exports of many **developing countries** also registered strong growth in 2000—16.3 per cent and 15 per cent, respectively, for the group as a whole. Terms-of-trade changes were mostly related to the upturn in energy prices: the terms of trade for most oil exporters improved, but they deteriorated for many oil importers. Particularly hard hit were oil-importing developing countries that also depend for most of their export revenues on agricultural products, whose prices continued to decline during 2000.

Leading the trade performance of developing countries as a group were several economies in East and South Asia, as well as China[2], whose international trade expanded by more than 20 per cent in real terms, driven in particular by the stronger-than-expected economic recovery from the 1997-1998 financial crises in the area. Imports of Latin America and the Caribbean grew by 9.3 per cent in 2000 following the sharp contraction in 1999, while exports surged by 11.6 per cent. Many economies in Western Asia also registered robust growth

[2] China's imports as reported grew by more than 30 per cent, owing in some degree to the Government's efforts to suppress smuggling and to bring that trade into the formal economy.

in their international trade, boosted mainly by high prices of oil during 2000, allowing for stronger growth of import than of export volumes.

A notable exception among developing countries was Africa, whose trade growth was barely one fifth of the pace for the world as a whole. Export growth remained especially mediocre but import volume surged by 5.7 per cent, nearly four times the rate in 1999. The annual growth of Africa's exports, particularly those of sub-Saharan Africa, has lagged that of world trade by about 2 percentage points on average throughout the last decade. As Africa's share in world markets continued to decline, many countries in the region became further marginalized, failing to participate in the acceleration of global economic integration that has occurred since the early 1990s to the same degree as many other developing countries.

Many factors are responsible for the loss of market share of Africa in world trade. Some are intrinsic to the low level of economic development of these countries, as their exports consist largely of primary commodities for which world demand has grown generally much more slowly than GWP. Second, in spite of some progress over the years, domestic policies in many of these economies have failed to improve the efficiency and competitiveness of export sectors and to foster closer linkages between them and the domestic economy. There were also problems with the "market institutions" that support participation in global trade, ranging from inadequate transportation and communication infrastructures, to poor export promotion and financing facilities. Furthermore, import restrictions in many economies, especially developed economies, tend to be comparatively high for the products, including agricultural and other labour-intensive goods, that many African countries can advantageously export. Unless these long-term problems are tackled on a sustainable basis and eventually removed, Africa's trade growth will not match that of the rest of the world and the region will continue to be excluded from the most dynamic components of global economic integration.

Notwithstanding the strong and widespread expansion in world trade in 2000, the large trade imbalances among major economic groups persisted. The trade deficit of the United States deteriorated to $450 billion at the end of 2000, up from $340 billion in 1999 (see table A.20). Japan continued to register a sizeable external surplus in 2000, in contrast with the large external deficits of Australia and New Zealand, while Europe's current account deteriorated notably because of the increased oil bill.

Owing to the higher prices of oil during 2000, the shifts in trade and current-account balances were sharply in favour of oil-exporting developing countries, but disadvantaged oil-importing developing countries. The trade balance for oil-exporting developing countries increased by about $100 billion in 2000, whereas that of many oil-importing developing economies in Asia deteriorated for two reasons: the higher prices of oil and the increased oil demand as these economies recovered. The trade balances of many Latin American economies improved in 2000, but current-account deficits remained high relative to GDP for several of the large economies.

For the economies in transition, a large increase in the external surplus of CIS, especially of the Russian Federation, contrasted markedly with the general deterioration in external deficits for most Central and Eastern European economies. Several major economies in this group had deficits of about 5 per cent of GDP in 2000. The Baltic countries other than Lithuania, however, experienced a substantial improvement in their current accounts in 2000, although they still recorded deficits.

Poorer prospects for 2001-2002

The strength of global trade began to peter out in late 2000 and the outlook for 2001-2002 is for significantly weaker growth. The economic downturn in the **developed economies** is critical because it is expected to cause the growth of their import volume to drop to almost 4½ per cent in 2001.

The marked deceleration in the growth of imports of the United States, a drop of more than 10 percentage points to only some 3 per cent in 2001, will be a major drag on the expansion in world trade. Measured in United States dollars, the country's share in global trade was about one fifth in 2000 so that this will have severe consequences for the rest of the world. The impact on individual countries and regions will depend on the importance of trade in their economies and on the share of exports to the United States in their total trade (see table II.2).

The slowdown in the trade of most European developed economies is likely to be less pronounced, with growth of import demand expected to moderate to about 6 per cent in 2001 and the growth of exports to be slightly higher. Internal demand is likely to support trade expansion: the deceleration will be due largely to external shocks. However, weakness in aggregate growth in Western Europe may make the trade downturn more endogenous as time goes by and may affect the expansion of intraregional trade, which accounts for more than 60 per cent of Western Europe's total trade.

The growth of import demand of other developed economies is expected to decelerate to varying degrees. The contraction is likely to be most significant for Canada, with growth dropping from 12 per cent in 2000 to 1 per cent in 2001, largely on account of the substantial share of intra-industry trade

Table II.2.
EXPORTS TO THE UNITED STATES OF AMERICA AS
A SHARE OF TOTAL TRADE BY MAIN ORIGIN, 1999

Percentage of United States dollar values in 2000	
World	18.8
European Union	9.4
Canada	87.4
Japan	29.7
Economies in transition	5.9
Eastern Europe	4.5
Developing countries	26.9
Latin America and the Caribbean	53.3
Africa	16.3
Western Asia	15.7
Eastern and Southern Asia (including China)	23.1

Source: Table A.14.

between Canada and the United States. The deceleration in the growth of imports by the United States from Canada will simultaneously induce a slow-down in Canadian imports from the United States. Growth in the volume of Japanese imports is also expected to slow markedly, to about ½ per cent in 2001, because of weakening domestic demand and the depreciation of the yen.

The growth of import demand of most **developing economies** is also expected to slow to about 7 per cent in 2001, or less than half the rate recorded for 2000. Since this rate remains above the average for global imports, these countries will on balance be supportive of world economic activity in 2001. In general, import growth of many oil-exporting developing economies is expected to decelerate less, as the increased revenues from the higher oil prices in 2000 and 2001 continue to support import demand. Import growth in other developing economies, however, is expected to ease more pronouncedly.

Because the United States is the destination for more than a quarter of their overall exports, growth of exports from developing countries is expected to slow to about 5½ per cent in 2001. Across the sub-groups, export growth of Eastern and Southern Asia is expected to drop to 6¼ per cent in 2001. Other groups are expected to see their growth of exports lowered by 3 to 5 percentage points below 2000 levels. However, several developing countries (notably the Republic of Korea, Taiwan Province of China and Thailand) will have even greater decelerations in their export growth because a large share of their exports consists of ICT-related products. Latin America is expected to experience a moderation in export growth to 7 per cent in 2001.

For many developing economies with a large share of so-called processing trade, including China, Mexico and other countries in Asia and Latin America, both their exports and imports are likely to decelerate significantly in the current global downturn. The processing trade depends directly on business prospects within the TNCs that contract for or directly manage such trade. When their export orders become less buoyant, imports of parts and materials also suffer. A contraction in the volume of processing trade may not have a comparable impact on GDP growth, however, since value added in the trade tends to be low. However, unemployment would rise and could have negative indirect effects on GDP growth.

The direct impact of the downturn in the United States is expected to be limited for both exports from and imports by most **economies in transition**, especially the Baltic and Central and Eastern European economies.

A significant upturn or downturn in the global economy usually involves an adjustment in external balances across countries. The current downturn could signal the beginning of the adjustment in the United States trade deficit, the significance of which depends on the magnitude of the adjustment and the manner in which it is brought about (see box I.1). As the total value of imports of the United States is about one third larger than the value of its exports, exports need to grow much faster than imports over many years to correct the deficit.

For the developed economies as a group, a small improvement in the external balance is expected in 2001, but some deterioration is expected for almost all developing economies. The surplus of the Russian Federation is forecast to decline somewhat in 2001, while deficits for the Baltic and Central and Eastern European economies are expected to remain at about the same level as in 2000.

SOFTENING COMMODITY PRICES

During the 1997-1998 international financial crises, prices of most commodities reached their lowest levels in decades. Since then, prices have recovered somewhat, but with sharp divergences in trends among commodities. Prices of oil recovered fully from their 1997-1998 decline by 2000, and were sustained at increased levels for more than a year, but prices of metals and minerals had recaptured only about half their earlier losses by the end of the year and prices of many agricultural commodities remained near the low levels reached during the crises.

The weak state of global economic activity is expected, on average, to exert downward pressure on commodity prices. There has been some softening in prices since the onset of the downturn, notably for metals and oil, but the probability of a replay of the deep deflation in a broad range of commodity prices that was experienced during the Asian financial crisis is not considered to be high.

Fuel prices

Prices for many fuel products were under upward pressure in the course of 2000 and remained high in early 2001. One major contributor to this was the management of supplies, notably oil and gas, whose prices are interrelated. Prices of oil have been unusually volatile for awhile. After soaring from a trough of $10 per barrel (pb) in February 1999 and touching $38 pb during September 2000, oil prices declined to an average of $28 pb in the first quarter of 2001 (see figure II.1) and are expected to moderate to about $25 pb by the end of 2001.

Figure II.1.
OIL PRICES, 1999-2001 (OPEC BASKET)

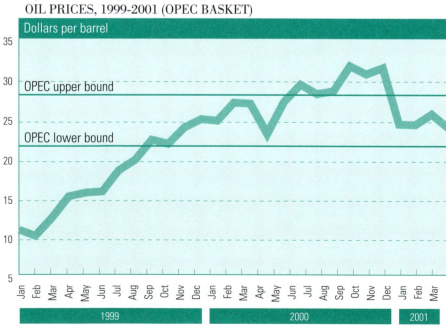

Source: *Middle East Economic Survey,* http://www. mees.com/Energy_Tables/basket.htm. Accessed on 26 June 2001.

The high volatility of the prices of oil since early 1999 has been caused by many factors. First, on a number of occasions, the expectations of agents concerned about world demand for oil diverged from actual changes in oil markets. Adjustments in supply that, with hindsight, should not have taken place, played a considerable role. Enhanced Organization of the Petroleum Exporting Countries (OPEC) control over marginal supply in the short run was another factor. This was made possible in part by other factors not directly under the control of the cartel's members, such as low inventories and the inelasticity of supply with respect to sudden changes in demand. Third, there was considerable mismatch in inventories, in terms of both composition and location. Finally, the replenishment of inventories has been discouraged by the fact that prices for oil to be delivered in the more distant future have been persistently lower than those for delivery in the near future; this has added to pressures on current prices.

These factors remain crucial for the course of oil prices in the near term. After a solid recovery during 1999 and the first three quarters of 2000, growth of world oil demand fell short of expectations in the last quarter of 2000 as a result of a milder-than-expected weather in Europe and Asia, the slowdown of the United States economy, and the weaker-than-anticipated demand for oil in several South-East Asian economies. Low inventories in the developed economies also contributed to the spike in prices in 1999 and 2000. In early 2001, stocks in the developed economies remained low by the standards of past decades, potentially leading to volatile prices.

Supply adjustment, especially on account of OPEC intervention, is the dominant factor behind prices, at least in the short run. Following the declared aim to maintain prices within a target range of between $22 and $28 pb from March 2000, OPEC increased production quotas four times in 2000 in attempts to lower prices to within the target range. Several other oil producers, including Mexico, Norway and the Russian Federation, geared their production and exports with a view to assisting OPEC's price stabilization efforts. These collective effects came to bear on the market only by the end of 2000. Confronted with softening oil prices at the beginning of 2001, OPEC cut production quotas twice in the first quarter, reversing two thirds of the increments agreed during the previous year.

Factors other than the direct impact of the global cyclical downturn make it hazardous to predict oil prices. It is unclear whether all members of OPEC will comply with their agreed output quotas as well under downward price pressures as they did when there were upward price pressures. In the latter case, only a few countries had the spare capacity required to increase output in an effort to contain the upward price movement. With downward pressure on prices, however, a growing number of countries will have to lower production, and will thus gain spare capacity and lose revenues. OPEC members facing heavy debt burdens, rapid population growth, and stagnant domestic economies may be especially tempted to breach the agreed limits in an effort to maintain their oil revenues. Second, non-OPEC production and export capacity continue to rise, generally among smaller producers who seek to maximize their export revenues rather than join OPEC's price maintenance strategy. Third, the volume of Iraqi exports is uncertain. Finally, expectations among economic agents about the depth and the duration of the global economic downturn influence market participants' behaviour, notably in the volume and composition of petroleum and products kept in reserve.

In the longer run, if present oil prices are sustained for some time, exploration and supply in non-OPEC countries are expected to expand. On present knowledge (see table A.18), however, the volumes likely to be brought to international markets from non-OPEC sources will remain small compared with global demand, as most proved reserves are held by OPEC countries. As the world economy is expected to recover in 2002 and beyond, demand for oil may once again outgrow supply.

Non-fuel commodities

Prices for other commodities reacted differently from those for fuels to the upswing during most of 2000 and the deceleration in demand since the latter part of 2000.

Food and beverages

Although prices of **food** commodities increased by an average of 6 per cent in 2000, the price index is still 25 per cent below that of 1996 (see figure II.2) because of successive declines over four years (see table A.17). The recovery in 2000 was partly due to production cutbacks for many of these commodities over the past few years in response to the erosion of prices. It was, however, also driven by increases in demand, notably from a number of oil-exporting countries, economies in transition, and developing countries in Asia. The price recovery, however, was far from homogeneous among the commodities in this category. Prices of some commodities, such as those for bananas and sugar, have rebounded significantly, while others, such as those for maize and rice, have continued to decline.

Prices of food commodities are expected to continue a slow recovery. The income elasticity for most commodities in this group is low, and so overall demand is not likely to be affected to the full extent of the slowdown in global growth. Also, adverse developments in food supplies in developed market economies in Europe are having an impact on supply, placing upward pressure on prices of some products (see chap. III).

Among food commodities, sugar prices rose 30 per cent in 2000 from the 14-year low in 1999. The recovery was due to an increase of import demand in such countries as the Russian Federation, as well as reduced production in Brazil on account of drought. While sugar prices remained firm in early 2001, high stocks make further increases unlikely. Similar developments explain banana prices: there was increased demand from such countries as China and Japan and Central and Eastern European countries and a decline in production in several Latin American countries due to adverse weather conditions. Banana prices are expected to continue to rise over the next two years, as growers are cutting back production because of increased costs and low returns.

Prices of grains, which had declined steadily since 1996, registered a mixed trend in 2000: prices of maize and rice continued to fall, while prices of soybeans and wheat recovered somewhat. Declining maize prices were largely due to the record crop in the United States. Rice prices dropped to their lowest level in almost two decades, as the price slide continued in Thailand, the largest rice

Figure II.2.
NON-FUEL COMMODITY PRICES, 1994-2000

Source: UNCTAD, *Monthly Commodity Price Bulletin*

exporter. In contrast, wheat prices recovered moderately in 2000, owing to increased demand from oil-exporting countries and weaker-than-anticipated production in Canada and the United States. Prices of grains are expected to recover slowly as the adjustment in production and stocks over the past few years creates a closer match to world demand.

Prices of major **beverages**, especially coffee and cocoa, registered another year of large declines in 2000. Weaker demand and increased production led to large stock accumulations, resulting in a substantial drop in coffee prices for the third year in a row. With a continued decline in the first quarter of 2001, coffee prices were 50 per cent lower than their peaks of 1997. Oversupply is due to increased production in such countries as Ethiopia, Mexico, Uganda and Viet Nam, and favourable weather conditions in 2000, except in Brazil. Despite the export-retention plan launched by the Association of Coffee Producing Countries (ACPC) to prevent further price erosion, persistently high production in the presence of sizeable inventories is bound to prevent any significant recovery in coffee prices in the near term.

Cocoa prices also suffered from restrained demand and increased production. Excess cocoa production was reported as a record 3 million tons in 2000,[3] mainly owing to the expanded production of Ghana and Nigeria and in spite of reduced output in Côte d'Ivoire, the world's largest exporter. An increase in cocoa prices is also unlikely in 2001, given current production levels and the expected recovery in the supply from Côte d'Ivoire.

Prices of tea recovered slightly in 2000, after a four-year decline. Demand for tea has been increasing, particularly from such countries as Iraq, the Russian Federation, Saudi Arabia and the United Arab Emirates. According to the International Tea Committee, however, the trend in global production of tea is firmly upward, suggesting a limited further recovery in tea prices.

Prices of **vegetable oil seeds and oils** continued their decline in 2000, although prices for some commodities in the group appeared to be stabilizing in late 2000 and early 2001. Prices of palm and soybean oil have dropped by 50 per cent since 1998, leaving the price index for the group at its lowest level in decades. Palm oil production, for example, has doubled over the past decade. While prices are expected on average to fall further, prices of commodities such as copra and groundnut oil may start to stabilize owing to increased consumption (in response to lower prices) and output adjustments.

Agricultural raw materials

Prices of this category recovered moderately in 2000 but stalled in late 2000. Further softening in prices of these commodities is expected, at least until the latter part of 2001.

Prices of cotton and rubber, while having risen by about 10 per cent in 2000, remain 40 to 50 per cent off the peaks reached in 1997. The recovery in cotton prices was due largely to reduced stockholding and production in China and to the expectation of lower crops in India and Pakistan, offsetting an increase in production from Brazil. A further slight increase in cotton prices is possible because of continued excess demand in the near term, but expanded planting in such countries as Argentina, Australia and the United States is likely to fill up the gap in the medium to long run.

[3] "Press release: *Quarterly Bulletin of Cocoa Statistics*" (London, International Cocoa Organization, 15 February 2001, http://www.icco.org/press/010215press).

Metals and minerals

Prices of base metals have paced the evolution of global industrial production. The recovery in prices begun in early 1999 continued in the first half of 2000. Since then, however, prices have been softening along with the downturn in global industrial production. The price index for this group recovered 13 per cent in 2000, led by prices of aluminium, copper and nickel, with the latter jumping by 40 per cent. Prices of other commodities in the group, such as gold and silver, have been relatively stable.

The recovery of metal prices during 1999-2000 was driven not only by the pickup in demand, especially from Asia, but also by supply problems and production cutbacks. For example, the surge in nickel prices was due partly to the increase in steel production, which uses nickel as an alloying admixture; delays in bringing new capacities on-stream; and the rundown in inventories. Meanwhile, energy-related supply constraints in the production of aluminium and copper, resulting from the high prices of energy, also provided price support. Prices are expected to remain volatile in the near term as stocks of many of these commodities are low. The demand for these commodities is highly correlated with the fluctuations in a few manufacturing sectors and, after a decline in the first half of 2001, prices of metals and minerals are expected to firm when the recovery in manufacturing in the major economies gets under way later in 2001.

DEVELOPMENTS IN MULTILATERAL TRADE NEGOTIATIONS AND THE WORLD TRADE ORGANIZATION

Despite the wide and frequent swings in the dynamics of global trade during the past several years, few signs of any major aggravation of protectionism have come to the fore. The progress made with trade liberalization during the 1990s, including the implementation of the agreements reached during the Uruguay Round,[4] of multilateral trade negotiations remains largely intact. Efforts are being made to build further upon these achievements.

Towards a new multilateral round of trade negotiations?

Since the impasse at the Third Ministerial Conference of the World Trade Organization in Seattle in November-December 1999, various calls for reconsidering the intended inauguration of a new round of trade negotiations have been made. Acting upon these calls has been complicated by a range of objections by both proponents and opponents of a new round. Most Governments opposed to a new round are not against embarking on new multilateral trade negotiations per se, but rather insist that all countries, and especially the developed economies, honour in full their previous commitments, particularly those made during the Uruguay Round as "best efforts" to bolster market access. Proponents of a new round among World Trade Organization member Governments now recognize that, in order to include the developing countries, they will have to present more than a tentative agenda that largely revolves around new issues, such as those tabled at Seattle.

Views on what the new round should tackle remain divided among broad country groups; the divergence is particularly pronounced between developed

[4] See *Legal Instruments Embodying the Results of the Uruguay Round of Multilateral Trade Negotiations, done at Marrakesh on 15 April 1994* (GATT secretariat publication, Sales No. GATT/1994.7).

and developing countries. Some developed countries have proposed that negotiations focus on trade liberalization in new domains and that such issues as labour standards, human rights, and protection of the environment be addressed. There has been an extensive debate in the international community on whether the latter three issues should be taken up in the context of trade negotiations, either in a new round or even within the World Trade Organization at all.

In contrast, many developing countries continue to be primarily concerned about effective market access for traditional goods and services, both as promised in earlier rounds and in terms of possibilities for a new round. Their priority for negotiations is the removal of barriers to market access in developed countries for products in which developing countries have a comparative advantage, notably agricultural and labour-intensive products.

EU has affirmed that the new round "must be directed at strengthening access to markets, at developing and strengthening the rules and disciplines of the World Trade Organization and at promoting a better integration of developing countries into the Multilateral Trading System". The objective of "a new round should be to increase transparency and predictability in trade relations, to reduce the risk of protectionism and unilateralism and to respond to the rapidly integrating international economic environment."[5] EU also deemed it important to strengthen the technical and institutional capacity of the developing countries, including the least developed countries, through World Trade Organization cooperation schemes with the goal of enhancing their capacity to participate in multilateral trade negotiations.[6]

Implementation of the agreements reached at the Uruguay Round since the mid-1990s, together with many unilateral trade liberalization measures, has reduced barriers to international trade. Nevertheless, the multilateral trading system is far from complete, and the range of unfinished business continues to be very wide as significant impediments to trade remain. Among the most heavily protected products are those of greatest interest to many developing economies, especially the least developed countries. These products include agriculture, textiles, clothing, footwear and many other labour-intensive manufactures.

Unfinished business from the Uruguay Round

Since the Seattle Conference at the end of 1999, some progress has been made in advancing outstanding issues, notably those left over from the Uruguay Round, in particular trade in agricultural products and services. Progress has also been booked on other issues, including those that figured in Seattle, and countries that oppose a new round have insisted that some of the above-cited topics be dealt with on a priority basis. There is some optimism, notably on the part of the United States and the European Commission, that the next World Trade Organization Ministerial Conference in Qatar could launch a new round.

Agriculture trade

Commenced in March 2000, the first phase of the deliberations on agriculture, as called for under the Uruguay Round agreements, was successfully concluded in March 2001, at which time all parties agreed on a work programme for the second phase. An unprecedented number of Governments participated

[5] "EU and candidate countries: joint declaration on WTO issues at ministerial meeting in Ljubljana" (Ljubljana, European Commission, 12 May 2001, http://europa.int/comm/trade/whats_new/enlarg .htm), pp. 1 and 2.

[6] This commitment was first agreed upon at the first Ministerial Conference of the World Trade Organization held at Singapore in 1996, but implementation of the Integrated Framework for Trade-related Technical Assistance, including for Human and Institutional Capacity-building, to Support Least Developed Countries in their Trade and Trade-related Activities (WT/LDC/HL/1/Rev.1), has fallen short of expectations.

actively in the first phase, with 125 World Trade Organization members, out of 140, submitting negotiating proposals. Most proposals were submitted within the context of the Agreement on Agriculture, reached during the Uruguay Round. That Agreement aimed at the continuation of the reform of trade in agricultural products by enacting progressively more substantial reductions in agricultural support and protection. The new proposals cover many issues in such areas as market access, export competition, and domestic support. Many of these proposals also include some related topics not directly pertaining to trade as such, including the environment, food safety, sustainable rural development, poverty alleviation, and consumer protection.

The special concerns of the least developed countries and net food-importing developing countries have been raised in many proposals from developing countries, as well as in some of those tabled by developed countries. For example, the joint proposal of the World Trade Organization's African Group stresses that trade reform should ensure market access that allows for competition on a commercial basis for all agricultural products originating in developing countries.[7] It also endorses efforts to level the playing field in the international trading system, taking into account different structural constraints among countries. The Group proposes that developed countries provide tariff-free and quota-free market access for exports from the least developed countries.[8] It also suggests an agricultural safeguard mechanism for developing countries, as a form of special and differential treatment. The Group urges that many special concerns of least developed countries and net food-importing developing countries (such as food aid, accession to financing facilities, and technical and financial assistance aimed at the improvement of agricultural productivity and infrastructure) be fully addressed during the negotiations.

At the Third United Nations Conference on the Least Developed Countries (Brussels, 14-20 May 2001), there was general agreement among all developed countries to expand the "Everything but Arms" initiative of EU.[9] This was part and parcel of broader initiatives in support of the least developed countries' development efforts because often the impediments to exports from LDCs comprise not only lack of market access but also weak domestic supply and the absence of effective trade-promotion institutions.

Given the wide range of interests and the complexity of many of the issues, the second phase of the negotiations on agricultural trade is expected to be difficult. The work programme includes further in-depth elaboration of all the proposals, with focus in the short run on such issues as tariffs, export subsidies, export credits, State-trading enterprises, food security, food safety, and rural development.

Trade in services

The post-Uruguay Round negotiations on these issues have gathered momentum since being formally launched at the beginning of 2000. The adoption of the negotiating guidelines and procedures by the World Trade Organization Council for Trade in Services (Services Council) in March 2001 marked a move forward from the "rules-making" phase, during which new rules for services on subsidies, safeguards and government procurement had been negotiated, to the "request and offer" phase, during which facilitating further market

[7] "WTO African Group: Joint Proposal on the Negotiations on Agriculture" (World Trade Organization, G/AG/NG/W/142, March 2001).

[8] The European Union (EU) has recently endorsed the position whereby least developed countries will have free access to the single European market for all goods but armaments. For some products, however, some transition regimes have been put in place; but by 2006, there should be full access.

[9] "EU succeeds in promoting market access in favour of LDCs" (Brussels, European Commission, 21 May 2001, http://europa.int/comm/trade/miti/devel/ldcmkacc.htm), p. 1.

access will be negotiated. Some 40 members had submitted about 70 proposals in the year following adoption of guidelines.

The newly adopted guidelines stress that the ongoing negotiations should aim at increasing the participation of developing countries. They emphasize that there should be flexibility for individual developing countries, with priority granted to the least developed countries; they also call for consideration to be given to the needs of small and medium-sized service suppliers, particularly those of developing countries.

Requests for accession

During 2000, the World Trade Organization General Council approved the accession of several new members, although 28, including China and the Russian Federation, continue to negotiate for accession. A key issue in designing the format for accession to the World Trade Organization by developing countries, especially the least developed countries and economies in transition, is whether there can be "special and differential" treatment for them or for sub-groups of them. There are concerns that new applicants are called upon to accept higher levels of obligations than existing members.

Dispute settlement

Despite the differences with regard to the agenda for a new round of global trade negotiations, efforts to build upon the present multilateral trading system have continued. One example has been the progress in solving disputes among trading partners, even though nearly 100 cases were pending under the World Trade Organization's provisions in early 2001.[10] In April 2001, there was a resolution of the long-standing dispute between the United States and some Latin American economies, on the one hand, and the European Commission, on the other hand, centring around the latter's banana regime (see box II.1). This dispute had dampened cooperation between the United States and EU, inter alia, on resolving other problems of the multilateral trading system and on a number of related issues of bilateral and multilateral interest. That dispute is now on its way to full settlement.

GLOBAL FINANCIAL FLOWS

Reflecting developments in international trade, there was a sharp rise in the net outward transfer of financial resources[11] from developing countries as a group in 2000 (see table II.3). The net outward transfer from countries in Eastern and Southern Asia moderated significantly, as robust economic recovery strengthened import growth and their repayments of bank loans bottomed out. At the same time, the net inward transfer of financial resources to Latin America, which had dwindled in 1999 in the aftermath of the macroeconomic adjustment to the financial crisis in Brazil, was reversed in 2000, owing to substantial growth in oil-related export earnings, as well as restricted access to credit in Argentina late in the year. There was a swing to a large outward net transfer from Western Asia in 2000, reflecting the rise in oil export revenues, which substantially exceeded the increase in import demand. The net inward transfer of resources to Africa as a whole was also reversed in 2000, owing to

[10] The fact that the member States are resorting to multilaterally agreed dispute settlement mechanisms, in lieu of resorting to bilateral negotiations, can be considered progress in itself.

[11] The net transfer of financial resources comprises the net capital inflow less the net outflow of investment income; it finances the balance of trade in goods and services and net private outward transfers (largely workers' remittances).

Box II.1

TOWARDS A RESOLUTION OF
THE DISPUTE CONCERNING
THE EUROPEAN UNION'S
BANANA REGIME

In April 2001, the Government of the United States of America and the European Commission reached an agreement to resolve their dispute over the latter's import regime for bananas. This was subsequently extended to Ecuador, the other major party in the dispute with the European Commission. Formal disputes were also lodged under the World Trade Organization's rules by Guatemala and Honduras, in one case, and Mexico, in another. A settlement with these countries, as well as an arrangement with Costa Rica and Venezuela, has not yet been reported.

The dispute between the European Union (EU) and, chiefly, the United States, which was acting on behalf of its companies with interests in banana production and trade, began with the establishment of the single European market in 1993, which called for eliminating internal barriers to market access among member countries. As a result, EU decided to adopt a single regime for banana imports.[a] Although it removed barriers within EU, the new regime benefited EU's African, Caribbean and Pacific partners and erected new barriers to other banana exporters, mainly from Latin America, including United States companies. Both sides negotiated for several years to secure relief for the aggrieved parties without finding a mutually satisfactory solution.

Following this failure, the United States and four Latin American countries (Ecuador, Guatemala, Honduras and Mexico) filed a case against EU's banana regime with the World Trade Organization in May 1997.[b] Utilizing its dispute settlement mechanism, a World Trade Organization panel adjudicated EU's regime to be illegal, notably according to the provisions of the General Agreement on Tariffs and Trade (GATT)[c] for the non-discriminatory administration under the various Lomé agreements of quantitative restrictions (article XIII). The grounds for this judgement were that EU had reserved a share of its market for bananas for imports from its African, Caribbean and Pacific partners by issuing licences that did not completely eliminate discrimination vis-à-vis agents from other countries.

In 1998, EU proposed some changes to this regime, but the World Trade Organization rejected them. In view of EU's continued non-compliance with the original findings, in April 1999 the World Trade Organization authorized the United States to impose trade sanctions with an annual value of $191 million. The United States implemented this by levying a 100 per cent duty on a number of products from members of EU, excluding Denmark and the Netherlands. Its sanction regime, however, had been put in place as of March 1999, before the WTO's authorization to levy extra tariffs was issued.

Owing to the failure to reach some form of agreement based on the historical distribution of import licences, the European Commission proposed in October 2000 that a transitional tariff quota system, meaning a regime with low tariffs for transactions within the quotas and higher tariffs otherwise, be managed on a "first come, first served" basis. After adopting this, the European Commission made clear that it remained open to further proposals and negotiations.

The new transitional regime was scheduled to take effect in July 2001 and will turn into a tariff-only system by January 2006. During the transition period, bananas will be imported into EU through import licences distributed on the basis of past

[a] The import regime consisted of (a) a tariff quota of 2 million tons (raised in 1994 to 2.1 million and in 1995 to 2.2 million tons, following the banana framework agreement, and an additional tariff quota of 353,000 tons also introduced in 1995 for Latin American countries and non-traditional African, Caribbean and Pacific exporters); (b) quantities allocated to traditional African, Caribbean and Pacific banana suppliers totalling 857,700 tons at zero duty; and (c) a quota duty of 75 euros per ton for Latin American countries and zero duty for African, Caribbean and Pacific countries.

[b] "Trade representative welcomes appellate victory in WTO banana dispute: sees broader benefits for U.S. trade" (Washington, D.C., Office of the United States Trade Representative, 9 September 1997), p. 1.

[c] GATT secretariat publication, Sales No. GATT/1986-4 (Geneva, July 1986).

Box II.1 (continued)

trade and the United States will suspend sanctions currently imposed on some EU exports. As part of this free-standing agreement, the United States will support EU's request for a waiver of World Trade Organization rules in order to allow EU to reserve a fixed quantity of bananas exclusively for its African, Caribbean and Pacific partners during the transition regime.

This agreement is fully compatible with World Trade Organization rules. It offers EU's African, Caribbean and Pacific partners, notably those of Africa and the Caribbean, a transition phase of nearly five years to adjust to more open global competition for EU's banana market. It is likely eventually to allow the non-traditional exporters of bananas among the African, Caribbean and Pacific countries to secure a larger market share since they will be able to compete on an equal basis in EU, especially once the tariff-only regime comes into effect in 2006.

By late April 2001, a similar agreement was reached between EU and Ecuador, the largest exporter of bananas among the developing countries. It is expected that this will be extended to the three other Latin American countries that joined in the World Trade Organization case and the two other banana exporters mentioned earlier.

The new regime will also enhance the exporting opportunities for Ecuadorian and other Latin American exporters of bananas into EU, since it abolishes the latter's import allocation on a country quota basis. Inasmuch as countries can now compete for a market share in EU, non-traditional banana exporters to EU can capture part of that market relying on their inherent comparative advantage. This is likely to hold in particular once the transitional period regime will have been replaced by a tariff-only system by 2006.

Table II.3.
NET TRANSFER OF FINANCIAL RESOURCES TO DEVELOPING COUNTRIES, 1993-2000

Billions of dollars

	1993	1994	1995	1996	1997	1998	1999	2000[a]
Developing countries	66.2	34.3	39.9	18.5	-5.7	-35.2	-111.2	-169.8
Africa	2.5	5.1	6.0	-5.1	-3.3	17.0	6.3	-14.5
Sub-Saharan (excluding Nigeria and South Africa)	19.2	3.7	10.1	12.2	12.9	13.1	16.4	15.8
Eastern and Southern Asia	10.0	1.9	22.9	24.6	-28.1	-127.7	-125.8	-102.9
Latin America	14.7	18.1	-1.6	-1.3	20.8	42.0	7.9	-1.6
Western Asia	39.0	9.2	12.6	0.2	4.9	33.5	0.4	-50.8
Memorandum item: Heavily indebted poor countries (HIPC)	13.0	10.7	11.8	11.9	13.6	16.5	12.8	9.2

Source: UN/DESA, based on International Monetary Fund (IMF), *World Economic Outlook, May 2001*, and IMF, *Balance of Payments Statistics*, various issues.

[a]   Preliminary estimate.

the higher capacity to pay for imports out of export earnings for several large oil-exporting countries. Inward resource transfers to oil-importing African countries to finance their trade deficits continued in 2000, while the net transfer to the heavily indebted poor countries (HIPC) was the smallest in the past several years.

These developments were mirrored in the subdued net financial flows to developing countries in 2000 (see figure II.3). Both private and official flows declined in the aggregate in 2000. Net private financial flows are expected to increase at best only slightly in 2001, dampened by the global economic slowdown and continued uncertainty. Total official financial flows are expected to rise in 2001, largely owing to commitments under the International Monetary Fund (IMF)-led assistance programmes to Argentina and Turkey. ODA declined in 2000 and prospects for a resumption of increases are uncertain.

Private financial flows

The low level of net private financial flows to developing countries and economies in transition in 2000 reflected persisting investor aversion to risk in these countries. Financial flows were concentrated in a small number of large developing countries (such as Brazil, China and, until its crisis, Turkey), amplifying the concentration observed since 1997.

Participants in global financial markets became more cautious in the second half of 2000. The tightening of monetary policy in developed countries raised interest rates, and thus the returns on alternative placements of funds in low-risk instruments. Increasing concerns about the overvaluation of equity prices, especially of ICT companies, exacerbated risk aversion. As investors sought to rebalance their overall risk exposure, they reduced demand for a wide range of high-risk investments, including emerging-market securities.

Figure II.3.
NET FINANCIAL FLOWS TO DEVELOPING
AND TRANSITION ECONOMIES, 1990-2000

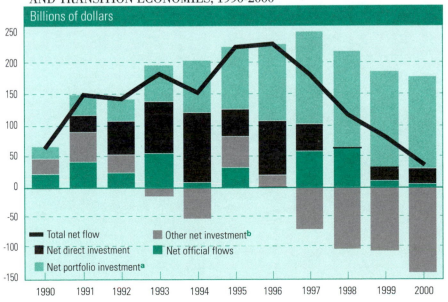

Source: International Monetary Fund, World Economic Outlook Database (online), May 2001.

a Including portfolio debt and equity flows.
b Including short- and long-term bank lending. It may include some official flows owing to data limitations.

The result was a significant widening in the "spread" between the yield on emerging market bonds and that on the standard risk-free benchmark instrument, United States Treasury bonds. This was particularly visible in the spreads on Asian bonds (see figure II.4) and on the bonds of a number of countries in Latin America (such as Argentina, owing to deepening financial concerns; Brazil, as a result of spillover from Argentina; and Peru, owing to political developments). However, this trend was not universal. For example, spreads on bonds of the Russian Federation benefited from the successful restructuring of private debt, the improvement in macroeconomic performance, and the increase in export revenues on account of higher fuel prices.

At the end of 2000, overall investor sentiment towards emerging markets improved somewhat. As a result, investment in emerging market bonds rose into the beginning of 2001. However, with increasing evidence of a spreading economic slowdown, international investor confidence weakened again during the first quarter of 2001, in spite of the continued easing of international interest rates.

Investors closely monitored the evolving economic crises in Argentina and Turkey and the solutions under discussion (see chap. III). The new programmes will benefit from international financial assistance packages led by IMF. The latter's commitment has helped to bolster investor confidence in both countries.

Influenced by persisting uncertainty about the two reform programmes, as well as about global economic conditions, bond spreads for emerging market economies in April 2001 remained relatively high. Thus, despite the easing of base interest rates on non-risky credits, owing to policy easing in the major economies, the average cost to developing countries and economies in transition of borrowing on international capital markets increased from their levels in early 2000, both for new bonds and for commercial bank loans.[12]

[12] *Global Development Finance, 2001: Building Coalitions for Effective Development Finance, Analysis and Summary Tables* (Washington, D.C., World Bank, 2001), p. 45.

Figure II.4.
YIELD SPREADS ON EMERGING MARKET BONDS,
3 JANUARY 2000-25 JUNE 2001

Nevertheless, there has not been a recurrence to date of the large-scale contagion with massive capital flight that occurred during the 1997-1998 international crises.

Private credit flows

There was a substantial net outflow of private credit from developing countries and economies in transition in 2000 (see figure II.3). This continued a trend set in motion in 1997 by the financial crises in several of these economies. One consequence has been a decline in the debt-to-GDP ratio and the share of short-term debt in the total debt of these countries as a group.

Net repayments to international commercial banks accounted for a large part of the net outflow, especially in East Asian countries. Net flows of bank credit to countries in other regions, such as Argentina, Brazil and Turkey, were subdued although these countries saw a rise in new syndicated loans in 2000, mainly for telecommunications, oil and energy projects. However, the volume of new loans plummeted in early 2001, and the net retrenchment in international bank lending to the developing countries and economies in transition is expected to continue.[13]

The net flow of non-bank credit to developing countries and economies in transition was basically unchanged in 2000 and gross bond issuance matched 1999 levels.[14] Latin American countries—with Argentina, Brazil and Mexico in the lead—dominated gross bond issuance, which was concentrated in the early part of the year. Activity dwindled to a very low level by the last quarter, as such countries as Argentina and Turkey dropped out of the primary market. There was a rebound in bond issuance in early 2001, mainly by Latin American countries, as spreads on emerging market bonds narrowed. Asian countries have generally been relatively inactive as their demand for external credit remained low. With the exception of a number of large privatized companies, corporations in the region are still in the process of reducing their leverage. Smaller net flows of non-bank credit are expected in 2001 as international investors remain risk-averse and financial uncertainties keep the cost of funds high.

Portfolio and direct equity investment flows

Foreign direct investment (FDI) continued to be the mainstay of private financial flows to emerging market economies in 2000, albeit at a slightly reduced level.[15] Investment for cross-border mergers and acquisitions levelled off while investment in "greenfield" projects continued to stagnate, owing to persisting excess capacity in many developing countries. The share of global direct investment flows going to developing countries continued to decline: it fell to 17 per cent in 2000, in marked contrast to the high of about 37 per cent in 1997.[16]

The small decline in net FDI flows was the combined result of the end of a wave of asset sales in crisis-affected Asian countries, particularly the Republic of Korea and Thailand, and continued strong flows to countries undertaking large-scale privatization, such as Brazil, Peru and Poland. Overall direct investment flows to Africa declined in 2000. FDI flows to the region have been concentrated in a small number of countries, such as Egypt, South Africa and the United Republic of Tanzania, with substantial privatization programmes, particularly in natural resource and infrastructure sectors. In Asia and Latin

[13] *Emerging Market Financing: Quarterly Report on Developments and Prospects* (Washington, D.C., International Monetary Fund, 10 May 2001), p. 13.

[14] *BIS Quarterly Review* (Basle, Bank for International Settlements, March 2001), p. 29; and *Emerging Market Financing: Quarterly Report on Developments and Prospects …*, p. 9.

[15] For further details on FDI, see UNCTAD, *World Investment Report, 2001* (United Nations publication, Sales No. E.01.II.D.12).

[16] UNCTAD FDI/TNC database.

America, the top 10 recipients of FDI flows accounted for 74 per cent of the total in 2000. Only 2.5 per cent of total FDI flowing to developing countries went to the least developed countries, and it was concentrated in the resource-based sectors of a small number of countries.[17]

17   *Global Development Finance, 2001 …,* p. 40.

Direct investment flows are expected to remain basically unchanged in 2001, with investment in privatization projects moderating. Investment for other activities is not anticipated to strengthen significantly, given the deteriorating international economic environment. A notable exception could be an increase in investment flows to China in anticipation of its accession to the World Trade Organization, possibly later this year.

There was a small increase in the net flow of portfolio equity investment to developing countries and economies in transition for 2000 as a whole but the strong rise in prices of emerging-market stocks ended in the second half of 2000 and there was a retreat by international investors. Declines in portfolio equity investment flows became widespread, with the sharpest fall in several Asian economies. In the few countries with a substantial increase in net investment flows, such as Brazil and China, the main impetus came from the international placement of equity issues of large State companies in the ICT and energy sectors.

Weakness in equity markets in emerging economies has generally paralleled price declines in equity markets of developed economies, as the downward revision of the earnings prospects of stocks in the ICT sector in particular spread to similar stocks in emerging markets. The effect was more pronounced in Asian and Latin American markets that had a high share of these stocks. Compounding this was the growing concern about the vulnerability of developing countries to the global economic slowdown. Global stock prices continued to decline in the first quarter of 2001 as pessimism about the global economy outweighed the effect of monetary easing.

Official finance for development

Most of the changes in total official financial flows to the developing countries and economies in transition in the past two years reflected the abatement of the financial emergencies of the late 1990s. While this is a positive sign, the continuation of reduced levels of development assistance is a highly negative aspect.

International Monetary Fund and the World Bank

For the second year in a row, there was a net flow of funds to **IMF** from the developing countries totalling $6.7 billion in 2000 (see table A.23), chiefly on account of repayments of earlier loans to Argentina, Brazil, Mexico and Venezuela. There was also a net flow of funds from the economies in transition because of repayments by the Russian Federation, Ukraine and Uzbekistan (see table A.24).

Fund commitments to the developing countries, however, rose, from $13.0 billion in 1999 to $22.1 billion in 2000, chiefly on account of a standby facility for Argentina in support of its 2000-2002 economic adjustment programme. Commitments to the economies in transition fell from $5.6 billion in 1999 to only $0.3 billion in 2000. The Republic of Moldova received almost half of these commitments in the form of a loan from the Poverty Reduction and Growth Facility (PRGF).

IMF has been undertaking a major review of its operations and policies. In early 2001, the Executive Board approved a streamlining of the conditionalities in IMF assistance programmes in response to criticisms that the Fund had allowed the policy conditions associated with its programmes to expand beyond what was required. As an interim arrangement now in effect, conditions for loans are restricted to measures deemed "critical" (as opposed to "important" or "relevant") to the achievement of the objectives of the adjustment programme. The number of formal conditions associated with steps leading to a structural reform are also being reduced. The new approach focuses the role of IMF on policies within the core areas of its mandate and expertise, and relies more on other institutions, such as the World Bank and regional development banks, to address programme aspects outside these core areas.

IMF instituted a number of changes in November 2000 with regard to the policy of making substantial liquidity available to pre-qualifying countries threatened by contagion from financial crisis in other countries. Some of the terms and conditions of the Contingent Credit Line (CCL) were changed to encourage countries to use the facility. These modifications include lowering the surcharge over the standard loan rate and reducing commitment fees paid upon securing the facility. The release of the first disbursement of committed resources is also to be made more automatic to a qualified country affected by contagion. Thus far, no country has applied for a CCL under either the original or the enhanced terms.

Parallel to IMF, the **World Bank** is making efforts to streamline, focus and prioritize its loan conditionalities, including use of the Poverty Reduction Support Credits (PRSCs), a facility available to the low-income countries that implement reforms outlined in their Poverty Reduction Strategy Papers (PRSPs). The Bank and Fund are also working to clarify the respective roles of the PRSC and the PRGF.

IMF and the World Bank continue to seek to bolster the capacity of developing countries and economies in transition to improve their financial sectors so that these countries will prospectively be better able to withstand financial shocks. A major effort has been the Fund/Bank cooperation on Financial Sector Assessment Programmes and the associated Reports on Observance of Standards and Codes. To strengthen its work in this area, IMF has created a new International Capital Markets Department. This is intended to deepen the Fund's understanding of the workings of capital markets, as well as strengthen its capacity to address systemic issues and provide early warning of potential stress in financial markets.

Other multilateral development institutions

Total resources committed by **other multilateral development** institutions declined in 2000 for the second year in a row, by about 10 per cent in dollar terms (about 8 per cent measured in constant prices and exchange rates), to $42 billion (see table A.27). The decrease mainly reflects the end of the emergency surge in lending operations by the multilateral banks in the aftermath of the Asian financial crises, particularly non-concessional loans to middle-income countries. However, lower loan volumes were also the result of the gradual downsizing of the operations for which the loans were made. There has also been a shift from large infrastructure projects towards smaller projects in support of institution-building and human development. There was a slight increase in International Development Association (IDA) lending. The average size of IDA loans, like the non-concessional ones, was smaller in 2000 than in 1999.

There were some positive developments in 2000 regarding concessional resources for the major multilateral financial institutions. At the Asian Development Bank, negotiations have been under way for concessional funding for 2001-2004 through the eighth replenishment of the Asian Development Fund (ADF VIII). Donors agreed on a $5.6 billion replenishment, an increase of almost 10 per cent over the seventh replenishment (ADF VII). The first meeting, in February 2001, to discuss the thirteenth replenishment of IDA resources (IDA 13) got off to a positive start when broad agreement on some issues, such as those pertaining to IDA eligibility, was reached.

Contributions to the core and regular resources for the programmes of the operational agencies of the United Nations system declined slightly in 2000. Contributions to the United Nations Development Programme (UNDP) recorded another year of decline, but there was a rise in the financing provided to the United Nations Children's Fund (UNICEF). World Food Programme (WFP) resource commitments rose, while those of the United Nations Population Fund (UNFPA) fell by almost a third.

On the other hand, in one important area of concern, prospects for heightened international financial cooperation to fight human immunodeficiency virus/acquired immunodeficiency syndrome (HIV/AIDS) improved in the first half of 2001, when the call by the Secretary-General and others to mobilize resources for a united Global Fund to Fight AIDS, Malaria and Tuberculosis began to receive a sympathetic hearing. The total amount of resources necessary to combat HIV/AIDS effectively has been estimated at $7 billion to $10 billion per year. The trust fund is envisioned to be a key tool to help meet some of the large increase in outlays the Secretary-General has called for. It is therefore being constructed to be flexible enough to accept contributions by Governments, the private sector and individuals. If it materializes, part of the $7 billion to $10 billion is likely to be spent via traditional bilateral methods, as the Global Fund is intended to house only a small portion of the total financial effort.

Official development assistance

After two consecutive years of increases, ODA from the DAC member countries fell from $56.4 billion in 1999 to $53.1 billion in 2000, a decline of 6 per cent in nominal terms or 1.6 per cent if the effects of inflation and exchange-rate changes are removed[18] (see table II.4). Coupled with the relatively strong economic growth in the OECD countries in 2000, there was a fallback of ODA as a share of the DAC members' combined GNP to 0.22 per cent in 2000 from 0.24 per cent in 1999, far below the target of 0.7 per cent of GNP called for in various United Nations forums.

A major factor behind the fall in ODA in 2000 was that the aid of the largest donor, Japan, contracted by almost 18 per cent in 2000, largely as a result of the end of the exceptional contributions to the Asian Development Bank in the

18 One factor in the decline in ODA in 2000 is definitional: DAC no longer classifies assistance to certain countries or territories as ODA. The countries and territories that have been excluded are Aruba; French Polynesia; Gibraltar; the Republic of Korea; the Libyan Arab Jamahiriya; Macao; China; the Netherlands Antilles; New Caledonia; the Northern Mariana Islands; and the British Virgin Islands. The effect of this reclassification is most apparent in the ODA of France.

Table II.4.

OFFICIAL DEVELOPMENT ASSISTANCE (ODA) OF THE MEMBER COUNTRIES OF THE DEVELOPMENT ASSISTANCE COMMITTEE (DAC), 2000

	ODA (millions of United States dollars)	ODA/GNP[a] (percentage)	Real change, 1999 to 2000[b] (percentage)
Australia	995	0.27	9.3
Austria	461	0.25	-0.1
Belgium	812	0.36	21.7
Canada	1 722	0.25	-2.2
Denmark	1 664	1.06	7.3
Finland	371	0.31	0.1
France	4 221	0.33	-13.9
Germany	5 034	0.27	5.9
Greece	216	0.19	28.7
Ireland	239	0.30	7.3
Italy	1 368	0.13	-14.3
Japan	13 062	0.27	-17.9
Luxembourg	116	0.70	9.1
Netherlands	3 075	0.82	10
New Zealand	116	0.26	-0.4
Norway	1 264	0.80	-9.6
Portugal	261	0.26	6.7
Spain	1 321	0.24	8.3
Sweden	1 813	0.81	22.3
Switzerland	888	0.34	0.1
United Kingdom	4 458	0.31	35.6
United States	9 581	0.10	2.7
Total DAC	53 058	0.22	-1.6
Average country effort (unweighted)	..	0.39	-
Memorandum items:			
EU countries combined	25 431	0.33	6.4
European Commission	4 876	-	12.6

Source: Organisation for Economic Cooperation and Development, news release, OECD On-line, Paris, 23 April 2001.

[a] DAC members are progressively introducing the new System of National Accounts. This is leading to slight upward revisions of gross national product (GNP) and corresponding falls in reported ODA/GNP ratios.
[b] Taking account of both inflation and exchange-rate movements.

wake of the Asian financial crises. Fiscal austerity has also become a factor affecting the outlook for Japan's ODA.

On the other hand, aid from the United Kingdom of Great Britain and Northern Ireland jumped by almost 36 per cent in real terms, more than compensating for the 11 per cent fall in its ODA in 1999. Belgium, Greece, the Netherlands and Sweden also recorded strong increases in ODA in 2000. Germany and the United States increased their aid as well, while that of Canada fell slightly. Luxembourg joined the ranks of DAC countries that attained or exceeded the ODA target of 0.7 per cent of donor GNP. The others were Denmark, whose ratio reached a high of 1.06 per cent, the Netherlands, Norway and Sweden.

The prospects for total ODA flows remain uncertain. Among the major donors, the United States is expected to record only a modest rise in ODA in the next few years. For some other DAC members, however, prospects are more encouraging. ODA from the United Kingdom is on a rising trend. Belgium and Canada (despite a slight fall in the latter's ODA) have announced increases for the medium term. Such outstanding performers as Denmark, Luxembourg, the Netherlands and Norway are expected to remain among the DAC's most generous contributors of ODA.

An increase in ODA is widely recognized as indispensable if the United Nations Millennium Declaration goals are to be achieved. At present, national ODA efforts, measured as the ratio of ODA to GNP of the donor country, remain highly uneven. Increasing the ODA of donor countries with a low ODA effort is one of the main financing challenges facing the international community today.

The international treatment of excessive debt burdens

The international community has continued to address the debt difficulties of low- and middle-income countries, with separate approaches for the problems of each group.

Of the 41 heavily indebted poor countries (HIPC), the Executive Board of IMF and the Board of Executive Directors of the World Bank had approved debt reduction programmes for 22 countries under the Enhanced HIPC Initiative by 31 December 2000, triggering the requisite commitments of all the relevant creditors. Following this "decision point", interim relief is given, but full relief is granted only later, at the "completion point". Only Uganda had reached that point by the end of April 2001.

The 22 countries will receive about $34 billion of debt relief when their programmes are completed, accounting for two thirds of the international expenditure required for the initiative when applied to all eligible countries. Combined with traditional debt relief and additional bilateral debt forgiveness, total debt-service relief is estimated at $53 billion. The debt relief committed under the Enhanced HIPC Initiative will halve the outstanding debt stock of the 22 countries, reducing it by $20.3 billion in net present value terms. Debt-service payments will be reduced by about a third. Debt as a proportion of exports of these countries will decline to an average of 126 per cent which, although high, is about half the level that prevailed prior to debt relief and is comparable with that of other developing countries.[19]

Although the implementation of the Enhanced HIPC Initiative gained momentum in late 2000—half of the 22 countries received approval in December—there remain obstacles to bringing other eligible countries to the decision point and all of them, other than Uganda, to the completion point. One concern is the low level of funding of the HIPC Trust Fund. Paid-in bilateral contributions, for instance, totalled 37 per cent of the pledged amount at the end of March 2001.[20] IMF's commitments to the initiative are expected to be covered by about $800 million from its off-market gold sales in 1999. Donor countries and the institutions themselves provide funding to cover the reduction in servicing obligations on debt to the World Bank and regional development banks, and this has been arranged largely on a "pay-as-you-go" basis. It is therefore critical for the smooth operation of the HIPC debt-relief process that the necessary funds be contributed to the HIPC Trust Fund on a timely basis.

The prompt disbursement of debt relief to countries that have reached the decision point also needs to be assured. Difficulties can arise because commit-

19 For a detailed analysis of the effects of debt relief on selected debt indicators of the 22 countries, see the report to the Development Committee (Joint Ministerial Committee of the Board of Governors of the Bank and the Fund on the Transfer of Real Resources to Developing Countries), "Heavily indebted poor countries (HIPC): progress report" (Washington, D.C., International Monetary Fund, 19 April 2001).

20 Ibid., table 15.

ments to cover the agreed programmes in full are needed before the programmes start. In particular, difficulties in arranging relief by relatively small creditors can hold up implementation. Such delays were the case for Honduras and Nicaragua, which received HIPC assistance from IMF only in March 2001, although the decision point had been reached in December 2000.

In addition, about a dozen countries that are eligible for the HIPC initiative are experiencing problems that impede their ability to initiate a programme of debt relief. These countries either are involved in or have recently emerged from domestic or cross-border armed conflict, while some other countries are encountering governance problems. An IMF programme for emergency post-conflict assistance can accelerate these countries' progress in qualifying for debt relief. There is broad agreement that the HIPC Initiative is flexible enough to accommodate the special conditions of these countries by taking into account other factors, such as their track record in macroeconomic policy and institutional development, in respect of qualifying them for the HIPC Initiative.[21]

As part of the strengthening of the HIPC programme, the international community required that countries prepare PRSPs with the participation of all relevant stakeholders in a country. In order to expedite the qualification process for debt relief, interim PRSPs, which require less detail and are easier to complete, were introduced in 2000. Flexibility can also be exercised in implementing the HIPC framework by giving credit to a country's track record in sound macroeconomic policies and institutional reforms so as to facilitate the progress of qualified countries to the completion point.

The aim of the Enhanced HIPC Initiative is to reduce the debt-servicing burden of participating countries to a sustainable level. There have been, however, questions about the validity of the assumptions used to set the target for post-HIPC debt levels, such as the projections of exports and government revenues upon which the calculations of external debt sustainability are based.[22] There is a possibility that an individual country that has received debt relief could fall back into an unsustainable debt situation if there were a significant and protracted decline in export revenues or increase in import costs. Additional assistance needs to be provided to cover such contingencies.

There is broad agreement that debt relief under the Enhanced HIPC Initiative needs to be complemented by other resources to help the beneficiaries accelerate the pace of feasible growth and reduce poverty, while maintaining debt sustainability. So as not to divert resources from financing for development, debt relief needs to be complemented by increased ODA, mainly in the form of grants and highly concessional loans.

Involvement of the private sector in debt crisis resolution and prevention

Since the 1997-1998 international financial crises, there has been growing consensus in the international community that private creditors should contribute more to the resolution of debt crises in emerging market economies. Sometimes a country faces a large short-term financing requirement, but private markets are unwilling to lend, or its debt burden becomes unsustainable and requires restructuring. It has been recognized that, in such cases, the

[21] As at March 2001, the countries that were deemed for HIPC Initiative purposes to be involved in armed conflict were Angola, Burundi, the Central African Republic, the Congo, the Democratic Republic of the Congo, Guinea-Bissau, Myanmar, Rwanda, Sierra Leone, Somalia and the Sudan. Ethiopia emerged from an armed conflict situation after having signed an agreement to end hostilities on 18 June 2000. See also "Communiqué of the joint session-International Monetary and Financial Committee and Development Committee" (Washington, D.C., International Monetary Fund, 29 April 2001), para. 10.

[22] See "The challenge of maintaining long-term external debt sustainability" (Washington, D.C., International Monetary Fund and World Bank, 20 April 2001), executive summary, p. 1.

country's private creditors should be brought together to reach a collective agreement to limit their demands for immediate repayment and to bring about the orderly restructuring of the country's debt obligations.

Beyond this general understanding, however, there is not much clarity. "Clear rules" on how to involve the private sector are not in sight. Some analysts prefer "constructive ambiguity" so that creditors better appreciate the uncertainty of a bailout and will therefore be more careful in extending loans. In addition, it is not clear how to overcome the "collective action" problem (where each individual creditor knows the debtor does not have enough funds to service all its creditors, and so has an incentive to collect on its loan before funds run out). If the creditors can be brought together, they will realize that they have a better chance of collecting at least some of their loans if they work together rather than at cross purposes. With the greater use of bond financing and the consequent increase in the number of creditors, this problem has become more cumbersome than when a small number of banks arranged large syndicated loans.

Recent debt crises suggest that both the official sector and private creditors have drawn lessons from the crises of 1997-1998, but major challenges remain. There were three instances of comprehensive restructuring of sovereign debt owed to private creditors in 2000: in Ecuador, the first country to default on Brady bonds, in Pakistan and in Ukraine. The success of the restructurings may reflect several factors. In all cases, there was extensive interaction with creditors, the importance of which is now much better understood by most debtors. The bonds of Ecuador and Pakistan were rather narrowly held, which made it easier to establish close collaborative contacts with bond holders. In contrast, Ukraine's case was more complex because mobilizing the numerous individual bond holders in Western Europe required a massive public relations effort. All the restructuring bids were characterized by their comprehensiveness as opposed to a more piecemeal approach. For instance, Ecuador included in the restructuring proposal all $6.65 billion of its existing Brady and other international bonds, insisting that there would be no side deals with particular groups of creditors. This might have provided one additional incentive for the creditors to participate.

All three countries restructured their international bonds with the endorsement of IMF, which made it clear that private sector involvement would be necessary. The creditors also realized that the external positions of the crisis countries were unsustainable and that their losses could have been much bigger without the restructuring agreement; for example, there was a danger of default by both Pakistan and Ukraine.

Also, the bonds of Pakistan and Ukraine contained collective action clauses (CAC). By specifying a requisite majority (as opposed to unanimity) in order to change the terms of the bond, these clauses may facilitate restructuring. They were activated for Ukraine, but not for Pakistan. According to IMF, CAC might have helped to facilitate the restructuring, but only at the margin.[23] In Ecuador's restructuring, "exit consents" were used, by which a simple majority of bond holders could change those terms of a bond not directly related to the repayment schedule in such a way as to encourage bond holders' agreement and avoid litigation.

[23] "Resolving and preventing financial crises: the role of the private sector" (Washington, D.C., International Monetary Fund, 26 March 2001, http://www.imf.org/external/np/exr/ib2001), p. 9.

Despite these success stories, agreeing on general procedures to address the collective action problem remains a major challenge, as illustrated by the Peruvian case. A single, small holder of Peruvian bonds, instead of taking part in Peru's Brady plan debt restructuring in the 1990s, sued Peru for full payment of the face value of the debt. In June 2000, the bond holder secured a restraining order in a United States court on Peruvian official assets, making the country temporarily unable to pay interest on its Brady bonds. In order to avoid being forced into default, Peru paid the full amount in September 2000 to get the restraining order lifted, allowing it to make interest payments to the other bond holders. An appropriate set of contractual obligations would have forced the recalcitrant creditor—in this case, a speculative investor—to participate in the collective agreement.

ANNEX

REGIONAL INTEGRATION: RECENT DEVELOPMENTS IN WEST AFRICA AND LATIN AMERICA

Regional trading arrangements have continued to increase. In 2000, an estimated 20 new preferential trading agreements were at various stages of deliberation. Movements to strengthen or revise existing regional trading arrangements, as illustrated by the Economic Community of West African States (ECOWAS) and the Southern Cone Common Market (MERCOSUR) in Latin America (see below), have also been launched. Some broader common features can be extracted from these recent developments in regional bloc formation.

First, traditional forms of regional blocs, such as a customs union or free trade area, which focus narrowly on regional trade, seem to have become inadequate for the purpose of enabling the participants to address the latest aspects of global economic integration. Many existing regional trading blocs have therefore made efforts to extend their trade arrangements to encompass a broader agenda of economic integration, including financial and monetary linkages, movement of factors of production, and macroeconomic policy coordination.

Second, the leadership of many existing regional arrangements has sought to enlarge them by co-opting additional members or merging with other trading blocs. However, the process of forming larger regional trading blocs is complex, often because of asymmetries between an existing bloc and potential new members.

Finally, the evidence from recent developments on whether regional blocs individually or collectively constitute "building blocs" or "stumbling blocs" in the process of global multilateralism remains unclear. Seen as building blocs, regional integration arrangements are a prelude to broader global integration, serving, in time, to enhance the multilateral trading system. In contrast, when seen as stumbling blocs, regional trading arrangements undermine the multilateral system and inhibit its further development.

Regional trading arrangements, by definition, discriminate against non-members. However, a number of these arrangements have enabled many developed countries, such as the members of EU, to lower their trade impediments over time, even if for some sectors, notably agriculture, the discrimination remains welfare-reducing. Such arrangements have also allowed many developing countries to phase in their integration into global markets more gradually than the abrupt acceptance of the global rules of the game would have permitted. This may have allowed them to enter the global economic framework better prepared for competition, inter alia, in higher value added products, than would otherwise have been the case.

Economic integration in West Africa

In the course of 2000, ECOWAS launched several initiatives to reinvigorate cooperation among its member countries and to extend the areas of cooperation beyond trade and related activities.

Founded in 1975, ECOWAS consists of 15 members: Benin, Burkina Faso, Côte d'Ivoire, Guinea-Bissau, Mali, the Niger, Senegal and Togo, which are all members of the West African Economic and Monetary Union (WAEMU)[a] and part of the long-standing Communauté financière africaine (CFA) franc zone; and Cape Verde, the Gambia, Ghana, Guinea, Liberia, Nigeria and Sierra Leone.[b]

Until recently, there had been limited progress in integrating ECOWAS countries. At the summit in Lomé (Togo) in December 1999, however, an ambitious initiative was agreed upon to create a single regional market in West Africa, based on the following principles: a common currency; a common external tariff; free movement of goods, services, capital and persons; and the harmonization of economic and financial policies among member States. ECOWAS is also aiming to increase its capacity to negotiate access to the markets of developed countries.[c]

Since the Lomé summit, WAEMU and ECOWAS have undertaken measures to harmonize their separate trade integration schemes in order to accelerate the creation of a West African common market. As of 1 January 2000, a common external tariff (CET) has been in place in WAEMU, while the other members of ECOWAS are currently working towards the introduction of their own CET. The ultimate goal is to create a single CET for the whole of ECOWAS. Furthermore, six of the seven countries that are not members of WAEMU have embarked on a fast-track approach towards setting up a monetary zone alongside WAEMU by 2003. Once in place, it is hoped that this new undertaking can be merged with WAEMU in 2004 to form a single ECOWAS monetary zone, though one member—Cape Verde—will remain outside any such arrangements, at least initially.

The impact of ECOWAS integration on regional trade

Trade integration in ECOWAS aims to promote a more efficient pattern of production, distribution and consumption based on comparative advantages. It also seeks to overcome some of the limitations of small domestic markets, so as to allow economic agents to reap economies of scale and to stimulate more diverse consumption and production structures.[d]

The direct benefits of trade integration in West Africa should not, however, be overstated. Intraregional trade in ECOWAS is generally low, as many West African countries have a comparative advantage in the production of similar goods, often limited to a few primary commodities that are exported mainly to developed countries. The larger share of their trade is with the developed countries,[e] reflecting both the composition of their exports and their dependence on developed countries for imports of manufactured products, especially capital goods. The direct gains from additional trade and broader economic cooperation following the creation of a customs union are thus likely to be small.

Moreover, the creation of a customs union may bring additional costs for some countries. For example, countries that rely for their fiscal revenues on import tariffs may find it difficult to replace those revenues with other taxation instruments. Moreover, competition in a larger market may temporarily idle resources. The most significant potential drawback arises when a customs union leads to replacement of cheap imports from outside the union by more expensive imports from within. This is one form of trade diversion, costly to the coun-

[a] The Treaty establishing the West African Economic and Monetary Union was signed in 1994. In it, the signatories committed themselves to extending their long-standing integration in monetary affairs to the whole economic sphere.

[b] Before its withdrawal from ECOWAS in 2000, Mauritania belonged to this second group.

[c] This is particularly relevant after the signing of the Cotonou agreement, as regional economic areas will be the relevant entity with which EU henceforth negotiates economic partnership agreements (see World Economic and Social Survey, 2000 (United Nations publication, Sales No. E.00.II.C.1), box II.1). For the text of the Cotonou agreement, see http://www.europa.eu.int/comm/development/cotonou/agreement_en.htm.

[d] Alexander J. Yeats, "What can be expected from African regional trade arrangements?", Policy Research Working Paper, No. 2004 (Washington, D.C., World Bank, November 1998).

[e] Intraregional trade in ECOWAS accounts for about 11 per cent, while trade with EU accounts for more than 40 per cent.

try concerned. If, on the other hand, joining the customs union leads to the replacement of high-cost domestic production by cheaper imports from within the customs union—one form of trade creation—then the country gains. The net effect will be positive if the gains from trade creation accruing through changes in production, consumption or terms of trade, and possibly all three, exceed the costs of trade diversion. The effects for the various ECOWAS countries will depend on the formulation of the common commercial policy. In general, the lower the external trade barriers for the customs union, the less trade diversion there will be and the more beneficial regional integration will be.

Regional economic integration may also promote a clustering of economic activities, thereby enhancing the advantage of having a headstart in a specific location. In West Africa, for example, economic centres that have already attracted a critical mass of industry, such as Abidjan and Dakar, have started to develop business networks and the forward and backward linkages that tend to lock related manufacturing activities into those locations. Such regional trade integration may benefit members more unevenly than multilateral trade liberalization.

Even though the direct trade effects may be limited, regional trade integration may have indirect benefits. First, the customs union may allow for more effective participation of ECOWAS in multilateral trade negotiations, in particular in achieving increased market access in developed countries. Second, EU's record shows that trade integration at the regional level can make it easier for national Governments to override or to forestall the emergence of domestic groups opposed to trade reforms. Third, regional trade integration is often one element in a package of policy measures with positive mutual synergies. In ECOWAS, trade integration forms part of a wider agenda for overall economic integration. Its merits, therefore, cannot be assessed in isolation. Finally, since the initiative is promoted by the member States, rather than imposed from the outside, such synergies are more likely to materialize, allowing for the firmer anchoring of reforms in national policy-making processes.

If trade diversion can be held to a minimum, the dismantling of regional barriers to trade is also likely to entail trade gains that are not directly related to the reduction of intra-group tariffs or the establishment of a CET. Regional cooperation to improve, for example, the communication and transportation infrastructure, which is of very poor quality and a significant impediment to growth in regional trade, would support this process. Furthermore, these gains can increase over time as specialization according to comparative advantage proceeds across the region in a dynamic process. As indicated above, the conventional static gains attainable by the removal, either simultaneously or over time, of customs duties, for example, are unlikely to be significant for these countries, but their principal aim, given their ambition to foster catch-up modernization, should be to reap dynamic gains from trade and broader cooperation.

More importantly, the process of regional trade integration, when well designed and purposefully implemented, is not necessarily incompatible with multilateral trade liberalization. At the very least, it should be seen as a complement to rather than a substitute for multilateral trade liberalization along the lines of most-favoured-nation principle. The ECOWAS countries are likely to achieve a higher return on their comparative advantages through multilateral trade liberalization and increased access for their exports to markets in developed countries than from regional trade integration in the short to medium run. Increased trade integration with advanced industrialized countries through multilateral channels is also likely to foster better transfer of technology, as well as to generate greater assistance in locking in economic and political reforms, than is regional integration alone.

The benefits and costs of a monetary union for ECOWAS

The expected gains from the creation of a monetary union in West Africa are chiefly lower and more stable inflation, enhanced credibility of monetary policy, a more stable macroeconomic environment, lower real interest rates, and reduced transaction costs. These gains are conducive to investment, trade and economic expansion. Furthermore, the ECOWAS members view monetary union as necessary to realize the full benefits of a common market in the region. At issue is whether these gains would be large enough to offset the costs of giving up monetary policy and the exchange rate as policy instruments in individual countries. More specifically, two questions need to be answered: (a) will the union facilitate real adjustment to country-specific shocks in the absence of the exchange rate as a policy instrument? and (b) will the institutions of the monetary union and the commitment of the members be strong enough to secure the benefits of such a union?

The conditions under which a group of countries benefit from giving up their own monetary policy[f] and creating a monetary union have been widely discussed.[g] The benefits of a monetary union will be larger if: the countries are primarily affected by common shocks; real adjustment to asymmetric shocks is facilitated by flexible prices and wages, or mobility of labour among participating countries; there is a high level of intraregional trade that increases the gains of integration; there is a mechanism for fiscal transfers at the regional level to counter asymmetric shocks; and the credibility of monetary policy outside the monetary union is low, rendering the exchange rate a less potent policy instrument.

ECOWAS fares better with respect to some of these criteria than others. On the positive side, mobility of labour across some of the ECOWAS countries is significant. Also, wages and prices are relatively flexible, in particular in the informal sectors of these economies. Thus, real adjustment to asymmetric shocks can be facilitated through changes in relative factor and product prices and movement of labour, rather than by modifying exchange rates. In addition, the credibility of monetary policy is low in many of the members of ECOWAS that are not members of WAEMU, so that the gain from the improved credibility associated with a monetary union could to some degree compensate for the loss of the exchange rate as a policy instrument.

On other scores, however, abandoning the exchange rate as an instrument for facilitating adjustment to shocks would involve costs. First, ECOWAS countries are generally vulnerable to asymmetric shocks because their production structures are quite varied.[h] For example, as a major oil exporter, Nigeria, which accounts for 40 per cent of the group's gross domestic product (GDP), is generally affected by different shocks than those experienced by the oil-importing ECOWAS countries. Second, as intraregional trade will remain limited for the foreseeable future, gains from trade will be small and are unlikely to outweigh potential adjustment costs arising from asymmetric shocks. Third,

[f] The members of WAEMU do not have an independent monetary policy, given their fixed exchange-rate link to the French franc until 1998 and since then to the euro.

[g] The seminal article on optimum currency areas is Robert A. Mundell, "A theory of optimum currency areas", *The American Economic Review*, vol. 51, No. 4 (November 1961), pp. 509-517.

[h] Paul Masson and Catherine Pattillo, "Monetary union in West Africa (ECOWAS)", *Occasional Paper*, No. 204 (Washington, D.C., International Monetary Fund, February 2001).

there is no mechanism for fiscal transfers between the member States to cushion and spread the adjustment costs of asymmetric shocks. Finally, the level of political integration and the commitment to the institutions and policies of the monetary union are thus far limited.

A successful monetary union requires investment in institutions that ensure the irrevocability of the fixed exchange rates, until a common currency is adopted, and that facilitate the conduct of a single monetary policy. Generally, it is necessary both to reduce the scope for individual Governments to breach the rules and to make exit from the union costly. More specifically, a necessary condition for a viable single monetary policy in ECOWAS is the establishment of a central bank for the region that has a clear mandate for conducting monetary policy, is free from pressures to finance government deficits, and can act decisively according to agreed upon criteria for the conduct of monetary policy.

The choice of monetary policy regime and monetary anchor for an eventual common currency in ECOWAS has yet to be decided. A decision will be needed no later than when the monetary union is expanded beyond the present WAEMU arrangements. Tying in the broader monetary union to the euro with a link through the French Treasury, as under the present CFA regime, may not be optimal for the monetary union or desirable for the French Treasury, or it may be neither optimal for the one nor desirable for the other. At that stage, various options need to be contemplated.

The issue of monetary policy regimes for developing countries has been widely discussed in recent years,[i] and there is no consensus on what constitutes the optimal monetary policy regime for a currency area such as ECOWAS. Because of the limited integration of the ECOWAS economies with international financial markets, ECOWAS is likely to have a range of options for managing its external exchange rate (although internal exchange rates will be fixed after the agreed upon transition period). For example, the new common currency could establish a hard peg to the euro. This would preserve the long-standing link of many countries in ECOWAS to the French franc and, since 1999, to the euro. This has enabled them to import, since 1999, the euro zone's monetary policy credibility and to ensure exchange-rate stability for more than half of the trade of ECOWAS members. The euro zone and ECOWAS are, exposed however, to different types of external shock. A peg to the euro implies that ECOWAS could be forced to accommodate negative external shocks by means of a recession rather than through relaxing its monetary policy, if the prevailing degree of product and factor price flexibility and labour migration turned out to be insufficient.

Another option is to adopt an inflation-targeting regime, in which case the exchange rate could accommodate some of the external shocks these countries are likely to sustain. Such a regime is demanding, in the sense that it requires strong political and institutional commitments. It also needs a stable relationship between monetary instruments and inflation, one that can be projected quantitatively in a credible manner. Otherwise the transparency, hence the credibility, of the monetary policy would suffer.

These countries could also establish an intermediate regime with a fixed but adjustable, crawling or managed exchange-rate peg. Such a regime would be less demanding in terms of the required institutions and the guidelines for operating such a monetary union. As several experiences of developing countries

i   See, for example, Michael Mussa and others, "Exchange rate regimes in an increasingly integrated world economy", *Occasional Paper*, No. 193 (Washington, D.C., International Monetary Fund, August 2000).

have demonstrated, such regimes are prone to instability, particularly if the currency area is highly integrated with international capital markets and its domestic supervisory institutions and prudential regulations are underdeveloped. This issue will become more relevant when the ECOWAS area is more integrated into the global economy.

In addition choosing a monetary regime, a well-functioning monetary union requires consistency between the single monetary policy and the fiscal policies pursued by individual member States. The creation of a monetary union does not in itself ensure this. The experience of the European Economic and Monetary Union (EMU) indicates that a rule-based approach to fiscal policy can promote fiscal prudence. This involves limits on debts and deficits, a prohibition against monetary bailouts, mechanisms for macroeconomic surveillance, peer reviews, and a strong political commitment to the institutions created.

It has been recognized by ECOWAS that the harmonization of economic and fiscal policies is a necessary condition for fully reaping the benefits of a common market and a monetary union. In April 2000, the six ECOWAS countries aiming to create a secondary monetary zone adopted a set of convergence criteria to be achieved by the end of 2003. Members of WAEMU have had in place convergence criteria, and have thus conducted mutual surveillance of economic policies, for a number of years. The two sets of convergence criteria are similar, and include limits on inflation, fiscal deficits, government debt, central bank financing of fiscal deficits, and international reserves (see annex table II.1). The WAEMU countries, partly reflecting their longer history of cooperation and mutual surveillance, are generally much closer to meeting their convergence criteria than the ECOWAS countries that are not members of WAEMU.

The experience of EMU indicates that the building of new institutions, the ensuring of effective governance therein, the technical preparations involved, and the achievement of convergence criteria are complex and time-consuming.

Annex table II.1.
MACROECONOMIC INDICATORS FOR WAEMU MEMBERS
IN RELATION TO CONVERGENCE CRITERIA

	Position in 1999		
	Basic fiscal finance (as percentage of GDP)	Inflation (annual percentage rate)	External public debt as percentage of GDP)
WAEMU	0.5	0.2	99.2
Benin	3.6	0.3	58.3
Burkina Faso	-0.5	-1.1	66.5
Côte d'Ivoire	-1.5	0.8	115
Guinea-Bissau	-9.5	-2.1	411.6
Maii	1.6	-1.1	97.6
Niger	-5.2	-2.3	113.9
Senegal	1.8	0.8	74.4
Togo	-1.7	0	126.7
Convergence criteria for end-2002	≥ 0	≤ 3	≤ 70

Source: Commission of WAEMU.

The timetable for creating the monetary union in ECOWAS is ambitious and requires that countries adjust to a set of convergence criteria within a short period of time, leading to a number of concerns. First, the record of implementing agreed measures among the ECOWAS countries is mixed. This casts doubt on the timetable's realism. Second, some countries, such as Ghana and Nigeria, the key participants in the second monetary union, have a long way yet to go to meet several of convergence criteria (see annex table II.2). Third, a number of crucial decisions have still to be made, such as the choice of a common currency, the choice of monetary anchor, handling of the WAEMU's peg to the euro, and managing its link to the French Treasury and to the other half of the CFA zone. Finally, the conflict and tension in several ECOWAS countries undermine their ability to undertake monetary integration on this scale.

In summary, increased coordination of fiscal and monetary policies in ECOWAS, in particular for the members not belonging to WAEMU, would promote a more stable macroeconomic environment, conducive to investment and trade. The current push for integration is also seen as complementing the cooperation within ECOWAS in security and political matters. These benefits, however, are not dependent upon the immediate realization of a monetary union. The latter requires not only the will, but also the ability, to undertake the necessary adjustments and to fulfil the relevant conditions. A hastily constructed and poorly devised monetary union could easily falter and undermine the overall effort of regional integration. In the longer term, however, with a solid commitment to the integration initiative and its institutions, a monetary union could deliver the benefits the ECOWAS countries are hoping to reap.

New challenges for the Southern Cone Common Market (MERCOSUR)

As a regional integration project in South America's Southern Cone, The Southern Cone Common Market (MERCOSUR) has been under pressure from

Annex table II.2.
MACROECONOMIC INDICATORS FOR COUNTRIES IN THE SECOND MONETARY ZONE IN RELATION TO CONVERGENCE CRITERIA

	Position at end-1999			
	Overall fiscal deficit (as percentage of GDP)[a]	Inflation (annual percentage rate)	Gross official reserves (in months of imports)	Central bank advances (as percentage of tax revenue)
Gambia	4.8	1.7	5.7	32
Ghana	8.2	13.8	1.5	8.2
Guinea	5.1	4.6	2.6	29.6
Liberia	0.4	4.0	0	0
Nigeria	7.7	6.6	4.5	55
Sierra Leone	14.9	34.1	2.0	70.9
Convergence criteria for				
End-2002	< 5	< 10	> 3	-
End-2003	< 4	< 5	> 6	< 10

Source: IMF staff estimates.
[a] Excluding grants

growing economic disparity among its members, including heterogeneous exchange-rate regimes; divergent macroeconomic performances; and disagreement on the degree of common external protection, both on average and in terms of its distribution, including its CET. Some of these factors have threatened the survival of MERCOSUR since late 2000. The bloc has also been confronted with the challenge emanating from the forthcoming negotiations around the establishment of the Free Trade Area of the Americas (FTAA).

Created in 1991 by Argentina, Brazil, Paraguay and Uruguay, with Chile and Bolivia later becoming associate members, MERCOSUR has as its primary objective to establish a common market for goods and services (which will ultimately be extended to factors of production as well); to coordinate macroeconomic policies; and to harmonize national legislations. With intraregional customs duties having been gradually eliminated during 1991-1994, a CET was introduced in 1995 and the customs union came into existence.

Until recently, intra-bloc trade had boomed after the establishment of MERCOSUR on account of the removal of intra-group tariffs and again after the introduction of the CET: the value of exports in United States dollars within the area grew at an average rate of 16 per cent during 1990-1999, compared with 4 per cent for extra-bloc exports. As a result, the share of intra-group exports in total exports increased from about 10 per cent in 1990 to 25 per cent in 1998. It receded in 1999 because of the economic slowdown in major countries and some of the other difficulties cited, but rebounded somewhat in 2000.

Divergences in interests among the members, especially between Argentina and Brazil, the two largest, have been mounting since Brazil's currency crisis in 1999. The depreciation and floating of the real boosted Brazil's competitiveness vis-à-vis Argentina. In order to enhance the competitive position of its industrial sector, in March 2001 Argentina suspended the application of the CET by eliminating tariffs on imports of capital goods and raising those for consumer goods. Furthermore, the divergent interests of the members and associate members have been compounded by Chile's decision to negotiate a bilateral trade agreement with the United States; the occurrence of several trade disputes in recent years, notably between Argentina and Brazil; and slow progress in resolving such issues as the elimination of non-tariff barriers, the enactment of dispute settlement mechanisms, and the adoption of anti-dumping rules. Some of the challenges facing economic integration in MERCOSUR derive, however, from the way in which the preferential arrangement was set up and the manner in which it has been governed.

Since its inception in 1995, MERCOSUR's CET has remained incomplete. First, many products in such categories as capital goods and technology are not subject to the CET, leaving individual members with the discretion to set their own external tariffs for such products. Second, some other economic activities, such as the automotive sector, have been excluded from the customs union, in the sense that tariffs and non-tariff barriers have not been eliminated among the members. Third, Argentina's action to suspend the CET has further jeopardized the customs union.

The problems of MERCOSUR's CET are closely linked to a disagreement among its member States regarding the degree of protection for certain goods, notably capital equipment. Argentina, Paraguay and Uruguay favour lower protection for capital goods from outside the bloc and tend to see a high CET as an impediment to enhancing the efficiency and competitiveness of their economies. Brazil, which has a relatively developed capital goods sector, favours higher protection as a means of consolidating its role as a supplier of machinery and equipment for the area. With fairly high external protection, the entire conundrum of trade diversion in MERCOSUR, hence the benefits of the regional bloc to its members, becomes evident.[i]

Despite some recent progress, including an agreement for free intra-bloc trade for the automotive sector by 2006, many problems of MERCOSUR's CET remain to be tackled in order for the members to reap the potential benefits of regional integration. These can be seen as accruing from expanded markets, a reduction in the dependence of some of these countries on commodity exports through greater production diversification for the region, and a reduction in the area's vulnerability to external shocks. This potential, however, can be fully realized only if the members succeed in meeting the above-cited challenges head-on.

Macroeconomic policy coordination

Over the last decade, the members of MERCOSUR adopted different approaches in respect of addressing various external shocks. Domestic economic problems have led to heterogeneous exchange-rate regimes in the bloc: Argentina has maintained its currency board—an extreme form of a fixed exchange-rate regime, which was adopted in 1991; Brazil abandoned the exchange-rate policy of the so-called real plan—a crawling band exchange-rate regime, combined with other policy commitments such as fiscal consolidation and structural reforms, which was implemented in 1994—and let its currency float in early 1999; and the other two members and two associate members have four different exchange-rate regimes, ranging from free floating since 1999 (Chile) and managed floating (Paraguay) to a crawling peg (Bolivia) and a crawling band (Uruguay). As a result, real exchange rates among the members have fluctuated widely, causing misaligned relative purchasing powers among the members. The direct consequence of the increased volatility and the misalignment of exchange rates, as well as the recessions in some countries in 1999 and 2000, has been a sharp reduction in intra-bloc trade: it contracted by 25 per cent in 1999.[k] At the same time, macroeconomic performances among the members have also diverged (see chap. III).

Recognizing these problems, MERCOSUR countries have improved the coordination of their macroeconomic policies. In June 2000, the Ministers of Finance of MERCOSUR, as well as those of Bolivia and Chile, recommitted themselves at the Buenos Aires summit to fiscal solvency and monetary stability; agreed on the establishment of common macroeconomic targets and a convergence mechanism[l]; and created a Macroeconomic Monitoring Group (MMG) entrusted with establishing a set of harmonized economic indicators and with monitoring compliance with agreed targets.

Subsequently, at the Florianópolis (Brazil) summit in December 2000, the Presidents of the member States adopted a concrete set of targets and a mechanism for facilitating macroeconomic convergence. The year 2001 will be a transitional period, during which country-specific targets will be jointly announced. For later years, member States committed themselves to achieving the following common targets[m]: inflation below 5 per cent per year during

[i] Alexander J. Yeats, "Does MERCOSUR's trade performance raise concerns about the effects of regional trade arrangements?", *World Bank Economic Review*, vol. 12, No. 1 (January 1998), pp. 1-28.

[k] Data for 2000 are incomplete, but it is unlikely that intra-group trade regained its 1998 share.

[l] See MERCOSUR Common Market Council, *CMC/DEC No. 30/2000* (Buenos Aires, 29 June 2000).

[m] See Institute for the Integration of Latin America, *Carta Mensual No. 53* (Washington, D.C., December 2000).

2002-2005; the increase in the stock of net debt of the consolidated public sector not to exceed 3 per cent of GDP from 2002 on; and the stock of net debt of the consolidated public sector not to exceed 40 per cent of GDP by 2010. Transitional regimes have been granted to Brazil (for the variation of public debt target) and Paraguay (for the inflation target).

A member that misses a target for a given year is required to submit to the next MMG meeting a set of macroeconomic and possibly structural measures for converging to the agreed path in the course of the next year. Once a country has submitted a set of measures, the MMG will evaluate them and submit its opinion to the meetings of ministers and presidents of central banks of MERCOSUR.

In the long run, convergence in inflation rates and fiscal deficits can provide the necessary conditions for narrowing variations in exchange rates among the members and increasing economic stability in the area. Furthermore, if monetary integration is considered to be an implied long-run goal of the integration process in the region, the macroeconomic convergence agreements currently in place could provide an essential stepping stone.

MERCOSUR and the Free Trade Area of the Americas (FTAA)

At the third Summit of the Americas held in Québec (Canada) in April 2001, the heads of State of the western hemisphere committed themselves to completing negotiations for FTAA by 1 January 2005. Participants will be able to negotiate either independently or as a trade bloc. The latter will be the option for the members of MERCOSUR, as well as for those of the Andean Community and of the Caribbean Community.

Negotiating as a bloc may grant MERCOSUR countries greater bargaining power in the deliberations on certain issues of common interest to them, such as non-tariff barriers, agricultural subsidies, anti-dumping regulations, and the treatment of environmental and labour regulations. Moreover, if MERCOSUR can act effectively as a bloc, its role in the negotiations as a leader of the subcontinent is likely to be enhanced.

It is still unclear, however, whether MERCOSUR members will eventually opt for bilateral negotiations with the United States, following the example of Chile, which in November 2000 announced negotiations for a bilateral trade agreement with the United States based on the characteristics of the North American Free Trade Agreement (NAFTA). Chile has already signed bilateral agreements with the two other NAFTA partners—Canada and Mexico. Its decision to opt out of MERCOSUR's common stance in the FTAA negotiations reflects the country's preference for a more open, lower-protection approach than is currently the case in MERCOSUR.

Finally, MERCOSUR also needs to make progress with non-tariff barriers, anti-dumping rules, and dispute settlement mechanisms. As recent sectoral disputes between Argentina and Brazil have underlined, solutions are all too frequently found through ad hoc bilateral agreements reached at the highest political level, rather than by invoking established rules and regulations. The absence of clear ex ante rules and of an independent institutional structure to guarantee their enforcement needs to be remedied soon if integration is to progress.

III THE CURRENT SITUATION IN THE WORLD'S ECONOMIES

The world economy grew by 4.1 per cent in 2000, supported by 12.3 per cent growth in international trade. Economic growth accelerated in all country groupings analysed by the present *Survey,* but the performance of the group of economies in transition was particularly striking. These economies grew on average faster than the developing countries, which themselves sustained a robust rate of growth in 2000.

As anticipated, the fast pace of growth could not be sustained owing to pressures from imbalances and other fragilities in some key economies. Additionally, higher oil prices ignited fears of an acceleration in inflation, leading monetary authorities to tighten credit conditions. As a result, world growth started to decelerate by the end of 2000, led by the sharp slowdown of the economy of the United States of America and its negative impact on those economies largely exposed to United States markets.

The outlook for 2001 is cautious, as the world economy will not be able to count on one of the major factors that contributed to the fast resumption of growth after the Asian crisis, namely, United States import demand. Meanwhile, the Japanese economy remains weak, while domestic demand conditions are not yet strong enough to sustain fast growth in the near term in countries affected by the recent financial crises of 1997-1998.

DEVELOPED ECONOMIES

The growth of gross domestic product (GDP) in the developed economies continued to accelerate and reached 3.6 per cent in 2000, the fastest rate in a decade. The economic performance of the North American economies was particularly strong, driven by the robustness of their domestic demand, particularly of private investment. In Western Europe, growth was similarly sustained by domestic demand as lower unemployment kept consumer confidence high, while the fast growth of external demand was also a positive factor. GDP growth in Japan—albeit faster than in 1999—remained sluggish in 2000 and largely supported by fiscal stimulus, although private investment recovered somewhat.

Inflation accelerated in the developed countries in 2000 owing to the higher oil prices whose impact on consumer price inflation was aggravated in some countries by currency depreciation and some other adverse exogenous shocks. The increase in inflation was, however, modest. Central banks tightened their policy stance and raised interest rates. Japan was the exception among developed economies as the country witnessed its second consecutive year of deflation and monetary conditions remained loose.

Most developed countries experienced an improvement in their fiscal position and employment situation owing to faster growth. Japan is, once again, an exception with its large budget deficit and mushrooming public debt and its unemployment remaining at record high rates.

Since late 2000, the United States economy has been showing signs of weakness and has decelerated sharply. Growth of GDP is anticipated to slow markedly in 2001. Growth will moderate in Western Europe, but the region is expected to maintain momentum in 2001 owing to the strength of its domestic demand. Prospects are not encouraging for the Japanese economy. Severe structural problems yet to be addressed present serious downside risks to the modest growth forecast for Japan in 2001. In all, the developed economies are expected to decelerate and their average GDP growth will be below 2 per cent in 2001.

North America: preventing a recession

After a long period of robust growth, North America experienced a slowdown in mid-2000 that continued and intensified into 2001, particularly in the United States. Although both the United States and Canada eased their monetary policies substantially in early 2001, further stimulus is needed to halt the eroding consumer and business confidence, as well as to contain the spreading of the downturn in manufacturing to other sectors.

A significant moderation became noticeable in the United States in the second half of 2000 (see table III.1), led by a sharp deceleration in business investment, especially in information and communication technologies (ICT) (see figure III.1). The momentum of the downturn increased at the beginning of 2001, as firms cut capital spending further. As discussed in chapter I, the main factors behind the downturn are the tightening monetary policy from mid-1999 to mid-2000, the considerable drop in equity prices (particularly of technology stocks), higher oil prices, and the emergence of excess capacity in some sectors of the economy, especially ICT.

These factors led to a significant squeezing of corporate profits. In the last quarter of 2000, corporate profits declined by about 10 per cent, having grown at double-digit rates during prior years. As indicated in chapter I, a vicious circle has developed among corporate profits, capital spending, stock markets, and consumer and business sentiments in the economy. In order to restore profits, firms cut capital spending, shed inventory, and laid off labour. Reacting, more firms lowered their earnings projections, leading to a further decline in stock markets, and broadening the deterioration in consumer and business confidence. As a result, the initial slowdown in the ICT sector was spread and amplified to other sectors.

The slowdown in Canada appeared later than that in the United States. Average corporate earnings were still rising in the second half of 2000, while growth of personal disposable income accelerated in the fourth quarter to an annual pace of 6.4 per cent, the highest since 1990. With the deepening slowdown in the United States economy, however, a deceleration in business capital spending, a decline in industrial capacity utilization, slack in the goods market, and a sharp downturn in employment emerged in Canada at the beginning of 2001.

Table III.1.
MAJOR INDUSTRIALIZED COUNTRIES: QUARTERLY INDICATORS, 1999-2000

	1999 quarter				2000 quarter			
	I	II	III	IV	I	II	III	IV
Growth of gross domestic product[a] (percentage change in seasonally adjusted data from preceding quarter)								
Canada	4.8	3.3	6.5	5.1	5.1	4.7	4.9	2.6
France	2.8	3.6	4.1	4.4	2.6	2.7	3.2	3.0
Germany	3.2	-0.4	3.6	3.6	4.1	4.9	1.2	0.8
Italy	1.9	2.3	3.0	3.8	4.1	1.1	1.9	3.3
Japan	1.9	6.3	-0.3	-5.8	10.0	0.9	-2.4	3.0
United Kingdom	1.8	2.6	5.2	3.3	1.8	3.6	3.5	1.4
United States	3.5	2.5	5.7	8.3	4.8	5.6	2.2	1.0
Major developed economies	2.9	3.2	3.7	3.3	5.6	3.7	1.2	1.8
Euro zone	3.2	2.0	4.1	4.1	3.6	3.2	2.0	2.8
Unemployment rate[b] (percentage of total labour force)								
Canada	7.9	7.8	7.6	7.0	6.8	6.7	6.9	6.9
France	11.7	11.5	11.2	10.8	10.2	9.8	9.6	9.3
Germany	8.8	8.7	8.8	8.7	8.5	8.4	8.3	8.2
Italy	11.6	11.4	11.3	11.1	11.4	10.8	10.1	10.0
Japan	4.6	4.7	4.7	4.6	4.8	4.7	4.6	4.8
United Kingdom	6.4	6.1	6.0	5.9	5.8	5.5	5.4	5.4
United States	4.3	4.3	4.2	4.1	4.0	4.0	4.0	4.0
Major developed economies	6.3	6.2	6.2	6.0	5.9	5.8	5.7	5.7
Euro zone	10.3	10.0	9.9	9.7	9.4	9.2	9.0	8.8
Growth of consumer prices[c] (percentage change from preceding quarter)								
Canada	0.8	4.4	2.9	1.3	2.2	3.5	3.9	2.7
France	0.1	2.4	-0.3	1.7	2.3	2.3	1.3	1.7
Germany	0.1	2.2	1.7	-0.1	3.5	1.5	3.4	0.9
Italy	1.4	2.3	1.8	2.7	2.5	2.9	2.4	2.9
Japan	-3.9	1.3	-1.2	0.0	-2.7	1.1	-1.0	0.7
United Kingdom	-1.7	4.3	0.3	3.0	1.6	7.7	0.6	2.5
United States	1.6	3.9	2.5	2.5	4.0	4.3	3.2	2.2
Major developed economies	-0.3	2.9	1.1	1.5	1.8	3.1	1.8	1.7
Euro zone	1.2	2.7	1.2	1.2	2.7	1.9	3.4	2.7

Source: UN/DESA, based on data of IMF, *International Financial Statistics;* Organisation for Economic Cooperation and Development (OECD); and national authorities.

[a] Expressed at annual rate (total is weighted average with weights being annual GDP valued at 1995 prices and exchange rates).
[b] Seasonally adjusted data as standardized by OECD.
[c] Expressed at annual rate.

Figure III.1.

UNITED STATES OF AMERICA: ANNUAL RATE OF GROWTH OF REAL GDP AND SELECTED COMPONENTS, FIRST QUARTER 1999-FIRST QUARTER 2001

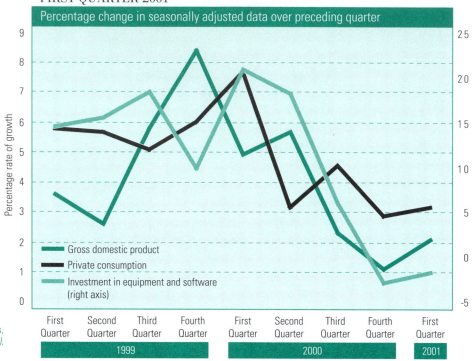

Percentage change in seasonally adjusted data over preceding quarter

Legend:
Gross domestic product
Private consumption
Investment in equipment and software (right axis)

First Quarter / Second Quarter / Third Quarter / Fourth Quarter — 1999
First Quarter / Second Quarter / Third Quarter / Fourth Quarter — 2000
First Quarter — 2001

Source: United States Bureau of Economic Analysis, *Gross Domestic Product: First Quarter 2001 (Advance)*, table 1.

Current economic situation and the outlook

A recovery in the region will depend on many factors, including the effectiveness of macroeconomic policy and a restoration of consumer and business confidence, particularly in the United States economy. Views are split on the outlook for the United States, with three different stylized paths: "V", "U" and "L", that is to say, a recovery of the economy as quickly as it went down, a slow recovery, and a situation where the economy will grow slowly at best, respectively.

Macroeconomic policies have become supportive of growth in the economies of both the United States and Canada most recently. As the downturn accelerated at the beginning of 2001, it became apparent that the risks for the economy had turned from a situation of exuberant demand to one of weakness. The United States Federal Reserve Bank (Fed) thus rapidly adjusted its policy stance, cutting interest rates four times in the first four months of the year by a total of 200 (basis points) bps (see figure III.2). In the same period, the Bank of Canada cut interest rates by a total of 100 bps. Given the continued deterioration in economic conditions, further monetary easing is expected for both economies in 2001.

Fiscal policies are stimulatory as well. In addition to a $1.3 trillion tax cut over the next 10 years, increased federal spending has been set for fiscal year 2001 in the United States. Meanwhile, spending of State and local governments has increased as a result of earlier revenue gains. In Canada, a new round of tax

Figure III.2.
EURO ZONE AND UNITED STATES OF AMERICA:
POLICY INTEREST RATES, JANUARY 1999-APRIL 2001

Percentage

— Euro zone
— USA

J F M A M J J A S O N D J F M A M J J A S O N D J F M A
1999   2000   2001

Source: United States Federal Reserve Bank and European Central Bank.

cuts was set in Budget 2000 and enacted in January 2001. The Five-Year Tax Reduction Plan will total about 100 billion Canadian dollars, including cutting tax rates for personal and corporate incomes, and reducing the capital gain-inclusion rate.

Growth for the first two quarters of 2001 is expected to be flat in the United States, followed by a rebound by the end of 2001. The GDP of the United States is expected to grow at 1¾ per cent in 2001 and 3 per cent in 2002, while that of Canada is expected to grow by 2¾ per cent in 2001, and 3½ per cent in 2002 (see table A.2)

Business investment has been the most volatile component of aggregate demand and it has decelerated rapidly. Capital spending on ICT has been reduced, as many firms have to consolidate excess capacity and to reduce inventory. Growth of investment in equipment and software is expected to slow from 13 per cent in 2000 to about 2 per cent in 2001 for the United States and a decline on a similar scale is expected for Canada.

In contrast, consumption spending has held up relatively well in both economies. While the growth of private consumption in the United States slowed from 5 per cent in 1998-1999 to 2.2 per cent in the fourth quarter of 2000, it is expected to be about 2.5 per cent in 2001-2002. Consumer sentiment and the performance of stock markets are the two key interlinked factors that may imply some risks for further weakening of consumer spending, at least in the short run. In the United States, the fall in equity markets cost households nearly 2 per cent of their net worth in 2000, the first decline in net wealth in a decade. Additionally, with the wealth effects from the large equity appreciation in the early years being reversed, the saving rate is expected to rise, leading to a lower propensity to consume out of current income.

In Canada, consumer spending remained buoyant at the beginning of 2001, after 4 per cent growth in 2000. The tax cut in January 2001 (see above) might provide some support, but a slowdown in private consumption is expected over the year as the spillover effects from weakening exports and a softening labour market reach the household sector.

On the supply side, both economies registered solid productivity growth in 2000. In the United States, productivity growth slowed. United States productivity growth dropped from an annual rate of 3.4 per cent in the third quarter to 2.2 per cent in the fourth quarter of 2000. Nevertheless, compared with the sharp deceleration in output, productivity growth has been holding up well, indicating that the ICT-driven productivity shift in the late 1990s was structural rather than cyclical. Productivity growth is expected to remain above 2 per cent for 2001, although it may be weak in the near term.

In the first quarter of 2001, the productivity of the non-farm business sector declined by 0.1 per cent in the United States. This added to the recent debate on whether the rise in productivity growth in the 1990s had reflected a structural improvement or only cyclical changes in productivity growth.[1] A review of the statistical data of the past few decades shows that quarterly productivity growth can be very volatile. This is particularly the case in periods when output fluctuates widely, as adjustments in the labour force (hours of all persons, which is used as the denominator for calculating productivity) usually move more slowly than output.[2] Therefore, given the latest decline in the growth of output, a dip in productivity growth in a couple of quarters should not be taken as a change in the trend. Even with the decline in the first quarter of the year, productivity still grew by 2.8 per cent when measured year over year.

Despite the slowdown, the United States labour market remained tight in 2000. Non-farm payroll employment increased by about 1.5 per cent in 2000, with employment creation in the service sector offsetting job reduction in manufacturing. Since the beginning of 2001, however, an increasing number of firms, especially many large ICT corporations, have announced plans for substantial lay-offs. As a result, the unemployment rate, which stood at 4.2 per cent at the beginning of 2001, is expected to rise to about 4¾ per cent by the end of the year. In Canada, labour-market statistics recorded the first decline in full-time jobs at the beginning of 2001 in four years, and the unemployment rate is expected to rise to 7 per cent in 2001 from 6.8 per cent in 2000.

Inflation increased in 2000 for both economies, mainly owing to higher energy prices (see table A.8). The upward pressure continued in early 2001, especially in the United States. In spite of some pass-through effects from energy prices, inflation in other sectors remained moderate in general. The rises in labour productivity, increased international competition, and a rapid expansion of capacity in manufacturing restricted the ability of firms to raise prices. Meanwhile, inflation expectations remain low and stable, and the rise in unemployment is expected to ease the wage pressure that built up in early 2001, especially in the United States. The inflation outlook for 2001 remains benign for the region, with the consumer price index (CPI) expected to rise less than 3 per cent and the increase in the core CPI remaining below 2½ per cent for the United States and about 2 per cent for Canada.

[1]   See *World Economic Situation and Prospects, 2001* (United Nations publication, Sales No. E.01.II.C.2), pp. 6-8.

[2]   For example, productivity growth registered only 1.6 per cent in the first quarter of 2000 when GDP grew by about 5 per cent. Since 1995, there have been two quarters when productivity registered a decline: the first quarter of 1995 (-0.8 per cent) and the third quarter of 1996 (-0.1 per cent).

The external sector of both economies registered strong growth in 2000. However, trade has decelerated sharply since the last quarter of 2000, with United States export demand contracting in real terms. The impact of the downturn in the United States on Canadian exports became apparent in the first of quarter of 2001, but more severe effects are expected later in the year. The growth of trade is expected to slow down substantially for both economies in 2001, to 3-4 per cent for both exports and imports in the United States, and an even lower rate for Canada.

The trade deficit of the United States reached nearly $450 billion (4.5 per cent of GDP) by the end of 2000. There is growing concern about the sustainability of the deficit and the risks of a sudden reversal (see chap. I). The deficit is expected to fall in the next few years, but only modestly. In contrast, Canada registered a trade surplus of over $30 billion in 2000 (equivalent to 4 per cent of GDP), but this is expected to moderate in 2001-2002.

The United States dollar continued to appreciate against most major currencies in 2000 (see table A.12) and in early 2001. Meanwhile, the Canadian dollar was on a weakening trend in 2000 until the fourth quarter. It is expected to remain relatively stable vis-à-vis the United States dollar in 2001.

Western Europe: how immune to the United States deceleration?

Growth in Western Europe in 2000 was the best in a decade. This marked a strong rebound from 1999, fairly balanced between domestic and foreign demand. Aggregate GDP of the 15 members of the European Union (EU-15) grew by 3.3 per cent in 2000 after 2.4 per cent in 1999. Mirroring other developed economies, growth is expected to decelerate to 2½ per cent in 2001 (see table A.2), owing primarily to external demand conditions, but also to the lingering effects of the increase in oil prices. Additionally, the region has been subjected to a number of adverse developments in the agricultural sector, where the outbreak of livestock diseases has resulted in mass slaughter of farm animals. This has pushed up food prices and also had substantial indirect effects on the rest of the economy owing to transportation problems and loss of tourism revenue. The region's robust domestic demand, however, is expected to soften the effects of these negative shocks on overall GDP growth. Boosted by the expected pickup of world demand in the second half of 2001, aggregate GDP of EU is expected to grow by 3 per cent in 2002.

One of the main uncertainties in the region's current outlook revolves around the extent, duration and impact of the United States slowdown, which may be amplified if economic conditions deteriorate further in Japan, and contagion spreads to other parts of the world. For Europe, four possible transmission channels stand out: trade, through both direct and indirect effects; the earnings of European companies with a large United States exposure; consumer and business confidence; and the behavior of the euro. The overall impact will also depend on the whether domestic demand retains its current strength.

While growth in 2000 as a whole was robust, the quarterly pattern revealed some stresses from both external and internal shocks as the economy slowed in the second half of the year (see table III.1). Private consumption decelerated sharply as sustained higher energy prices impacted on real incomes. Nevertheless, consumption should provide a cushion to growth in 2001. Tax cuts implemented in many countries in early 2001, continuing employment growth, and moderate gains in wages together with declining inflation, as well as the dissipation of the effects of the higher oil prices, should raise disposable incomes. Continuing strength in consumer confidence argues for stable saving rates.

Growth of fixed capital formation was volatile during 2000, with the second half of the year slower than the first, as the positive effects of buoyant demand and relaxed financing conditions early in the year gave way to increasingly restrictive monetary policy and a less favourable external environment. Investment growth is expected to remain low in the first half of 2001. Despite the anticipated loosening of monetary policy, financing conditions may not ease substantially in the immediate future. Firms with a strong international presence have already seen a marked deterioration in their balance sheets, which affects their ability to raise capital. The telecommunications sector in particular, in which Western Europe plays a leading role, has been hard hit owing to the large amounts of debt incurred in financing the acquisition of third-generation mobile phone licences, as well as the impact of ICT as the focus of the current slowdown in world demand. Finally, in a number of countries, investment behaviour is tightly linked to export performance. Investment spending, however, is expected to pick up in the second half of 2001 into 2002 with the anticipated recovery in world growth, the easing of financing conditions, and high levels of capacity utilization in many countries.

Exports grew by 11 per cent in the region as a whole (see table A.13) and were the other driving force behind the strong performance in 2000. Despite the slowing of external demand in the latter half of the year, export growth accelerated in the last two quarters of 2000, boosted by the further weakening of the euro. This strong performance carried over to the beginning of 2001. It is expected to be affected by the movements in world demand since then, with a marked slowdown in the first half of 2001, a modest recovery in the second half, and a strengthening into 2002. A moderate appreciation of the euro is expected and will lead to some loss in competitiveness, but the currency would remain highly competitive.

The extent of the vulnerability to the United States slowdown is a matter of considerable debate. Western Europe, particularly the euro zone, is a relatively closed trading area, but there are differing levels of exposure for the countries in the region. The share of EU-15 trade to the United States is about 9 per cent (see table A.14), but for a number of countries the exposure is higher—close to 15 per cent in the case of the United Kingdom of Great Britain and Northern Ireland and 10 per cent for Germany. Given that these are the largest economies in the region, there may be significant second-round effects for the region as a whole.

Imports also grew at double-digit rates in 2000, supported by robust domestic demand. This dampened the positive contribution of net exports to overall GDP growth. Import demand is expected to slow in 2001 in line with the movements in domestic demand, but to be boosted moderately by the expected euro appreciation, so that the contribution of net exports to growth will narrow significantly.

Growth performances were more uniform in 2000 than in prior years, with no major outliers on the downside. A number of the smaller economies–Belgium, Finland, Greece, Luxembourg, the Netherlands and

Spain—grew above 4 per cent, while Ireland recorded another remarkable performance with GDP growing by almost 11 per cent (see table A.2). In contrast to the recent past, all of the large economies grew by 3 per cent or slightly above 3 per cent in 2000.

France's growth exceeded 3 per cent for the third year in a row. Much of this can be attributed to the continued strength of domestic demand, whose roots lie in the turnaround in the labour market during the 1990s, with solid employment growth and a significant drop in the rate of unemployment. Structural reforms initiated in the 1990s, including large-scale cuts in payroll taxes that targeted unskilled workers, have increased labour-market flexibility. The development of part-time, temporary and fixed-term contracts have led to a much more job-intensive growth pattern. Paradoxically, the structure of labour contracts under the 35-hour workweek regulations has also, at least in the short run, increased flexibility in labour markets. Owing to the robustness of domestic demand, France is expected to ride out the current slowdown relatively painlessly.

In 2000, the German economy experienced a remarkable rebound from 1999 and its best performance since 1990 (see table A.2). Strong export growth, which also boosted investment in equipment, was the principal driving force and responded well to the robust world demand and the low value of the euro. Growth was also supported by supply-side measures of tax reforms, a decrease in unit labour costs, and low real interest rates. On the negative side, private consumption proved especially sensitive to the oil price increase, and investment in construction shrank further owing to overcapacity. Germany's dependence on trade and the weakness of its domestic demand are a major reason why growth is expected to decelerate substantially in 2001.

The external environment is similarly relevant for the Italian economy and raises risks during the current slowdown. During the East Asian crisis, the drop in export demand affected GDP growth significantly, in part because domestic demand was extremely weak. Conversely, domestic demand was robust in 2000 and is expected to slow only moderately in 2001, cushioning the impact of falling exports.

Growth in the United Kingdom in 2000 was characterized by robust private consumption growth and a resilience of exports that was surprising given the continuing strength of the currency (see table A.12). The low level of unemployment and moderate wage gains supported consumption. The latter also benefited from wealth effects stemming from the sustained high prices in the real estate market. The United Kingdom economy is expected to slow in 2001 owing to the deterioration in external demand and the impact from continuing problems with livestock diseases. Domestic demand, on the other hand, is expected to maintain solid, boosted by increased government spending.

Faster GDP growth and country-specific factors contributed to lower unemployment in the region. Countries that have pursued labour-market reforms (for example, France) have achieved high rates of employment growth and lower rates of unemployment. The improvement in employment created a virtuous circle. It led to strong consumer demand and, in turn, to increased demand for labour. The region's unemployment rate was below 9 per cent by the end of 2000 (see table A.7). Much of this improvement has been in the service sector, with employment growing by more than 2.5 per cent on an annual basis; industrial sector employment has been less dynamic. Even though the rate of decline in unemployment slowed in the second half of 2000 and there was some deterioration in some countries in early 2001, unemployment should continue to fall over the medium term.

Inflation has been a policy concern since mid-2000. In the euro zone, the annual increase in the Harmonized Index of Consumer Prices (HICP), which is the operational target for the European Central Bank (ECB), rose above 2 per cent in June 2000 and has remained above this upper bound of the target range (see figure III.3). The acceleration was due mainly to external impulses over the course of 2000, primarily the increase in oil prices. Additionally, the decline of the euro during the year, which boosted import prices in general, amplified the increase in the euro-denominated price of oil. The effect of these impulses could be clearly seen in the behaviour of producer prices, but core inflation (which excludes the prices of energy, food, alcohol and tobacco and therefore captures the more fundamental trend in inflation) was much lower, indicating that the pass-through from these impulses had been limited. Wage pressures remained moderate.

Since the end of 2000, oil prices have moderated and the euro, while remaining weak, has not depreciated further, although in both cases there has been significant volatility. The effects of the earlier external impulses have been dissipating as they gradually feed through the system, and producer price inflation has decelerated since the third quarter of 2000. The HICP, however, moderated only slightly, largely owing to increases in food prices, particularly for meat. Core inflation, however, has continued gradually to increase during the first quarter of 2001 (see figure III.3).

Figure III.3.
EURO ZONE: SELECTED PRICE INDICES, JANUARY 1999-MARCH 2001

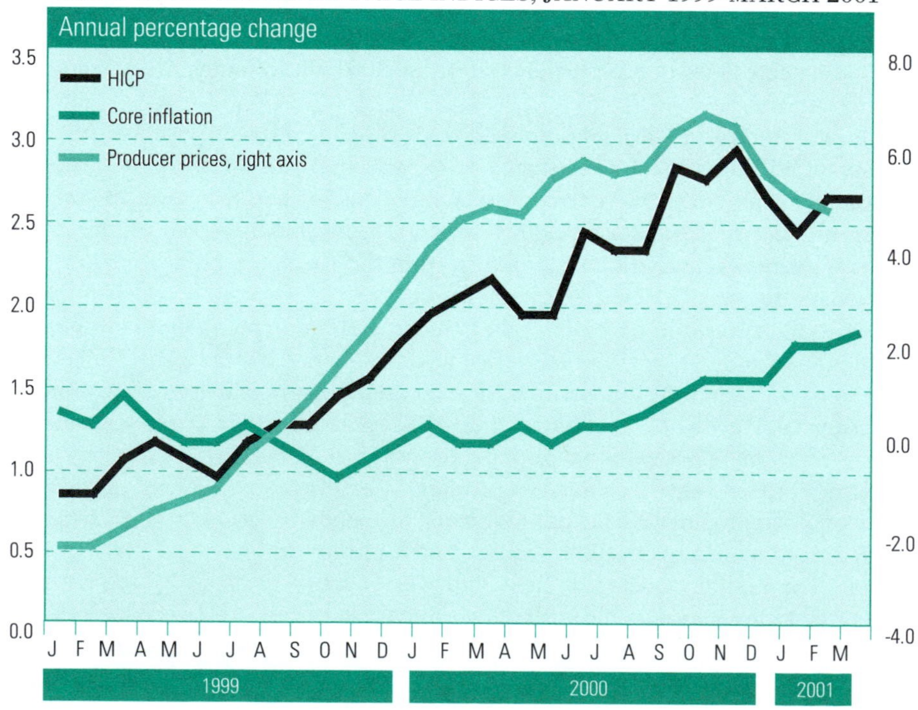

Annual percentage change

HICP
Core inflation
Producer prices, right axis

1999   2000   2001

Nevertheless, diminishing inflationary pressures are forecast for the near term. Energy prices are expected to decline further during 2001, and the euro to appreciate. Inflationary pressures will be further subdued by the anticipated moderation in growth. Finally, there should be sufficient room for some moderate upward movement in wages, owing to increased productivity, although there is no expectation of aggressive wage claims. Thus the rate of change of the HICP is expected to move below 2 per cent towards the end of 2001 and to decelerate further in 2002.

There is, however, significant dispersion across countries in the inflation picture. Inflation has been low in France and Germany, but well above the 2 per cent target in Finland, Greece, Ireland, the Netherlands, Portugal and Spain (see table A.8). This is less of a problem in Greece, Portugal and Spain, where relatively high rates of inflation are a by-product of catching up to EU average levels of productivity. However, it is a concern for Ireland as the country enters the later stages of the catching-up process, and the inflationary pressure has more to do with cyclical pressures, as is the case in the Netherlands.

Fiscal balances continued to improve in 2000 owing to robust economic growth. Most countries achieved their target of fiscal balance, even though the policy stance was slightly expansionary. Fiscal policy in 2001 will continue to be mildly expansionary across Western Europe. Most countries are aiming to reduce taxes as a part of supply side-structural reforms. Tax cuts, however, are not taking place in the context of reduced expenditures. In terms of the budget goals outlined in the Stability and Growth Pact, seven euro-zone countries had not achieved budget balance in 1999, while eight had debt-to-GDP ratios greater than 60 per cent. According to the most recent stability programmes submitted by member States, it will not be until 2004 that all countries will have achieved budget balance, with three still registering debt-to-GDP ratios significantly above 60 per cent.

In contrast with fiscal policy, monetary policy tightened in 2000. In the course of the year, the ECB raised interest rates six times for a cumulative 175 bps, bringing the short-term policy interest rate to 4.75 per cent, where it remained from October 2000 until early May 2001 (see figure III.2). This sustained tightening aimed at moving policy first to a more neutral stance, as growth rebounded following the East Asian crises, and then to a more restrictive stance as growth firmed and inflation began to inch up. With the slowdown in external demand and the slowing of activities in the euro zone itself, there was mounting pressure for a loosening of policy. With the substantial easing by the Fed and rate cuts elsewhere in Europe, the ECB was, until early May, the only major central bank not to have submitted.

The outlook indicates diminishing inflationary pressures, on the strength of falling oil prices, an appreciation of the euro, and moderating growth. In addition, the growth in the broad money supply (M3), the first pillar of the ECB's monetary policy, which has run well above its reference value of 4.5 per cent since the beginning of monetary union, has moderated substantially over the past year and is expected to move below the reference value in the near future.

The short-term evidence, however, is less compelling. The HICP remains above its upper target limit of 2 per cent, with no clear downward direction in the past few months of 2001. As noted above, core inflation continued to move upward, and there was no sign of a convincing turnaround in the value of the euro. Furthermore, the ECB is aware that, as a new institution, it needs to build a track record of success in controlling inflation. There might therefore be a perceived risk in lowering policy interest rates prior to having clear signs of decelerating inflation.

Nevertheless, there is also an element of risk in not easing soon. The preponderance of the economic risks is to the downside, in the nature both of the United States slowdown and of its impact on the euro-zone economy. With a V-shaped recovery in the United States, growth in Europe is expected to slow only moderately; but if the United States was to have a U-shaped recovery, the impact on Europe could be much larger. The trade effects would be more substantial, with the possibilities of more serious second-round effects from asymmetric impacts. Stock markets would also be further depressed and their impact on consumer and business confidence is unknown. While the wealth effect of stock markets on consumer behaviour, for example, is typically estimated to be far less significant in Europe then in the United States, owing to the smaller share of stocks in household wealth, this share has been rising so its impact could be greater than expected. There are similar questions as regards the effects on business investment. Finally, in the event of a U-shaped recovery in the United States, there would also be the risk that the appreciation of the euro could occur abruptly as a result of the collapse of the United States dollar, and this would add significantly to deflationary pressures.

The euro: continued weakness

The euro continued its slide during 2000. Although there were some rallies, they could not be sustained. The euro reached record lows in September 2000, which prompted a coordinated Group of Seven (G-7) intervention on the initiative of the ECB on 22 September. This stabilized the currency for a few weeks, but shortly thereafter there was renewed downward pressure. The ECB continued to intervene in foreign exchange markets in November.

The continued weakness of the currency counters all previous predictions and is increasingly at odds with the fundamental determinants of currency values. The principal argument for the current strength of the United States dollar has been based on relative growth differentials between the United States and the euro zone. Expected returns on investments in the United States have been more attractive owing to its stronger economic growth. Therefore, Europeans have invested heavily in the United States to capture the benefits of the faster-growing economy. It was argued, however, that this behaviour would change as the United States economy slowed and European growth maintained its pace; the euro was expected to appreciate as investment flows reversed.

This has been repeatedly delayed as the United States continued to register stronger than-expected-growth. This changed in the last quarter of 2000 when, for the first time since the inception of monetary union, the euro zone grew faster than the United States. Also, the outlook for the United States economy in the first half of 2001 deteriorated significantly. Accordingly, the euro began to rebound in December and January, but then stalled and subsequently fell back. Among the explanations, the principal one was that the Fed's prompt action restored confidence that the downturn would be brief, but this reasoning has become increasingly less convincing. By the second quarter of 2001, interest rate differentials, current and expected growth differentials (at least over the next year), inflation differentials, and the relative sizes of the current-account deficits, were all in favour of the euro, but they produced no sustained upward movement in the currency.

Nevertheless, the current outlook calls for a gradual appreciation of the euro towards parity with the United States dollar over the next two years. This is because the most probable explanation of the euro's weakness has to do with confidence. Amid the euphoria of the single currency's launching, the difficulties of building confidence in the euro and its supporting institutions may have been overlooked. Central bankers believe that confidence and credibility are earned over time by building a track record of successful performance; this may take a long time.

From this point of view, one cause of the current weakness of the euro is a lack of confidence in the new and evolving institutions. This has caused an overshooting of the euro's value relative to medium- and long-term economic fundamentals. As confidence in the new institutions improves over time, the overshooting should diminish and the euro should begin to more fully reflect underlying fundamentals.

Developed Asia and the Pacific: renewed threat of recession in Japan

After having registered 1.7 per cent GDP growth in 2000, the Japanese economy is facing the possibility of another contraction. At the beginning of 2001, several indicators signalled a sharp downturn in a broad range of economic activities. The outlook for GDP growth is ¾ per cent in 2001 and 1¼ per cent in 2002. Weakening domestic and external demand, and plummeting equity values are a drag on the economy in the short run. Meanwhile, structural problems, such as non-performing loans (NPLs) of the financial sector, excessive capacity in the corporate sector, and the large government debt, continue to pose downside risks for the medium- and long-run outlook. Therefore, policy makers are facing the challenge of devising measures to prevent the economy from sliding into another recession in the short run, and yet support structural adjustments.

The performance of the Japanese economy in 2000 was better than in the previous two years, as the economy continued to recover gradually from the 1998 recession. The recovery, however, was uneven during the year: strong growth in the first quarter was immediately followed by a deceleration as the government stimulus package ran out of steam, although another rebound occurred in the fourth quarter (see table III.1). The recovery was also unbalanced across sectors: profits of the corporate sector improved markedly, but demand of the household sector remained weak; investment in information technology was strong, while excess capacity prevailed in traditional economic sectors.

Business fixed investment, which grew by 4.5 per cent in 2000, was the leading domestic factor in the recovery. Investment in ICT was particularly strong, with an increase of about 8 per cent. Business investment is expected to continue growing as corporate profits improve further; however, its pace will be curbed by adjustment of excess capacity and reduction of debts of many firms.

Commentators have argued that the growing investment in ICT would eventually lift the Japanese economy to a higher growth path, as happened in the

3 So far, the ratio of investment in ICT to GDP stands at about 4 per cent in Japan, behind the United States by just a few years.

4 A third of all mortgaged Japanese homes are estimated to have a negative net equity. In March 2001, the stock market, as measured by the Nikkei 225 index, fell to its lowest level in 16 years.

United States in the 1990s.[3] The accumulation of ICT capital, however, is only one necessary condition for boosting the productivity and potential GDP growth of an economy. Many other factors, such as a flexible labour market, an efficient financial system, and an accommodative regulatory framework, are equally important. All this suggests that more economic restructuring will be needed before the Japanese economy can benefit substantially from the ICT revolution.

Consumer spending in Japan remains weak, with private consumption having grown by only 0.5 per cent in 2000. Lacklustre household demand resulted from several factors, such as unfavourable employment and income conditions, and the negative wealth effects from a decade-long deflation in real estate and equity prices.[4] The outlook for consumer spending remains weak, as no significant improvement is expected in these underlying forces any time soon.

The general deflationary trend continued in 2000, with both the CPI and the GDP deflator registering a decline for the second consecutive year. Despite higher prices of oil, the prices of manufacturing goods and services continued to decline. Besides weak demand, some supply-side factors—technological innovation, the streamlining of distribution channels, and increased competition from deregulation—might have driven prices down. Inflation is not foreseen as a problem, but halting and reversing the deflationary spiral remain a crucial policy challenge.

The unemployment rate reached 4.7 per cent in 2000 (see table A.7). Though the ratio of job offers to applicants rose moderately by year-end, the mismatch between labour supply and demand remained considerable: the continued corporate downsizing contrasts with the shortage of high-skilled labour in the ICT sector. While many obstacles to labour mobility persist, the number of part-time and temporary workers increased, and the labour market is expected to become more flexible over time. The outlook for employment in the short run, however, is not optimistic.

Japan's foreign trade was very buoyant in 2000, as exports rose by 11 per cent in real terms and imports increased by nearly 6.3 per cent (see table A.13). The trade balance, despite a slight deterioration due to higher oil prices, reached a surplus of $120 billion. Meanwhile, the yen remained relatively stable against the United States dollar until November 2000, when it began to depreciate owing to the sharp slowdown in Japanese exports brought on by weakening economic growth in the United States and elsewhere. Growth of both exports and imports is expected to slow to 2-3 per cent for 2001-2002.

Policy measures adopted so far have not been effective in revitalizing the weak economy. Fiscal policy had been expansionary over the past decade when, on average, one stimulus package was launched per year. These packages, each at least 10 trillion yen (about $80 billion), often included public spending on infrastructure projects; loans for small and medium-sized enterprises; and financing for job creation, employment stability, and housing. As each package began to be implemented, GDP growth usually increased for one or two quarters. Once public spending slowed, however, growth decelerated. This cyclical pattern was particularly pronounced in 1999-2000.

While these stimulus packages did not lead the economy to sustained recovery, the budget deficit mushroomed and reached about 8 per cent of GDP in 2000. As a result, outstanding government debt has climbed to about 120 per cent of GDP, the highest ratio among the major developed economies. As a result, Japanese sovereign bonds have been downgraded in international capital markets.

Given the economic downturn at the beginning of 2001, the Government released another economic package in April. Different from previous packages, this one focuses on structural reforms, instead of stimulus spending, in five categories: a financial and industrial revival; structural reform of the securities market; revitalization of urban areas and increase in land liquidity; job creation and a safety net; and tax system reform. The package includes some drastic measures, such as urging banks to write off, within two years, their NPLs that are considered to be at high risk of failure; promoting corporate reorganization; limiting banks' shareholdings in order to reduce the vulnerability of banks to stock market fluctuations; and creating a Bank Equity Purchasing Corporation (BEPC) to purchase excess shares from banks. While an increase in financing is expected, for some measures in the package, such as the revitalization of urban areas, the large budget deficit would limit its size. More importantly, the inevitable task of fiscal consolidation in the future will become more formidable.

The traditional monetary policy measures adopted in Japan have not produced their desired effects either. After maintaining a zero-interest rate policy for about a year and a half, the Bank of Japan raised the targeted overnight rate by 25 bps in August 2000—its first monetary tightening in a decade. Since the beginning of 2001, however, the Central Bank has reversed this action by reducing interest rates, along with the introduction of a standby lending facility ("Lombard-type"), through which the Central Bank could extend loans at the request of financial institutions at the official discount rate and under certain pre-specified conditions.

As economic conditions deteriorated sharply, some unorthodox monetary policy measures were taken in March 2001. First, the Central Bank shifted the target of monetary policy from the overnight interest rate to its current-account balance on money market operations. With a 25 per cent increase of the Central Bank's current-account balance, the stance is equivalent to the zero-interest-rate policy. Moreover, the Central Bank decided to use the CPI as the guideline for monetary easing, at least until a sustainable positive annual CPI rate prevailed. However, a formal inflation-targeting framework was not adopted. Finally, the Central Bank would increase its outright purchases of long-term government bonds to ensure a smooth supply of liquidity.

Growth prospects of the Japanese economy face considerable downside risks. In addition to the fallout from the slowdown in the United States, the turmoil in Japanese financial markets carries some risks, particularly for the banking sector. Stocks often collateralize commercial loans and banks are the largest owners of cross-shareholdings among financial institutions and business corporations. Therefore, the fall in the stock market in early 2001 might have pushed many commercial banks, which were already vulnerable became of large NPLs, into crisis. Moreover, if some large Japanese banks became insolvent, the "systemic risk" for the global financial system would rise. The credit relationship between Japanese banks and other large banks of major developed economies would be disrupted, causing havoc in the derivatives markets.

GDP growth decelerated in Australia and New Zealand in 2000 (see table A.2). The slowdown was more pronounced in Australia, particularly in the second half of the year. It reflected the impact of fiscal reforms mainly on construction, with negative labour-market effects, as well as the adverse effects of higher oil prices and negative wealth effects on domestic demand brought about by lower or stagnating real estate prices. Domestic factors also constrained faster demand growth in New Zealand, as the new Employment Relations Act and tighter monetary stance delayed new investment, whereas oil prices took a toll on real disposable incomes and affected confidence. In both economies, external demand was a major source of growth in 2000. Both countries benefited from faster growth of international trade, higher commodity prices, and increased competitiveness brought about by the depreciation of their currencies. Further deceleration in growth is expected for 2001 owing to the less favourable international environment.

Inflation accelerated in both countries in 2000 owing to higher oil prices and depreciated currencies (see table A.8). Year-end headline inflation surpassed established targets, but core inflation was kept under control and it is expected to remain stable in 2001. Monetary policy was tightened in 2000. Both economies increased their policy interest rate by 150 bps, starting in November 1999. These increases, however, were subsequently partially reversed, as inflation expectations abated and the international environment deteriorated. Nonetheless, the two economies face different inflationary pressures and New Zealand has been more cautious in its approach. By the end of April 2001, it had cut interest rates by 50 bps, while Australia had reduced its policy rate by a total of 125 bps.

Both economies recorded a budget surplus in 2000. Fiscal policy will remain neutral in New Zealand and mildly expansionary in Australia in anticipation of upcoming elections. The fiscal balance in both economies is expected to remain positive, leaving room to manoeuvre in case the international environment worsens more than expected.

Despite faster export growth, New Zealand's current-account position is a source of concern as its deficit, although lower than in 1999, remained about 5.5 per cent of GDP. Australia, on the other hand, registered faster improvement in its current-account balance as its deficit declined to about 3 per cent of GDP by the end of 2000. The competitive exchange rates in both economies may help to support further reductions in the current-account gap, if external demand does not collapse.

ECONOMIES IN TRANSITION

The economies in transition recorded a remarkable recovery in 2000, with average GDP growth reaching 6.1 per cent from 3.0 per cent in 1999. All countries of the group had achieved positive growth for the first year since transition began, with the Commonwealth of Independent States (CIS) economies, in particular the Russian Federation,[5] witnessing a sharp acceleration (see table A.3).

Faster growth in 2000 was attributable to several factors. In the CIS countries, it was due largely to the benefits of the currency devaluations in the aftermath of the Russian crisis; these encouraged not only exports but also a switch from imports to domestic supply. The improved prices of oil and gas and other commodities exported by the region were also a factor. The recovery of the

[5] Record tax revenues in the Russian Federation might in part reflect some legitimization of the "shadow economy" in 2000. If so, the rate of GDP growth would be overestimated.

Russian market, in turn, was positive for the other CIS economies, as well as for the Baltic countries. Dynamic international trade elsewhere, particularly import demand by Western Europe, was also beneficial for countries in Central and Eastern Europe and the Baltics.

Growth, however, is expected to decelerate in 2001, with the slowdown anticipated to be more marked in CIS than in the other groups of countries. Meanwhile, many countries continue to face the challenges of restructuring their economies and addressing macroeconomic imbalances, with progress being unsatisfactory in some of them. The deceleration in growth will make the implementation of these tasks even more difficult.

Central and Eastern Europe: strong exports, subdued consumption

Economic growth in Central and Eastern Europe accelerated markedly in 2000 and was far stronger than in previous years, owing to the favourable external environment. Following the strong economic performance of EU, the region's major trading partner (see table A.14), GDP grew by 4 per cent in 2000. In 2001, however, the demand for exports from the region will decelerate, following the weakening in the EU. Furthermore, weak equity markets will discourage portfolio and direct investment inflows into the region. GDP growth is forecast to moderate to 3½ per cent in 2001 (see table A.3).

Increased external demand from EU and continuing inflows of foreign direct investment (FDI) boosted industrial production and exports in 2000. The strong economic expansion, however, was unevenly distributed among sectors and reflected a "dual economy" phenomenon, even in economies that have been most advanced with their transformation. The upswing in external demand favoured export-oriented sectors, especially those with a substantial FDI presence[6], while domestic demand, particularly private consumption, remained subdued throughout the region. Agriculture— in addition to the weakness of domestic demand—was adversely affected by harsh weather conditions almost everywhere in the region. This necessitated imports of foodstuffs, and exerted upward pressure on food prices.

The reasons for sluggish domestic demand are several. Tight macroeconomic policies adopted when some economies, Hungary and Poland in particular, faced the risk of overheating in 2000 led to lower consumption and investment spending. The effects of such policies are still being felt. Other countries, notably Romania and Slovakia, have experienced high unemployment owing to enterprise restructuring. Additionally, almost all countries faced a conflict between fiscal and monetary policies, with central banks resisting monetary easing in the light of a possible fiscal expansion.

Growth of investment in the region has so far been correlated with FDI inflows. Most countries have continued to have low domestic savings and assets of poor quality plagued domestic banks. Bulgaria and Hungary registered high rates of investment in 2000, owing to the strong investment demand and monetary loosening. In Poland, however, growth in fixed investment dropped from 6.5 per cent in the previous year to 3.1 per cent in 2000 on account of monetary restraint.

Signs of weakening GDP growth were already evident by the end of 2000. A sharp deceleration in exports and industrial production occurred in the last

6   For example, both in the Czech Republic and Slovakia, growth in 2000 was mainly due to a small number of foreign-controlled enterprises in the automotive and electronics industries.

quarter of 2000, not only in the largest economy of the region, Poland, but also in the best performing one, Hungary. Owing to the weakening external environment, domestic demand will have to support growth in 2001 if the momentum is to be maintained. This will present a difficult challenge for macroeconomic policies in the region in view of the subdued domestic demand and the existing imbalances.

The marked slowdown in Poland in the last quarter of 2000 was due to the appreciation of the currency, reduced external demand by EU, and weak domestic demand due to very tight monetary policy. Prospects for the Polish economy are not encouraging until consumption spending recovers. Lower oil and food prices, however, may stimulate domestic demand. Conversely, Hungary may continue its strong growth, owing to growing consumer confidence and the relatively small loss of competitiveness in external markets.

Strong FDI inflows and investment-led domestic demand pulled the Czech Republic out of its three-year recession. Towards the end of 2000, the country became one of the leading industrial performers of the region, as manufacturing benefited from both the easing of the credit crunch and large FDI inflows. The Slovak economy, in contrast, performed worse than expected in 2000. Despite the surge in exports, austerity measures and economic restructuring, with fragilities in both the enterprise and financial sectors, continued to hold down domestic demand. Both economies are expected to grow by about 3 per cent in 2001. Growth in the Czech Republic will also have positive effects on the Slovak economy, given the strong trade linkages between the two countries.

South-eastern European countries are still introducing incisive, socially disruptive structural changes. Increased demand for their exports boosted growth in Bulgaria and ended the three-year recession in Romania. Both countries are expected to register positive growth in 2001, despite the less favourable external environment. The latter will include a loss of competitiveness for Bulgaria since its economy is tied to the euro and is affected as well by the adverse impact of the recent financial turmoil in Turkey (see section on Western Asia below). The devaluation of the Turkish lira implied a loss of competitiveness for Bulgarian products in Turkish markets, as well as increased competition from cheaper Turkish exports (especially clothing and textiles) in third markets. Romania, on the other hand, is in a relatively better position owing to the devaluation of its currency in 2000.

Strong international trade also benefited the successor States of the former Yugoslavia, with the exception of the Federal Republic of Yugoslavia, where the economy, under international sanctions, remained in deep stagnation until late 2000. Despite the partial restoration of regional trade and the revival of the tourism industry in parts of the Balkans, international assistance remains of crucial importance for this subregion, but has been forthcoming only slowly.

The change of the Government in the Federal Republic of Yugoslavia in October 2000 and the normalization of the country's external relations should be favourable for the region as a whole, by changing investors' perceptions, facilitating privatization and stimulating financial inflows. Furthermore, the revival and gradual improvement of traditional trade routes will promote both intra- and interregional trade. The lifting of trade sanctions and the provision of aid will help Yugoslavia to overcome its current economic difficulties. However, the implementation of a comprehensive programme of economic reconstruction in Yugoslavia will require inflows of foreign capital on a much larger scale than that of the emergency short-term funds, chiefly from official sources, currently contemplated. The Government faces the difficult task of dismantling the State-run economy, encouraging private-sector development, and establishing a legal and institutional framework to make the country attractive to foreign investors. Additionally, the country faces balance-of-payments difficulties and has a substantial external debt.

The positive export performance resulted in only a slight improvement in the employment situation in Central and Eastern Europe. Labour productivity growth in manufacturing and continuing enterprise restructuring are the main reasons. There are especially high rates (about 14-20 per cent) of unemployment in Bulgaria, Poland and Slovakia, as well as in many of the successor States of the former Yugoslavia. Prospects for a reduction in unemployment in the medium term are not promising (see table A.7).

Increased export revenues improved the current-account balances of the region only marginally in 2000, owing to strong import growth (see table A.21). In Hungary, increased profit repatriation by foreign investors represented another source of pressure on the current account. In Poland, the current-account deficit remained high at 6.6 per cent of GDP at the end of 2000. Despite the tightening of monetary policy, Poland, unlike the other economies of the region, experienced a domestic demand that remained robust during the first half of the year, thus sustaining imports, but decelerated sharply towards the end. FDI inflows have financed the external deficit. Nonetheless, as privatization revenues are expected to decline in 2001, the Polish economy may become vulnerable if external balances do not improve.

Despite the expected moderation of oil prices and a contraction of imports due to tight macroeconomic policies, a significant reduction in the current-account deficit not only for Poland but also for other countries in the region is unlikely. Expectations are that current-account deficits will be fully covered, as in the recent past, by FDI inflows. The volume of the latter, however, will depend not only on the region's maintaining its attractiveness to foreign investors but also on economic developments in EU, the largest foreign investor in Central and Eastern Europe.

Consumer and producer prices increased throughout the region in 2000, mostly owing to the surge in oil prices and the rebound of food prices (see tables III.2 and A.9). The impact of imported inflation was compounded by the depreciation of the euro against the United States dollar (see section above on Western Europe) for most countries. Annual inflation of about 45 per cent was registered in Romania, owing to lax fiscal policies and currency depreciation, and of about 76 per cent in the Federal Republic of Yugoslavia, where monetary policy remained expansionary in 2000. Elsewhere, official inflation targets of most countries were overshot: compared with targets of 6-8 per cent, most economies registered a 10-12 per cent increase in their CPI.

The Czech Republic and Poland have adopted direct inflation-targeting as the framework for monetary policy. The initial target for the year-end core inflation rate (excluding administered prices and indirect taxes) in the Czech Republic for 2000 was increased in August, following external price changes. The revised target was undershot, and the Central Bank came under criticism for the poor quality of its inflation forecast. As a result, the Czech Republic adopted the headline inflation rate as the policy target for 2001. In Poland,

Table III.2.
ECONOMIES IN TRANSITION: QUARTERLY INDICATORS, 1999-2000

	1999 quarter				2000 quarter			
	I	II	III	IV	I	II	III	IV
Rates of growth of gross domestic product[a]								
Belarus	0.7	3.1	2.2	7.2	6.5	2.3	6.4	7.9
Czech Republic	-3.7	-0.8	0.4	1.0	4.3	2.1	2.2	3.9
Hungary	3.5	3.9	4.5	5.9	6.6	5.8	4.5	4.2
Kazakhstan	-7.4	-3.9	6.3	15.3	9.4	1.8	11.0	6.5
Poland	1.6	3.0	5.0	6.2	6.0	5.2	3.3	2.4
Romania	-4.5	-4.2	-3.0	-3.2	0.9	3.5	1.6	0.0
Russian Federation	-2.7	2.2	10.8	10.5	9.0	8.6	8.8	6.8
Ukraine	-4.7	-1.6	0.2	3.1	5.5	4.5	5.7	9.0
Growth of consumer prices[a]								
Belarus	248.4	311.7	344.9	275.4	212.0	191.0	164.6	108.0
Czech Republic	3.0	2.2	1.3	2.0	3.6	3.8	4.0	4.1
Hungary	9.5	9.1	10.6	10.8	9.8	9.2	9.7	10.1
Kazakhstan	-0.2	5.5	11.9	16.1	20.7	10.6	10.1	9.8
Poland	6.2	6.3	7.4	9.3	10.3	10.1	10.8	9.3
Romania	35.4	43.3	49.5	53.1	53.7	44.4	44.9	41.6
Russian Federation	102.6	116.7	98.2	47.4	22.4	20.2	18.6	20.1
Ukraine	21.2	25.4	26.0	18.7	26.9	30.3	31.7	25.6

Source: IMF, *International Financial Statistics;* and ECE.

[a] Percentage change from the corresponding period of the preceding year.

where headline inflation is targeted, the year-end target was overshot in 2000, as inflation was driven by external factors (see table III.2). While it is still too early to assess the suitability and efficiency of direct inflation-targeting for economies in transition, the experience of the Czech Republic and Poland highlights the difficulties that central banks have in forecasting inflation and using short-term interest rates as an instrument of monetary policy to address external price shocks.

Oil prices are expected to weaken in 2001 and the euro is expected to appreciate (see chap. I). Inflation in the region will decelerate only moderately, however, as the impact of the improvement in terms of trade will be offset by a rise in administered prices and relative price adjustments. There are also indications that producer price inflation is about 2-3 per cent higher than consumer price inflation, and these pressures will feed into consumer prices. The outlook for inflation in 2001 depends also on monetary and fiscal policies.

High double-digit inflation is expected in Romania and the Federal Republic of Yugoslavia again in 2001. In the former, this will be due to the Government's limited capacity to finance the deficit in a non-inflationary way. In the latter, high inflation will reflect the ongoing economic reform measures, such as the liberalization of electricity prices, especially in the first months of the year. Comparatively low inflation is forecast for the Czech Republic, as domestic credit-induced inflation is subdued and imported inflation is easing.

Accelerated inflation, combined with the uncertainty of fiscal positions in many countries, undermined attempts to relax monetary policy in 2000. Some central banks, in particular in Hungary and Slovakia, undertook monetary loosening at the beginning of 2000 in order to discourage speculative capital inflows. They could not, however, cut interest rates further owing to accelerating inflation, and the perception of lax fiscal policies, as well as monetary tightening by the ECB. Many central banks (in particular, in the Czech Republic, Hungary and Poland) warned about the possibility of monetary tightening if Governments in these countries were to continue to improve their fiscal positions by relying only on the cyclical upturn (that is to say, by generating additional fiscal revenues through faster economic growth without addressing expenditure rationalization and other necessary reforms). The Central Bank of Poland, in particular, took an especially strong stance on monetary policy. Higher interest rates, however, encouraged speculative capital inflows and expanded the money supply owing to the Central Bank's limited ability to sterilize these inflows.

Monetary stances were reversed at the beginning of 2001. The Czech, Hungarian and Polish Central Banks reduced their key interest rates with the aim of stimulating domestic demand and promoting exports as growth expectations deteriorated. This monetary loosening may not be sustainable in 2001, given the fiscal-monetary dilemma faced by these countries. Furthermore, lower interest rates do not necessarily lead to increased credit availability— lending has remained subdued in most of these economies.

Fiscal positions of most Governments of the region remained precarious in 2000, with budget deficits exceeding initial targets, owing to large off-budget spending (for example, the recapitalization of the banking sector in the Czech Republic), increased social security payments to offset the social cost of transition, and the accumulation of tax arrears in some States, including Romania. Most Governments attempted to use the economic upturn, and the rise in inflation, as well as the proceeds from privatization, to improve public finances and to meet their deficit targets. Comprehensive structural reforms, in particular of social security, are still to be implemented however.

Many of the proposed budgets for 2001 rely on optimistic growth and inflation projections. Failure to reduce budget deficits in 2001 will increase the cost of debt-servicing and compromise progress with inflation. Because several of these countries have presidential or parliamentary elections in 2001-2002, significant fiscal tightening is unlikely. If further monetary tightening was applied to offset fiscal laxity ahead of elections, it would discourage the private sector. In the long run, failure to address the problems of public finance will jeopardize macroeconomic stability and increase the vulnerability of these economies to external shocks.

The policy tasks for Central Europe in 2001 include financial stabilization, lowering inflation, increasing export competitiveness, and maintaining high rates of investment. For South-eastern Europe, macroeconomic stabilization should be accompanied by structural reforms, including the privatization of enterprise and financial sectors, attracting strategic investors, and implementing infrastructure programmes.

The main short-term risk to the region emerges from the impact on EU of any prolonged slowdown of the United States economy. On the domestic side, problems may arise in some countries from political uncertainties and the determination with which policy makers will pursue reforms as pressures for early elections mount. Additional risks emerge from the possibility of renewed political instability in South-eastern Europe.

Commonwealth of Independent States (CIS) countries: fast but unsustainable growth

Following the economic upturn that started in mid-1999, GDP growth in the CIS countries accelerated to 7.9 per cent in 2000—about double the rate anticipated at the beginning of the year. This has been the best performance of the region since transition started and for the first year in a decade, all countries in the group experienced positive growth. The slowdown in the world economy, terms-of-trade losses and appreciation in national currencies will bring overall growth in the region down to 3¾ per cent in 2001, as improvements in consumer demand will be insufficient to offset deteriorating exports. Meanwhile, investment will be constrained by the slow implementation of structural reforms and the continuing weakness of the financial sectors.

Two major factors drove the strong growth in 2000. First, the real currency depreciations in 1998-1999 provided significant cost advantages to domestic producers, at least with respect to most non-CIS markets. This encouraged import substitution, which continued in 2000. Although real exchange rates in the major economies of the region (Kazakhstan, the Russian Federation and Ukraine) appreciated in 2000, they did not return to their pre-crisis levels, thus keeping domestic production competitive. Region-wide growth in industrial output, led by the mining and processing of oil and metals, ranged from 2.3 per cent in the Republic of Moldova to almost 15 per cent in Kazakhstan. Agricultural production, however, was constrained by severe drought in some countries, especially Armenia, Georgia and the Republic of Moldova.

Second, higher fuel prices in 2000 and increased buoyancy in international trade gave a boost to export revenues of producing countries and had strong ripple effects throughout their economies, leading to increased production, reduced pressure on fiscal and external balances, and higher profits in the corporate sector. CIS countries are highly dependent on exports of both fuel and non-fuel commodities (see figure III.4). The favourable external environment was therefore a crucial determinant for the acceleration in growth in 2000. The effect also spilled over to non-fuel commodity exporters, as the strong recovery in the Russian Federation benefited other CIS countries, which had suffered from the collapse of the Russian market after the rouble devaluation in August 1998. Also, the Russian Administration emphasized improving intraregional trade, facilitating faster growth of exports into Russian markets. The share of Russian imports originating in CIS increased from 28 per cent in 1999 to 35 per cent in 2000.

The positive impact of these two factors gradually waned in 2001 and, in some countries of the region, expanding domestic demand has been increasingly contributing to GDP growth. Capital investment increased in 2000 in all CIS countries, except Belarus, with the three largest economies enjoying the

Figure III.4.
COMMONWEALTH OF INDEPENDENT STATES (CIS)
COUNTRIES: SHARE OF COMMODITIES
IN TOTAL EXPORTS, 1999

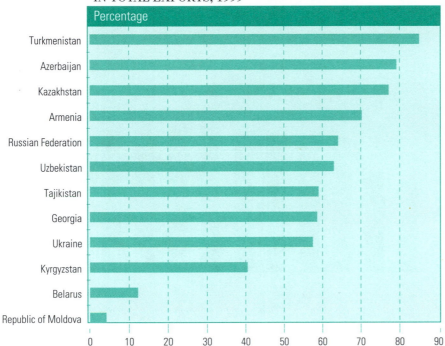

Source: European Bank for Reconstruction and Development.

Note: Data for Azerbaijan, Georgia, Kyrgyzstan, the Russian Federation, Tajikistan and Ukraine refer to 1998.

strongest growth.[7] In Kazakhstan, for example, investment grew by almost 30 per cent in 2000 owing to the construction work of the Caspian Pipeline Consortium (CPC), which is linking the Tengiz oilfield to the Russian terminal at Novorossiysk.[8] In the Russian Federation, investment increased by almost 18 per cent in 2000, financed largely from earnings. While estimated capital flight rose in absolute terms, it decreased as a percentage of total profits. On average, Russian businessmen chose to channel a larger part of their increased profits into domestic investment, demonstrating improved confidence in the country's economy. Private consumption also increased in Kazakhstan and the Russian Federation, with real incomes growing in 2000 by 5.3 per cent and 7.2 per cent, respectively, and wage arrears being substantially decreased.

Despite the second consecutive year of positive growth, the overall GDP level in the CIS countries is still 16 per cent lower than in 1993 (see figure III.5) and poverty remains a major social problem. Unemployment in the region continued to be high, although it was significantly reduced in the Russian Federation, where it had declined from about 12 per cent in 1999 to 9.7 per cent in 2000. Prospects in this area are not encouraging as growth decelerates in 2001.

Economic growth began to slow in the Russian Federation in the final quarter of 2000. Despite the strong annual performance (up by 8.3 per cent), industrial production decelerated towards the end of 2000 and was weak in the early months of 2001. GDP growth decelerated to 4 per cent in the first quarter of

[7] Armenia's capital investment grew by 26 per cent in 2000, but from a low base.

[8] On the economic impact of the Caspian pipelines, see *World Economic and Social Survey, 2000* (United Nations publication, Sales No. E.00.II.C.1), box III.2.

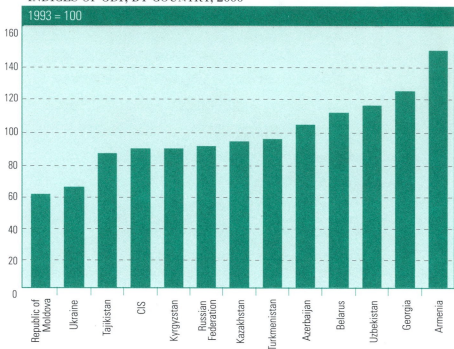

Figure III.5.
COMMONWEALTH OF INDEPENDENT STATES (CIS) COUNTRIES:
INDICES OF GDP, BY COUNTRY, 2000

1993 = 100

2001, as exports slowed. For the year as a whole, growth is expected to be about 3½ per cent. In Ukraine, where most of the economic expansion in 2000 was induced by an export-led increase in metallurgy and heavy equipment production, GDP growth remained strong in the first four months of 2001. However, it might decelerate later in the year because of weaker external demand and slower structural reforms. Kazakhstan's GDP growth will decelerate in 2001, but remain strong owing to continued growth in FDI and export revenues. Despite easing oil prices, Kazakhstan's export revenues are expected to rise because its oil exporting capacity will double with the opening of the CPC pipeline. Georgia and the Republic of Moldova are the only CIS countries likely to record faster growth in 2001, mostly from a low base.

The external situation remained uneven across the CIS region. All fuel-exporting countries (Azerbaijan, Kazakhstan, the Russian Federation and Turkmenistan) enjoyed current-account surpluses in 2000. In some cases, the improvement in the external balance was dramatic. For instance, Azerbaijan's current-account balance moved from a deficit of 15 per cent of GDP in 1999 to a 2 per cent surplus in 2000. These countries' external balances are expected to worsen in 2001, as a result of the deterioration of their terms of trade and possible cutbacks in export volumes. Conversely, unsustainably large current-account deficits persisted in some of the smaller, fuel-importing countries (such as Armenia, Georgia, Kyrgyzstan, the Republic of Moldova and Tajikistan). These continuously high trade deficits, coupled with heavy external debt burdens, make these countries exceptionally vulnerable to external shocks.

The export revenues of the Russian Federation grew by about 40 per cent, surpassing $100 billion, in 2000, mostly owing to the rise in export prices; export volume rose by only 10 per cent. Imports increased by 12 per cent in nominal terms. As a result, the trade surplus more than doubled, reaching $61 billion. Nonetheless, in the fourth quarter of 2000, the growth of export revenues decelerated to about 20 per cent on an annual basis. Conversely, imports grew faster in late 2000, owing to strengthening domestic demand and continued appreciation of the rouble. With the anticipated easing of oil prices and further upward pressure on the rouble, this trend is expected to continue in 2001.

Inflation in the region decreased dramatically in 2000 (see table A.9). The most impressive drop was recorded in the Russian Federation, where average annual inflation plummeted from about 86 per cent in 1999 to about 20 per cent in 2000. Stable exchange rates in most countries (except for Belarus,[9] Tajikistan, Turkmenistan and Uzbekistan) were partially responsible for the lower rates of inflation.

Since the collapse of fixed exchange-rate regimes during the Russian crisis in 1998, most central banks of the region have been implicitly targeting the nominal exchange rate. In 2000, Kazakhstan and the Russian Federation were committed to preventing the currency from appreciating in an attempt to preserve the competitiveness of domestic production. Interventions by the central banks, aimed at absorbing large, export-related, foreign currency inflows, led to an expansion of the domestic money supply. In the Russian Federation, some of this increased liquidity was absorbed by higher demand for money. This was due to the increased volume of transactions in the expanding economy, a decline in the proportion of barter exchanges and a dramatic drop in velocity, indicating greater local confidence in the currency. However, continuing such interventions without an active sterilization policy risks higher inflation. Inflation was already accelerating by the end of 2000 (see table III.2). In the first quarter of 2001, annual average consumer price inflation continued to rise and reached 23.8 per cent, up from 20.1 per cent in the last quarter of 2000, thus pointing to a substantially higher annual rate in 2001 than the 14-16 per cent forecast by the Government. In such countries as Belarus, Turkmenistan and Uzbekistan, loans to non-viable enterprises are likely to continue to exert upward pressure on inflation.

Most countries introduced fiscal austerity measures after the Russian crisis. The improvement in fiscal balances gained momentum in 2000. Oil-producing countries, except Azerbaijan, enjoyed fiscal surpluses owing to high export revenues. The Russian fiscal turnaround was the most impressive, as the federal budget deficit of 1.7 per cent of GDP in 1999 became a 1.3 per cent surplus in 2000, despite continued servicing of external debt. The sustainability of this improvement, however, is questionable owing to the heavy reliance on public revenues from commodity exports. Azerbaijan and Kazakhstan have taken steps to protect their economies against adverse shocks from fluctuations in oil prices by establishing national stabilization funds supplied from oil revenues when prices surpass the budgeted level. The Russian Federation recently started considering such funds as well. In some non-oil exporting countries, including Armenia and Georgia, traditionally large fiscal imbalances persisted because of the failure to improve revenue collection.

[9] Belarus pegged its currency to the Russian rouble on 1 January 2001. It is not clear whether this arrangement is sustainable since it is based on an assumption that Belarus will be able to secure a new loan from the Russian Federation; however, the loan will be forthcoming only if Belarus tightens its monetary policy.

Furthermore, the substantial external debt-servicing burden of most of the CIS countries undermines their fiscal position. It is questionable whether the small economies (such as Armenia, Georgia, Kyrgyzstan, the Republic of Moldova and Tajikistan) will be able to service their debt. For the Russian Federation, despite the failure to have rescheduled Soviet-era debt with the Paris Club in January 2001, total debt repayments due in 2001 (estimated at slightly above $13 billion) seem manageable, given the large fiscal and external surpluses. However, as the country's fiscal and external balances deteriorate later in the year and the growth in fiscal revenues slows, debt-servicing may become a heavier strain on the budget. The Russian Federation's external debt payments will peak in 2003 and might become increasingly difficult to service in the light of coming parliamentary and presidential elections. For Ukraine, the recent suspension of multilateral lending could exacerbate the fiscal strain in 2001, leading the Government to loosen its monetary policy and undermining the relative stability of the hryvnia. Overall, the recent fiscal stabilization was mainly a consequence of the favourable external situation rather than of fiscal reform so that the danger of fiscal imbalances remains and poses a potential threat to macroeconomic stability in the region. Already CIS countries' fiscal positions are expected to worsen in 2001.

The pace of reforms in the CIS region has been slow in 2000 and no substantial improvement can be expected in 2001. Although the Russian Federation embarked on a reform programme in mid-2000, little progress has been made in most areas, except for tax reform. The new Tax Code entered into force on 1 January 2001, but it does not include the most controversial chapter, related to corporate taxation. The Government and the State Duma are still negotiating over this issue. Custom reform remains high on the agenda, as it is necessary for the Russian Federation's accession to the World Trade Organization. The Government introduced a new and simplified system of import tariffs in January 2001 and a new Customs Code is to be considered by the Parliament later this year. However, the country has failed to take advantage of its oil revenues to reform the banking sector and natural monopolies.

Many structural reforms, especially in the energy sector, are still needed in Ukraine. However, substantial progress in 2001 seems unlikely owing to persisting political turmoil. Uzbekistan's economy has been left practically unreformed since the collapse of the Soviet Union. The Government's repeated reluctance to reform, including the failure to implement an agreement with the International Monetary Fund (IMF) to introduce a unified exchange rate by the end of 2000, made the Fund decide to minimize its presence in the country. This, in turn, is unlikely to encourage foreign investment in the Uzbek economy, which would be crucial in achieving growth and trade diversification.

Baltic Countries: a broadly based recovery

The Baltic economies recovered from the 1999 recession caused by the Russian crisis and grew by about 5 per cent in 2000. Increased external demand from EU and the Russian Federation, giving a stimulus to industrial output, was the major factor behind the strong growth. In 2001, growth is expected to decelerate, but only to 4¾ per cent (see table A.3).

While the recovery was initiated by exports, in the course of 2000 it became increasingly broadly based, particularly in Estonia and Latvia. Low interest rates, increased credit availability, and rising real wages supported the acceleration of private consumption and investment in 2000. In Lithuania, however, domestic demand remained subdued. The country's recovery was slower than that of the other Baltic countries owing to its large trade links with the Russian Federation and the strength of the litas, its currency, which is pegged to the United States dollar.

On the supply side, surging industrial production, particularly of machinery and communications equipment, was the basis of GDP growth in Estonia. Industrial output growth was also robust in Lithuania, despite a sharp contraction in the second quarter caused by disruptions in deliveries of oil from the Russian Federation. In Latvia, forestry was the fastest growing sector, reflecting the growth in external demand, as wood and wood products account for almost one third of Latvian exports. The services sector performed well in the whole region, owing mainly to the increase in transit freight, mostly oil and oil products from the Russian Federation.

Despite faster growth, the unemployment situation did not improve, although employment outcomes were quite diverse. Lithuania has the highest level of unemployment among the three countries and it continued to rise in 2000 as a result of moderate economic growth and enterprise restructuring. Latvia's unemployment fell by almost 1.5 percentage points in 2000, while in Estonia it remained virtually the same as in 1999 (see table A.7).

Domestic demand is expected to be the major source of growth in 2001. Investment is expected to pick up in response to further economic restructuring and improvement of the business climate. Particularly strong acceleration of investment growth is predicted for Estonia. This is due to the positive outlook for its Scandinavian neighbours and also increased public and private investment in the communication and transportation sectors in preparation for integration into EU. Even in Lithuania, whose growth so far has been driven almost exclusively by exports, internal demand is expected to edge up in 2001, as growth spills over from the external sector to the domestic economy, aided by the further consolidation of Lithuania's public finances.

Average inflation in the region was only 2.4 per cent in 2000, in part because of the currency-board arrangements that these countries maintain. Average inflation is not expected to increase in 2001. In 2000, Estonian and Latvian international reserves increased, resulting in low interest rates and credit expansion.

Public finances improved dramatically in 2000, following the austerity measures to correct the fiscal slippage of early 1999. Among the three economies, Estonia is the most advanced in consolidating its public finances and is heading for a fiscal surplus in 2001-2002. In the other economies, further fiscal improvements depend on additional cuts in expenditures and renewed efforts at increasing tax collection. For Lithuania, the major focus of fiscal policy will be the implementation of the reform of the social security fund already approved by the parliament. Further improvement in Latvia's public finances, given general and presidential elections in 2002, seems unlikely.

Privatization has slowed as it entered into the politically sensitive phase of selling large infrastructure enterprises, mostly in the transportation and energy sectors. Constrained by political opposition, privatization in 2001 is likely to proceed slowly, further impeding FDI. On the other hand, the prospect of accession to EU by 2004 at the earliest is encouraging further institutional and structural reforms and greater fiscal discipline.

The current-account deficit increased in Estonia but declined substantially in Latvia and Lithuania in 2000 owing to the favourable external environment. In Lithuania, weak domestic demand was also a factor. However, imports will increase as investment and private consumption accelerate. The regional current-account deficit, therefore, is likely to increase in 2001-2002.

A number of contingencies may affect the outlook for these economies. The major one is related to the depth and duration of the deterioration in the external environment. Another stems from the fact that the Russian Federation's new oil-exporting terminal in Primorsk is scheduled to be completed at the end of 2001. The fact that this would greatly reduce the Russian Federation's reliance on Baltic ports is thus likely to have negative impact on the generation of transit revenues for these economies.

DEVELOPING ECONOMIES

Developing countries grew by 5.7 per cent in 2000, a performance that matches their best annual outcome in the last 10 years (see table A.4). External demand was a major source of growth for these economies in 2000. External financing conditions facing this group of countries did not improve, however, and spread premiums charged on developing countries' sovereign debt increased during the year.

East Asia and China, the largest participants in international trade, grew the fastest among the developing economies in 2000. The external environment was also a major factor in the economic recovery in Western Asia as higher oil prices supported demand and investment in the oil-exporting countries of the region. Latin America and the Caribbean also benefited from the higher oil prices and faster growth of international trade, while domestic demand in several countries remained constrained by high unemployment and tight credit availability. Africa registered the slowest rate of growth among the developing regions, barely above the rate of population growth. Adverse weather conditions, low prices for some important commodities exported by the region, political uncertainties, and limited financial resources inhibited growth in several countries.

Towards the end of 2000, however, economic growth started to decelerate as international trade cooled and uncertainties regarding prospects for the world economy increased. Domestic demand in a number of countries, particularly in East Asia, is still not robust enough to pick up the slack left by external demand and growth is expected to decelerate to 4 per cent in developing countries as a whole in 2001. While slower growth will be noticeable in all developing regions, with the exception of Africa, the deceleration will be relatively sharper in East Asia (excluding China) and in Western Asia (see table A.4). Conversely, growth in Africa is anticipated to accelerate somewhat, with favourable weather conditions. Meanwhile, new financial and payments crisis emerged in some large developing economies, with significant negative implications for growth in these countries in particular. The possibility of contagion to neighbouring economies compounds the downside risks to the present forecast.

Africa: insufficient growth

Africa's GDP grew barely above 3 per cent in 2000 (see table A.4). This was the fourth consecutive year that African growth gravitated around a rate of 3 per cent, which was only slightly higher than the rate of population growth in the continent. Output growth is expected to accelerate to above 4 per cent in 2001. This improvement will be due to the recovery of agricultural output, the stabilization in the prices of some key African export commodities, and the relatively high oil revenues that will continue to support consumption and investment in oil-producing countries. External demand for African exports, chiefly in EU, will be a contributing factor as well, provided EU realizes the growth forecast above.

In 2000, economic performance in many African countries was largely influenced by developments in international markets, weather conditions, and political factors. With international trade expanding at a robust rate, higher oil and metal prices and increased external demand were among the positive growth impulses. Oil-exporting countries supported the region's performance to a large extent, as increased oil production and higher prices had a positive impact on their economies. In the large oil-exporters (Algeria, Angola, the Libyan Arab Jamahiriya and Nigeria), GDP growth accelerated owing to increased production and investment in the hydrocarbon sector, higher public spending, and increased private consumption. GDP growth was marginal in Gabon owing to lower oil output; and in Egypt, which is less dependent on oil revenues, growth decelerated, to 4 per cent, owing mainly to tight macroeconomic policies.

While GDP growth accelerated in oil-importers as a whole in 2000, individual economic performance was not uniform. GDP growth decelerated in 12 of Africa's 30 oil-importing countries monitored by the Secretariat. Low international prices for coffee, cocoa and other agricultural commodities, for example, depressed export earnings and contributed to slower growth in most West African countries. Conversely, higher prices for a few minerals and base metals contributed to increased export earnings in Zambia and other mineral-exporting countries. Strong external demand contributed to increased manufacturing output in Mauritius where GDP grew by 7 per cent, one of the best performances among the developing economies in 2000. The South African economy rebounded from weak growth in the first half of the year to record better-than-expected growth of 3.1 per cent in 2000 (see table A.4).

Africa continues to be vulnerable to weather conditions, as agriculture remains one of the major economic sectors in most of the continent. In 2000, adverse weather led to lower-than-anticipated GDP growth. Heavy rains and flooding caused extensive damage to crops in Madagascar, Mozambique and South Africa. Similarly, drought led to sharp reductions in agricultural output in Algeria, Eritrea and Ethiopia (in addition to the disruptions caused by the war between the latter two countries), Kenya, Morocco for the second consecutive year, and Tunisia.

Armed conflicts and political instability continued to disrupt economic activity in many African countries in 2000. Countries facing conflict situations have consistently performed rather poorly (see figure III.6). In some of them, however, GDP growth was positive but largely sustained by industries operating in isolation from the rest of the economy, usually in the mining and hydrocarbon sectors.

Figure III.6.

AVERAGE ANNUAL RATE OF GDP GROWTH IN AFRICA AND CONFLICT-AFFECTED COUNTRIES,[a] 1985-2001

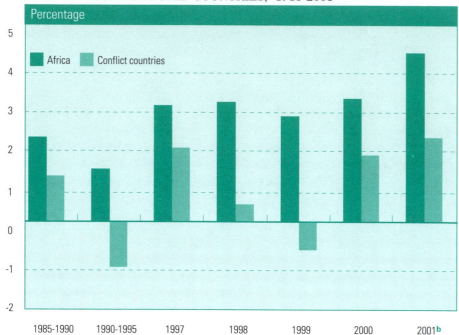

Source: UN/DESA.

a The term "conflict countries" refers to those countries with a United Nations peacekeeping, peacemaking or peace-building operation in 2000. They were Angola, the Central African Republic, the Democratic Republic of the Congo, Eritrea, Ethiopia, Guinea-Bissau, Liberia, Sierra Leone, Somalia and the Sudan.
b Forecast.

In addition to the countries identified in figure III.6, Algeria, in 2000, experienced civil unrest that again undermined investor confidence and lowered private consumption. In Côte d'Ivoire, economic difficulties brought about by further declines in the prices of tropical beverages were exacerbated by the military coup in December 1999, following which external financial assistance was suspended; GDP contracted by 2.0 per cent in 2000. In Guinea, the escalating conflicts in the border regions with Liberia and Sierra Leone discouraged investors and depressed aggregate demand. In Nigeria, religious tensions and social unrest, combined with stagnation in the non-oil sectors of the economy and acute shortages of refined petroleum products, kept the rate of growth of GDP below 3 per cent in 2000.

The recession in Zimbabwe that had started in 1999 deepened in 2000 as political instability increased and the country became more isolated from official sources of finance. The International Monetary Fund (IMF) and donor countries suspended financial assistance to Zimbabwe because of disagreement with the Government's land reform programme. The ensuing lack of foreign exchange led to shortages of essential imports, large budget deficits, excessive money supply growth, and sharp increases in both the inflation and unemployment rates. Zimbabwe's GDP contracted by an estimated 4 per cent in 2000. The civil and political disturbances undermined investor confidence in the entire southern African region and caused substantial capital flight from South Africa at the beginning of the year. As noted, the South Africa economy recovered its momentum later in the year.

Some major developments in 2000 renewed hopes for an early resolution of at least two of the major regional conflicts. First, the end of the war between Eritrea and Ethiopia improved prospects for a resumption of normal economic activity in both countries. Second, political developments in the Democratic Republic of the Congo revived the internationally sponsored peace process and created a more favourable environment for ending the civil war in that country.

The outlook for 2001 is cautiously favourable. EU is a major importer of African products (see table A.14) and should sustain some demand growth in 2001. That only a moderate decline in oil prices is expected would mean a continuation of high export and fiscal revenues which should support investment and consumption in oil-producing countries. The moderation of oil prices and the expected stabilization of the prices of some non-fuel commodities should lead to some improvement in the terms of trade and in the export revenues of oil-importing countries.

The recovery of agriculture in countries affected by adverse weather conditions in 2000 —particularly Morocco and Tunisia, which are among the largest economies of the region— should be another positive factor. Furthermore, the advances in the implementation of the Heavily Indebted Poor Countries (HIPC) Initiative towards the end of 2000 should relieve balance-of-payments pressure and support investment and consumption in some countries in the next few years (see chap. II). Further gains from economic reform should also stimulate growth in the region.

While improved growth is expected, there are a number of risks to the outlook. There are low-level political tensions in many countries or subregions. An upsurge of political instability or violence in a country can depress investors' and consumers' confidence and compromise external assistance, with spillover effects on neighbouring countries. In terms of economic policy, failure to address structural weaknesses, inter alia, in the stability of power supply and expenditure management in the public sector, may hamper the recovery in many countries. Additionally, it is anticipated that commodity prices will stabilize in 2001, but, if the impact of the United States slowdown becomes more severe than expected or if Europe is affected more than anticipated, commodity prices are likely to remain depressed or fall even further. Finally, since weather conditions are unpredictable and yet a chief determinant of economic performance in many countries in Africa, there is an element of uncertainty to the forecast.

The annual average inflation rate for the region increased only marginally in 2000 (see table A.10). Individual country performances, however, diverged markedly. Most countries that had adopted tight monetary policies and maintained stable exchange rates were successful in controlling inflationary pressures. Inflation remained low in the Communauté financière africaine (CFA) franc zone, for example, despite higher oil prices and the depreciation of the CFA franc vis-à-vis the United States dollar owing to the weak euro. The two regional central banks kept inflation rates in this group of countries below 3 per cent.

Inflation increased, however, in countries that suffered from severe food shortages, currency depreciations, or large fiscal deficits. In Ghana, for example, loose fiscal policy and a deterioration of the country's terms of trade triggered a large depreciation in 2000, which led to higher inflation. Triple-digit inflation persisted in Angola and the Democratic Republic of the Congo as a result of the collapse of monetary and fiscal control and the disruption of markets in areas of conflict and instability.

Inflation accelerated in South Africa, particularly in the first half of 2000 owing to higher oil and food prices. Later on, however, inflation moderated, owing in large measure to the recovery in agriculture and increased domestic food supplies. Average annual inflation was about the same as in 1999 (see table A.10). An inflation-targeting framework for monetary policy has committed South African policy makers to maintaining inflation (growth in the overall CPI, excluding mortgage interest rate costs) within a range of 3 to 6 per cent. The expected decline in oil prices should keep inflation at relatively low levels in most countries, although for the region as a whole, inflation is expected to accelerate somewhat in 2001.

Many countries in the region maintained their strong commitment to the implementation of economic reforms and pursued those reforms with the general objectives of achieving stable, non-inflationary growth in their money supplies and stable exchange rates. In Egypt, for instance, monetary policy was tight during early 2000 owing to pressures on the exchange-rate peg vis-à-vis the United States dollar, which were brought about in part by the appreciation of the latter in relation to other major currencies. As a result, liquidity in the financial markets declined and the business sector was hurt. In May 2000, the Government decided to allow the Egyptian pound to depreciate gradually for the remainder of the year, with the result that Egypt's external competitiveness improved. On 30 January 2001, however, the Government introduced a new foreign exchange regime. The pound was allowed to fluctuate within a narrow band (+/- 1 per cent) around the central rate set by the Central Bank. Since then, liquidity has tightened again.

In South Africa, monetary policy was credited with restoring stability to the domestic financial sector in the aftermath of the 1998 international financial crisis. The repurchase rate, which had been adopted as the main instrument of monetary policy in March 1998, soared following of the Asian crisis, but than declined steadily from over 25 to 12 per cent by November 1999. A further cut of 25 bps was adopted in January 2000, but reversed later in the year to contain the second-round effects on inflationary expectations of higher oil prices and the lower rand.

Within the framework of the Economic Community of West African States (ECOWAS), the Gambia, Ghana, Guinea, Liberia, Nigeria and Sierra Leone decided in April 2000 to establish a monetary zone by end-2003, with the aim of merging with the West African Economic and Monetary Union (WAEMU) in 2004. However, in both Ghana and Nigeria, the principal sponsors of this initiative, inflation was higher than in the other West African economies in 2000 owing to loose monetary and fiscal policies. Both countries therefore need to redirect macroeconomic policy to achieve the convergence necessary for the establishment of the proposed monetary union (see chap. II, annex).

Fiscal policy was conservative in most oil-importing countries in the region in 2000. Many countries continued their efforts to bring their fiscal balances onto a more sustainable trajectory by broadening their tax base, making their tax systems and tax collection more efficient, and improving expenditure management in the delivery of public services. The continuing liberalization of trade diminishes tariffs as a source of revenue, amplifying the need to mobilize revenue from other sources.

Exogenous shocks impaired some countries' ability to consolidate their fiscal finances. In Morocco, for instance, emergency measures necessitated by the drought exerted a strain on the State budget in 2000. Assuming normal weather conditions, the fiscal deficit is likely to decrease significantly in 2001. Budget deficits also widened in Angola, Kenya, Madagascar, Zimbabwe and other countries that experienced difficulties in obtaining external financing for budgeted and emergency expenditures. Despite tight fiscal policies and reforms, many African countries will depend on the privatization of state assets, as well as external assistance, to balance their budgets in 2001.

In a departure from its policy in recent years, the Government of South Africa announced an expansionary fiscal policy in its budget proposals for 2001. The budget contained significant increases, in real terms, in capital spending and spending on health, education, housing and other social services over the next three years. Tax cuts for individuals and tax incentives for businesses were aimed at increasing domestic savings and investment in enterprises that were likely to accelerate private sector job growth. Large proceeds from future privatizations, a widening of the tax base through improved collection methods, and savings from public sector reforms were expected to provide some of the funds to finance the increased spending commitments.

In the oil-exporting countries, increased oil revenues led to the adoption of expansionary policies but in 2000 most countries sustained improvements in their fiscal positions. For this group of countries, however, fiscal balances will deteriorate in 2001 as a high level of spending and investment in the public sector coincides with lower oil revenues.

Some oil-exporting countries are trying to reduce their budgetary reliance on oil revenues by broadening their revenue base and insulating budgetary expenditures from variations in oil revenues. As in 2000, if oil exceeds the price of $19 per barrel (pb) assumed in the budget, Algeria will channel all additional revenues received to a stabilization fund to support subsequent budgets, should prices slump. Similarly, in Nigeria, the Government intends to transfer surplus oil earnings in 2001, based on an assumption of an oil price of $22 pb, into an Excess Crude Petroleum Reserve Account.

Many countries, especially the countries benefiting from the HIPC Initiative, have shown a strong commitment to the implementation of structural reforms supported by the international financial institutions. Also, most North African countries are pursuing structural reform policies such as privatization, foreign direct investment (FDI) promotion and trade liberalization. In the case of Morocco and Tunisia, the reform effort has been heavily influenced by these countries' Association Agreements with EU. However, a number of other countries, such as Kenya and Zimbabwe, have experienced setbacks in the implementation of reforms.

East Asia: recovery halted

East Asia (excluding China) grew by 7.3 per cent in 2000. In most countries of the region, GDP growth was supported by strong external demand. Domestic demand continued to recover in many countries, particularly in the first half of the year, but its growth was more muted. The region's recovery had progressed

10   The share of exports to the United States in total exports of most of these economies exceeds 20 per cent.

11   The price of the standard 64-megabyte dynamic random-access memory (DRAM) fell by 60 per cent in 2000.

12   In the Republic of Korea, for instance, the unemployment rate reached 4.1 per cent (seasonally adjusted) in December 2000, almost twice the pre-crisis level.

13   See *World Economic and Social Survey, 1999* (United Nations publication, Sales No. E.99.II.C.1), chap. III, sect. entitled "Asia and the Pacific: macroeconomic policies: easing the crunch".

briskly from early 1999, but came to a halt in the fourth quarter of 2000, mainly as a result of the slowdown in the United States.[10] The downturn continued into 2001. The deceleration has been broad but varied across countries. It was steep in the Republic of Korea and Taiwan Province of China, while a moderate recovery continued in Indonesia until the end of 2000.

The slowdown in East Asia is expected to continue until the latter half of 2001, when it should reverse if the United States economy rebounds. Aggregate GDP growth of the region is forecast to decelerate to 3¾ per cent in 2001, but to recover to 5 per cent in 2002. Hong Kong Special Administrative Region (SAR) of China, the Republic of Korea, Malaysia and Singapore, economies that grew particularly strongly in 2000, will exhibit the sharpest deceleration (see table A.4).

The rapid downturn of the export boom in the fourth quarter of 2000 was the primary cause of the slowdown. The rapid cooling of the United States economy, combined with sluggish demand in Japan and the ensuing weakening in intraregional trade, curtailed growth of exports. Reduced ICT investment in the United States, and the sharp fall in world semiconductor prices[11] in particular, adversely affected exports of electronics, a major item for East Asian countries.

A few adverse factors hindered growth of domestic demand. First, having already exhibited patchy signs of deceleration in early 2000, domestic demand was further weakened by the slowing exports late in the year. Second, household income has been growing slowly, as the unemployment rate, though improved in many countries in 2000, has not returned to its pre-crisis level;[12] and the jobless rate rose again in early 2001. Third, the negative wealth effects from the equity and property markets constrained household spending. Equity markets, which had recovered relatively quickly, did not sustain these gains as stock prices plunged again in 2000. Finally, the persistence of inadequate credit conditions, higher oil prices, and heightened political uncertainties in 2000 also discouraged consumption and private investment.

On the supply side, the manufacturing sector slowed sharply throughout the region in the fourth quarter of 2000, primarily in response to slowing exports. Growth of the service sector was healthy through the third quarter of the year, led by ICT-related activities and tourism, but was adversely affected thereafter by the economic slowdown. Agricultural output growth was positive in most countries, except the Republic of Korea and Thailand where there were unfavourable weather conditions.

Inflation began to rise modestly in the second half of 2000, owing to higher fuel prices, increases in administered prices and, in the case of Indonesia, the Philippines, the Republic of Korea and Thailand, currency depreciation (see table III.3). The rising trend in inflation continued into early 2001. Except for Indonesia and the Philippines, where annual inflation was over 6 per cent in early 2001, softening demand, lower high oil prices, and increased competition should keep inflation at low levels.

Macroeconomic policies in the region remained broadly accommodative in 2000. Previously, fiscal stimulus had been a major factor contributing to the recovery of crisis-hit countries[13] and fiscal positions deteriorated and the public debt increased. In 2000, increases in cyclical revenue resulted in smaller deficits than had been anticipated. However, an increasing number of countries made greater use of lower interest rates to support growth from late 2000

Table III.3.
MAJOR DEVELOPING COUNTRIES: QUARTERLY INDICATORS, 1999-2000

	1999 quarter				2000 quarter			
	I	II	III	IV	I	II	III	IV
Rates of growth of gross domestic product[a]								
Argentina-	2.7	-5.2	-5.1	-0.5	0.5	0.2	-0.5	-2.0
Brazil	0.7	-0.2	0.5	3.4	3.8	3.5	5.1	4.4
Chile	-2.8	-3.7	-1.8	4.0	5.5	6.0	5.6	4.5
China	8.3	7.6	7.4	7.1	8.1	8.3	8.2	8.0
Colombia	-5.7	-6.8	-3.6	-1.0	2.4	3.4	3.1	2.1
Ecuador	-5.4	-7.2	-8.0	-8.5	-2.2	2.0	3.6	6.0
Hong Kong (SAR)	-2.9	1.1	4.3	9.2	14.1	10.8	10.8	6.8
India	7.2	7.1	6.2	6.0	7.2	6.3	6.5	5.7
Indonesia	-4.1	3.5	2.4	5.0	4.2	5.2	4.4	5.2
Israel	0.9	2.1	2.2	3.1	6.3	6.3	7.6	3.0
Korea, Republic of	5.4	10.8	12.8	13.0	12.7	9.6	9.2	4.6
Malaysia	-1.4	5.0	8.6	11.0	11.8	8.4	7.8	6.5
Mexico	1.8	3.1	4.3	5.2	7.9	7.6	7.0	5.1
Philippines	1.6	5.0	3.0	4.6	3.2	3.2	4.6	3.7
Singapore	1.3	6.9	7.4	7.7	9.8	8.4	10.3	11.0
South Africa	0.8	1.3	2.3	3.1	3.1	3.1	3.2	2.9
Taiwan Province of China	4.2	6.4	4.7	6.4	7.9	5.4	6.6	4.1
Thailand	0.1	2.7	7.8	6.5	5.2	6.2	2.8	3.1
Turkey	-9.1	-1.7	-6.0	-3.4	5.4	6.2	8.0	8.3
Venezuela	-8.5	-7.4	-4.3	-4.1	1.1	2.7	3.4	5.6
Growth of consumer prices[a]								
Argentina	0.0	-1.1	-1.8	-1.8	-1.3	-1.1	-0.8	-0.6
Brazil	2.3	3.3	5.5	8.4	7.9	6.6	7.6	6.2
Chile	3.8	3.9	3.2	2.5	3.2	3.6	4.0	4.6
China	-1.4	-2.2	-1.2	-0.8	0.1	0.1	0.3	0.4
Colombia	16.7	9.9	9.1	9.6	9.0	10.6	9.4	8.9
Ecuador	45.6	54.6	54.0	53.8	83.2	96.5	104.8	97.3
Hong Kong (SAR)	-1.8	-4.0	-5.9	-4.1	-5.1	-4.4	-2.9	-2.2
India	9.0	7.1	2.8	0.5	3.7	5.3	4.1	3.0
Indonesia	55.9	30.9	6.6	1.7	-0.6	1.1	5.7	8.8
Israel	7.3	5.9	6.0	1.9	1.5	2.0	1.0	0.0
Korea, Republic of	0.7	0.6	0.7	1.3	1.5	1.4	3.2	2.9
Malaysia	4.0	2.7	2.3	2.1	1.5	1.4	1.5	1.7
Mexico	18.6	17.9	16.5	13.7	10.5	9.5	9.0	8.9
Philippines	10.0	6.8	5.5	4.5	3.0	3.9	4.5	5.9
Singapore	-0.7	0.0	0.3	0.5	1.1	0.8	1.5	2.0
South Africa	8.5	7.3	3.3	2.0	2.8	5.2	6.3	6.2
Taiwan Province of China	0.7	-0.1	0.3	0.0	0.9	1.4	1.1	1.5
Thailand	2.7	-0.4	-1.0	0.1	0.8	1.6	2.2	1.6
Turkey	64.4	63.7	64.9	66.1	68.8	61.7	52.7	42.3
Venezuela	29.1	23.9	22.2	20.1	18.2	17.1	15.6	14.2

Source: IMF, *International Financial Statistics,* and national authorities.

[a]   Percentage change over the same quarter of previous year.

onwards. Indonesia and the Philippines are exceptions to this trend: both countries raised interest rates in the second half of 2000 amid increased political uncertainty and pressure on their currencies. The Philippines, however, reversed these increases starting in December 2000.

Fiscal policy in the region remains expansionary; but with the slowdown, countries are likely to contemplate additional policy measures in 2001. The scope for fiscal manoeuvre, however, is limited owing to the increased public debt. In most countries, increased fiscal expenditures, combined with the large debt-servicing obligations and the cyclical decline in revenues, will further aggravate fiscal positions in 2001. The Philippines, in particular, faces the challenge of dealing simultaneously with a large fiscal deficit and a slowing economy.[14] Fiscal imbalances may prevent the Thai administration from introducing sufficient fiscal stimuli to offset the weakening of exports. More imminently, policy makers will need to address fiscal imbalances as soon as their economies are back on a recovery track in order to avoid the higher interest rates associated with the financing of the public debt and their damaging effects on investment and growth in the longer run.

In Hong Kong SAR, the Basic Law mandates the SAR Government to maintain fiscal balance so that fiscal stimulus is feasible only within limits. As in other countries of the region, fiscal policy was used over the past few years to mitigate the adverse effects of the Asian financial crises. Public expenditures, especially for social welfare due to the high unemployment rate, continued to increase in 2000 and there was a fiscal deficit. This was less than 1 per cent of GDP and is expected to narrow. Discretion in the Region's monetary policy is similarly limited, owing to the currency board. Interest rates usually follow those in the United States, as the Hong Kong dollar is pegged to the United States dollar. The monetary easing in the United States is therefore expected to help reduce interest rates in the Region.

Economic restructuring has continued in most of East Asia. There are increasing signs that the Democratic People's Republic of Korea, for instance, is contemplating reforms, particularly in external trade and foreign investment, to overcome its economic stagnation (see box III.1). Nonetheless, the process of restructuring has been relatively more dynamic in those economies affected by the financial crisis. The financial and corporate sectors still exhibit considerable fragility, which impedes normal lending and therefore investment and stable growth. Crisis-hit countries are still saddled with sizeable low-quality loans and profit performance has been poor. Progress in Indonesia and Thailand has been slower than elsewhere. In all countries, however, corporate restructuring has lagged behind financial restructuring.

The Republic of Korea is most advanced in the consolidation of the financial sector, but it still faces problems:[15] the share of non-performing loans (NPLs) is still high and there is a continuing need to strengthen the regulatory and supervisory frameworks. The Government has initiated a second round of financial restructuring by creating a financial holding company. It also provided additional funds of 40 trillion won (about $35 billion) to strengthen the capital base of banks and to augment the loss provisions of non-bank financial institutions. In Thailand, NPLs fell from 39 per cent in January 2000 to 18 per cent by year-end, largely owing to reschedulings and debt transfer to asset-management companies. The Government has planned to buy up banks' NPLs

14 Rosario G. Manasan, *The President's Budget for 2001: Depleted Economic Choices* (Philippine Institute for Development Studies, Discussion Paper Series, No. 2000-43, November 2000).

15 Ministry of Finance and Economy, Republic of Korea, *Financial Statistics Bulletin*, second quarter, 2001, pp. 64-83.

Box III.1

ECONOMIC TRANSITION IN THE
DEMOCRATIC PEOPLE'S
REPUBLIC OF KOREA:
DELAYED PASSAGE TO
OPEN MARKET ECONOMY

In the past decade, the Democratic People's Republic of Korea struggled to overcome severe economic difficulties. The shocks from the collapse of its trade with socialist countries in the early 1990s and disastrous floods in the mid-1990s sharply exacerbated the problems of the already sagging economy, resulting in declining output for nine consecutive years and acute shortages of food and energy[a] (see table). However, these exogenous factors were not the only reasons behind the country's persistent deterioration. Structural inefficiencies owing to the country's centrally planned economic system have also constrained economic growth since the early 1980s.

A series of reforms have been adopted since the mid-1980s. Reforms in the external sector were more significant than in the domestic sector, reflecting the profound changes in external conditions and the Democratic People's Republic of Korea's changing perceptions on the importance of the external sector. The measures included the extension of industrial associations[b] in 1985, the transformation of cooperative farms into State farms in 1994, the improvement of material incentives in team units in 1996, the decentralization of trade management in 1984 and in the early 1990s, the introduction of joint venture law in 1984, and the establishment of the Rajin-Sunbong free trade zone in 1992.

Despite these reforms, the economy of the Democratic People's Republic of Korea remains in a dire situation and faces a daunting task of transition. A major problem with past reforms is that they were only partial. Furthermore, the measures adopted were geared mainly to management inefficiencies but did not tackle fundamental structural problems or succeed in reversing economic deterioration.

Since September 1998, there have been signs of new thinking about the process of opening up the economy. The newly introduced measures have included pragmatic as well as traditional ideological elements, such as labour competition and self-reliance. The main elements of the new reforms include abolishing the industrial associations, promoting export industries, emphasizing science and technology, allowing special economic zones (SEZs) in multiple locations, and the second-round "Chunrima" movement.[c] There has been some reversal of earlier decentralization effort but also signs of further opening.

Since 1998, the Democratic People's Republic of Korea has consolidated central control in the industrial sector by abolishing industrial associations and strength-

[a] Bank of Korea, "Recent situation in the Democratic People's Republic of Korea economy", Research Department, March 2001.

[b] These are giant groups of firms based on vertical integration and were first introduced in 1973. They are similar to Kombinat in the former German Democratic Republic and the Russian industrial associations.

[c] This is a mass movement originally introduced in 1958. Its method is to increase labour productivity through the use of non-material incentives.

Box table III.1.
DEMOCRATIC PEOPLE'S REPUBLIC OF KOREA: REAL GDP AND INTERNATIONAL TRADE, 1989-2000

	1989	1990	1991	1992	1993	1994	1995	1996	1997	1998	1999	2000
GDP[a]	..	-3.7	-3.5	-6	-4.2	-2.1	-4.1	-3.6	-6.3	-1.1	6.2	1.3
Exports[b]	1.91	1.96	2.01	1.03	1.02	0.84	0.74	0.73	0.9	0.56	0.52	0.56
Imports[b]	2.89	2.76	1.71	1.64	1.62	1.27	1.32	1.25	1.27	0.88	0.96	1.41
Trade balance[b]	-0.98	-0.8	0.3	-0.61	-0.6	-0.43	-0.58	-0.52	-0.37	-0.32	-0.44	-0.85

Source: Bank of Korea.

[a] Annual percentage change.
[b] Billions of dollars.

Box III.1 (continued)

ening the authority of the Cabinet. By January 2000, 44 industrial associations had been dismantled and individual firms had been put under the de facto direct control of the Cabinet. As the Government was also downsized significantly, however, this may eventually strengthen accountability by individual firms. Conversely, since September 2000, the Democratic People's Republic of Korea has restored more than 20 large industrial associations in heavy industry. This change aimed at reorganizing factories and firms into industry-based associations, for example, in the metal, machinery and extractive industries. As a result of these more recent changes, the Democratic People's Republic of Korea appears to be positioning itself to deal with external competition more effectively by letting the associations handle not only production but also distribution and trade of their products.

In the agricultural sector, farmers were allowed to own simple farming tools and cattle in 1998. This measure, if it leads to the separation of land ownership and usage rights, could facilitate the introduction of the household production responsibility system as adopted in China and Viet Nam, particularly in view of the free disposal of excess production by team units introduced in 1996. There is, however, one important contrast: there is still no market-oriented reform in the Democratic People's Republic of Korea.

Additionally, the Democratic People's Republic of Korea reformed its trade management system in late 1998. It sharply reduced the number of trade companies, which were under the local government, and placed them under the direct control of the Cabinet. The role of local governments in trade was thus reduced substantially.

In June 2000, a historic summit between the Democratic People's Republic of Korea and the Republic of Korea took place and a cooperation agreement was signed. The summit agreement provided additional momentum for the Democratic People's Republic of Korea to intensify its economic cooperation with the Republic of Korea, to improve its relationship with developed countries, and to take bolder steps towards opening. If its open door policy moves successfully, this may encourage the Democratic People's Republic of Korea to start market-oriented reforms. Nonetheless, the measures adopted so far have stressed only opening the economy; in contrast with China and Viet Nam, Democratic People's Republic of Korea is still silent about fundamental domestic reform.

The road to reform, however, is a long one and many options can be considered. Initially, the Democratic People's Republic of Korea may attempt to use a combination of the SEZ (or similar arrangements) and economic cooperation with the Republic of Korea as main instruments to break through its economic impasse, while remaining cautious about domestic reform. The resources required to finance this undertaking, however, are beyond the capacity of both economies and will require external finance. At the beginning, the Republic of Korea can play a limited but important role.

To facilitate economic cooperation, the Democratic People's Republic of Korea and the Republic of Korea agreed in November 2000 on investment guarantees, protection from double taxation, dispute settlement, and a payments clearance system. Firms from both economies were already allowed to operate in the Rajin-Sunbong free trade zone. In some cases, factories of the Democratic People's Republic of Korea were allowed even outside this zone. The prospect for trade between the Democratic People's Republic of Korea and the Republic of Korea is favourable in view of their strong complementarity in respect of resource endowments and stages of economic development and their common culture.

Box III.1 (continued)

Notwithstanding the above, the establishment of SEZs alone—albeit a significant step forward—is unlikely to put the economy on a sustainable growth track. The SEZ effort needs to be supported by a consistent and operational market environment for the entire economy. This will require extensive market-oriented reforms covering the ownership of means of production; liberalizing prices, trade and the activities of economic agents; and establishing the required institutional infrastructure.

These requirements are all closely interrelated and essential for the efficient functioning of the market system and cannot work well in isolation.[d] Nevertheless, their simultaneous implementation is a complex and challenging task. Some of the necessary measures take more time and cost more than others to put into effect (for instance, privatization and the creation of banking and tax systems). Their political and social consequences are also quite diverse. The impacts of reforms of the price system and of State-owned enterprises (SOEs) on income distribution and employment are cases in point.

When deciding about which reform path to take, the Democratic People's Republic of Korea may draw on the diverse experiences of transition economies, as well as those of market economies. Two major patterns of transition can be identified: the radical or "big bang" approach, which began in Poland and was followed by other transition economies in Europe, including the Czech Republic and the Russian Federation; and the gradual approach adopted by China. It is likely that the Democratic People's Republic of Korea, constrained by its concern about political security, would choose gradualism, possibly a variant of China's initial model of economic reforms, if only because this proved that market-oriented reforms could be compatible with the existing political system. The timing, scope, speed and sequence of the reform programme will have to be adapted and take into account the Democratic People's Republic of Korea's initial conditions[e] as well as developments in political and other local factors.

Initial conditions differ from those in China in several respects. First, the Democratic People's Republic of Korea has less political momentum for reform than China had in the late 1970s owing to the weight of its political legacy and the latent competition with the system of the Republic of Korea. Second, the Democratic People's Republic of Korea has a smaller share of population in the agricultural sector than China.[f] Consequently, this sector would have limited effectiveness as a leader in the transition, particularly as a source of unlimited cheap labour and as a generator of domestic saving.[g] Third, in contrast with China, the Democratic People's Republic of Korea's current economic difficulties will make it difficult to carry out major reform programmes in the near term. Fourth, and in respect of this it also differs from China, the Democratic People's Republic of Korea does not have many expatriates living abroad who would be in a position to mobilize significant amounts of capital inflow.

In sum, there are increasing signs that the Democratic People's Republic of Korea is quickening its pace of opening, although it is still uncertain whether it will embark on more comprehensive, fundamental domestic economic reforms in the near future. In any case, the Democratic People's Republic of Korea's approach will be consistent with its paramount concern about the security of its political system. However, efforts at external liberalization, if successful, may trigger more extensive reforms. This possibility will depend crucially not only on how the Democratic People's Republic of Korea perceives the impact of the economic reforms on its socio-political system but also on the unfolding security environment in north-eastern Asia.

[d] Daniel Gros and Alfred Steinherr, *Winds of Change*, (London, Longman, 1995), pp. 90-112.

[e] Jeffrey Sachs, and Wing Thye Woo, "Structural factors in the economic reform of China, Eastern Europe and the former Soviet Union", *Economic Policy*, vol. 18 (April 1994).

[f] In China, the rural population accounts for 70 per cent of total population and SOEs account for only 19 per cent of total employment.

[g] Arthur Lewis, "Economic development with unlimited supplies of labor", *Manchester School of Economic and Social Studies*, vol. 22 No.2 (1954).

through the new Government-owned Central Asset Management Company (CAMC). The Government, however, has faced difficulties in setting the discount rate for these purchases in view of the rising fiscal burden, as well as the possibilities for moral hazard. Progress in Indonesia has been the slowest, although the NPL ratio in the banking system fell sharply to about 20 per cent by the end of 2000. This was due largely to the transfer of NPLs from banks to government agencies, in this case the Indonesian Bank Restructuring Agency (IBRA). Very few assets have been disposed of. As a result of the massive infusion of public funds in the financial restructuring process, the Indonesian Government ended up owning about 80 per cent of the banking system's total assets, far more than in other countries. Debt-servicing costs arising from bank restructuring now absorb 40 per cent of public revenues in Indonesia.

Progress in corporate reform has been slow throughout the region. In the Republic of Korea, the corporate sector is still heavily indebted although the disposal of commercially non-viable firms is in progress. Nonetheless, further advances in this area may be constrained by opposition from the labour unions and the presidential election in December 2002. In Indonesia, corporate restructuring has been delayed because of debtors' resistance, political uncertainty, asset-valuation problems, and the weak judicial system. As of June 2000, total corporate debt was estimated at $117 billion, of which 64 per cent is non-performing; $85 billion was denominated in foreign currency. The Indonesian corporate sector, therefore, remains vulnerable to changes in interest rates and the exchange rate.

The region's economic deceleration will be broad-based. By early 2001, it had engulfed the entire region as exports and domestic demand weakened further in the first quarter. The downtrend in exports is expected to continue through mid-2001 in line with slowing world trade. ICT-related exports are the hardest hit, but other exports have also declined. The depreciation of currencies in many countries, except for Hong Kong SAR and Malaysia whose currencies are pegged to the United States dollar, will provide some support to their exports. On the other hand, depreciation, if excessive, would undermine the orderly servicing of these countries' external debt, fuel inflation, and jeopardize financial stability (see box III.2).

The widespread slowdown in domestic demand is expected to continue for at least the first half of 2001. Private consumption will be constrained by the collapsed stock prices, slowing real wage increases, rising unemployment, and lower consumer confidence. Sluggish export growth and limited credit availability will deter private investment. Unstable currency markets and, in Indonesia, political uncertainties continue to undermine investor confidence. Additionally, banks' reluctance to lend partially offsets the potential positive impact of lower interest rates on growth. In countries hit by the 1997 crisis, restructuring will continue to have deflationary short-term effects. It will, however, facilitate financial intermediation and bolster investor confidence and foreign capital inflows, as well as be conducive to more stable growth. Meanwhile, the proposed policy stimuli in several countries have been moderate owing to the constraints discussed above. They are unlikely to reverse the trend of slowing growth.

On the supply side, manufacturing output will continue to weaken in line with slowing exports. Although the slowdown will be particularly sharp in the ICT sector, other industries will also weaken. Similarly, the performance in the

Box III.2

RENEWED DEPRECIATION OF
SELECTED EAST ASIAN
CURRENCIES: CAUSES
AND IMPACT

The currencies of an increasing number of East Asian countries —first Indonesia, and later Thailand, the Philippines and the Republic of Korea— began to depreciate after early 2000. The main causes of these exchange-rate movements differed among countries.

In the case of Indonesia and the Philippines, political uncertainty was the prime reason, although the depreciation was also linked to such other factors as the interest differential vis-à-vis the United States economy, as well as the strength of the dollar relative to the Japanese yen. As the political crisis receded in the Philippines, the peso stabilized and recovered some of its lost value (see figure). On the other hand, political uncertainty kept the rupiah weak and unstable. In March 2001, panic dollar buying —out of fear that Bank Indonesia (BI) would impose capital controls— drove the rupiah to another record low against the United States dollar. BI's subsequent intervention calmed the markets but the situation remained fragile. Finally, the Korean won began to depreciate rapidly in December 2000, owing to the slowdown in Republic of Korea exports and growth, the depreciation of the yen, and news about delays and problems in the restructuring of the economy. Increased demand for United States dollars to repay debts added to the pressure on the won. Similar factors were behind the depreciation of the Thai baht.

In addition to these conjunctural factors, structural elements were also at play. The continued liberalization of the foreign currency and capital markets in these countries since the Asian financial crisis had provided the institutional environment for the wider fluctuation of their currencies.

SELECTED EAST ASIAN COUNTRIES: REAL EFFECTIVE EXCHANGE RATES,
JANUARY 1999-APRIL 2001

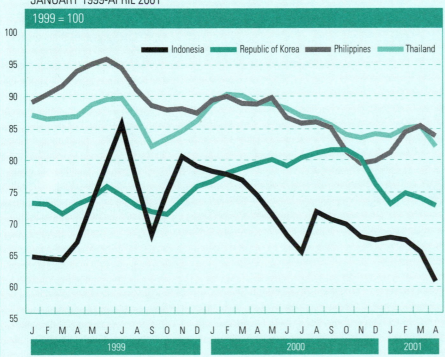

Source: J.P. Morgan.

Box III.2 (continued)

While the greater flexibility of the exchange rates has allowed these currencies to better absorb the demand and supply pressures in foreign currency markets, the thin and immature nature of local foreign exchange and financial markets has left these economies vulnerable to volatile movements of portfolio capital, which have contributed to excessive exchange-rate fluctuations. Even minor pressures from capital movements or currency speculation can cause large fluctuations in the exchange rates of these countries.

A sharp depreciation can benefit exports because it improves competitiveness, but it also hurts industries that have a large share of imported inputs or that carry a large foreign debt. Indonesia, in particular, is vulnerable because of its large foreign debt. In countries where the import content of exports is high, the net direct gain from a depreciation can be small. This is the case for the Philippines, where electronics is a dominant export and has a high import content.

The gain in export competitiveness has also been offset by the depreciation of the currencies of major competitors. The currencies of the Republic of Korea and Taiwan Province of China, for instance, appreciated against the Japanese yen in early 2001, and these economies lost competitiveness in a wide range of exports in which they compete directly with Japan for export markets—the overlap is about 40 per cent. Exports can be hurt further if the yen keeps depreciating or if other competitors adjust their peg to lower the price of their exports so as to maintain their market shares.

A large depreciation also constrains monetary and fiscal policy by fuelling inflation, increasing the debt-service burden, and destabilizing capital markets. It was a major cause of the rise in inflation in Indonesia, the Philippines and the Republic of Korea in 2000/early 2001 and forced BI to keep the interest rate high.

These three countries intervened in currency markets when the depreciation exceeded a given level. They had adequate foreign reserves to weather excessive currency attacks. Moreover, their financial system is more resilient than three years previously and their short-term debt has declined since the financial crisis. Nevertheless, their foreign reserves are not unlimited and regional cooperation was called for to improve these countries' ability to prevent further currency crises.

In May 2000, a group of East Asian countries launched the Chiang Mai initiative.[1] It included, among other things, the enlargement and strengthening of existing mechanisms of financial cooperation in the region (the Association of Southeast Asian Nations (ASEAN) Swap Arrangement) to provide liquidity in the event of temporary balance-of- payment difficulties. Funding for the ASEAN Swap Arrangement was increased and all 10 ASEAN members are now included. Moreover, additional support mechanisms are being developed through a network of bilateral currency swap arrangements with China, Japan and the Republic of Korea.[2] These latter arrangements, however, are yet to be fully tested.

[a]   It includes Brunei Darussalam, Cambodia, Indonesia, the Lao People's Democratic Republic, Malaysia, Myanmar, the Philippines, Singapore, Thailand and Viet Nam, which are ASEAN members, plus China, Japan and the Republic of Korea.

[b]   Joint Ministerial Statement of the Fifth ASEAN Finance Ministers' Meeting, 7 and 8 April 2001, Kuala Lumpur, Malaysia (http://www.aseansec.org/economic/jps_5afmm.htm).

service sector will be adversely affected by slowing demand and exports. On the other hand, prospects for agriculture are positive in most countries.

A broad-based moderate recovery is expected to start in the second half of 2001. Exports will pick up if the United States recovers, as expected, with positive spillover effects on domestic demand. Softer oil prices will also contribute to the recovery.

Nevertheless, there are considerable uncertainties about the timing and strength of the recovery. First, the stock market of the United States economy will have a decisive effect on East Asian growth because of its importance for both the real and financial sectors of the region. Second, there is a high degree of uncertainty about the severity and duration of the downturn in the global electronics cycle. Third, although the resilience of the East Asian economies has improved, slowing economic growth can expose their structural weaknesses. This is of particular concern to Indonesia, where many marginal financial institutions and firms still carry large NPLs and have low profitability. Furthermore, the political situation is unstable in several instances. Structural weaknesses, if not rectified, could trap these economies in a protracted economic stagnation or a prolonged period of unstable growth.

China: strengthening domestic demand

Despite some downside risks, particularly a weakening of external demand, the outlook for the Chinese economy remains optimistic, as economic policies continue to focus on strengthening domestic demand. After 8 per cent in 2000, GDP growth is expected to moderate to about 7 per cent in 2001. The same pace is forecast for the next few years. According to the five-year development plan for 2001-2005, policy measures in the years ahead will emphasize both the quality and the quantity of economic growth through structural reform, rather than aim at high growth per se. The reform agenda, however, continues to be challenging and some uncertainties remain.

Economic efficiency improved notably in 2000, as indicated by the 86 per cent increase in corporate profits in the manufacturing sector. The overall efficiency index for industrial enterprises had reached its highest level since the early 1990s. Profits of State-owned and State-holding enterprises increased by 140 per cent, while the total losses of the money-losing enterprises in the same group declined by 26 per cent.

Output growth in 2000 was more balanced across sectors: industrial production increased by more than 9 per cent and the services sector grew by almost 8 per cent. Within the agricultural sector, however, grain output declined by 9 per cent, owing to drought in some areas and measures introduced to reduce the sown grain area in order to optimize the agricultural product mix.

On the demand side, the growth of both consumption and investment accelerated in 2000, as several stimulus measures carried out in the past few years started to produce results. Consumer spending, which had weakened after the Asian financial crisis, was stimulated by cutting interest rates, expanding consumption loans, taxing interest earnings, raising the wages of government employees and instituting longer public holidays. Meanwhile, improvements in the social security system reduced some uncertainties, and enhanced consumer confidence. A few adverse factors remain, however: the growth of the disposable income of rural residents, who still account for more than 60 per cent of the total population, has moderated recently; and pressures on the labour market persist in conjunction with the ongoing enterprise restructuring. The number of laid-off workers from State-owned enterprises (SOEs) increased in 2000, reaching over 6.5 million.

16 Total fixed investment grew by about 9 per cent in 2000, but spending on technological innovations to improve energy and raw-material efficiency increased even more rapidly. ICT-related investment surged by more than 30 per cent.

17 FDI increased by only 1 per cent to about $40 billion in 2000, but new commitments jumped by 50 per cent to about $62 billion, implying solid growth in the short term. FDI accounted for 14 per cent of total fixed investment in 2000.

Investment growth has been strong and driven by such measures as direct government spending on infrastructure (financed by long-term bond issues totalling 360 billion yuan ($45 billion) in the past three years) and investment tax credits.[16] A noticeable improvement in 2000 was the catch-up of investment growth of the non-State sector, which had earlier lagged. Supported by continued fiscal spending, along with improved business confidence and the ongoing housing reform, investment is expected to remain strong in 2001. Adding to the strength is the positive outlook for FDI as China is likely to join the World Trade Organization in the near future.[17]

The inflation outlook remains benign. The two-year period of deflation ended by late 2000, as most price indices rose. The CPI edged up by 0.4 per cent, compared with a decline of 1.4 per cent in 1999. The upward pressure, however, is expected to be limited. Excess capacity exists in the domestic economy and international competition is likely to increase with further cuts in import tariffs. Annual inflation for the next few years is forecast to be within the range of 1 to 2 per cent.

China has maintained a robust external balance for many years. Both exports and imports accelerated very rapidly in 2000, by 27 per cent and 35 per cent in United States dollar terms, respectively. As a result of a deterioration in the terms of trade, higher prices for petroleum imports being one factor, the trade surplus declined slightly from that of 1999 to $24 billion. Foreign reserves continued to rise and reached $165 billion, while the exchange rate of the yuan vis-à-vis the United States dollar remained stable. A further decline in the trade surplus is likely for 2001-2002, partly because of the substantial weakening of external demand, especially from the United States, and partly because of an expected boost to China's imports from its anticipated entry into the World Trade Organization. While the ratio of exports to GDP for China is relatively high (22 per cent), the impact of slowing external demand on China's overall economic growth is unlikely to be as large as that for many other Asian economies. One reason is that a substantial proportion of China's exports consists of simple processing of imported materials with low value-added.

Expansionary macroeconomic policies over the last few years have played a crucial role in reviving domestic demand and are expected to remain pro-growth. Interest rates have been maintained at low levels since mid-1999, after several reductions in the previous three years. The non-banking financial sector, particularly export markets, had a good performance in 2000. The ratio of total market capitalization to GDP reached 50 per cent by the end of the year, 82 per cent above 1999, and the two stock markets in China (Shanghai and Shenzhen) ranked at the top of the few stock markets in the world registering positive returns in 2000.

Fiscal policy has been expansionary and is expected to remain so in 2001. Despite increased government spending over the past few years, the fiscal position is relatively sound. While total spending rose by more than 20 per cent in 2000, revenues grew by 16 per cent, with the deficit increasing to $260 billion yuan, or 2.9 per cent of GDP. The central government debt stood below 20 per cent of GDP in 2000. In the 2001 budget, another long-term bond issue of 150 billion yuan (about $19 billion) is planned to finance public investment in infrastructure. Other expenditure increases include higher wages for civil servants, improvements in the social security system, and a rise of 17 per cent in military spending.

The reform agenda, especially for the financial sector, remains a crucial and difficult task for policy makers. Some progress has recently been made, with debt-equity swaps to reduce SOEs' indebtedness while improving the balance sheets of State-owned banks. More significant initiatives are expected in the coming years to prepare for opening China's financial sector to international competition after the country's entry into the World Trade Organization, as well as to improve the efficiency of allocating financial resources. These measures include liberalization of interest rates, development of other institutional investors, reform of the pension system, and opening of a National Association of Securities Dealers Automated Quotations System (Nasdaq)-type stock market to encourage venture capital. Despite the expected long-term benefits, these reforms entail costs and risks.

The debate on whether China should widen its exchange-rate band has revived with views split on the impact of a more flexible exchange rate. Pressure for a devaluation of the yuan is much less than during the Asian financial crisis as the real effective exchange rate has depreciated over the past two years owing to domestic deflation and the rebound of many Asian currencies. Moreover, China continues to have large foreign reserves. In the outlook, the yuan is expected to maintain the current peg to the United States dollar.

South Asia: growth remained strong

South Asia extended its strong performance to 2000: GDP growth for the region as a whole reached 5.8 per cent, barely below the rate of growth recorded in 1999. Despite some adverse factors, including political uncertainties and higher oil prices, growth accelerated in most countries in 2000, but not in India. The growth of that country, which accounts for 70 per cent of total output of the region, unexpectedly decelerated in 2000. In 2001, economic growth in South Asia is forecast to slow to 5½ per cent (see table A.4).

The main thrust for growth in most countries in 2000 came from strong exports. This reflected the expansion in world demand and the region's improved export competitiveness as a result of the depreciation of several currencies. Additionally, a preferential trade agreement between India and Nepal, and the bumper cotton crop in Pakistan provided a further boost to these countries' exports.

Domestic economic performances were mixed in 2000, mainly reflecting natural calamities and political uncertainties. Agricultural output growth in Bangladesh, Nepal and Pakistan was favourable. On the other hand, India experienced bad monsoons in some provinces, while Sri Lanka had a poor rice crop. Manufacturing was weaker than earlier thought in a number of countries. In India, the recovery of the industrial sector faltered during 2000 and the boom in the ICT sector began to fade in late 2000. In Pakistan, industrial output stagnated, owing mainly to the sharp contraction in the sugar industry. Conversely, robust exports of manufactures supported industrial output, particularly textiles, in Nepal and Sri Lanka. The service sector sustained growth in most countries.

Inflation in the region, after a rapid fall in 1999, began to rise moderately during 2000 in line with higher oil prices, the devaluation of national currencies, and increases in administered prices (see table A.10). It continued to increase in early 2001, rising faster in Pakistan and Sri Lanka than elsewhere. Inflation remains, however, below the historical trend in these countries. In Pakistan, inflation has been rising rapidly as the devaluation of the currency fed into production costs and agricultural support prices increased. The petroleum price adjustment and the expected levy of the 18 per cent goods and services tax (GST) on agricultural inputs and retail trade are also likely to add inflationary pressures in the near term.

Low inflation in the region allowed monetary policy to be accommodative through early 2000. Later in the year, however, a number of countries raised their key interest rates to curb pressures on their currencies and inflation. In India, Pakistan and Sri Lanka, which were under increasing inflationary pressures from fiscal deficits and depreciation, key interest rates were raised significantly during the second half of 2000.[18] In early 2001, the Reserve Bank of India (RBI) reversed some of these increases by lowering its key interest rate by 100 bps to boost the slowing economy.[19]

Fiscal spending was expansionary in most of these countries in 2000. Governments continued unsustainably large fiscal deficits, crowding out private investment and constraining growth. To reduce these deficits, several countries have stepped up fiscal reforms, both revenue increases and expenditure rationalization. Progress, however, has been slow.

Fiscal imbalances are particularly serious in India and Sri Lanka. Despite plans to reduce the deficit in fiscal 2000/01, India incurred additional public expenditures, including increased fuel price subsidies and the rehabilitation costs associated with heavy flood damages. The Government's target for fiscal 2000/01 may therefore not be met.[20] The new budget for fiscal 2001/02 envisages a deficit target of about 4.0 per cent of GDP. In view of the slowing economy, the Government adopted a mixture of fiscal stimuli, increased spending on infrastructure, and budget-rationalization measures, such as downsizing government and speeding up privatization. In Sri Lanka, the fiscal deficit reached 10 per cent of GDP in 2000[21] owing to an increase in military expenditure and lax budget management in the run-up to the election. After the election, the Government introduced new measures, such as raising key administered prices and speeding up privatization, to increase revenues. These measures are unlikely to reduce the deficit drastically, because of the large debt-service burden and the increased cost of government administration.

Some of these countries are also facing serious external financial constraints. In Bangladesh, Pakistan and Sri Lanka, foreign reserves are very low and chronic current-account deficits continue to strain their import capacities. In Pakistan, despite a narrow current-account deficit in 2000, the balance-of-payments situation remains precarious. With the Paris Club rescheduling in January 2001, Pakistan barely escaped another liquidity crisis.

Prospects for South Asia have cooled somewhat and uncertainties have increased, mainly because of the slowing of exports as a result of the United States slowdown and the weakening of world demand since late 2000. Faltering exports and tight external payments conditions will hamper growth in domestic demand and production in most countries, causing growth to moderate in

18 IMF, "Pakistan: 2000 Article IV Consultation and Request for Stand-by Arrangement—Staff Report", 26 January 2001, pp. 20-25. (http://www.imf.org/external/pubs/ft/ser/2001/cr0124.pdf).

19 Reserve Bank of India, press release: 2000-2001/1220.

20 India planned to reduce the central Government's fiscal deficit from 5.6 per cent of GDP in fiscal 1999/2000 (ending March) to 5.1 per cent in fiscal 2000/01.

21 Excluding grants. See letter of intent of the government of Sri Lanka to IMF, 19 March 2001, p. 2. (http://www.imf.org/external/np/101/2001/ika/01/index.htm).

2001 in India; manufacturing output and ICT-related services are likely to weaken, while Pakistan may suffer a setback because of the protracted drought and the deteriorating external environment.

Poor winter harvests in Nepal and Pakistan, and political uncertainties in a number of countries will also have adverse effects. Owing to their large deficits, the room for fiscal policy stimuli is limited: in India, Pakistan and Sri Lanka, ongoing fiscal consolidation, if seriously pursued, will be an additional factor restraining demand.

Western Asia: accelerated growth and increased tensions

Economic activity accelerated sharply in Western Asia in 2000. The region's GDP grew by almost 6 per cent from less than 1 per cent in 1999 (see table A.4). Internal and external balances improved markedly in many countries. Some countries, however, experienced higher inflation, mounting unemployment, and an increased external debt burden. Prospects for the region have deteriorated since the end of 2000. Turmoil in Israel and the Occupied Palestinian Territory since late 2000 has been negatively affecting also neighbouring countries such as Jordan and Lebanon. At the end of 2000, Turkey faced severe banking, liquidity and financial crises. In February 2001, massive capital outflows led to the collapse of its exchange-rate regime, undermining its stabilization programme.

The region's economic growth is likely to decelerate to about 2½ per cent in 2001 and 4 per cent in 2002. Oil prices are forecast to decline somewhat in 2001, reducing government revenues and expenditures in oil-exporting countries. Additionally, the Organization of the Petroleum Exporting Countries (OPEC) has cut production quotas twice this year (see chap. II) and might reduce them further. The prospects for oil-importing countries will also deteriorate, owing to the weakening of external demand and the persistence of hostilities in the region.

Much of the economic growth in the region in 2000 came from the oil sector, as oil production increased following the various OPEC agreements concluded during the year. Additionally, oil prices rose by 60 per cent in 2000, yielding sizeable foreign exchange earnings and fiscal revenues for oil-exporters. Agriculture also contributed to the region's growth as major producers, with the exception of the Islamic Republic of Iran, recovered from the drought of 1999. In many countries, industrial production increased in response mainly to fiscal relaxation. Recovering export markets in South-East Asia also provided a boost to export growth for some countries in the region.

Among the oil-importing countries, the economic recovery in Israel that had started in late 1999 continued through the third quarter of 2000 (see table III.3). The recovery was mostly export-led (particularly by high-tech industry), but increased tourism revenues, together with rising private and public consumption, also contributed. Investment rose, responding to the buoyant economy. However, the momentum came to an end when political tensions in Israel and the Occupied Palestinian Territory erupted in October 2000. As a result, tourism collapsed and fiscal revenues declined. The slowdown of the United States economy towards the end of 2000 also contributed to the deceleration of growth in late 2000, owing to the fact that some 35 per cent of Israel's exports flow to the United States.

The impact of the violence also exerted a negative effect on neighbouring economies. The damage was pronounced for the territories under the jurisdiction of the Palestinian Authority. Prior to the increased violence, the Palestinian economy had been recovering strongly at about 5.0 per cent, creating many new employment opportunities. With the escalation of violence, economic activity came to a standstill as shops closed and the movement of labour and goods between Israel and the occupied territories was suspended. The trade disruption devastated the Palestine economy as Israel used to absorb 95 per cent of its exports and furnish 75 per cent of its imports. Infrastructure has been damaged or destroyed. Israel also employs a significant portion of the Palestinian labour force. The closure of the border deprived the economy of vital income needed to finance both consumption and investment. As a result, the economy is estimated to have contracted by about 8.0 per cent in 2000.

Economic growth remained modest in Jordan in 2000. While agricultural production recovered from the 1999 drought, other sectors performed poorly. Tourism arrivals collapsed, and manufacturing and mining output declined as a result of reduced investment. Consumer confidence and demand dropped sharply.

In oil-exporting countries, higher oil revenues led to a shift in policy stance as many countries moved from restrictive to expansionary fiscal policies in early 2000. Public spending increased as many large-scale investment projects, mainly downstream activities such as refining, gas liquefaction and petrochemicals, were reactivated. Despite the expansionary fiscal policy, all oil-exporting countries, except Oman and the United Arab Emirates, recorded a budget surplus in 2000, after many years of deficits. For 2001, lower oil revenues will compel most of them to adopt a more cautious fiscal policy and government expenditures will barely grow. Nevertheless, most oil-exporting countries are expected to maintain a budget surplus, though one that is much smaller than in 2000.

Fiscal policy remained tight in most oil-importing countries of the region in 2000. Fiscal deficits declined in most of these countries, on account of improved tax collection procedures and full implementation of tax reforms. In Israel, the fiscal position improved during the first three quarters of 2000. As the economy grew at a brisk pace, tax receipts increased, exceeding their targets. This was most pronounced for the income tax, which was boosted by the rise in real wages. With the eruption of unrest in late 2000, however, expenditures rose and budget revenues fell, leading the budget into a deficit of 0.6 per cent of GDP in 2000. Similarly, tax collection in the Palestinian economy slumped with the emergence of disturbances. Caught between sinking budget revenues and unplanned expenditures, the fiscal deficit soared to an estimated 20 per cent of GDP in 2000. Part of current expenditures is being financed by international assistance.

After several years of reducing inflation through fiscal consolidation, inflationary pressures emerged again in the region in 2000. Increased aggregate demand, together with the gradual removal of subsidies, fed inflation in most oil-exporting countries. However, inflation remained subdued in oil-importing countries mainly owing to the continued tight fiscal and monetary policies.

Israel's monetary authorities cut nominal interest rates during 2000 in line with declining inflation expectations. Nonetheless, nominal interest rates were kept well above expected inflation, yielding positive real interest rates and attracting capital inflows. The shekel appreciated, mainly during the first half of 2000, and contributed to lowering inflation. By year-end, inflation was around 1.1 per cent, well below the Government's target range of 3-4 per cent.

Restrictive monetary policies in Jordan, while reducing inflation and monitoring the currency peg to the United States dollar, were not conducive to growth. As a result, unemployment continued to rise and economic recovery remained weak, causing the Jordanian monetary authorities to adopt a more relaxed stance in mid-2000. Interest rates were cut twice and the reserve requirements of commercial banks were reduced. Despite the relaxation of monetary policy and higher oil prices, the CPI grew by less than 1 per cent in 2000. Other factors were at play as well. Weak domestic demand and the strength of the United States dollar against the euro reduced the domestic cost of euro-denominated imports. In addition, the public budget absorbed much of the increase in fuel prices, thus contributing to containing inflation.[22]

The region's balance of payments benefited from the increase in both the price and the volume of oil exports in 2000. Most oil-exporting countries recorded current-account surpluses in 2000 (see table A.22). Non-oil exports also increased, thanks to the general revival of economic activity in the region. In some oil-importing countries, however, increased debt-service payments and lower private transfers offset the increased trade surplus and their current-account balances did not improve much in 2000. The region's export receipts in 2001 might trail their 2000 high, but will still be a stimulus to growth, and most oil-exporters will therefore register a current-account surplus in 2001.

The Turkish crisis: a short-lived stabilization attempt

During 2000, Turkey held to its commitment to the IMF-backed stabilization programme, which aimed at reducing inflation to the single-digit level by the end of 2002. The programme included measures to bring down the chronic budget deficit, which had been a constant source of inflation and a constraint on growth,[23] structural reforms and a new framework for monetary policy. The exchange rate was chosen as the nominal anchor of the stabilization programme. Initially, movements in the exchange rate were to follow a pre-announced crawling peg established in line with a (declining) inflation target. Subsequently, a gradually widening band was to be introduced to allow greater flexibility for policy-making, as well as an orderly exit from the peg framework. Events in late 2000 and early 2001, however, halted the implementation of this strategy.

Year-end annual inflation for 2000 declined to about 33 per cent compared with 60 per cent in 1999. Nonetheless, it remained above the 20 per cent target and led to a real appreciation of the currency as the nominal depreciation of the currency during the year had been in line with the lower inflation target and did not reflect the observed inflation. Interest rates fell during the first half of 2000, reflecting lower inflation expectations, and reduced government debt-servicing. Economic growth was strong (see table III.3), driven by post-earthquake reconstruction work, increased domestic demand, and lower real interest rates. The current-account deficit, however, reached 5 per cent of GDP in 2000, from less than 1 per cent in 1999. Imports rose owing to increased oil prices, growing domestic demand, and the overvalued currency. The latter mirrors developments

[22] The budget deficit reached 6.7 per cent of GDP in 2000 and was financed largely by external aid, mostly grants.

[23] The consolidated budget deficit reached 11.7 per cent of gross national product in 1999 from 7.1 per cent in 1998. Turkey has a large domestic debt. The servicing of this debt (about $5 billion per month on average in 2000) represents a large drain for the Treasury and a constant pressure on interest rates. See Central Bank of the Republic of Turkey, *Monthly Economic Bulletin*, March 2001.

in similar stabilization programmes based on currency pegs, such as those in Brazil and Mexico, in the 1990s, which also had dramatic endings.

Confidence in the programme declined owing to the large current-account deficit, delays in the implementation of structural reforms, and prominent weaknesses in the domestic banking system. The widening of the current account led to higher interest rates to curb domestic demand, while delays in the privatization programme undermined confidence in the Turkish authorities' commitment to the stabilization programme. Meanwhile, liquidity problems emerged in the banking system as some institutions started to face increased difficulties in financing their positions.

Assuming that interest rates would fall, some banks had invested heavily in long-term instruments, relying on short-term financing. As interest rates rose, these institutions had to sell their assets at a loss to cover their short-term positions. Investigations of corruption allegations in banks under the control of the Deposit Insurance Fund further undermined confidence in the banking system. Eventually, domestic interbank lines of credit disappeared as a troubled bank started to default domestically and foreign banks reduced short-term credit facilities to local banks. Initially, the Central Bank reacted by injecting liquidity into the system, but banks converted this into foreign exchange in order to cover their foreign-currency positions. International reserves fell and the Central Bank withdrew from the money market owing to the need to comply with monetary targets agreed with IMF. Interest rates skyrocketed in November 2000. A revised and enlarged ($10 billion) programme with IMF[24] restored confidence and allowed the maintenance of the currency peg, but only temporarily.

Interest rates, while falling, remained above the pre-crisis level, further undermining banks' positions and increasing borrowing costs for the treasury. In addition to the existing deposit guarantees, guarantees were introduced by the Government on banks' foreign liabilities and the Deposit Insurance Fund took over troubled banks. Both actions were perceived as potential strains on public finances and on inflation, as well as possible deviations from the targets agreed with IMF. A new financial crisis erupted in February 2001, this time triggered by political differences within the Government, but with similar developments; market sentiment soured, interest rates soared again, liquidity disappeared as interbank payments almost came to a halt, and a massive run on the Central Bank's reserves resulted. The curb of liquidity by the Central Bank did not prevent another loss of international reserves. As a result, the Government decided to float the currency, thereby abandoning its stabilization programme.

By mid-April 2001, the Turkish lira had lost over 40 per cent of its nominal value vis-à-vis the United States dollar (see figure III.7), and interest rates declined but remained high, while inflation accelerated. A new stabilization package was negotiated with IMF, but near-term prospects for the economy are not encouraging. The banking system has been further weakened by the crisis and is in need of restructuring. A deterioration in economic conditions could lead to an increase in NPLs and renewed difficulties in the banking system. The fiscal stance may tighten owing to higher interest payments if the interest rate fails to decline. This may constrain the economy beyond the needs of bringing the current account back to a more sustainable position. Moreover, the devalu-

24 This included the undisbursed portion (about $2.9 billion) of the previous standby loan and a new loan (about $7.5 billion) from IMF's Supplemental Reserve Facility. Additionally, the World Bank approved a new Country Assistance Strategy for Turkey amounting to up to $5 billion during a three-year period.

Figure III.7.
TURKISH LIRA EXCHANGE RATE VIS-À-VIS THE
UNITED STATES DOLLAR, JANUARY 1999-APRIL 2001

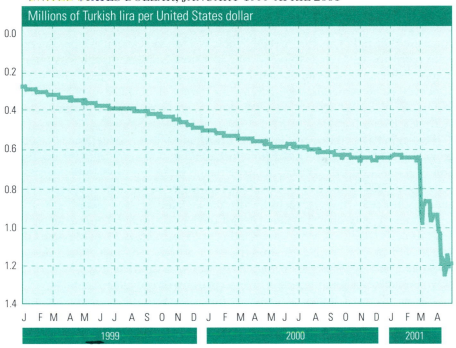

Millions of Turkish lira per United States dollar

1999   2000   2001

Source: Central Bank of the Republic of Turkey.

ation of the lira will make the servicing of the country's external debt more costly for both private and public debtors. GDP is forecast to contract by 3 per cent in 2001.

Latin America: a sustainable recovery?

After almost no growth in 1999, Latin America rebounded in 2000 and recorded a 3.8 per cent increase in aggregate GDP. The fundamental factor behind the recovery was the surge in external demand, especially from the United States, for the region's exports, which grew above 11 per cent in real terms (see table A.13). Domestic demand accelerated in a few countries of the region, notably Brazil and Mexico, and supported growth in these economies but remained subdued elsewhere. The slowdown in the United States therefore has an important bearing on growth prospects in 2001. Latin American countries, however, are likely to produce varying outcomes, since not all of them are equally dependent on United States import demand. GDP growth for the region is expected to decelerate to about 3 per cent in 2001 (see table A.4).

The wide gap in economic performances between economies of South America and those of the rest of the region contracted in 2000, as the former gradually recovered from recession while the latter sustained their growth rates. Nonetheless, within each of these two groups, outcomes diverged. Among the South American economies, Brazil and Chile experienced a strong rebound, whereas the other countries recovered at more moderate rates. Argentina and Uruguay, however, remained in recession. Among the northern economies, growth accelerated in the Dominican Republic and Mexico but declined sharply in Costa Rica, largely reflecting lower output by the micro-processor industry.

Oil-exporters benefited from increases in oil-revenue windfalls, which improved their external and fiscal balances while providing support for domestic demand. This was notably the case for Venezuela, which emerged from recession through a strong fiscal expansion. Similar, though less intense trends characterize Colombia and Ecuador. The favourable evolution of the prices of some minerals and increased external demand also helped boost export revenue, and ultimately GDP growth, in some other countries, especially Chile and Peru.

The region's two largest economies, Brazil and Mexico, experienced healthy growth in 2000. Brazil benefited from the stimulus stemming from the devaluation of the real in early 1999 as its exports and industrial production expanded strongly in 2000, leading to a recovery in real wages in the industrial sector. The latter, combined with an expansion of credit to the private sector as well as lower interest rates, contributed to faster growth of consumer demand during the year. Brazil's GDP grew by 4.2 per cent in 2000 (see table A.4). In Mexico, GDP accelerated in 2000 owing to strong growth not only of exports but also of investment and consumer spending. The latter was supported by lower unemployment, increased real wages, and an expansion of consumer credit.[25]

25 Economic Commission for Latin America and the Caribbean (ECLAC), *Preliminary Overview of the Economies of Latin America and the Caribbean, 2000* (United Nations publication, Sales No. E.00.II.G.138).

The recovery of domestic demand, however, was disappointing in most South American countries, owing in part to the pervasiveness of high unemployment rates (see below). Other factors were at play as well. For instance, structural problems in the financial sector, which in many countries are reflected in high real lending rates, heavily constrained credit to the private sector. In Peru, a deep political crisis virtually paralyzed the country in the second half of 2000 and depressed investment.

Open urban unemployment reached 8.6 per cent for the region as a whole in 2000, similar to the level in 1999. Over the past few years, unemployment in Latin America has consistently increased despite economic growth (see figure III.8), which suggests that unemployment in the region is largely of a structural nature. Labour markets in the region, however, have undergone considerable deregulation and should not be a major factor behind the increasing rates of unemployment. On the other hand, structural reforms may not have so far produced the anticipated outcomes. The alternative explanation is that the pattern of economic growth is not labour-intensive enough.

In Argentina, urban open unemployment reached about 15 per cent of the workforce and prospects for a reduction in the near term are not encouraging. In many of the Andean countries, recovery in 2000 did not generate a sufficient number of jobs. Colombia is a case in point: the unemployment rate averaged over 15 per cent in 2000 and rose to about 20 per cent in the first months of 2001. In Brazil, urban unemployment decreased throughout 2000, and stood at 6.4 per cent at the beginning of 2001, although some of this improvement is due to a decrease in the participation rate. The unemployment rate, however, remains significantly higher than in the early 1990s.

Gross fixed capital formation grew above 4 per cent in 2000 after contracting 6 per cent in 1999. The regional average, however, conceals diverse country performances. While fixed capital formation accelerated in Mexico to 11 per cent growth, in the Andean countries and Chile it either remained stagnant

Figure III.8.
LATIN AMERICA: GDP AND URBAN UNEMPLOYMENT, 1991-2000

Sources: UN/DESA and Economic Commission for Latin America and the Caribbean (ECLAC).

or its recovery was insufficient to offset the contractions in 1999 and previous years. Further expansion of capital formation is required if capacity constraints and pressures on the current account are to be averted when recovery gathers strength.

The slowdown in the United States economy will affect growth prospects for 2001 of countries with large exposure to the United States markets, such as Mexico and most of the economies of Central America and the Caribbean. In Mexico, a substantial deceleration in exports and industrial production was already evident at the end of 2000.

Recovery will continue in Brazil in 2001, led by dynamic internal demand and stronger investment, albeit at a more moderate pace than in 2000. The potential effects of the Argentine crisis (see below) on the Brazilian economy will continue to condition short-term economic prospects for Brazil and the region as a whole. Argentina, however, is expected to recover by the second half of the year, provided the recent economic measures are effective in restoring external competitiveness, and financial turmoil or a debt default is averted.

In the Andean countries, recovery will continue at a similar pace in 2001. Peru is an exception to this trend as growth will substantially slow down in 2001, owing to last year's political crisis. Nevertheless, a recovery is expected towards the end of the year. In Venezuela, internal demand will continue to support growth in 2001, while in Ecuador capital formation, largely associated with new investments in oil exploration and transportation, will lead growth.

Despite higher oil prices, inflation in the region in 2000 remained subdued, barely inching above the 1999 level (see table A.10). Prudent monetary policies in most countries and weak domestic demand in some economies predicated this outcome. A further moderate reduction in inflation is expected for 2001. Most countries were successful in keeping inflation within established targets in 2000. At the extremes, Argentina experienced deflation for the second consecutive year, while Ecuador witnessed a sharp increase in inflation. Fuelled by the slide in the exchange rate during 1999 and the first months of 2000, inflation spiralled in Ecuador and prices continued to surge despite the official dollarization of the economy. The average annual inflation was over 100 per cent in the third quarter of 2000 (see table III.3). A substantial moderation was already apparent at the end of the year and persisted in 2001. Inflation, however, remains relatively high in the country.

Among the countries with an inflation-targeting framework, Brazil achieved its target for the year (between 4 and 8 per cent). In Chile, year-end inflation exceeded the Central Bank's medium-term target range (2 to 4 per cent), owing to the effects of higher oil prices. Inflation is expected to fall to 3 per cent by December 2001, thus making increases in interest rates unlikely.

In 2000, most central banks of the region tended to maintain flexible monetary policies to support the recovery. In doing so, they were helped by progress on the inflation front and additional degrees of freedom due to the floating of the exchange rate in several countries.

In the wake of the 1997-1998 financial crises, monetary authorities in several countries of the region, notably Brazil, Chile and Colombia, abandoned their fixed or crawling pegs to the United States dollar. As a result, many of the region's biggest economies are now floating their currencies, allowing their monetary policies greater flexibility and increasing their ability to adjust to external shocks.

Nonetheless, the move towards freely floating currencies has not been the general trend in the region.[26] For example, Ecuador, El Salvador (see below) and Panama have the United States dollar as legal tender, and dollarization is being considered by some Central American economies. With another exchange-rate arrangement, Argentina keeps the peso pegged to the dollar under a currency board (see discussion below). Venezuela, on the other hand, maintains a crawling band arrangement under which the bolivar continued to appreciate in real terms in 2000 and into 2001. Strong oil revenues and the favourable evolution of foreign reserves continue to shield the currency from external pressures.

Ecuador adopted the United States dollar as legal tender in March 2000 in a context of deep financial crisis. Between January 1999 and January 2000, the sucre had lost more than 70 per cent of its value relative to the United States dollar. However, the fixing of the exchange rate and the subsequent dollarization did not prevent internal prices from increasing, as reflected in table III.3. As a result, Ecuador's real effective exchange rate has appreciated over 70 per cent from February 2000 (when the country fixed its exchange rate to the United States dollar) to March 2001. This evolution should be a matter of concern, since in a dollarized economy, the absence of exchange rate adjustments implies that sustained current-account deficits have to be corrected in the medium term via adjustments in domestic absorption and that this will continue until domestic product and factor (mostly wages) prices decline sufficiently to restore the real effective exchange rate.

[26] On exchange-rate policy developments in Latin America, see *World Economic and Social Survey 2000* (United Nations publication, Sales No. E.00.II.C.1), box III.4 entitled, "Rethinking exchange-rate regimes in Latin America".

El Salvador adopted the United States dollar as legal tender in November 2000, becoming the third Latin American country to officially dollarize its economy. In contrast with Ecuador, however, El Salvador had already pegged its currency to the dollar (at a fixed exchange rate) for the previous eight years and its economy was not in crisis when the plan was announced. El Salvador's dollarization could be interpreted as a "natural" step forward in the country's foreign exchange policy, aiming at eliminating speculative attacks on its currency; achieving greater economic stability; lowering domestic interest rates; and attracting foreign investment. However, shortly after dollarization entered into force, a strong earthquake hit the country in January 2001, leaving hundreds of thousands homeless; causing widespread damage to infrastructure; and inflicting serious disruptions on agricultural activity. The direct cost of the earthquake has been estimated officially at $1 billion, but the total economic impact will be much higher. Balanced fiscal accounts are all the more crucial in the context of dollarization, but the reconstruction effort will put considerable pressure on fiscal expenditures over the medium term. Additionally, the colón had appreciated vis-à-vis the United States dollar over the previous years, thus posing additional challenges for improving the competitiveness of the economy.

Monetary policies in most countries of the region are no longer formally constrained by the need to defend exchange rates. However, there was only cautious monetary relaxation in 2000. The Brazilian Central Bank gradually relaxed monetary policy throughout the year, as allowed by improvements in the fiscal balance and developments on the external front. In contrast, in Mexico, a restrictive monetary stance was adopted to prevent the economy from overheating, as the growth of internal demand has been considered incompatible with inflation objectives by the monetary authority.

Monetary easing in the United States at the beginning of 2001 should provide increased room for manoeuvre in the region's monetary policies, though this benefit will be partially offset by the persistence of external imbalances and unfavourable external financing conditions for the region. A case in point is Brazil, where the Central Bank reversed its monetary stance in March 2001 by increasing the policy interest rate. The move followed a significant depreciation of the real because of the poor trade balance and spillovers from the crisis in neighbouring Argentina.

Most Governments continued with fiscal consolidation in 2000, and deficit-to-GDP ratios improved as growth recovered. The increase in the price of oil provided an important boost to public finances in Mexico, Venezuela and the main oil-exporters in the Andean region. It was particularly relevant for Ecuador, given its dollarization and the difficulties in implementing fiscal reforms agreed with IMF. On the expenditure side, prudence was the norm, but there were exceptions. In Peru, the strong fiscal expansion during the run-up to the August 2000 elections was followed by a tough adjustment which fell mainly on public investment expenditure. In Venezuela, the increased oil revenue funded a strong fiscal expansion. In Mexico, the Government disclosed in late February 2001 the existence of previously unaccounted-for liabilities which could lead to substantial revisions of the deficit reported earlier (1.1 per cent of GDP). Brazil, on the other hand, recorded a substantial improvement in its fiscal position helped, in part, by lower interest rates.

A number of Governments in the region, notably those of Colombia, Ecuador and Mexico, are pursuing comprehensive tax reforms, aiming at expanding revenue bases, simplifying tax codes and eliminating large-scale tax fraud. In some of the oil-exporting countries, tax reform reflects concerns over the evolution of oil prices in 2001 and its potential impact on fiscal revenues. International prices are already close to the reference price built into many budget projections and a further decline would worsen the fiscal balance unless offset by additional revenue from other sources.

Turning to the external sector, the strong export performance reduced the trade deficit in 2000, even though imports also grew vigorously (see table A.13). The latter largely reflected the impact of the surge in economic activity on imported intermediate and capital goods for the industrial sector. The reduction of the trade deficit also reflected more favourable terms of trade, which improved moderately in 2000 compared with 1999 for several countries, mainly as a result of the increase in the price of oil and advances in the prices of metals. Net oil exporters, notably Colombia, Ecuador and Venezuela, recorded marked improvements in their trade balances.

Despite higher interest payments and profit repatriations, the regional current-account deficit also improved in 2000 (see table A.22) and fell to 2.5 per cent of the region's GDP, compared with 3.1 per cent in 1999. However, if it had not been for Venezuela's increased oil revenue and its impact on the external accounts in 2000, the region's trade and current-account deficits would not have improved in 2000. The current-account deficit is set to widen again in 2001 as export earnings reflect the impact of the global economic slowdown and softer commodity prices, while imports continue to grow along with still-recovering internal demand, and payments of interest on loans and profit repatriation continue to increase.

The external imbalance will remain an issue of concern for the region. With current-account deficits still high and widening as recovery gathers strength, notably in large economies such as Mexico and particularly Brazil, the region remains very dependent on capital inflows, and therefore vulnerable to conditions in international capital markets (box III.3).

The crisis in Argentina: recession persists

In sharp contrast with most of the region and contrary to early forecasts, Argentina failed to recover in 2000. A rebound is not likely before the second half of 2001.

Since mid-1998, Argentina has been facing economic difficulties. These have been largely due to the negative impacts of the 1997-1998 financial crises, particularly the limited availability and adverse terms of external finance; sharp terms-of-trade losses; and the drop in external demand in 1999. Moreover, the competitiveness of its economy has been negatively affected by the continuous strengthening of the United States dollar, to which the peso is pegged, during the past few years, as well as the devaluation of the Brazilian real in early 1999. The limited policy options available to the country owing to its currency board compounded the problem. A financial package negotiated with IMF in early 2000 had a strong fiscal component aimed at reducing the financial requirements of the public sector.[27]

[27] Argentina had negotiated a three-year Extended Fund Facility (EFF) with IMF of about $2.8 billion in early 1998. The standby credit of about $7.2 billion negotiated in March 2000 replaced EFF.

Box III.3

LATIN AMERICA: LIBERALIZATION WITHOUT SUSTAINED GROWTH

Despite 15 years of reforms, Latin America has not yet overcome its chronic current-account problem, and its dependence on external finance has not declined. In most countries of the region, any acceleration of growth leads to a quick deterioration of the (merchandise) trade balance. The increasing deficit eventually puts a brake on the expansion as foreign investors become concerned about its sustainability and restrict flows to the region. Countries have then to adjust by generating a surplus in their trade balance, necessarily by compressing aggregate absorption, which may trigger a recession. Demand is curbed, imports fall and, eventually, the trade balance becomes more manageable until the next boom. This usual pattern for Latin America intensified in the 1990s.

Developments in the trade balance can be traced to liberalization and modernization efforts, as well as to the region's pattern of insertion into the global economy. Trade liberalization (as well as appreciating currencies) led to a surge of imports in the 1990s, which quickly eroded the region's trade surplus, despite the robust growth of exports, aggravating its current-account position (see figure box III.3a).[a] Imports of capital goods soared and played an important role in the industrial modernization, with a noticeable change in regard to specialization in production.

The region's vast natural resources provide the basis for such specialization. The manufacturing sectors of many economies, especially in South America, have concentrated on the processing of agricultural products and other natural resources (such as steel, cellulose and paper), while import-substituting manufacturing has been declining, particularly production of capital goods in the three

[a] The volume of imports increased at an annual average rate of 13 per cent during the past decade while the volume of exports grew slightly over 10 per cent. In the 1980s, the volume of imports contracted by an annual average rate of 0.6 per cent while exports grew by 7 per cent.

Figure box III.3a.
LATIN AMERICA: CURRENT ACCOUNT, 1985-1999

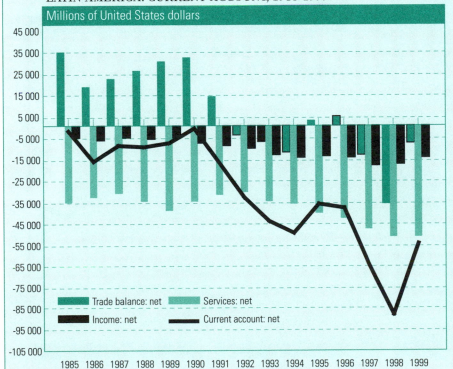

Source: IMF, *Balance of Payments Statistics*, various issues.

Box III.3 (continued)

b   The automotive industry is an exception as it has consolidated its presence in the three countries.

c   The word "maquilador" or "maquila" describes any partial activity in a manufacturing process, such as assembly or packaging, carried out by an entity other than the original manufacturer. Currently, "maquiladora" means "assembly plant or factory" and refers to a Mexican (or Central American or Carribean) company operating under a special customs regime that allows the company to temporarily import, on a duty-free basis, machinery, equipment, materials, parts and components and other items needed for the assembly or manufacture or finished goods for subsequent export.

d   ECLAC, *Latin America and the Caribbean in the World Economy*, 1998 ed. (United Nations publication, Sales No. E.99.II.G.3).

largest economies (Argentina, Brazil and Mexico).[b] In Central America, the Caribbean and Mexico, manufacturing has largely developed around the *maquila* sector,[c] with an increasing dependence on the United States market.

Despite some diversification away from the production and export of unprocessed commodities, the latter still account for over 40 per cent of the region's total export revenues. This share is significantly higher in most countries though not in Brazil, Costa Rica and Mexico. The region therefore continues to be exposed to the erratic behaviour of commodity prices, which have declined along a secular trend. As a result, and despite the fact that the region's exports grew, on average, above the rate of growth of world exports in the 1990s, the share of Latin American export receipts in the world total remained about 5.5 per cent from 1990 to 1999. This contrasts with the share of Eastern and Southern Asia, which jumped from 16.1 to 19.1 per cent during the same period (see table A.15).

At the same time, import expenditures grew faster than export receipts but only in part on account of trade liberalization. Foreign exchange policies adopted during the stabilization efforts of the 1990s were also an important factor. Several countries used the exchange rate as the nominal anchor to bring down inflationary expectations by adopting a crawling peg or a fixed rate. Inflation did come down but at the cost of overvalued national currencies. Inflation differentials between Latin American countries and their major trading partners remained (see table A.12). Latin American exports lost competitiveness while producers catering to the domestic market faced cheaper imports, made possible not only by the lower tariffs but also by the overvalued currency.

Other factors have been at play as well. Imports of intermediate goods, for instance, tend to increase as output grows.[d] This happened in Brazil in 2000. The country generated an unexpected trade deficit owing to the need to import inputs as manufacturing recovered from recession of 1999. Nonetheless, the Brazilian deficit also stems from the limited productive capacity in the country: it cannot supply the domestic market when the latter is not in recession **and**, at the same time, generate sufficient export revenues to pay for imports of intermediate inputs and the modernization needs of the economy.

Such constraints are present in several other Latin American economies and are compromising growth in the region. Mexico, for instance, has been forced to cool down its economy since late 2000 with restrictive monetary policies. This is due in part to the current-account constraint, as increased domestic demand would add pressures to its trade balance at a time of expected lower export revenues. The country therefore cannot use countercyclical measures to mitigate the effect of reduced import demand by the United States in 2001.

The region has also shown a big appetite for imported consumer goods whenever growth resumes and credit conditions improve. This phenomenon suggests "repressed demand" and, once again, insufficient investment effort. In most countries, trade surpluses have been generated only under hardship and have usually been a sign of difficult economic times, with Chile being an exception. This implies that, under "normal circumstances", imports soar as domestic absorption recovers and the region is dependent on external capital to cover the merchandise trade deficit, its permanently negative service balance and its increasingly negative

Box III.3 (continued)

income balance (see figure box III.3a). The increasing trade deficits that the region so often confronts may therefore reflect limited productive capacity, that is to say, lack of investment.

Capital flows returned to the region in the 1990s, facilitated by the Brady initiative, low real world interest rates, and a more welcoming domestic policy environment. The composition of such flows changed considerably during the decade. Initially, portfolio inflows (equity and debt securities such as bonds and notes) dominated. The relative importance of such flows, however, has declined since 1993, while foreign direct investment (FDI) has become more prevalent.[e] Other net investment flows, such as trade credits and official and commercial bank loans, remained negative during most of the decade. The latter reflects, on the one hand, commercial banks' flight from the region and, on the other hand, the schedule of disbursements and payments related to International Monetary Fund (IMF)-led financial operations.

The return of capital inflows has increased the region's external debt, particularly the debt of the private sector in countries such as Brazil, Chile, Colombia and Mexico. In Argentina, however, the public sector also experienced a substantial increase in its external debt. As the external debt grew, so did the region's external debt-service obligations and its dependence on additional inflows of foreign capital to refinance maturing liabilities.[f] The surge of FDI in the late 1990s has eased this problem somewhat. Such flows may recede some day, if only because the opportunities for privatization and mergers and acquisitions by large transnational corporations will have ended. Additionally, FDI will eventually generate additional pressures on the current account as profits are repatriated. FDI is welcome for the embodied new technology and the increased efficiency it brings. A significant share of these flows (roughly 50 per cent in most large economies), however, has been directed towards the non-tradable sectors (services and infrastructure) that were closed to foreign participation. Foreign currency to finance profit repatriation will have to be generated elsewhere.

Although capital inflows and gross domestic product (GDP) growth are strongly correlated in the region (see figure box III.3b), the resumption of capital inflows in the 1990s did not lead to a noticeable increase of investment.[g] While net capital flows increased sharply (from $17 billion in 1990 to $78 billion in 1998), the ratio of investment to GDP remained relatively stable at about 20-22 per cent (see table A.6). Naturally, the regional aggregate masks individual country performances, and some countries did succeed in increasing investment during the period. Nonetheless, by 1998, Chile was the only country among the large economies in the region with an investment ratio above 25 per cent of GDP. On the whole, investment remained depressed, preventing faster growth and increased domestic savings.

Foreign capital inflows have often leaked into consumption and intensified the cycles of boom and bust so common in Latin America.[h] Several factors underlie this phenomenon. The burst of short-term inflows in the early 1990s led to a relaxation of financing constraints as domestic bank credit, mostly for financing consumption, expanded at a time when prudential regulation and supervision were inadequate. Capital inflows led to a rapid rise in the price of domestic securities and real estate which, together with the real appreciation of the exchange rate, created a wealth

[e] On the recent inflows of FDI to Latin America, see Eduardo Fernandez-Arias and Ricardo Hausmann, "Is FDI a safer form of financing?", and "Foreign direct investment: good cholesterol?" (papers presented at the Annual Meetings of the Board of Governors, Inter-American Development Bank and Inter-American Investment Corporation, New Orleans, March 2000).

[f] Accordingly, much of the progress in terms of improved debt indicators brought about by the Brady Plan has stopped or been reversed in some countries. For instance, among the larger economies of the region (Argentina, Brazil, Mexico and Peru), the ratio of total debt service to both exports of goods and services and the gross national product deteriorated from 1990 to 1998.

[g] Ricardo Ffrench-Davis and Helmut Reisen, eds., *Capital Flows and Investment Performance: Lessons from Latin America*, Paris, OECD, 1998.

[h] Andras Uthoff and Daniel Titelman, "The relationship between foreign and national savings under financial liberalization", in Ricardo Ffrench-Davis and Helmut Reisen, op. cit.

Box III.3 (continued)

Figure box III.3b.
LATIN AMERICA: NET TRANSFER OF FINANCIAL RESOURCES AND ANNUAL RATE OF GDP GROWTH, 1985-2000

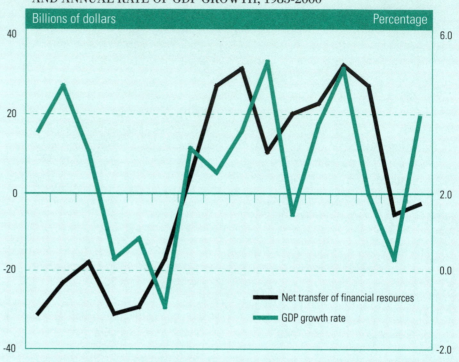

Source: ECLAC.

[i] Manuel R. Agosin and Ricardo Mayer, "Foreign investment in developing countries", UNCTAD Discussion Paper, No. 146, February 2000.

[j] On possible anti-cyclical policies for Latin America, see Jose Antonio Ocampo, "Developing countries' anti-cyclical policies in a globalized world", Comisión Económica para América Latina y el Caribe (CEPAL) Temas de Coyuntura, No. 13, November 2000.

[k] Dani Rodrik, "Saving transitions", The World Bank Economic Review, vol. 14, No. 3 (September 2000), pp. 481-507.

effect and stimulated consumption. Additionally, despite financial reforms, Latin America still suffers from a lack of satisfactory instruments, particularly of a long-term nature, with which to channel resources into investment. Access to finance is often a prerogative of relatively large firms, and capital markets remain thin.

The surge of FDI during the second half of the 1990s, in turn, did not cause a corresponding increase in domestic investment because most of these inflows went to the acquisition of existing assets. Little new capacity was added. Moreover, in certain instances, FDI failed to crowd in domestic investment, because it either displaced domestic producers or did not create enough linkages with the domestic economy.[i] Insufficient investment therefore continues to constrain growth.

Latin America has to confront several tasks. Better management of capital inflow booms is one.[j] Deepening of capital markets is another. Nonetheless, raising the volume and the efficiency of investment, preferably in areas that offer greater growth potential for exports and generate more value added, is key to sustainable growth and eventually reduced dependence on external finance. Countries that have sustained high rates of growth have achieved noticeable increases in investment, often as a result of policies that raised the expected profitability (and therefore the attractiveness) of investment for the private sector.[k] The region could learn from these experiences and consider similar approaches.

The Government initially adopted a tight fiscal stance to meet the deficit target of 1.5 per cent of GDP for the year 2000,[28] as agreed with IMF. The Government had hoped to receive additional revenues as a result of the expected recovery. However, the fiscal adjustment itself had a dampening effect on internal demand as price deflation and high unemployment persisted. Additionally, there was a growing lack of confidence in the Government's ability to steer the country out of recession. The resulting poor fiscal performance fed into investors' concerns about a possible debt default or the abandonment of the currency-board regime. Such worries intensified during the year. As a result, interest spreads on Argentine debt reached new highs in the fourth quarter of 2000.

These developments highlight the urgency of putting in place an effective pro-growth strategy. However, the currency board substantially reduces the Government's room for policy manoeuvre. The country needs to grow in order to generate fiscal revenues to close its budget gap. It also needs foreign currency to service its expanding external debt and reduce its dependence on external capital inflows. So far, Argentina has been able to cover the fiscal and the current-account gap owing to a continuous inflow of external capital through FDI and increased indebtedness. These options are not sustainable in the long run. The country's total external debt, for instance, reached $147 billion at the end of 2000 and interest payments on that debt consumed about 40 per cent of Argentina's export revenues in 2000.[29] Exports grew modestly in 2000, and were not enough to pull the country out of recession, while the conditions of external financing remained restrictive.

Amid growing worries that the Government would not be able to meet its scheduled public debt repayments of about $26 billion for 2001, Argentine leaders negotiated a new financial package with IMF in December 2000. It entailed financial commitments of about $40 billion by multilateral and bilateral donors, as well as several domestic financial institutions. The negotiation of the package included a new set of fiscal and reform measures, notably a compromise whereby the provincial governments would freeze their primary spending for the next five years, and sweeping reforms of the public pension and health-care systems. The Government also relaxed its fiscal stance for the medium term somewhat, as it is now expected to produce a fiscal balance by the end of 2005 rather than 2003, as originally envisaged.

Although investor anxiety eased after the conclusion of the IMF package deal in December 2000, markets reacted nervously when apparently unrelated episodes, such as the Turkish devaluation in the first quarter of 2001, occurred. As a result, spreads tended to widen (see chap. II). Furthermore, preliminary figures for the first months of 2001 indicated that the fiscal target for the first quarter of the year would not be met, and a renewed confidence crisis hit the country in March 2001.

A new economic team, which took office in March 2001, embraced emergency measures to tackle the fiscal imbalance and improve the competitiveness of Argentina's industry without devaluing the peso. It temporarily eliminated the application of the common external tariff of the Southern Cone Common Market (MERCOSUR) on imports of capital goods and raised tariffs on consumer goods, among other measures (see chap. II, annex). Moreover, it tried to exercise some degree of expansionary monetary policy—despite the current monetary regime—by reducing banks' reserve requirements.

[28] This target refers to the central government balance.

[29] ECLAC, *Preliminary Overview of the Economies of Latin America and the Caribbean, 2000* (United Nations publication, Sales No.E.00.II.G.138), table A.19, p. 105.

Several alternatives are potentially available for Argentina in terms of adjusting its foreign exchange regime. As a sign that the new team leaves all options open, it submitted a proposal to Congress in April 2001 that foresees a change in the exchange-rate mechanism by including the euro in the currency board. According to the authorities, this move would not imply any devaluation of the peso or the abandonment of its parity with the United States dollar in the medium term, for the switch would take place only when the euro itself reaches parity with the dollar. While it may be preferable for Argentina to have the peso pegged to a basket of currencies, as this would better reflect the structure of its trade, the measure does not solve the problem of the overvaluation of the peso, particularly vis-à-vis its main trading partner, Brazil. Furthermore, the measure risks further undermining the competitiveness of the Argentine economy owing to prospects for the evolution of the euro/dollar exchange rate (see sect.above on Western Europe).

Another possibility is to float the peso by abandoning the currency board; this would restore competitiveness to the country's exports and boost growth. It would also give Argentina greater flexibility with which to cope with external shocks. However, many regard the currency board as an indispensable guarantee against the hyperinflation that was so customary in the past. Moreover, in a country where a large part of liabilities are dollar-denominated, a devaluation would be costly, even though many economic agents have already hedged against the prospect of a devaluation by shifting their assets into dollars.

Full dollarization is another option, at least in theory. However, it would not solve the competitiveness problem. Neither does it seem optimal in light of certain considerations: Argentina is a sizeable economy that is not highly integrated with the United States,[30] and it is subject to asymmetric economic shocks and asynchronous economic cycles vis-à-vis that country.

[30]   Only 11 per cent of Argentina's exports were destined for, and 20 per cent of its imports originated in, the United States in 1999.

A GLOBALIZING WORLD: RISKS, VULNERABILITY AND OPPORTUNITY

OVERVIEW

Part two of the *World Economic and Social Survey, 2001* discusses various aspects of vulnerability at the level of the country. Vulnerability may be defined as the "risk of being negatively affected by shocks".[1] There are shocks that come from nature, such as cyclones, earthquakes, droughts and locust invasions, and economic shocks that are outside a country's control, such as the rapid decline in the price of a major export, changes in interest rates on international capital markets and reduced access to credit. At the level of the country, vulnerability has been one of the criteria used, within the United Nations system, in determining whether a country should be classified as "least developed".[2]

Vulnerability is an especially important concept for the poorest countries, as shocks can set back their growth for many years and the effects on the poorest, and therefore most vulnerable, members of the society can be especially severe. Although this aspect of vulnerability within countries—the fact that the most vulnerable members suffer the most during a downturn—will not be discussed at length in this *Survey*, which looks at vulnerability at the level of the country as a whole, its importance can hardly be exaggerated.

The reaction—or lack of reaction—of economic actors, including especially Governments, to shocks can themselves provide a further adverse shock to the system on top of that coming from the purely outside sources. It is essential, then, that Governments be prepared "through the exercise of appropriate policies at the micro- and macrolevels to reduce vulnerability and to mitigate the consequences of economic shocks".[3] What the appropriate policies are, on the national and international fronts, in the present globalized economy will be the focus of this part of the *Survey*. This is necessarily a matter of trade-offs between the advantages of greater globalization, primarily wealth creation and enabling human, physical and social capital to be augmented, and the possible disadvantages of greater vulnerability, primarily fluctuations in income flows. Poor countries and poor groups within countries are vulnerable and suffer disproportionately when change is rapid, especially when there is a downturn brought about by an unexpected shock.

It is especially opportune now to examine the appropriate policies to be adopted when confronting vulnerability because of the changing views of policy makers on the appropriate limits of government action, at the national and international levels, to counteract the effects of the free play of market forces, and the recent exposure of many economies to sudden changes in their economic environment. Vulnerability is, to some extent, a fact of life: prices—of shares, computer chips, bauxite ore, and currencies, and of borrowing money

[1] See *Vulnerability and Poverty in a Global Economy: Report of the Committee for Development Policy on the first session (26-30 April 1999)* (United Nations publication, Sales No. E.99.II.A.5), para. 38.

[2] See *Poverty amidst Riches: The Need for Change, Report of the Committee for Development Policy on the second session* (3-7 April 2000) (United Nations publication, Sales No. E.00.II.A.4), chap. III and annex I.

[3] *Vulnerability and Poverty in a Global Economy ...*, para. 41.

4 Two of the objectives of the proposed Integrated Programme for Commodities were "to achieve stable conditions in commodity trade, including avoidance of excessive prices fluctuations" and "to improve and sustain the real income of individual developing countries through increased export earnings, and to protect them from fluctuations in export earnings, especially from commodities" (see UNCTAD resolution 93 (IV), sect. I, paras. 1 and 2). The text of the resolution is contained in *Proceedings of the United Nations Conference on Trade and Development, Fourth Session, Nairobi, vol. I, Report and Annexes* (United Nations publication, Sales No. E.76.11.D.10), part one, sect. A.1.

5 *Vulnerability and Poverty in a Global Economy* ...., para. 42.

itself—always fluctuate in a market economy. However, a solution proposed less than 30 years ago for the problem of the volatility of commodity prices, namely, an Integrated Programme for Commodities, is one that is not active in current discussions.[4] On the other hand, the wisdom of attempting to fix the price of one currency in terms of another currency or a basket of other currencies is currently very much a live issue. The consequences of the volatility of prices must still be confronted by Governments. The problem has not disappeared, although the feasible or accepted solutions might have changed.

As "the extent of vulnerability at any one time depends partly on initial conditions and partly on the policies subsequently pursued to reduce vulnerability",[5] the past reactions to real or perceived vulnerability must be examined in order to design the appropriate policies to counter present-day vulnerability. One example is the discussion on diversification. Diversification is often seen as an appropriate policy to be pursued in the face of the type of vulnerability that comes from relying heavily on the production and export of one commodity or industrial sector. Yet, inappropriate diversification, directed at reducing vulnerability but resulting in the creation of industries that are not in line with a country's true comparative advantage and that therefore cannot survive in an open-market environment, could itself have adverse economic consequences. This, in turn, increases vulnerability. In general, the appropriate strategy for a country to adopt in order to deal with vulnerability entails exploiting its true comparative advantages as much as it can.

Chapter IV addresses issues of vulnerability in the financial sector. Rather than assist wealth creation, the financial sector has sometimes contributed to a massive loss in income through the shocks emanating from banking and currency crises. Indeed, such shocks as the Asian financial crisis have given the increasing integration of global financial markets, and the problems that might ensue, a very high profile in the public's eye. Chapter IV examines whether the vulnerability that comes from greater integration in global financial markets can be reduced. The policies that countries should adopt as they liberalize their financial markets are addressed. The development of vibrant and modern banking sector that can allocate savings to their most effective uses should be the aim of all countries. However, this is only one element in a successful market economy. Other elements, such as good bookkeeping, serious analysis of the risks involved in prospective investments and an understanding of the nature of the industry that is seeking funds, are required. These can be built up only over time, particularly in countries that did not operate a regular market economy in the past. Similarly, the capacity to regulate the financial system so that the relevant information is available to interested parties for the purpose of enabling them to make an informed decision on the wisdom of a financial transaction and to gauge whether the overall financial system is not being exposed to excessive risks, is acquired only over time. Thus, an attempt to liberalize the operations of the financial system so as to obtain the benefits of a more efficient use of capital can backfire if the regulatory system is not in place and ready. The *Survey* thus calls for progress on all fronts—namely, opening up the economy to the interplay of modern market forces, liberalizing the financial sector, and refining the regulatory mechanisms.

Another source of shock is through trade—specifically rapid changes in prices and demand for goods and services. Chapter V looks at the interrelationship between trade and vulnerability. This occurs on two fronts. To begin with, trade has a role to play in promoting growth. Countries that grow and become wealthier are better able to cope with the inevitable shocks that occur in an open and increasingly globalized world economy. The chapter examines the evidence of the trade-induced growth relationship. It discusses what measures have been taken to increase market access, especially for the least developed countries, to enable them to participate more fully in the global trading system. Moreover, many poorer developing countries are heavily reliant on the export of a few primary commodities, rendering them vulnerable to sudden price or demand changes. This is the second aspect of the trade-vulnerability relation. Chapter V therefore next examines how countries have tried to lessen the possibility or severity of trade shocks. Past attempts to control the fluctuations in prices through international commodity agreements have, on the whole, failed. Now efforts are concentrated on the mechanisms for hedging the risks involved, though these can be complicated instruments.

The above-mentioned two chapters, which cover generalized shocks, are followed by two chapters that focus on the responses to specific shocks. Chapter VI looks at the shocks that hit three countries—Armenia, Kyrgyzstan and Mongolia—as they moved from a centrally planned system to a market economy, at the same time as their former trading relationships were severely disrupted. Armenia and Kyrgyzstan had the further shock of being suddenly, and unexpectedly, torn away from a larger State and becoming landlocked countries. What makes these three countries especially worthy of close examination is that they are largely remote or cut off from their main potential markets, unlike some of the other economies in transition, such as the Baltic States, for whom problems of transport links have not been important. They have considerable mineral resources and are encouraging the development of those resources in partnership with private enterprise. However, they do not enjoy mineral rents on the scale of the fuel producers which could, perhaps, have made possible a policy of State-assisted growth. Rather, they are relying on private investment to determine the future direction of their economic growth. As they are otherwise in a disadvantageous geographical position, they have set out to become extremely attractive to foreign investment. They have the most liberal foreign trade regimes in the world, and have actively promoted regional initiatives to improve trade.

Chapter VII examines how a country can handle a natural disaster. The example studied is Bangladesh, a densely populated country that suffers from regular flooding. The issue is one not simply of coping with a crisis, but of ensuring that the highest level of economic activity can be maintained over long periods of time in this otherwise hostile environment. In the case of Bangladesh, a huge nationwide scheme to protect the country from flooding by, as it were, keeping the waters out, was impractical on the grounds of capital and maintenance costs. It could also have even deterred some economic activities. The answer was to assign to the local communities the task of arriving at the correct coping mechanisms, in terms of both physically controlling the inflow of water and choosing the economic activities that were best suited to the particular environment in this flood-prone country.

In any analysis of vulnerability, especially of the poor countries, the role of international aid and the accompanying policy advice must be addressed. A country that is hit by a sudden shock can be expected to seek financial, and sometimes technical, help from the international community. In the case of balance-of-payment shocks, the international institutions have had a variety of compensatory financing schemes. As for natural disasters and humanitarian crises, the United Nations provides a framework for mobilizing assistance. It is essential, however, that the country reduce its long-term dependence on external assistance and build up the capacity to handle future crises. In the case of an earthquake-prone country, for instance, domestic capacity is needed to predict an occurrence, to put in place and enforce codes to ensure that buildings are as safe as reasonably feasible, to evacuate the population at risk and to supply emergency assistance in the event of a disaster. For countries that are particularly vulnerable to economic shocks, domestic capacity is still essential if those countries are to put in place the appropriate micro- and macroeconomic policies that will enable them not only to ride out the crisis, but also to grow over the long term.

In sum, Part two of the *Survey* highlights the importance of managing vulnerability. In many cases, risks associated with vulnerability can best be borne by the private sector, and appropriate agents for confronting diverse risks involved in economic activities are private sector investors, domestic or foreign, who feel that they will be rewarded by making a profit. In other situations where the impact of vulnerabilities is felt by households or small producers, for example, the role of government is crucial. In all cases, however, there is a need for a public policy that supports activities and institutions that can understand and anticipate risks, provide insurance where possible and a public safety net where necessary.

Managing vulnerability has its counterpart at the international level. Thus, the risks that underlie the profits of large corporations have to be borne by the owners of these corporations. But beyond that, international arrangements are necessary to understand and anticipate risks; to provide compensation (in the areas of trade or finance) where the scale of the shock requires them; to make available adjustment assistance when the depth of transformation being undertaken is very substantial; and to secure the commitment to provide a safety net, particularly for natural disasters and humanitarian crises.

The challenge of vulnerability lies not in change per se, but in the effectiveness of national and international policies to cope with the uncertainties arising from change.

IV FINANCIAL VULNERABILITY IN A GLOBALIZING WORLD

The globalization of financial markets during the 1990s has had profound implications for the world economy. This development creates the prospects for a more efficient worldwide allocation of financial resources than was possible in the past. While such prospects have certainly widened, the several financial/banking crises that erupted during the course of the 1990s have raised the issue about increased vulnerability of financial markets and even countries as a whole. This period also saw stronger linkages among national financial markets through computer-aided communications technologies and the introduction of more sophisticated financial products.

One of the essential features of the market economy is a financial system where economic agents can make free decisions as to the allocation of credit: granting and denying credit on the basis of judgements as to profitability and the likelihood of repayment. For instance, a financial system that simply funnels the savings of the population to enterprises without any appraisal of their future profitability is defeating the purposes of the market economy—to allocate the limited savings of the population to enterprises likely to thrive, and to restrict credit to those that cannot survive in a competitive environment. Based on these principles, the financial system should ensure that society's savings are put to the most profitable use. Many actors are involved in the allocation of credit according to market principles—primarily the borrower, according to whose calculations the expected return will be greater than the cost of borrowing, and the lender who must assess whether these calculations are realistic and if, in fact, the lender is likely to be repaid. Both borrowers and lenders will, of course, use the services of many other agents to assess the risks and to spread them if necessary. What the financial system in effect does is to transform short term funds into longer-term capital. For instance, a person deposits in a bank funds that could have been used today for consumption and the bank lends those funds to, say, an agricultural enterprise whose production and therefore repayment will materialize only after some years.

Over time the market economies have been developing or improving institutions, including regulatory institutions, that enabled lenders and borrowers to be brought together while seeking to ensure that the likelihood of "shocks", their effects on the overall economy when they occurred and the opportunities for abuse were minimized. This has necessarily involved different levels of Government, as a well-functioning financial system can be considered to be as essential as physical infrastructure for overall economic performance and so a legitimate concern for Government. Governments need not undertake the necessary functions themselves, but could assign them to independent bodies or allow the market participants to set up bodies to regulate their own activities.

Several important principles were established. Borrowers were expected to be motivated to provide a full and accurate statement of relevant information to potential lenders and could be penalized for knowingly providing false information or withholding vital information. All those lending funds should be treated equally—with no one group of lenders having privileged information that would enable them to withdraw their credit before others had an equal chance, or to insist on payment before other creditors. The underlying principle of the market-based financial system—that people want to ensure that they are paid for the goods and services that they have already delivered, and therefore if there is a likelihood that they will not be paid, that they should be the first in the queue to collect payment—implies that there will be considerable disturbance when threats of non-payment arise. Those with a claim to payment will rush to be first in the line and to switch their assets to a safer venue (known as "herding" behaviour). This attempt to switch assets to a safer venue could result in the liquidation of assets in a country or enterprise that appeared to have some of the same characteristics as the suspect country or enterprise (what is known as the "contagion effect").

The developing countries, in particular, have much to gain from becoming modern, market-based economies with an efficient financial system that can attract domestic and foreign savings and put them to the most productive use. However, a modern financial system cannot operate in a vacuum. It needs a whole array of institutions and talents that govern not just banking but all other aspects of the economy. It requires, for instance, analysts who can assess the feasibility of a business project or who can judge whether prices of one asset, such as housing, have risen to unrealistically high levels and regulators who have an understanding of the nature of the industry to which banks are extending loans. In even the most advanced countries, judgements on these matters that have been based on extensive past experience have frequently been proved wrong and considerable funds have been wasted. Experience and institution-building are vital. It would, then, be impractical to suggest that the financial system of a developing country should replicate that of a developed country which had in place all the talents and institutions, in not just the financial, but also the industrial, marketing and research fields, that helped ensure that funds were wisely invested.

In many cases, those wishing to borrow funds, including the Government, could not raise the quantities required from the domestic public. Agents might also want repayment to be not in terms of the domestic currency, but in terms of what they considered a more sound or convenient currency. Thus the rise of the modern industrial economy has been accompanied by a growth in international financial transactions and liberalization of financial transactions between countries.[1] This has not been a smooth or even one-directional process.

In more recent times, the difficulties that the financial system, like other sectors of the economy, has encountered in adapting quickly enough to the

1 For an account of the evolution of international banking in the modern era, see Niall Fergusson, *The House of Rothschild: Money's Prophets 1798-1848* (New York, Penguin Books, 1998), and *The House of Rothschild: The World's Bankers, 1849-1998* (New York, Penguin Books, 2000).

needs of the market-driven global economy can help explain why global-ization has apparently led to greater vulnerability stemming increasingly from financial shocks. The experience of the past two decades demon-strates that international financial markets are subject to unpredictable swings, contagion, and costly financial crises. These crises had a large impact on the real economies and social conditions, especially in develop-ing countries. Accordingly, prevention and mitigation of crises pose a great challenge to both national Governments and international organizations.

ISSUES SURROUNDING THE LIBERALIZATION OF FINANCIAL FLOWS

The causes of the financial crises of the last two decades have occupied aca-demic researchers, market participants and policy makers.[2] While there are still disagreements about the causes, it is clear that the role of financial markets in causing crises has increased; in contrast, macroeconomic policies played a larger role in earlier crises. There could be two reasons for this. First, domes-tic and external financial liberalization can, in themselves, increase the risk of a financial crisis. Second, a crisis elsewhere is more likely to lead to a domes-tic crisis as a result of the strengthening of economic and financial linkages between countries, that is to say the risk of contagion has increased.

Financial liberalization in developing countries has been given greater atten-tion, as a result of two seminal studies on financial development in the early 1970s.[3] These studies pointed out that government intervention in financial markets, particularly interest rate controls, created distortions in credit alloca-tion, which adversely affected economic development. Policies towards the financial sector therefore focused primarily or even entirely on liberalization, particularly of interest rates, with relatively scant attention being paid to insti-tutional development.[4]

The arguments in favour of financial liberalization are based largely on the analogy between those goods for which there is instant settlement (cash in exchange for a standard good) and financial markets which ultimately depend on the goods and services produced in the real economy, but where the con-nection is not so direct and instant. This analogy, it is further asserted, could be misleading in that it ignores one crucial difference between the two markets: such direct markets for goods are not subject to asymmetric information, adverse selection and external effects to the same extent as financial markets, if at all. Also, because such factors as herding are known to prevent the market from achieving an efficient allocation of resources, it is argued that the recog-nized benefits of liberalization in goods markets cannot be assumed to apply to the same extent in the case of financial markets.[5]

It has been argued that removing controls on interest rates and regulations on credit for particular sectors, freeing entry into the financial sector and allowing private ownership of financial institutions should lead to a better allo-cation of investment, more savings and financial deepening. Yet, the evidence on these results of liberalization are mixed. For example, one survey conclud-ed that "financial liberalization has yielded positive results in terms of greater financial depth and increased efficiency in the allocation of investment but it has not brought the boost in saving" that had been predicted.[6] In Africa, the

2 For a summary discussion, see *World Economic and Social Survey 1999* (United Nations publica-tion, Sales No. E.99.II.C.1), chap. IX.

3 See Ronald I. McKinnon, *Money and Capital in Economic Development*, (Washington, D.C., Brookings Institutions, 1973); and Edward S. Shaw, *Financial Deepening in Economic Development* (New York, Oxford University Press, 1973).

4 See, for example, John Williamson, "What should the World Bank think about the Washington Consensus?", *The World Bank Research Observer*, vol. 15, No. 2 (August 2000), pp. 251-264.

5 See, for example, Jagdish Bhagwati, "The capital myth: the difference between trade in widgets and dollars", *Foreign Affairs*, vol. 77, No. 3 (May/June 1998), pp. 7-12.

6 See John Williamson and Molly Mahar, "A Survey of Financial Liberalization", *Essays in International Finance*, No. 211 (November 1998), p. 63.

7 See Henk-Jan Brinkman, "Financial reforms in Africa and the lessons from Asia", in *Global Financial Turmoil and Reform: A United Nations Perspective*, Barry Herman, ed. (Tokyo, United Nations University Press, 1999), pp. 213-246.

8 See, for example, John Eatwell and Lance Taylor, "The performance of liberalized capital markets", *CEPA Working Paper Series*, No. 8 (New York, Centre for Economic Policy Analysis (CEPA), The New School University, August 1998).

9 Whereas theory suggests that capital should flow from rich to poor countries because the return to capital should be highest in the poorest countries where capital is most scarce, actual financial flows have not followed this pattern. See, for example, Robert E. Lucas, Jr., "Why doesn't capital flow from rich to poor countries?", *The American Economic Review*, vol. 80, No. 2 (May 1990), pp. 92-96.

10 See Asli Demirgüç-Kunt and Enrica Detragiache, "Financial liberalization and Financial Fragility", *World Bank Policy Research Working Paper*, No. 1917 (Washington; D.C., World Bank, May 1998), p. 5.

11 See Williamson and Mahar, loc. cit.

results have been disappointing.[7] The characteristics of financial markets in Africa, such as high administrative and transaction costs compared with loan size, lack of collateral and the difficulties banks have in assessing credit risk, have precluded an increase in bank lending for investment potentially resulting from financial liberalization. Moreover, financial liberalization in Africa did not lead to financial deepening and improved credit allocation where some of the bases for a functioning market-based financial system were absent—that is to say, in cases where non-performing loans took up a large share of the loan portfolio and where insider lending and government interference persisted.

At a global level, the argument in favour of free capital movements is based to a large extent on the principle of allocative efficiency, namely, that the world's efficiency could be maximized by allowing capital to move to places where it can secure the highest return. The evidence, however, suggests that capital flows have not always conformed to the principle of allocative efficiency. The bulk of global financial flows, for example, over the past few decades have flowed to the United States of America. It is unlikely that these flows are guided solely by the rate of return, even if the return is adjusted for risk.[8] Among the developing countries, private capital flows have mainly concentrated on a small number of middle-income countries.[9]

While the evidence on the benefits of financial liberalization is mixed, most observers agree that financial liberalization increases the risk of a domestic financial crisis in cases where the institutional arrangements are weak. For example, a crisis is more probable when capacity for prudential regulation and supervision, accounting and legal systems and risk management systems is not adequate. "To summarize, financial liberalization, by giving banks and other financial intermediaries more freedom of action, increases the opportunities to take on risk. This tends to increase financial fragility, but it is not necessarily bad for the economy, as high-risk, high-return investment projects may dominate low-risk, low-return ventures. However, because of limited liability, compounded with other forms of implicit and explicit guarantees, bankers' appetite for risk is likely to be greater than what is socially desirable. If prudential regulation and supervision are not effective at controlling bank behaviour and at realigning incentives, liberalization may increase financial fragility well above what is socially desirable."[10] Thus, "the danger that liberalization will lead to (a financial) crisis is by far the most important drawback in the process."[11] Indeed, a number of studies have found that, even after controlling for the macroeconomic fundamentals, the probability of a banking crisis increases in liberalized financial environments. This is particularly the case when the capital account is liberalized and if prudential regulation and supervision are weak.

Financial liberalization can increase the risk of a financial crisis in several ways. Removing controls on the interest rate for loans might lead banks to engage in riskier ventures in search of higher returns. Deregulation of directed credit can also lead to lending for riskier projects. Thailand, for example, abolished limits on lending to the real estate sector; that led to an increase in loans to the sector, many of which went bad. However, deregulation of directed credit cannot provide all the explanation as it took place in an environment of weak banking supervision and regulations, cross-lending and large capital inflows. In general, financial liberalization often means higher interest rates; this should, in theory, promote efficiency in encouraging capital to go to those projects with the highest expected rate of return. It can, though, lead to riskier lending and exacerbate moral hazard and adverse selection problems. Higher interest rates are particularly a problem if banks have high debt-equity ratios.

Financial liberalization often leads to higher volatility of interest rates, asset prices and capital flows. As a result, banks face increased interest rate risk, liquidity risk and credit risk. Liquidity risk is likely to increase because, if asset prices are low, a bank might not be able to sell assets at the expected price when it wishes to raise cash. Credit risk is higher because higher volatility in financial and asset markets affects the creditworthiness of borrowers.

Allowing entry of new domestic or foreign firms into the financial sector will enhance competition in the sector. Increased competition, however, can lead to lower profitability and reduce the "franchise value" of the bank, that is to say, the profits that banks derive from their reputation. This can mean that, searching for higher returns, domestic banks will lend to more risky projects especially if foreign banks "cherry-pick" the best credits.[12] On the other hand, the arrival of foreign banks as a result of liberalization can be helpful in cases where domestic banks previously enjoyed above-normal rents owing to their monopolistic or oligopolistic position. Moreover, foreign banks can transfer financial management know-how and technology to domestic banks.

The possibility of a financial crisis is particularly large after the country is opened up to external financial flows, particularly short-term flows. The result may be excessive surges of potentially reversible capital flows into the recipient countries. Short-term external borrowing was a key source of instability in the Asian financial crisis of 1997-1998, and the Mexican peso crisis of 1994-1995. Countries are particularly vulnerable to the negative effects of capital inflows if their banking system is unsound because these inflows expose banks to exchange-rate risk on top of their other difficulties. Inflows could also lead to more risky lending by banks.

In an era of globalization, the probability of a domestic financial crisis can increase if there is a crisis elsewhere. This "contagion" can result from several factors. It can be a result of a common shock, such as an increase in international interest rates or a change in the exchange rates between key currencies.[13] Changes in United States interest rates have been particularly important for Latin America, leading up, for example, to the crisis in Mexico in 1994. Similarly, the appreciation of the United States dollar against the yen during 1995 and 1996 was one factor behind the weakening export performance of East Asian countries, which contributed to the financial crises in 1997.

Trade linkages can also propagate a crisis. If a country suffers a financial crisis that leads to a drop in its demand for imports, its trading partners will experience a fall in exports. This has historically played a role, particularly within a region where intraregional trade linkages are strong.[14] Bilateral trade links are generally less relevant in explaining contagion across regions, say, from Asia to Latin America, because interregional trade usually accounts for a smaller share of total trade than intraregional trade.

A related channel is through competitive devaluations, as occurred during the 1930s. When a country devalues, other countries that compete in the same export markets lose competitiveness and might be forced to devalue as well. Some have argued that the devaluation of the Chinese yuan renminbi in 1994 precipitated the currency crises in East Asia in 1997 because of competition in

[12] See, for example, Christian Weller, "The supply of credit by multinational banks in developing and transition economies: determinants and effects", DESA Discussion Paper, No. 16, March 2001, http://www.un.org/esa/papers.htm.

[13] See, for example, Paul Masson, "Contagion: Monsoonal Effects, Spillovers, and Jumps between Multiple Equilibria", IMF Working Paper, No. WP/98/142 (Washington, D.C., September 1998).

[14] See, for example, Reuven Glick and Andrew K. Rose, "Contagion and trade: why are currency crises regional?", Journal of International Economics, vol. 18 (1999), pp. 603-617.

[15] For an examination of this argument, see *World Economic and Social Survey, 1998* (United Nations publication, Sales No. E.98.II.C.1 and Corr.1), box III.1, sect. entitled "Actual developments in relative exchange rates".

[16] See Graciela L. Kaminsky and Carmen M. Reinhart, "On crises, contagion, and confusion", *Journal of International Economics*, vol. 51, No. 1 (June 2000), pp. 145-168.

[17] See, for example, Sebastian Edwards, "Contagion", *The World Economy*, vol. 23, No. 7 (July 2000), pp. 873-900.

third-country markets.[15] Similarly, despite their strong macroeconomic situations, the currencies of Singapore and Taiwan Province of China depreciated after the East Asian crises. One factor was the need to maintain competitiveness in third markets.

Yet another case in which a financial crisis in one country can lead to a financial crisis in another is when a creditor bank, typically located in a developed country, has outstanding loans to various developing countries all located in the same region. Because a creditor bank tends to treat assets located in different countries but in the same region as a basket of assets within its overall financial portfolio, it tries to "unload" the financial basket altogether when a crisis hits even just one of the countries. An example is the Japanese banks' involvement in Thailand in the 1990s. As of December 1996, 54 per cent of Thai liabilities had been to Japanese banks and, on the reverse side, 22 per cent of Japanese claims on emerging markets were on Thailand.[16] When the Thai crisis erupted, Japanese banks began to call loans, not only in Thailand, but in other East Asian countries as well.

Moreover, a crisis in one country can trigger a crisis in another country if investors perceive macroeconomic or financial situations to be similar. This could also result in the recognition of weaknesses that were not recognized before—a so-called wake-up call. Yet a crisis in one country can also spread to another country through a shift in market sentiment that is not based on economic fundamentals.

The portfolio structure and liquidity problems of international investors can also contribute to contagion. Managers of mutual funds often allocate certain proportions of their investments to specific countries and instruments. If the value of one investment declines, the manager might sell assets of other countries to keep the proportions intact. Moreover, fund managers might encounter liquidity constraints if the investments in one country decline in value: this might force the sale of assets of other countries.

The possibility of contagion has increased the likelihood that some countries that do not experience a deterioration in their economic fundamentals may nonetheless be affected by a financial crisis somewhere else in the world. These countries could be termed "innocent bystanders". For example, during the Russian crisis in August 1998, the yield spreads between the United States Treasury bills (the international benchmark) and dollar-denominated bonds issued by developing countries increased dramatically. Suddenly, developing countries and their firms had to pay more interest on their newly incurred foreign debt or on their variable rate debt, even though nothing else had changed.

The effect of contagion is often detected through the correlation of volatility across countries during a crisis. Asset prices or interest rates in the two countries may not correlate during a tranquil period, but the movements of these variables suddenly become highly correlated as a crisis breaks out in one of them and asset prices experience wide swings.[17] For example, Hong Kong Special Administrative Region (SAR) of China and Chile had not jointly experienced any period of high volatility between 1994 and late 1997. Yet, in October 1997—during the Asian financial crises—both economies experienced rapid shifts in the same direction in asset prices and in interest rates.

This has critical consequences for the financial sector. Financial sector participants determine the size and composition of their portfolios in order to optimize the combination of expected returns and risks that best meets their objectives. Risks are partly minimized by diversification across assets whose returns are not positively correlated: if the price of one asset does fall, the prices of other assets need not; but if during a crisis the correlation of returns suddenly becomes positive, the assumptions underlying the model used in the portfolio break down, with possibly severe results for the solvency of financial sector institutions. This happened during the Russian crisis.

EFFECTS OF FINANCIAL CRISES

The costs of a financial crisis can be staggering to a country.[18] A crisis in the financial system is different from that in any other industry. It necessarily reverberates throughout the economy, affecting every aspect of economic life. When depositors feel that they will not be able to recover their deposits from the institutions to which they entrusted them or sellers fear that the financial system will not be able to remit to them the amount the buyer owes, the whole basis of commercial activity is put in jeopardy. The ultimate breakdown would occur if the economy reverted to only instant cash payments or even barter.[19] The Government, then, has to ensure that it has a functioning financial system, even if this means a considerable commitment of public funds.

As one study found: "There have been more than 65 developing-country episodes during 1980-95, when banking systems' capital was completely or nearly exhausted; the public-sector bail-out costs of resolving crises in developing countries during this period have been estimated at around $250 billion. In more than a dozen of these banking crises, the public-sector resolution costs amounted to 10 per cent or more of the country's gross domestic product (GDP). In the latest additions to the list of severe banking crisis, the cost of bank recapitalization for the countries most affected in the ongoing Asian financial crisis is expected to be huge—on the order of 58 per cent of GDP for Indonesia, 30 per cent for Thailand, 16 per cent for the Republic of Korea, and 10 per cent of GDP for Malaysia."[20] The adverse effects of financial crises are also felt in the extent and the duration of actual output's going below the trend output level: the average cumulative output loss, relative to trend, among 30 developing countries that were effected by financial crises during 1975-1997 is estimated to have been 8.3 percentage points. Moreover, GDP growth, even three years after a crisis, had not returned to the average growth rate in the last two years prior to the crisis in a sample of 25 emerging and industrialized countries during 1975-1995.

Indicators such as GDP growth and the fiscal costs of a crisis tell only part of the story. The financial crises of the 1990s have had a huge impact on poverty and unemployment. The large changes in interest rates, exchange rates, output and government expenditures affect all income groups. These changes affect the demand for labour and real wages. The impact on poor people is particularly harsh. Poor people have fewer capital assets (human, financial or physical) with which to cope with a shock and almost no insurance to smooth consumption.[21] Although some evidence shows that poor households do not suffer from higher income volatility than others during an economic crisis, even small income volatility affects poor people much more because they possess limited means to mitigate the effect of volatility.[22] In the crisis countries in East

[18] This section is partly based on Jahangir Aziz, Francesco Caramazza and Ranil Salgado, "Currency Crises: In Search of Common Elements", IMF Working Paper, No. WP/00/67 (Washington, D.C., April 2000); and Morris Goldstein, Graciela L. Kaminsky and Carmen M. Reinhart, Assessing Financial Vulnerability: An Early Warning System for Emerging Markets (Washington, D.C., Institute for International Economics, 2000), pp. 1-2.

[19] It could be noted that the dire effects of financial crises have long been appreciated. The actions of the Rothschilds in 1825 in delivering gold to the Bank of England had averted a crisis in which, according to William Huskisson, President of the Board of Trade, the country came within 48 hours of "putting stop to all dealings between man and man except by barter". See Niall Fergusson, The House of Rothschild: Money's Prophets 1798-1848 (New York, Penguin Books, 1998), p. 137.

[20] See Goldstein, Kaminsky and Reinhart, op. cit, pp. 1-2.

[21] See, for example, Jonathan Morduch, "Income smoothing and consumption smoothing", The Journal of Economic Perspectives, vol. 9. No. 3 (summer 1995), pp. 103-114.

[22] See, for example, Guillermo Perry, "Financial globalization in Latin America and the Caribbean: mitigating the impact of volatility on the poor", presentation at the conference on "Financial Globalisation: Issues and Challenges for Small States", 27 and 28 March 2001, Saint Kitts and Nevis, mimeo (Washington, D.C., World Bank).

[23] See, for example, United Nations, *World Economic and Social Survey, 1999...*, box III.2.

[24] It subsequently declined to 11.4 per cent in August 1999, which was about equal to the level of February 1996. See Asep Suryahadi and others, "The Evolution of Poverty during the Crisis in Indonesia, 1996-99", *World Bank Policy Research Working Paper,* No. 2435 (Washington, D.C., September 2000).

[25] See, for example, Nora Lustig, "Life is not easy: Mexico's quest for stability and growth", *The Journal of Economic Perspectives,* vol. 15, No. 1 (winter 2001), pp. 85-106.

[26] See, for example, World Bank, *World Development Report 2000/2001: Attacking Poverty* (New York, Oxford University Press, 2001), p. 163.

[27] Ibid., table 9.2.

[28] See, for example, Administrative Committee on Coordination (ACC)/Subcommittee on Nutrition (SCN), *Fourth Report on the World Nutrition Situation* (Geneva, ACC/SCN, 2000); Robert W. Fogel, "Economic growth, population theory, and physiology: the bearing of long-term processes on the making of economic policy", *The American Economic Review,* vol. 84, No. 3 (June 1994), pp. 369-395; and United Nations Children's Fund (UNICEF), *The State of the World's Children, 2001* (New York, UNICEF, 2000).

[29] See, for example, report of the Secretary-General (E/CN.5/2001/2) entitled "Enhancing social protection and reducing vulnerability in a globalizing world", 8 December 2000; and *World Economic and Social Survey, 1999* ..., chap. VII entitled "Bringing financial services to the poor".

[30] See, for example, Guillermo Perry, loc. cit.; and *World Development Report 2000/2001,* pp. 166-170.

Asia, the impact was most severely felt among the urban poor.[23] The low-skilled workers in manufacturing and construction suffered particularly from lower real wages or unemployment. In rural areas, farmers have generally been less affected because they have received more for their cash crops as a result of the devaluations. On the other hand, many migrated from urban areas back to the rural areas of origin, putting downward pressure on wages there.

In the crisis countries in East Asia, poverty rates and unemployment shot up immediately after the Asian crisis in 1997-1998. For example, in the Republic of Korea, which publishes nationwide (rather than urban-based) unemployment rates, the rate jumped from 2.0 per cent in 1996 to 6.8 per cent in 1998. In Indonesia, the poverty rate increased from 7.6 per cent in August 1997 to 20.2 per cent at the end of 1998, which amounted to about 25 million people falling into poverty in a short period of time. It subsequently declined to 11.4 per cent in August 1999, which was about equal to the level of February 1996.[24] Yet, real manufacturing wages were in March 2000 still below the level recorded four years earlier. Similar effects of a financial crisis were recorded in Mexico.[25] Between the end of 1994 and July 1997, real wages fell by 30 per cent and they have only very slowly increased subsequently. In Latin America, however, poverty rates have remained higher than they were before the crises.[26]

Households employ different kinds of mechanisms to cope with the effects of shocks. These coping mechanisms might have long-term consequences. Poor households might sell some or all of the few assets they have, including productive assets, such as livestock and equipment. Yet, without these assets, households can be stuck in a poverty trap. The fact that when people become unemployed they lose skills and might become stigmatized makes it harder for them to become employed again. Households might also assume debt, which could lead to a debt trap. Moreover, families might take their children out of school during an economic crisis. For example, the dropout rate among the poorest quartile in Indonesia increased from 1.3 per cent in 1997 to 7.5 per cent in 1998 among children ages 7-12 and from 14.2 to 25.5 per cent during the same period among children ages 13-19.[27] Most importantly, child mortality might increase and child malnutrition might worsen. Child malnutrition, even if temporary, has long-term consequences. Lack of the proper nutrition at the crucial phases of brain development, for example, affects cognitive ability during the rest of a person's life. A period of malnutrition also has negative effects on the incidence of morbidity and mortality later in life.[28] In fact, this negative cycle can already start in utero. Low-birth weight increases the risk of dying at a young age and has lifelong negative consequences, if the infant goes on to survive childhood.

Financial crises can never be completely prevented, but their permanent negative impacts on human beings can be largely mitigated. Governments should have a broad social safety net in place to avoid these impacts, for example, through unemployment insurance, public employment programmes and microfinance (credit and insurance) schemes.[29] Moreover, Governments should make every effort to protect budget expenditures on these programmes and other social areas, such as education and health care, during a crisis, particularly those expenditures that benefit the poor. In order for Governments to be able to do this, they need to save during good times so that it is possible to increase expenditures during bad times.[30]

PREVENTION AND MITIGATION OF CRISES

Assessing external vulnerability: early warning systems

After the recent financial crises, increased attention has been paid to the identification of vulnerabilities that might lead to a crisis. Different approaches have been developed. One method is based on the fact that the economy behaves differently on the eve of a crisis and sends out signals that can be interpreted as an early warning.[31] For example, a currency crisis is usually preceded by an overvaluation of the exchange rate and/or a high ratio of short-term debt in foreign currency to GDP. A banking crisis is often precipitated by a fall in asset prices, such as house prices. Predicting financial crises with models is not foolproof. Typically the models predict a crisis accurately half the time: in half the cases, a crisis was predicted and actually occurred within the next two years; but this has no value for market participants. Yet, in about 60 per cent of the cases, the typical model predicted a crisis but none occurred in the next two years.[32] This, however, could be a sign that the model had done its work: it had predicted a crisis and the authorities took the proper measures to stave it off. On the other hand, an early warning, especially if it comes from reputable actors, could result in a crisis's occurring through self-fulfilling prophecies. This is a serious concern, given the fact that a change in market sentiment can trigger a financial crisis. It is possible that more transparency and information can lead to a crisis, rather than prevent it. Yet a small crisis early on is probably better than a crisis later on when the imbalances have been allowed to build up.

In addition to being poor in determining the time of a crisis, early warning models do poorly in predicting a crisis "out of sample", that is to say, for a period or for countries that the model was not designed for. For example, almost nobody predicted the East Asian crises, and in particular their timing, because their causes had not previously been recognized as important. The major financial crises over the past several decades have brought different elements to the fore, with theory running behind, trying to catch up with reality.

Over time, and with the improvement of macroeconomic policies, the role of the particularities of financial markets has gained in prominence in the explanation of financial crises.[33] Macroeconomic imbalances, such as budget deficits and exchange-rate overvaluation, and exogenous shocks (terms-of-trade shocks, interest rate increases and economic slowdown in many developed countries) were seen to be the main causes of the debt crisis of the 1980s. Domestic financial sector fragilities received very little attention in the analyses of this crisis. The Mexican crisis of 1995 was partly explained by self-fulfilling prophecies, which had been made possible, however, by weak macroeconomic fundamentals, such as an overvalued exchange rate in combination with the accumulation of dollar-denominated short-term debt. Again, financial sector fragilities were hardly emphasized. This changed in the Asian crises. Macroeconomic imbalances were largely absent or minor, except in Thailand where the real exchange rate had appreciated unsustainably. However, the fiscal position was sound and inflation was low in all the crisis countries. After the crisis erupted, weaknesses in the financial sector came to the fore and have been at the core of the explanations of the crises.

As the role of the financial sector in causing financial crises has increased, crises have become harder to predict. Self-fulfilling crises are particularly dif-

[31] See, for example, Goldstein, Kaminsky and Reinhart, op. cit.

[32] See, for example, Andrew Berg and others, "Anticipating Balance of Payments Crises: The Role of Early Warning Systems", *Occasional Paper*, No. 186 (Washington, D.C., International Monetary Fund, 1999). The percentages do not add up because the denominator is not the same. In the first case, the denominator is the total number of actual crises. In the second case, the denominator is the number of countries without a crisis.

[33] See, for example, Berg and others, loc. cit., pp. 5-7, and 27.

ficult to anticipate and models identify self-fulfilling crises only for a range of values of economic variables. Within this range a crisis may occur but is not inevitable. However, the task of determining that range for each economic variable that might possibly play a role in causing a financial crisis is still enormous. Moreover, there is no uniform set of variables that can predict crises. The most important variables differ from country to country and depend on the specific circumstances. Nevertheless, a number of variables turned up in most models as important leading indicators. They include real exchange-rate appreciation, short-term foreign liabilities (as percentage of reserves) and domestic credit expansion.

Macroeconomic policies

Macroeconomic policies play a crucial role in preventing a financial crisis and mitigating its effect if it occurs. They are particularly important for exchange-rate management. Poor macroeconomic policies that lead to external and internal imbalances, such as budget and current-account deficits, can directly cause a currency crisis or can make an attack on the currency more likely. Unfortunately, it is not always clear what good macroeconomic policy is. For example, hyperinflation is clearly a sign of failing macroeconomic policy, but this might not be the case for moderate inflation.

Over time, the role of macroeconomic policies in causing a financial crisis has decreased relative to other factors, perhaps partly as a result of improved macroeconomic policies in many parts of the world. For example, double and triple-digit inflation rates became much less frequent in the second half of the 1990s. Macroeconomic policies with regard to inflation, budget deficits and exchange rates were sound in almost all Asian countries that faced a financial crisis in 1997-1998; they are a necessary condition for the prevention of crises, but are recognized as not being sufficient.

While macroeconomic policies as such have become relatively less important, financial markets and the interaction between financial markets and macroeconomic policies have gained prominence in the recent financial crises. Partly because of this interaction, macroeconomic policy, particularly monetary policy and exchange-rate policy, continues to play a crucial role in the prevention and mitigation of financial crises. For example, a depreciating exchange rate increases the local currency liabilities of the private and public sectors if they have debt that is denominated in foreign currency. Higher interest rates have adverse implications for debt servicing, asset prices, balance sheets and economic activity. Moreover, higher interest rates can aggravate adverse selection and moral hazard problems. Such changes in interest and exchange rates can precipitate, cause or contribute to a financial crisis. Stabilizing them through proper macroeconomic measures can prevent and mitigate a financial crisis. On the other hand, it should be recognized that for a country with a well-developed financial system and a sound macroeconomic policy, allowing one variable to adjust to a shock can be the appropriate policy—Australia's exchange rate adjusted downward as a result of the Asian shock and the country rose out the crisis rather well.

Macroeconomic policy becomes particularly important when foreign capital flows into a country. Capital inflows fuel economic activity and, in this case, foreign direct investment (FDI) could be used to create new and competitive export industries. Yet the inflows are likely to put upward pressure on the exchange rate, endangering the competitiveness of existing exports, and exerting downward pressure on interest rates. Stabilizing interest and exchange rates, or neutralizing the effects of their changes, is a major task of macroeconomic policy in these circumstances. To this end, Governments have often sterilized capital inflows by selling bonds to offset the expansionary effect of capital inflows on the economy. This, however, pushes up the interest rate and the fact that, if it is done aggressively, domestic interest rates will be higher than before the capital inflows started, will encourage more foreign inflows, particularly of the short-term kind. Sterilization tends to become less effective and more expensive in fiscal terms over time. Even if sterilization is abandoned, the boom could continue, as the lower domestic interest rate will lead to higher demand for domestic credit. The boom is also fuelled by an appreciating exchange rate, which increases the returns on investment for foreigners. High returns could lead to expectations of further appreciation and encourage more capital inflows.

Fiscal policy can also partly counter the effects of capital inflows. Fiscal revenues are often pro-cyclical as tax revenues increase with the expansion of output. To avoid fuelling the boom, some cuts in government expenditures might be required. Discretionary spending, like public investment, is a possible target for cuts, but is not always politically feasible. As discussed at greater length in chapter V, an alternative is a stabilization fund in which revenues from capital inflows or commodity booms could be set aside to avoid cuts in government expenditures when the good times end. Part of these funds could, for example, be used to finance social safety nets.[34] These funds should, however, not be used for explicit or implicit guarantees for the private sector because this might only fuel the boom.

Dampening a boom and avoiding a bust cannot be accomplished by macroeconomic policy alone, but a greater effort to make macroeconomic policies counter-cyclical and flexible is needed. This is also of import in the wake of a crisis. It is now recognized, for example, that, after the onset of the crisis in East Asia, macroeconomic policies were too tight, exacerbating the economic downturn and the negative impact on the vulnerable poor.[35] Restoring confidence might require expansionary policies in the wake of a crisis to offset the negative effect on private consumption and demand.

Regulation and supervision

In respect of preventing financial crises, a great deal of emphasis has been placed on the regulation and supervision of the financial sector, largely because inadequate regulation and supervision have contributed to—or even caused—financial crises. In East Asia, for example, the capital inflows led to a growth in the number of banks and non-bank institutions and risky lending. Crucially, this growth occurred at a time when the capacity to supervise was inadequate and regulation outdated or not enforced.

Developing countries face large obstacles to the establishment of adequate prudential regulation and supervision.[36] In many developing countries, there is a dearth of professionals such as accountants, regulators, supervisors and managers. In some countries, accounting standards, rules for loan classification and loan-loss provisions, and reporting and disclosure requirements do not even

[34] See, for example, José Antonio Ocampo, "Developing countries' anti-cyclical policies in a globalized world", paper presented at a conference entitled "A broad agenda of crisis prevention and response: addressing global economic imbalances in the north and boom-bust cycles in the south", organized by the Forum on Debt and Development, Santiago de Chile, 1 and 2 March 2001.

[35] See, for example, Jack Boorman and others, "Managing Financial Crises: The Experience in East Asia", *IMF Working Paper*, No. WP/00/107 (Washington, D.C., IMF, June 2000).

[36] See, for example, S. Mansoob Murshed and Djono Subagjo, "Prudential regulation of banks in less developed countries", *World Institute for Development Economics Research Working Papers*, No. 199 (Helsinki, UNU/WIDER, July 2000).

37   See, for example, Martin Brownbridge, "The causes of financial distress in local banks in Africa and implications for prudential policy", *UNCTAD Discussion Papers*, No. 132, March 1998.

38   See, for example, Demirgüc-Kunt and Detragiache, loc. cit.

39   See, for example, Yilmaz Akyüz and Andrew Cornford, "Capital flows to developing countries and the reform of the international financial system", *World Institute for Development Economics Research Working Papers*, No. 190 (Helsinki, UNU/WIDER, July 2000).

40   See, for example, Joseph Stiglitz and Amar Bhattacharya, "The underpinnings of a stable and equitable global financial system: from old debates to a new paradigm", in *Annual World Bank Conference on Development Economics, 1999* (Washington, D.C., World Bank, 2000), pp. 91-130.

exist. Weak supervision and regulation and lack of professionals also had its counterpart at the level of the financial institutions.[37] Banks often suffer from inadequate expertise for screening and monitoring borrowers, and from poor loan documentation and internal controls. In some countries, insider lending is a major contributor to bank failures. Politicians or supervisors who are shareholders or directors often received loans from parastatals or other favours in return for deposits. Political connections are also used to obtain banks licenses or prevent action by regulators, reducing constraints on imprudent lending and worsening moral hazard problems.

The creation of the capacity to monitor, supervise and regulate financial institutions is essential before financial liberalization commences. For example, if interest rates are liberalized and rise, moral hazard and adverse selection problems increase, and if the banking system is unsound or prudential regulation inadequate, a financial crisis becomes more likely. Thus, banking crises are more likely when the financial system is liberalized but this effect is weaker—albeit still existent—when the supervision and regulation are strong.[38] It is quite unlikely that a repressed financial system would have enough human capacity in the areas of prudential supervision and regulation. These skills could be built up only over time. This implies that financial liberalization should take into consideration not only competition and efficiency, but also progress in capacity-building in terms of human capital and institutional infrastructure in the field of financial risk management.

The basic arguments for regulation and supervision are consumer protection, reduction in systemic risk and enhancement of the performance of markets. The support for better prudential regulation and supervision is (almost) universal. Nonetheless, the how, the scope, the limits and their success in preventing crisis remain controversial areas.

There are limits to what supervision can accomplish. Supervisions and regulation are, indeed, likely to always run behind technological innovation. Moreover, the values of the assets on a bank's balance sheet are susceptible to changes and regulators can hardly keep up with them in the rapidly evolving economic world.[39]

Also, there are disagreements on the scope of supervision and regulation. They pertain, for example, to whether or to what degree supervision and regulation can be extended to corporations, the international arena, non-bank financial institutions (such as mutual funds), offshore banking centres and highly leveraged institutions such as hedge funds. The accumulation of short-term debt by private corporations was as much a factor in the financial crisis in East Asia as the accumulation of similar debts by banks, both factors being largely unknown to the authorities. This raises the issue of the monetary authorities' preventing the overexposure of corporations. Some argue that this could be achieved indirectly through the strict regulation of banks that lend to them, for example, by restricting lending when corporations have accumulated a large share of short-term foreign debt. This, however, might not be sufficient and measures to regulate borrowing by firms might involve restrictions on foreign borrowing, inflow or outflow taxes and limitations on tax deductibility.[40]

Non-bank financial institutions, including highly leveraged institutions, have become large players in financial markets, but regulation and supervision are relatively weak. This issue has been taken up in a number of reports. For example, the Financial Stability Forum Working Group on Highly Leveraged Institutions recommended a number of measures that were mainly addressed at financial institutions that were counterparts, for example, banks that provided credit to the highly leveraged institutions.[41] It did not recommend an international credit register or direct regulation of the highly leveraged institutions that were currently unregulated, although it would reconsider these proposals in the future, particularly if the recommendations were not implemented.

The regulation and supervision of offshore banking centres and non-bank financial institutions are closely intertwined with the question whether regulation on an international level is adequate. The increased openness of capital markets, with large amounts of capital flowing across borders, has raised the need for international regulation. It is impossible for a national authority to know the exact risk exposure of all financial (and non-financial) institutions within its jurisdiction without information from other authorities. Since the 1970s, international regulation has been conducted through cooperation of national authorities. Some have argued that this leaves large gaps, which should be filled by the establishment of a new international regulatory authority.[42] Others have argued that this is unrealistic and that intensified cooperation among national authorities should be the approach.

The Bank for International Settlements (BIS) in Basel, Switzerland, has been the main institution for international cooperation and coordination regarding regulation. The Basel Committee on Banking Supervision launched in 1988 capital adequacy requirements for banks (1988 Basel Capital Accord). This Accord made a major contribution to the use of standardized risk-weighted capital-to-asset ratios by supervising authorities to assess banking safety, originally for internationally active banks of the Group of Ten (the original sponsors), but later across the world. Yet, over time deficiencies emerged. In fact, they might have contributed to the financial crises in the 1990s, as short-term lending gets a lower risk weighting and needs less provisioning capital, according to the 1988 Accord. Generally, the risk weighting system is rather crude. Moreover, with the advent of new risk-management techniques, the focus only on capital ratios became outdated. In June 1999, the Basel Committee issued a consultative document on a new capital adequacy framework. It is proposed that the new framework be based on three pillars: revised minimum capital requirements, the development of a supervisory review of banks' capital adequacy and more effective utilization of market discipline. The details of these proposals are still under consideration and it is hoped that the accord will be finalized during 2002 with a view to implementation in 2005.

The Basel Committee took another step towards improved international regulation with the publication of the Core Principles for Effective Banking Supervision in 1997. These principles, which were formulated with the participation of several developing countries and economies in transition, aimed at enhancing the quality of supervision within countries across the globe. The principles emphasized the importance of consolidated statements on exposures, which are critical in the case of transnational banks with subsidiaries all over the world.

There is a need to adopt counter-cyclical regulation, as currently regulation does little to dampen a boom. This could include setting predetermined rules that would set higher capital adequacy ratios in times of a boom, caps on the

[41] For more information see: http://www.fsforum.org/Press/Home.html.

[42] See, for example, John Eatwell and Lance Taylor, *Global Finance at Risk: The Case for International Regulation* (New York, The New Press, 2000); and United Nations, "Towards a new international financial architecture", report of the Task Force of the Executive Committee on Economic and Social Affairs of the United Nations, 21 January 1999.

acceptable value for collateral purposes of certain assets that are likely to be inflated during a boom period (such as real estate and stocks), and limits on lending to the real estate sector and construction.[43] Again, the case for counter-cyclical regulation has been challenged as mixing two separate issues: counter-cyclical macroeconomic policy with bank regulation.

Exchange-rate regimes

To many, the exchange-rate regime was one important cause of the crises in Mexico (1994-1995), East Asia (1997-1998), the Russian Federation (1998) and Brazil (1999). All the crisis countries had a pegged or managed exchange rate before the crisis.[44] In East Asia, for example, financial market participants perceived the stability of the rate as reducing the risk of devaluation and this fuelled capital inflows. Lending by foreigners and foreign borrowing by domestic banks and firms, made possible by the liberalization of the financial sector and capital account, were considered relatively safe as the exchange-rate risk was minimal. This behaviour might have been further encouraged by implicit or explicit government guarantees.[45] When the current-account deficit grew, partly as a result of the appreciation of the real exchange rate, short-term liabilities became large compared with the international reserves. Investors and lenders fled and the consequence was a currency crisis because the exchange-rate adjustment was not managed in a timely enough fashion.

These events have led to a questioning of the feasibility of an exchange-rate regime that is between the extremes of a completely freely floating exchange rate and a very hard pegged regime, such as a currency board, dollarization or a monetary union. The argument is that either of the two extremes is less vulnerable to financial crises because each removes the uncertainty with regard to policies. At either extreme, markets no longer have to guess what Governments will do because, in the fixed case, monetary policy is devoted solely to the defence of the parity and, in the floating case, policies to manage the exchange rate are not used at all. This has become the conventional wisdom although the official view of the International Monetary Fund (IMF) is now more cautious: "The usual approach by the IMF on this matter has been to abide by a member country's preferred exchange-rate regime and to tailor its overall policy advice accordingly."[46] In practice, the intermediate regimes have shrunk. Between 1991 and 1999, the number of countries with an intermediate exchange-rate regime declined from 98 to 63 per cent.[47]

The theoretical basis for the vanishing intermediate regime is a corollary of the "impossible trinity", which states that one can attain only two of the three following objectives: full capital mobility, fixed exchange rates and monetary autonomy. During the Bretton Woods era of fixed exchange rates that ended in the early 1970s, fixed exchange rates and monetary autonomy prevailed, while capital flows were restricted. Capital mobility and fixed exchange rates had been combined—and monetary autonomy sacrificed—during the gold standard period. The same now applies to countries with currency boards and the euro-area countries. The final option is to combine capital mobility and monetary autonomy, while exchange rates generally float.

In a world that is increasingly financially integrated, the choice appears to be between exchange-rate stability and monetary autonomy. According to this thinking, the room between the extremes of irretrievably fixed and completely

[43] See, for example, Stephany Griffith-Jones and José Antonio Ocampo, "Facing the volatility and concentration of capital flows", in *Reforming the International Financial System: Crises Prevention and Response*, Jan Joost Teunissen, ed. (The Hague, Forum on Debt and Development, 2000), pp. 31-63.

[44] The Philippines officially had a freely floating regime but in practice a managed one.

[45] The role of these guarantees, if there was one, is still unclear. In the Republic of Korea, for example, the Government did not bail out any chaebol (large family-owned business conglomerate) in the 1980s and 1990s and 3 of the 30 biggest went bankrupt between 1990 and 1997. See Eatwell and Taylor, op. cit. p. 48.

[46] See Michael Mussa and others, "Exchange Rate Regimes in an Increasingly Integrated World Economy", *Occasional Paper*, No. 193 (Washington, D.C., IMF, 2000), p. 48. It is a matter of dispute to what extent IMF has pressured countries away from the intermediate regimes. See Stanley Fischer, "Exchange rate regimes: is the bipolar view correct?", Distinguished Lecture on Economics in Government, delivered at the Meeting of the American Economic Association, New Orleans, Louisiana, 6 January 2001; and John Williamson, *Exchange Rate Regimes for Emerging Markets: Reviving the Intermediate Option* (Washington, D.C., Institute for International Economics, 2000).

[47] Fischer, loc. cit.

floating exchange rates, also referred to as the "corner solutions", has become smaller; to some, the possibility of an intermediate regime, such as a crawling peg or band, target zone or adjustable peg, has disappeared.

Nevertheless, there is some discord about the limited feasibility of intermediate regimes. First of all, the theoretical basis for it is rather weak. It is possible to have some capital mobility, some exchange-rate stability and some monetary autonomy. There is little theoretical justification for choosing for two of the three options in total rather than part of each.[48] Also, the evidence on the disappearing intermediate regimes is based on what countries say they do, rather than what they actually do. Thus, many countries that claim to have a freely floating exchange rate are, in reality, managing the rate.[49]

Moreover, the argument that intermediate regimes are more likely to generate financial crises is questionable. Indeed, intermediate regimes have been associated with financial crises, but this does not mean that they are the ultimate cause. The underlying cause might be the behaviour of financial market participants. For example, it seems unreasonable to "blame" the exchange-rate regime if banks and firms keep accumulating short-term unhedged liabilities because they wrongly assume that a pegged exchange rate is irretrievably fixed.

Furthermore, both purely fixed and freely floating exchange-rate regimes are vulnerable to financial crises. Under a fixed regime, such as a currency board, a currency crisis might be less likely, but only at the expense of banking crises as the banking sector is left without a lender of last resort.[50] An appreciating real exchange rate is a relatively good predictor of banking and currency crises.[51] However, this can occur under any exchange-rate regime.[52] Even freely floating and permanently fixed exchange rates can have extended periods of large misalignments and these can lead to financial crises.

When choosing an exchange-rate regime, a country has to balance credibility and flexibility. A permanently fixed exchange rate, such as dollarization or a currency board, is the most credible but the least flexible regime; the exchange rate cannot be adjusted after an exogenous shock, such as a fall in the terms of trade. The fixed exchange rate provides a credible nominal anchor for prices and stability for exporters and investors. In contrast, a freely floating exchange rate adjusts itself in case of an exogenous shock and is able to do so more easily than nominal prices and wages. However, flexibility might come at the expense of credibility. Credibility for a freely floating regime is established only if market participants are convinced that the authorities will not intervene, whatever the circumstances. Experience suggests that this can, on occasion, become a difficult policy to sustain.

If currency traders and in particular financial markets do not find the current policies of a Government credible and so believe that they will be abandoned, an attack on the currency becomes probable. Some argue that the corner solutions to exchange-rate regimes might be less vulnerable to an attack because they are more transparent and verifiable and their credibility is correspondingly larger.[53] In theory, corner solutions can be more easily verified by market participants as they can determine whether the value of a currency has changed in the case of a fixed parity, and whether the reserves of the central bank have been used to intervene in currency markets, in case of a float. Intermediate regimes are thus supposedly less transparent and therefore less credible. In contrast to the theory, some have argued that Governments prefer the lack of

[48] See, for example, Edwards, loc. cit., pp. 898-899; and Jeffrey Frankel, Sergio Schmukler and Luis Servén, "Verifiability and the Vanishing Intermediate Exchange Rate Regime", *NBER Working Paper*, No. 7901 (Cambridge, Massachusetts, National Bureau of Economic Research, September 2000).

[49] See Guillermo A. Calvo and Carmen M. Reinhart, "Fear of floating", mimeo, University of Maryland, retrieved from http://www.bsos.umd.edu/econ/ciecrp11.pdf, on 7 March 2001; and also Carmen M. Reinhart, "The mirage of floating exchange rates", *The American Economic Review*, vol. 90, No. 2 (May 2000), pp. 65-70.

[50] See, for example, Roberto Chang and Andrés Velasco, "Exchange-rate policy for developing countries", *The American Economic Review*, vol. 90, No. 2 (May 2000), pp. 71-75.

[51] See Goldstein, Kaminsky and Reinhart, op. cit.

[52] Few—if any—empirical studies of banking crises include the exchange-rate regime as a predictor.

[53] See, for example, Edwards, loc. cit., pp. 898-899; and Frankel, Schmukler and Servén, loc. cit.

transparency because it allows them to "act without the threat of informed criticism. They surely find life easier when there are no public benchmarks that can indicate failure".[54]

Many developing countries, however, find it hard to establish the level of credibility that is needed to reduce the volatility that would accompany a freely floating exchange rate. Floating exchange rates are particularly volatile in developing countries because these countries are more vulnerable to external shocks, as their currency markets are usually thin and capital flows, even if relatively small, have large effects on exchange rates. Developing countries usually prefer some exchange-rate stability for several reasons. First, it reduces uncertainty and encourages long-term investment. Moreover, preventing exchange-rate appreciation as a result of capital inflows maintains the competitiveness of exports and discourages further inflows in anticipation of a further appreciation. The inflows can also cause financial difficulties if a large proportion of private or public debt is denominated in foreign currency. Indeed, exchange-rate stability provides a nominal anchor against inflation. On the other hand, freely floating exchange rates have been advocated because the uncertainty they embody discourages short-term speculative capital flows.

In sum, choosing an exchange-rate regime is a balancing act, involving trade-offs between internal and external economic objectives and between credibility and flexibility. No single exchange-rate regime can satisfy all objectives at all times. The particular regime best suited for a country depends on the prevailing economic and political circumstances. For example, a peg regime might be the proper one for countries that have suffered from high and chronic inflation because credibility in domestic policy is low. For most developing countries, intermediate regimes, in combination with some capital controls, have advantages because they provide both some stability and some flexibility while avoiding the rigorous demands on credibility required for corner solutions.

Capital controls

It is generally recommended that domestic financial liberalization should commence only after macroeconomic stability has been established. Moreover, it was commonly accepted that external financial liberalization should be carried out at the end of the economic reform sequence, if it is to be pursued at all. Liberalization of international financial flows did not become a major policy concern until the mid-1990s when private capital flows to developing countries were surging.[55] IMF started to advocate that it should be given jurisdiction over the convertibility of the capital account of the balance of payments, which—in contrast to current-account convertibility—is not part of IMF's Articles of Agreement. However, the financial crises at the end of the 1990s caused this goal to be put on hold.

Capital flows from abroad, especially short-term flows, have been an important contributing factor in the financial crises of the 1990s. Capital controls can play a role in the prevention of a financial crisis, particularly during the transition period when supervisory and regulatory institutions or macroeconomic stability is still inadequate. Controls on short-term capital inflows are particularly important. They can dampen excessive inflows and prevent the overheating of an economy that puts macroeconomic policy to the test. Moreover, if

54   See John Williamson, "Exchange rate policy in Latin America: the costs of the conventional wisdom", paper presented at a conference entitled "A broad agenda of crisis prevention and response: addressing global economic imbalances in the north and boom-bust cycles in the south", organized by the Forum on Debt and Development, Santiago de Chile, 1 and 2 March 2001.

55   See, for example, Barry Herman and Barbara Stallings, "International finance and the developing countries: liberalization, crisis and the Reform Agenda", in *Global Financial Turmoil and Reform: A United Nations Perspective ...*, pp. 11-27.

they curtail the inflows, capital controls can reduce the rush to the exit when confidence changes. It has been argued that controls on outflows are harder to implement, especially when the crisis is already unfolding because they can be circumvented more easily. Nevertheless, Malaysia has made rather effective use of them.[56] Capital controls have also had success in several other countries. Chile imposed reserve requirements on foreign loans and foreign-owned deposits of short maturity, which lengthened the maturity of capital inflows. Brazil and Colombia have taxed short-term inflows and Colombia has imposed minimum stay periods for FDI. China's capital account is not convertible and India has used capital controls. It is thought that these controls on the capital account contributed to the fact that these countries were relatively insulated from contagion resulting from the East Asian crises.

Liquidity, the lender of last resort and the problem of moral hazard

Providing liquidity to the economy, or to particular financial institutions, has always been an important step in preventing and mitigating a financial crisis. If a country or a bank develops payment problems, or is perceived to have such problems, an infusion of liquidity can prevent or stop a run-out of the currency or on the deposits of the bank. The fundamental reason for providing a lender of last resort is to reduce "systemic risk", that is to say, the risk of a financial crisis to the economy (or society) as a whole, which is larger than the sum of the risks that each individual participant faces as a result of the external effects of a crisis.

The crucial questions for a lender of last resort are by whom, when, how much, to whom and at what rate.[57] These questions have been hotly debated for centuries. According to Walter Bagehot, the first editor of *The Economist*, liquidity should be provided seldom, at a penalty rate on sound collateral to illiquid but solvent institutions and in as great a quantity as the public asks for. The distinction between illiquid and insolvent institutions is not always easy to make but asking for sound collateral is a starting point.[58] The penalty rate should discourage borrowing by healthy institutions and reduce the risk of moral hazard. Overall, therefore, it can be argued that the lender of last resort should provide as much liquidity as is demanded by illiquid but solvent institutions at a penalty rate.

This answers the questions only partly. Providing liquidity in case of a (pending) crisis is more an art than a science, particularly with regard to timing. Too little, too late, which will worsen the crisis, and too much, too early, which will exacerbate moral hazard, are both indications of failure. After a crash, one has to find a balance between waiting for some time to let insolvent institutions fail and waiting so long that solvent ones also fail.

When transactions and debts are in the local currency, the central bank is usually the lender of last resort, but not necessarily. Private firms (coordinated, for example, by J.P. Morgan in 1907 in the United States) have also supplied liquidity. When some of the liabilities are in a foreign currency, the central bank can play a crucial role in a liquidity crisis because it can disburse foreign reserves for emergencies and should be able to borrow abroad more easily than private firms.

[56] See, for example, UNCTAD, *Trade and Development Report, 2000* (United Nations publication, Sales No. E.00.II.D.19), box 4.1.

[57] See, for example, Charles P Kindleberger, *Manias, Panics and Crashes: A History of Financial Crises* (New York, John Wiley and Sons, Inc., 2000); and Stanley Fischer, "On the need for an international lender of last resort", *Essays in International Finance*, No. 220 (Princeton, New Jersey, Princeton University, November 2000).

[58] This distinction is even harder in the case of countries. Technically, countries cannot go bankrupt. Yet, Mexico in 1995 and the Republic of Korea in 1997 constituted clear cases of illiquidity, as the quick repayment of emergency financing showed. See, for example, Manmohan S. Kumar, Paul Masson and Marcus Miller, "Global Financial Crises: Institutions and incentives", *IMF Working Paper*, No. WP/00/105 (Washington, D.C., International Monetary Fund, June 2000) . The IMF Articles of Agreement allow IMF to ask for collateral, but in practice it has rarely done so. See Fischer "On the need for an international lender of last resort" ..., p. 26.

[59] See, for example, Graham Bird, "Crisis averter, crisis lender, crisis manager: the IMF in search of a systemic role", *The World Economy,* vol. 22, No. 7 (September 1999), pp. 955-975.

[60] See, for example, Kenneth Rogoff, "International institutions for reducing global financial instability", *The Journal of Economic Perspectives,* vol. 13, No. 4 (fall 1999), pp. 21-42.

[61] See, for example, Fischer, "On the need for an international lender of last resort" …, p. 19.

[62] See, Articles of Agreement of IMF, article XVIII, sect. 1 (a).

[63] See, for example, Griffith-Jones and Ocampo, loc. cit.

[64] Risk-sharing is an important component of a strategy to reduce moral hazard. Someone with fire insurance who is responsible for part of the costs if his or her house burns down is supposedly more concerned about preventing a fire. Similarly, a private financial institution or firm that has to bear part of the burden in case of a crisis should act more prudently. Charging a high price for the funds provided under a rescue operation is one step. However, if the Government borrows from IMF at a penalty rate and uses the money to bail out the private sector, there is still a moral hazard problem regarding the behaviour of the private sector. It needs to share in the risk as well.

[65] See, for example, *World Economic and Social Survey, 1999...,* chap. IX, sects. entitled "The problem of moral hazard", and "'Involving the private sector' in crisis resolution".

Internationally, there is no clear-cut lender of last resort, but IMF comes closest to filling the role.[59] Central banks (often coordinated by BIS), other institutions and groups of (mostly developed) countries have also played that role, or acted in unison. Yet, there are several shortcomings to the current system entailing questions of sufficient resources, biases against (certain) developing countries, transparency and equity.[60]

The need for an international lender of last resort has increased in recent years because of the volatility of capital flows and the possibility of contagion of financial crises. An international lender of last resort is also critical for countries where a domestic one is absent or ineffective, either by choice (in the case of a currency board) or in practice (in the case of a small, highly open economy). The adequacy of IMF's resources should be judged in relation to these needs. Compared with the size of the world economy, or even with the potential borrower base, the quotas of IMF have declined since its inception in 1945.[61] As of 20 June 2000, quotas amounted to only some $300 billion, including weaker currencies which in practice cannot be lent. IMF has access to additional resources under the General Arrangements to Borrow, created in 1962, and the New Arrangements to Borrow, created in 1997. Moreover, IMF could reinvigorate the special drawing rights (SDRs), which were created in 1967. SDRs can be allocated, after an 85 per cent majority decision, "to meet the long-term global need, as and when it arises, to supplement existing reserve assets".[62] This possibility, however, has been rarely used. SDRs are the closest IMF can come to creating money, in parallel to a central bank in a domestic situation of lender of last resort. SDRs, however, cannot be created quickly enough in case of an emergency. Questions remain whether IMF has sufficient resources, whether the existing facilities adequately address the need for emergency funding, and whether they can be disbursed quickly enough to stem a crisis, particularly when conditions are attached.[63]

The answers to the questions posed above attempt to moderate the problem of moral hazard. If financial market participants know that liquidity will be forthcoming when they face payments problems, will they act irresponsibly? Moral hazard can never be totally avoided, but with proper incentives it can be reduced. Two strategies are usually employed: risk-sharing and regulation.[64]

The involvement of the private sector in the resolution of a financial crisis has gained momentum since the Asian crisis. During the 1990s, large amounts of internationally provided public funds were used to bail out private sector participants, foreign and domestic. This has raised issues of fairness in as much as equity investors incurred greater losses than banks and the rich benefited from these bail-outs more than the poor.[65] Private sector involvement is also critical because of a collective action problem. When a crisis seems likely, each creditor has an incentive to immediately attempt to cash outstanding credits with the threatened party; if all creditors do so, the debtor is unlikely to be able to meet all demands and all creditors will lose. On the other hand, if creditors jointly agree to roll over the loans, while an adjustment programme is implemented, each creditor will recover a much larger share of its loan. An agreement among creditors can be facilitated by international agencies. A similar result can be reached by including a clause about rescheduling and a stay of payments in bonds and other contracts. Other proposals in this area include arrangements that would, to all intents and purposes, declare a country bankrupt to protect it against creditors.

The second component of a strategy to minimize moral hazard is prudential regulation and supervision (see above). The creation of a safety net for the financial sector without supervision and prudential regulation is likely to encourage risky behaviour.

CONCLUSION

In the aftermath of the Asian crisis, a broad consensus quickly developed on the need to reduce excessive instability in international economic and financial activity. By the end of the decade, there was agreement on broad policy goals with respect to doing so, including a sound and stable macroeconomic environment and well-functioning and robust financial systems in both capital exporting and capital importing countries. There has also been considerable agreement on many of the elements needed to achieve these goals. Moreover, as argued above, many of the general conclusions reached over the last years are being turned into concrete policies and practices. This means not that there are no disputes, but rather that policy makers around the world are operating largely from a common assessment of what policies to implement in several areas. The major international financial institutions have also been rethinking how best to assist countries in this regard.

Despite significant progress in strengthening international economic and financial stability, there is no room for complacency. The recent crisis episodes in Argentina and Turkey are a powerful reminder that much more needs to be done, and that there still remain important gaps and asymmetries in the process of international financial reform. These asymmetries include (but are not limited to) the limited participation of developing countries in the decision-making for a new financial architecture, inadequate international regulation of private capital flows, and slow progress in exploring more effective ways of achieving international provision of official liquidity to control crises within countries and to prevent their spreading to other countries. Also, in the discussions on the design of a new international financial architecture, the highly important issues of appropriate external financing for low-income countries have been largely neglected.

Correction of these and other asymmetries requires complementary and enhanced exchanges among all the parties concerned. Here one of the outstanding issues is how to better integrate the views and needs of all countries into the process for further elaboration of a new international financial system that is responsive to the priorities of growth and development and to the promotion of economic and social equity. The United Nations should be among those actors that bring their own perspective to identifying emerging issues and policy gaps. It is playing a major role in convening and facilitating policy dialogue and consensus-building on global economic, financial and development problems among the relevant stakeholders. The International Conference on Financing for Development to be held in Monterrey, Mexico, in March 2002 will furnish one opportunity for the Organization to fulfil that role.

V TRADE AND VULNERABILITY

In recent years, it has frequently been maintained that the increasing globalization of the world economy has had a negative impact on its less well off members, especially the poorer developing countries and the economies in transition. It is pointed out that many of these countries have simply been excluded from the various benefits of globalization. Moreover, it is argued that poorer economies are rendered more vulnerable owing to their increased exposure to the fluctuations and vacillations of an increasingly open global economy.

The present chapter will discuss the question of vulnerability from the perspective of trade. There are two dimensions to this issue. First, trade is critical to development via its potential impact on growth, which is fundamental in overcoming vulnerability and poverty. Most, if not all, studies show a high positive impact of trade on economic growth. Trade is thus well positioned to be part of the solution, providing a mechanism whereby countries may grow and flourish, thereby reducing vulnerability.

Indeed, trade is one of the means whereby countries can link themselves to the world economy as part of the ongoing process of globalization. Critics of globalization contend, however, that, far from being part of the solution, trade may be part of the problem. Such detractors argue that the exogenous trade shocks to which small, open economies are exposed are inherently destabilizing, rendering countries more vulnerable than they otherwise would be. They further maintain that volatile world prices for primary commodities constitute a significant source of uncertainty and risk for many countries, especially the low-income economies, with a less diversified export base, that depend on such products for export revenue. These arguments embody the second dimension of the issue of trade and vulnerability.

That countries—and even population groups *within* countries—have not shared equally in the fruits of globalization is beyond a doubt. More contentious, however, is the extent to which international trade helps poorer countries to overcome their poverty and whether increasing trade is reducing or exacerbating their vulnerability.

This chapter will begin by addressing the role of trade as a response to vulnerability via its impact on economic growth. To this end, it briefly examines the recent growth of world trade and the universality of participation in this expansion. The chapter then assesses one aspect of the current backlash against globalization. This has taken place under the guise of attempts to discredit the trade-to-growth paradigm. The second part of

1   Mike Moore, Director-General of the World Trade Organization, "Open societies, freedom, development and trade", Plenary Opening of the World Trade Organization Symposium on Gender Issues Confronting the World Trading System, Geneva, 6 and 7 July 2001.

the chapter then turns to the shocks countries experience by virtue of their participation in the global trading system. The frequently maintained hypothesis in this regard is that poorer countries increase their vulnerability when they trade owing to their increased exposure to events beyond their control. Included here would be commodity price uncertainty and instability, currency devaluations by significant partners or competitors, and sudden shifts in capital inflows, as well as export market fluctuations and vacillations. The real issue, however, is not so much whether there is greater exposure since there are no real alternatives to being a fully participating member of the global economy. As the Director-General of the World Trade Organization recently pointed out, globalization "is a process, not a policy".[1] The concern, therefore, has to be what measures can be devised to minimize any problems that might ensue and to maximize potential benefits. The chapter concludes by looking at some such instruments and discussing policy considerations.

Most trade issues pertain to all developing countries. However, it is the poorest of the developing countries—the least developed—that warrant particular concern. Most of these countries have fared poorly as regards growth. Most have been marginalized as regards trade. The obstacles that they face in trying to integrate themselves into the world economy are of particular concern, therefore, as are the measures that could be taken to assist them in this endeavour. However, trade liberalization, though critical, is unlikely to be enough since these economies now face growing competition from freer markets and more successful developing countries. Thus, liberalized trade may be a necessary condition, but it is a far from sufficient one, for setting the least developed on the sustained growth paths that will enable them to integrate themselves into the global economy. In the presence of appropriate trade conditions and provisions, the decisive element will be their own policies in the coming decades.

THE GROWTH OF WORLD TRADE

Trade underwent a global boom during the entire second half of the twentieth century. The volume of world trade increased at an annual average rate of 6.2 per cent per annum between 1950 and 2000. Thus, it almost consistently outpaced the growth of world output, which grew about 3.8 per cent per year. Moreover, this trend actually escalated as of the 1980s. At least two questions present themselves here. First, why has this happened and, second, is this a global phenomenon or are only certain countries involved?

The phenomenon of expanding world trade—one of the linchpins of globalization—can be accounted for in a variety of ways, though no one explanation alone suffices to explain the vast expansion in international trade flows. Nevertheless, two factors that have played a huge role in motivating global trade are increasing liberalization and the great reductions in the costs of transport and communications.

Much as liberalization has driven trade, the eight rounds of multilateral trade negotiations, which took place post-Second World War and whose culmination was the Uruguay Round of multilateral trade negotiations, have driven liberalization. Though this has proceeded at differing speeds in different economies, the commitment to increased liberalization is now almost universal. The fact that the average tariff level declined from about 40 per cent in the late 1940s when the General Agreement on Tariffs and Trade (GATT) was established to under 6 per cent in the 1990s has played a role in increasing trade.[2] This trend towards greater openness will be discussed below.

The other key element in increasing trade stems from the declining costs of transport and communications. In recent years, average revenue per mile in air transport has fallen dramatically, as has the cost of a three-minute telephone call or electronic message between London and New York. Meanwhile, the unit cost of sea freight fell some 70 per cent in real terms between the beginning of the 1980s and 1996, making it far easier and cheaper to ship goods worldwide.[3] This sharp decline in the cost of shipping has been driven by at least three trends. First, a number of technological innovations, broadly referred to as "containerization", have prompted rapid improvements in productivity with respect to the handling of cargo. Second, the transport industry has undergone a considerable amount of deregulation commencing in the mid-1970s. The upshot, and third development, has been a trend towards greater competition, which, in turn, induced greater productivity and lower costs. Not only have the boundaries between different modes of transport been broken down, but capacity has also grown dramatically. For example, in 1980, world containership fleets had a capacity of half a million 20-foot containers. By 1996, the equivalent figure was over 3 million.[4]

Granted that trade has been booming in the post-Second World War period, a second issue is the universality of this trend. One approach to this question is to look at growth in the value of world merchandise trade by region (see table V.1).

Over the past half-century, the shares of North America and Latin America in world merchandise exports have declined, as has the share of Africa. Western Europe and Asia—most particularly China, Japan and the so-called Asian tigers—exemplify the countervailing trend, with shares that have risen dramatically. The fact remains, however, that Africa's share has declined most drastically. Indeed, in the past 25 years, only two regions have registered significant

[2] World Trade Organization, *The World Trade Organization* (Geneva, Information and Media Relations Division, 1995).

[3] *The Financial Times*, 1 October 1997.

[4] For further details, see *The Economist*, 15 November 1997, pp. 85-86.

Table V.1.
SHARE OF WORLD MERCHANDISE EXPORTS BY REGION,
1948, 1973 AND 2000

Percentage			
	1948	1973	2000
World	100	100	100
North America	27.5	17.2	17.1
Latin America	12.3	4.7	5.8
Western Europe	31.0	44.8	39.3
Transition economies	6.0	8.9	4.4
Africa	7.4	4.8	2.4
Middle East	2.1	4.5	4.3
Asia	13.8	15.0	26.7
China	0.9	1.0	4.0
Japan	0.4	6.4	7.7

Source: World Trade Organization, *Annual Report, 2001* (Geneva, 2001), p. 12, table II.2, and *Annual Report, 1998: International Trade Statistics* (Geneva, 1998), p. 12, table II.2.

declines in their trade shares: the transition economies (which are still recovering from the changes of the early 1990s) and Africa. Indeed, Africa's share has declined steadily since 1948.

It is thus clear why so much attention is now focused on Africa as regards trade marginalization. Over the past decade, Africa has lagged well behind the world average on the export front, with annual percentage change of only 3.4 per cent between 1990 and 2000, compared with a global average of 6 per cent. As a result, outside of the oil-exporters, there was not a single African country among the set of the leading exporters in world merchandise trade in 2000, this despite the fact that there were several other developing countries belonging to the set—including, for example, China in seventh place, as well as the Republic of Korea, Taiwan Province of China, Singapore, Malaysia, Thailand, Indonesia and Brazil.[5]

THE TRADE-GROWTH RELATIONSHIP

The benefits of liberalization, in terms of growth, have long been established. An open trade regime has the capacity to increase welfare and income in a variety of ways. As accepted as these tenets are, a number of concerns have emerged with regard to them. One empirical source of doubt is that attempts to estimate the impact on gross domestic product (GDP) have traditionally come up with very small numbers. From a theoretical perspective, another source of doubt is that the welfare effect of improved resource allocation is a one-time event. It thus may lead to a higher *level* of income, but not to sustained long-term growth (though there will be short-run growth as an economy moves to a higher income level).

Because of such concerns, extensive efforts have been undertaken to document the trade-growth relationship. By now, extensive empirical research exists showing that growth prospects, over very long periods of time, are greatly enhanced by trade openness, a finding that fits in neatly with the current focus on fully participatory globalization. For instance, one estimate of the tariff changes that five developing countries had been undertaking as part of their Uruguay Round commitments, found that a significant welfare gain could be realized.[6] An oft-cited cross-country study, which analysed how openness related to economic performance, found that "open" economies had grown at an annual average rate of 4.5 per cent over the 1970s and 1980s, while the closed economies in the sample grew at an average annual rate of only 0.7 per cent.[7] Regressions in this cross-country study further showed that open economies had adjusted more rapidly than closed economies to making the shift from being primary-intensive to being manufactures-intensive exporters. They also showed that closed economies had been *more* vulnerable to financial or inflation crises than were open economies. Of 13 economies that had been open throughout the 1970s, only 1 succumbed to such a crisis, while 57 of 70 developing countries that had been closed throughout the same period experienced crises.

However, such cross-country regression research has, of late, encountered criticism of sorts, bringing into question the conclusions of such analyses. This has, in turn, provided some ammunition for the current backlash against the process of globalization.[8] One such criticism is that there is a lack of conclusive evidence as to the direction of causality between openness and growth. A

5 See World Trade Organization, *Annual Report, 2001* (Geneva, 2001), p. 14, table II.3.

6 Thomas F. Rutherford and David G. Tarr, "Trade Liberalization and Endogenous Growth in a Small Open Economy: A Quantitative Assessment", *World Bank Policy Research Working Paper*, No.1970 (Washington, D.C., May 1998). The authors' estimates were based on an endogenous growth model.

7 Jeffrey D. Sachs and Andrew Warner, "Economic Reform and the Process of Global Integration", *Brookings Papers on Economic Activity*, No. 1 (Washington, D.C., 1995), pp. 1-95.

8 See, for example, Francisco Rodriguez and Dani Rodrik, *Trade Policy and Economic Growth: A Skeptic's Guide to the Cross National Evidence*, NBER Working Paper No. 7081 (Cambridge, Massachusetts, April 1999).

further shortcoming is said to be the fact that many of the openness measures, or proxies, used to test the openness-growth relationship do not solely reflect trade phenomena, but other policy variables that are actually more macroeconomic in nature as well. Also, the point is made that the results of studies assessing the effects of openness on economic growth are extremely sensitive to the choice of time period and/or sample countries. While these arguments have been resuscitated in the past few years, they are, in fact, not at all new. The shortcomings of such cross-country analyses were recognized more than a decade ago.[9]

Irrespective of the merits of cross-national analysis of this sort (and there appears to be general agreement that it is a clumsy tool at best), there remains the more important issue of the channels through which openness affects growth. Several such conduits are customarily highlighted.[10] First, by bringing incentives closer to international opportunity costs, liberalization promotes an optimum allocation of resources in production, reorienting resources to areas of comparative advantage. Second, optimality in consumption is also encouraged. Third, the incentive to engage in income-generating, but unproductive, activities associated with protection—such as smuggling, lobbying and tariff evasion—is minimized.[11] In addition, openness can affect both the level and the efficiency of investment. For example, an open regime can increase market size, thereby leading to investment in industries with increasing returns that would not have been viable if constrained by a smaller market. Openness also allows access to capital goods that might otherwise have been unavailable or too expensive, hence removing some structural constraints on investment and production. Moreover, openness may increase the efficiency of investment, minimizing the probability of an immiserizing outcome in the recipient.[12] Empirical research, looking at 57 countries between 1970-1989 and decomposing the effects of trade openness on growth, has suggested that increased investment may be the most important.[13] Finally, there may be a number of so-called grey area dynamic effects, which are intrinsically difficult to measure. Greater openness may encourage more innovation, for example, and greater X-efficiency, which is the production of output at the lowest possible cost.

A ROUTE OUT OF POVERTY: IMPROVING MARKET ACCESS FOR THE LEAST DEVELOPED COUNTRIES

The advantages of openness—as well as the success of many export-oriented economies—explain why the policy has so many proponents. The need to encourage the pursuit of such a policy in turn necessitates ensuring easy market access. This is especially essential for the poorest economies.

Developed-country tariffs and preferences

Organisation for Economic Cooperation and Development (OECD) markets serve as a major outlet for exports of least developed countries. In 1998, those markets accounted for 64 per cent of the latter's total exports. The highest rates of duty levied by developed countries on exports of least developed countries apply to manufactures. For example, these can be as high as 14 per cent (excluding preferences) and 9.9 per cent (including preferences) for

[9] See Jagdish N. Bhagwati, "Export-promoting trade strategy: issues and evidence", *World Bank Research Observer*, vol. 3, No. 1 (1988), pp. 27-57.

[10] For more details, see T. N. Srinivasan and Jagdish Bhagwati, "Outward-orientation and development: are revisionists right?", Yale University, New Haven, Connecticut, Economic Growth Center, Discussion Paper No. 806, September 1999.

[11] See Jagdish Bagwati, "Directly-Unproductive, Profit-Seeking (DUP) Activities", *Journal of Political Economy*, vol. 90, No. 5, October 1982, pp. 988-1002.

[12] See Jagdish Bhagwati, "The theory of immiserizing growth: further applications", in *International Trade and Money*, M. Connolly and A. Swoboda, eds. (Toronto, University of Toronto Press, 1973).

[13] Romain Wacziarg, "Measuring the Dynamic Gains from Trade", *World Bank Policy Research Paper*, No.2001 (Washington, D.C., May 1998).

14 For details, see World Trade Organization, "Market Access for the Least-Developed Countries: Where Are the Obstacles?" (WT/LDC/HL/19), paper prepared by the OECD secretariat, 21 October 1997. The share of exports of least developed countries directed to developed-country markets increased marginally from under 64 to almost 67 per cent between 1995 and 1998. (See United Nations Conference on Trade and Development (UNCTAD), *The Least Developed Countries: 1997 Report* (United Nations publication, Sales No. E.97.II.D.6); and *The Least Developed Countries: 2000 Report* (United Nations publication, Sales No. E.00.II.D.21).

15 See *Legal Instruments Embodying the Results of the Uruguay Round of Multilateral Trade Negotiations, done at Marrakesh on 15 April 1994* (GATT secretariat publication, Sales No. GATT/1994-7).

16 Azita Amjadi and Alexander Yeats, "Nontariff Barriers Africa Faces: What Did the Uruguay Round Accomplish and What Remains to be Done?", *World Bank Policy Research Working Paper*, No. 1439 (Washington, D.C., March 1995).

17 Duties on fresh bananas will be reduced by 20 per cent annually commencing 1 January 2002 and eliminated at the latest at the beginning of 2006. Duties on rice will be reduced by 20 per cent on 1 September 2006 and by 50 per cent on 1 September 2008 and totally eliminated a year later. Duties on sugar will be reduced by 20 per cent on 1 July 2006, by 50 per cent on 1 July 2007 and by 80 per cent on 1 July 2008 and totally eliminated at the latest a year later. See Michael Finger of the World Bank, cited in *Washington Trade Daily*, vol. 10, No. 42 (27 February 2001).

18 *The Washington Post*, 28 February 2001, p. E1.

19 See UNCTAD and Commonwealth Secretariat, *Duty and Quota Free Market Access for LDCs: An Analysis of Quad Initiatives* (London and Geneva, 2001), p. xvii and chap. III.

Bangladesh and 18.1 per cent (excluding preferences) and 11.7 per cent (including preferences) for Maldives. Such relatively high rates are explained by the fact that the majority of least developed countries in the sample of those that export manufactures have recorded a concentration of manufactured exports in the Multi-Fibre Arrangement-dominated textiles and clothing sectors. This does not hold for countries such as the Democratic Republic of the Congo and Zambia, whose exports of manufactures consist of processed forms of copper and other inputs into industrial production, rather than textiles and clothing. Consequently, these countries face far lower tariffs on their manufactured exports. Overall, nearly all exports of the fuels, forestry, minerals and mining sectors from least developed countries to developed markets enter duty-free or virtually so.

Exports of least developed countries into developed markets are also aided by a variety of preference schemes, although a number of studies that have measured statistically the trade effects of such European Union (EU) schemes as the Generalized System of Preferences (GSP) suggest that they have had only limited success in generating significant export growth or improving the trade shares of beneficiaries.[14] Nevertheless, least developed country beneficiaries of preferences under such arrangements as GSP, the Lomé Convention and the Caribbean Basin Initiative have expressed concerns that multilateral liberalization might harm them via preference erosion. A considerable loss in preference margins will have occurred in Quad (Canada, EU, Japan and the United States of America) markets once all of the Uruguay Round agreements[15] have been fully implemented. Much empirical work, however, suggests that the losses due to preference erosion are in many cases more than outweighed by multilateral liberalization, though there may still be problems of adjustment. It is apparent, for example, that as preferences are rolled back, and as liberalization increasingly takes hold, countries will face more vigorous international competition. Whether they can develop or maintain viable export sectors will be contingent on their achieving reforms aimed, for example, at cost competitiveness.[16]

EU took a further step to provide special trade treatment for the poorest developing countries when, on 28 February 2001, it rescinded quotas and duties on all products except military weapons from least developed countries—termed the "Everything but Arms" initiative. However, full liberalization of sugar, rice and bananas is subject to a transition period.[17] To compensate for the delay in full liberalization, EU has offered immediate market access to the least developed countries through duty-free quotas for sugar and rice, based initially on previous shipments from these countries during the 1990s, plus 15 per cent. EU intends to monitor imports of these three commodities and apply safeguard measures, if necessary, to prevent surges. There will also be strict monitoring to verify rules of origin as well as potential circumvention. According to one estimate, these EU measures, once fully phased in, would increase exports by the poorest nations to EU by from 15 to 20 per cent.[18]

The impact of this initiative, according to other recent estimates, however, will be only a small increase in exports from least developed countries. The benefits to least developed countries would be far greater if Canada, Japan and the United States followed the lead of EU.[19]

Developing-country markets

Since almost one third of exports of least developed countries are directed to *developing*-country markets[20], the latter's market access conditions—as measured by tariff rates that apply to products of export interest to least developed countries—are of particular concern. Overall applied rates on the current exports of least developed countries continue to be higher in developing countries and transition economies than in developed countries. This is true in all sectors: agriculture, as well as fisheries, fuels, forestry, minerals and mining, and manufactures. Cameroon, for example, faces developed market tariffs on agriculture of between 13.9 and 0.0 per cent (excluding and including preferences, respectively), compared with comparable developing market tariffs of between 19.1 and 17.7 per cent. As regards exports of manufactures, developing-country rates are often substantially higher. For example, Bangladesh faces rates of between 14.0 and 9.9 per cent in developed countries as compared with a rate of 23.7 per cent in other developing countries.[21]

The possibility of creating preferential trading schemes among least developed countries has been put forward as a means of expanding their markets and introducing economies of scale in production. The logic here is that as such countries expand their imports, and given their generally higher trade barriers, they may offer each other a promising avenue for least developed countries export growth. The issue is whether such groupings of least developed countries, with similar comparatives advantages, would be a viable proposition—at least from the perspective of the traditional costs and benefits of trade integration.[22]

Overall, however, barriers to export growth currently hinge to a very great extent on the policies and supply capabilities of the least developed countries and not just on market access problems. For example, it has been maintained that, in the sub-Saharan African countries, too high a proportion of foreign exchange earnings—earnings that should be invested in building productive capacity and transportation infrastructure—pays for Africa's high export transport costs. Such high costs, especially for processed products, often place African exporters at a competitive disadvantage. Not only do African countries use a far larger share of their foreign exchange earnings to pay for international transport services compared with other developing countries, but the relative importance of these payments has been increasing. In 1970, for example, net freight payments to foreign nationals absorbed 11 per cent of Africa's export earnings. By 1990, that ratio had increased to 15 per cent, compared with about 6 per cent for developing countries as a whole. For 10 landlocked African countries (Burkina Faso, the Central African Republic, Chad, Ethiopia, Malawi, Mali, the Niger, Uganda, Zambia and Zimbabwe), the 1990 figure averaged 42 per cent. These high transport costs are at least partially attributable to ill-advised Government polices. Evidence suggests that anti-competitive cargo reservation policies adopted by most African Governments have had an important adverse influence on freight costs, producing high "rents" for lines that have been shielded from the effects of competition. Similarly, the failure to maintain or improve transport infrastructure has also played a role.[23] It has been argued that these policy concerns far outweigh the role of OECD tariff and non-tariff barriers in accounting for Africa's poor trade performance.[24]

20 *The Least Developed Countries: 2000 Report ...,* annex, table 17.

21 World Trade Organization, Subcommittee on Least Developed Countries, "Market access for least developed countries WTO members" (WT/COMTD/LDC/W/17), 25 January 2000.

22 It has been noted, for example, that Africa's non-oil exports are highly concentrated in a very few products – none of which are important in regional imports. Sub-Saharan African countries appear to have relatively little to trade with each other. Furthermore, African trade is also highly concentrated within subregional geographical groups, with almost no trade occurring between East and West Africa. This finding makes the arguments that regional trade can help overcome problems associated with small domestic markets less compelling. See Alexander J. Yeats, "What Can Be Expected from African Regional Trade Arrangements? Some Empirical Evidence", *World Bank Policy Research Working Paper*, No. 2004 (November 1998).

23 Azita Amjadi and Alexander J. Yeats, "Have Transport Costs Contributed to the Relative Decline of Sub-Saharan African Exports? Some Preliminary Empirical Evidence", *World Bank Policy Research Working Paper*, No. 1559 (Washington, D.C., December 1995).

24 Azita Amjadi, U. Reinke and A. Yeats, "Did External Barriers Cause the Marginalization of Sub-Saharan Africa in World Trade?", *World Bank Policy Research Working Paper*, No. 1586 (Washington, D.C., March 1996).

THE DILEMMA OF EXPORT INSTABILITY, UNCERTAINTY AND SHOCKS

All countries that trade internationally are subject to trade shocks. Trade shocks may be defined as sudden, large and unexpected shifts, or fluctuations, in the value or volume of an economy's exports or imports. The quadrupling of oil prices in 1973 has perhaps embedded the notion of price variability in the public consciousness forever. Shocks in the international marketplace, however, can also occur in *volume* terms. The latter situation occurs either when an importer's supply of a product is suddenly cut off or, conversely, when a country is cut off from an established export market. An example of such a sudden shock was the imposition by the United States of a temporary ban, in mid-March 2001, on imports of all animals and animal products from EU because of indications of highly contagious foot-and-mouth disease in the region. Many trade shocks are thus country-specific and all trading economies—developed and developing, as well as those in transition—can be hit by a trade shock. Moreover, while a great deal of the literature on trade shocks has focused on primary commodities, the reality is that all exports—manufactures, as well as oil and non-oil primary commodities—are subject to sudden, unexpected fluctuations. Such oscillations, in short, are inevitable and normal, though they have come to be regarded, for a variety of reasons, as highly undesirable. The difficulty lies in determining an appropriate policy response.

Tariff and non-tariff barriers

As noted, declines in tariff and non-tariff barriers to trade, the mainstays of commercial policy, go a long way towards explaining recent trade growth.[25] Thus, tariff averages have fallen in a substantial number of developed and developing economies, as well as in a number of economies in transition, in the wake of the Uruguay Round of multilateral trade negotiations. Bound tariff rates have been reduced in all country groups. Two caveats are in order, however. The first qualification is that rates in developing countries continue to be almost 3 and 2 times the averages for the developed and the transition economies, respectively—and, as agreed in the Uruguay Round, they have fallen relatively less than tariff rates in the latter two groups (see table V.2). The significance of this lies in the fact that some 40 per cent of developing-country exports are directed to other developing countries. The second qualification is that tariff levels may not be where the vulnerability story lies. To the contrary, lower tariff levels have enabled countries to expand their trade, with all the advantages this brings in terms of increased growth and income. Moreover, tariffs seldom change abruptly. Therefore, while existing tariffs may constitute an obstacle to further increases in trade, they seldom create trade shocks.

Rather, from the perspective of shocks and vulnerability, the bigger issue at the present time may be non-tariff barriers to trade (NTBs). Such instruments, which include import quotas and voluntary export constraints, generally impede competition, sometimes at substantial costs in terms of economic efficiency and welfare. Moreover, they generate considerable trade tensions because of their ability to cut exporters off, often abruptly, from existing markets.

The success that has been achieved in reducing tariff barriers has raised the

[25] See, for example, Jagdish Bhagwati, *Protectionism* (Cambridge, Massachusetts, The MIT Press 1988).

Table V.2.
TRADE-WEIGHTED TARIFF AVERAGES, PRE- AND POST-URUGUAY ROUND

Percentage		
Grouping	Pre-Uruguay	Post-Uruguay
Developed economies	6.3	3.9
Developing economies	15.3	12.3
Transition economies	8.6	6.0

Source: GATT, as cited in OECD, "Trade and competition: frictions after the Uruguay Round, International Trade and Investment Division, Economics Department Working Papers, No. 165 (Paris, 1996).

Note: This table refers to trade-weighted bound most-favoured-nation (MFN) tariff rates in percentage terms. These are often higher than actually levied tariffs. Moreover, the Uruguay Round converted some non-tariff barriers to trade (NTBs) to tariff equivalents (for the sake of greater transparency) and this, in some instances, raised the apparent levels of average bound tariff rates. The so-called bound MFN tariff rate, which is the highest rate of duty levied on a product permissible under the GATT/World Trade Organization, differs from the applied MFN rate, which is the nominal tariff rate excluding preferential rates and exemptions.

The MFN principle requires that every privilege or concession granted by one contracting party to GATT/ World Trade Organization to a product of another contracting party be unconditionally granted to the like product of all other contracting parties. There are three important exceptions to the MFN principle that can be exploited by contracting parties - namely, customs unions, free trade areas and preferences to developing countries. Many OECD countries have introduced special preferences to developing countries. The Generalized System of Preferences (GSP) provides one mechanism for granting such preferences. Under the GSP, a developed country can grant non-reciprocal duty concessions to imports from developing countries. Each importer determines its own system, including product coverage and the volume of imports affected. For further details, see OECD, *Indicators of Tariff and Non-Tariff Trade Barriers* (Paris, 1996).

relative profile of NTBs. There are a large variety of such measures and these can essentially be separated into two broad categories. First, there are those NTBs that have a *direct* effect on importers' costs and prices. Customs surcharges, additional taxes and fees that discriminate against imports are included in this category, as are anti-dumping and countervailing actions and export price restraints.

The second broad group of NTBs, quantitative restrictions (QRs), include measures that involve quantity controls and thus have an *indirect* impact on import prices. QRs are designed to restrain the volume or value of imports of a particular commodity. The resulting scarcity tends, then, to raise the domestic price of this import, allowing domestic producers of import substitutes to charge higher prices than would have been possible in the absence of such restrictions.[26] Among the most frequently used QRs are import quotas, licensing schemes, prohibitions and "voluntary" export restraints (VERs). In the last case, an exporter "agrees" to curtail exports of a particular commodity to a specified level, either in value or in volume terms. Such arrangements may be formal agreements negotiated among Governments, or they may be unofficial. By the early 1990s, VERs, including those maintained under the Multi-Fibre Arrangement, had become a significant instrument of trade policy, particularly in EU and the United States. In 1992, for instance, OECD VERs encompassed almost 10 per cent of imports from developing countries. In particular cases, the trade coverage ratio was far higher, covering some 50, 60 and 30 per cent of textile yarn and fabric, clothing and footwear imports, respectively.[27]

[26] Until the early 1980s, it was customary in analytical discussions to argue that tariffs and quotas were equivalent in welfare terms. In other words, if a tariff were to be replaced by a quota equal to the import level associated with the tariff, the real outcome from a welfare angle would be identical. The only difference would be that, in the case of a tariff, the revenue would accrue to the Government, whereas in the case of an equivalent quota an equal amount of windfall premiums or "rents" would accrue to those receiving the import quotas. For a detailed exposition of this point, see Jagdish Bhagwati and T.N. Srinivasan, *Lectures on International Trade* (Cambridge, Massachusetts, The MIT Press, 1983), chap. 10. More recently, it has been suggested that they are not equivalent from a welfare perspective and that, in many - if not most - instances in the real (as opposed to theoretical) world, a quota will generally be more welfare-reducing that a tariff. One of the explanations for this is that quota schemes are hard to administer fairly. Those at the head of the queue reap windfall profits, while the fact that those handing them out may be tempted to share these profits is conducive to corruption.

[27] Patrick Low and Alexander Yeats, "Nontariff measures and developing countries: has the Uruguay Round levelled the playing field?", *The World Economy*, vol. 18, No. 1 (January 1995), pp. 51-68, table 2.

Despite some recent example of VERs, resort to quantitative restrictions has generally declined of late, thanks to the Uruguay Round negotiations. However, while the use of QRs has declined, interventions of other sorts have proliferated. Included here are anti-dumping (AD) and countervailing (CV) measures.

Moreover, developing countries have started to make greater use of trade remedies, such as anti-dumping actions. In part, this is explained by the fact that many young developing countries have patterned their trade regime laws on those of the United States.[28] As of mid-2000, 1,121 measures were in force, with Latin America accounting for about 217 of the total. As of the first half of 2000, developing countries accounted for roughly 32 per cent of the anti-dumping actions reported to the World Trade Organization. Argentina, for example, had 45 such measures in force, Brazil had 42 and Mexico had 80. However, Latin American economies were not the only ones using these measures. India, as of mid-2000, had 91 ADs in force, compared with 19 at the end of 1997.[29] There are no existing estimates of the costs such measures impose on targeted countries. However, extrapolation from work carried out as regards the Multi-Fibre Arrangement suggests that such instruments may generate substantial welfare losses for the targeted countries.[30]

Despite their drawbacks, ADs, CVs and even quotas are fairly transparent forms of NTBs. Thus, although it is not always easy to measure their impact on welfare—via their effects on prices, outputs and trade flows—it is not hard to detect their purpose. However, other forms of intervention, which are far less transparent, are gathering momentum. Included here would be many regulations pertaining to health, labour, safety and environmental standards. In many instances, these may constitute a subtle means whereby a Government can restrict trade. For example, inspection of imported fruits and vegetables is often perceived by the exporter as a means of keeping out imports, rather than as being part of an overall effort to boost food safety. Another example of such intervention is provided by a 1997 complaint filed under a relatively new trade law banning imports into the United States of goods produced by "abusive child labour". The complaint called for an investigation into hand-knotted carpets from India, Pakistan and Nepal.[31] In early 1998, a United States House of Representatives Committee on International Relations subcommittee approved legislation that would impose sanctions—including bans on Export-Import Bank of the United States financing as well as on Overseas Private Investment Corporation insurance—on countries and firms that did not prohibit child labour or ignored their own laws in this regard.[32] Yet another illustration is the complaint filed in 2000 by Australia and the United States against the Republic of Korea with regard to the latter's imports of fresh, chilled and frozen beef. The objection was to the fact that, in 1990, the Republic of Korea had established a "dual retail" system which required imported and domestic beef to be sold in separate stores or, in the case of large stores or supermarkets, in separate display areas.[33] Thus, many such regulations fall into a grey area, there being a fine line between imposing safety and health standards or ensuring consumer protection and simply resorting to this mechanism to restrict imports.

There was a marked rise in the number of trade disputes over standards brought to the World Trade Organization between 1995 and 2000. The majority centred on trade in agricultural products and obligations under the Agreement on the Application of Sanitary and Phytosanitary Measures (SPS).[34] Claims that

[28] Will Martin and Alan Winters, *The Uruguay Round and the Developing Countries* (Cambridge, United Kingdom, Cambridge University Press, 1996).

[29] World Trade Organization, Committee on Anti-Dumping Practices, document G/ADP/N/35/IND, 31 March 1998; and World Trade Organization, *Annual Report, 2001* ..., p. 65, table IV.5.

[30] Matthew J. Slaughter, "Protectionist Tendencies in the North and Vulnerable Economies in the South", *World Institute for Development Economics Research* (WIDER) *Working Papers*, No. 196 (UNU, September 2000).

[31] *Washington Trade Daily*, 6 November 1997.

[32] Ibid., 13 February 1998.

[33] World Trade Organization, *Annual Report, 2001* ..., pp. 76-77.

[34] The EU-United States dispute over hormone-treated beef fell under this rubric.

countries have violated provisions of the Agreement on Technical Barriers to Trade (TBT) have also increased since 1995. Included here are disputes over domestic regulations affecting process and production methods. As of the end of January 1999, the World Trade Organization Dispute Settlement Body had considered a number of disputes that referred either to the SPS or to the TBT Agreement. Though the majority of the complaints were from developed countries, a number of cases were brought by developing countries.[35]

In short, as is the case in many developed economies, the reduction in traditional trade barriers in many developing countries has coincided with pressures to resort to alternative measures to protect the affected import-competing producers. This has led to increased resort to anti-dumping or countervailing duty actions in many instances.

However, not all market "shocks" are due to the sudden imposition of *formal* trade barriers. Natural calamities—such as droughts, floods, crop blights, insects and diseases—all too frequently have sudden and unexpected consequences for a country's exports, as do changes in consumers' preferences. For example, a 1997 outbreak of hepatitis A in the United States, traced to Mexican strawberries, led United States authorities to temporarily ban imports, causing strawberry sales to the United States to plummet by between 75 and 80 per cent.[36] In 2000, potato farmers on Prince Edward Island in Canada, which accounts for one third of the country's potato production, found their entire potato crop in jeopardy when potato wart was found in a single field and their customary market, the United States, was abruptly cut off.[37]

Commodity price fluctuations and shocks

Sudden and unanticipated changes do not always occur in quantity terms, as in the cases of Mexican strawberries and Canadian potatoes mentioned above. Shocks may also occur via prices. Similarly, it is not only agricultural commodities that can be "shocked". One of the most spectacular examples was the dramatic fall, commencing in 1996, in the prices of some electronic and information equipment, particularly semiconductors. This drop in prices had dire consequences for several countries in Asia since electronic products account for large shares of the exports of Malaysia, the Philippines, the Republic of Korea, Singapore and Taiwan Province of China. For example, in the Republic of Korea, the unit value index for semiconductor exports, which had stood at 100 in 1995, dropped to 43 in 1996 and registered 13 in 2000. Such a shift has had a huge impact and entailed significant adjustment problems given the fact that semiconductor exports accounted for some 14 per cent of Korea's total exports in 1995.[38]

However, issues of adjustment are that much more significant and difficult for a poorer developing country. Because many of these countries tend to be heavily dependent on the export of one or two primary commodities, a major share of the academic and policy discussion on price shocks has focused on primary commodity prices.

The Prebisch-Singer hypothesis, which postulates a secular negative trend in the prices of internationally traded primary commodities vis-à-vis those of manufactured products, is one of the most intensively examined propositions in development economics.[39] Recent estimates, for example, suggest that pre-

[35] For details see Keith Maskus, J. Wilson and T. Otsuki, "Quantifying the Impact of Technical Barriers to Trade", *World Bank Policy Research Working Paper*, No. 2512 (Washington, D.C., December 2000).

[36] Sourcemex, 4 June 1997 (http://www.ladb.unm.edu).

[37] Canadian Broadcasting Company News, 26 April and 29 July 2001 (http://www.cbc.ca).

[38] Bank of Korea, *Monthly Statistical Bulletin*, May 2001.

[39] For details, see Hans W. Singer, "The Distribution of Gains Between Investing and Borrowing Countries", *American Economic Review*, Papers and Proceedings, vol. 40 (1950), pp. 473-485; and Raúl Prebisch, "The economic development of Latin America and its principal problems, mimeo, United Nations, 1950.

[40] Yael S. Hadass and Jeffrey G. Williamson, *Terms of Trade Shocks and Economic Performance 1870-1940: Prebisch and Singer Revisited*, NBER Working Paper, No. 8188 (Cambridge, Massachusetts, March 2001).

[41] Jacques Morisset, "Unfair Trade? Empirical Evidence in World Commodity Markets Over the Past 25 Years", *World Bank Policy Research Working Paper*, No. 1815 (Washington, D.C., August 1997). The author's hypothesis is that, in all major consumer markets, decreases in world commodity prices have systematically been transmitted to domestic consumer prices much less than have increases. This has limited the expansion of demand for commodities in these markets.

[42] See table 2 of the note by the Development Policy Analysis Division of the Department of Economic and Social Affairs on the impact of recent declines in primary commodity prices on commodity-dependent developing countries (A/CN.2/R.655/Add.2), of 17 May 2001: addendum to the note by the Secretariat on the implementation of General Assembly resolutions 55/5 B, C and F and decisions of the Committee on Contributions relating to the scale methodology, submitted to the Committee at its sixty-first session (11-29 June 2001) under agenda item 7 entitled "Methodology for the preparation of future scales of assessment".

1940 terms-of-trade deterioration had a negative, albeit small, impact on the growth of developing-country exporters.[40] The issue continues to be a crucial one because many developing countries—and, in particular, least developed countries—rely heavily on exports of primary commodities for income and export revenues. One estimate, for example, is that commodity-exporting countries lose some 100 billion dollars a year because of commodity price trends.[41] More recently, it has been approximated that commodity-dependent countries lost 9 per cent of their total trade value between 1995 and 2000 owing to changes in prices.[42]

The real price of non-fuel commodities, as a group, in terms of manufactures, appears to have declined over 1970-2000, after peaking sharply around 1973 (figure V.1). However, while looking at primary commodities, as a group, appears to reveal a downward bias, disaggregation tells another story (figure V.2). Disaggregating and examining individual commodities, there is a distinct lack of *any* trend in some instances—as, for example, in the cases of vegetable oilseeds and oils or minerals (figure V.2). Moreover, in the case of agricultural commodities, there is, if anything, a slight upward trend (figure V.2). A second point to be noted is that commodity price movements are positively autocorrelated. If nudged downward or upward, the trend tends to feed on itself. However, such shocks as do occur do not appear to have long-run effects. Real primary commodity prices revert to trend or, in most cases, to a long-run unchanging average. Indeed, recent research on wheat, rice and maize suggests that world real cereal prices do not exhibit behaviour that would imply the per-

Figure V.1.
REAL PRICE OF NON-FUEL COMMODITIES IN TERMS OF
MANUFACTURES, 1970-2000

Figure V.2.
INTERNATIONAL MARKET PRICES OF NON-FUEL COMMODITIES, 1970-2000

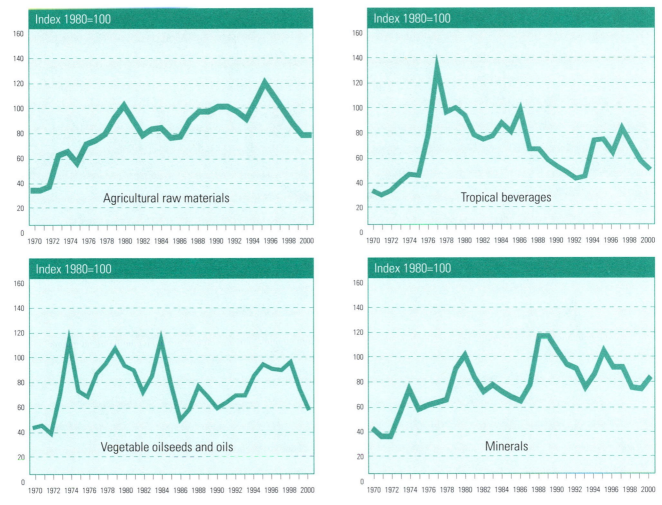

Source: UNCTAD, *Monthly Commodity Price Bulletin.*

petuation of shocks.[43] Third, prices of different commodities tend to move together, though the correlations are much closer for some pairs, such as coffee and cocoa (figure V.3), than for others, such as copper and gold.[44] As will be noted below, this tendency for prices of different primary commodities to move together has contributed to the lack of success of such price stabilization schemes as the Common Fund for Commodities.

A final point to be made with regard to commodity price movements is that it is critical to differentiate between *volatility and trend*. Long-run price declines (or increases, for that matter), which are regarded as fairly permanent, should raise quite different policy concerns than do short-run price gyrations.[45]

[43] Alexander H. Sarris, "World cereal price instability as a market-based instrument for LDC food import risk management, *Food Policy*, vol. 25 (2000), pp. 189-209.

[44] Angus Deaton, "Commodity prices and growth in Africa", *Journal of Economic Perspectives*, vol. 13, No. 3 (summer 1999), pp. 23-40.

[45] See, for example, David Sapsford and Hans Singer, "The IMF, the World Bank and commodity prices: a case of shifting sands?", *World Development*, vol. 26, No. 9 (1998), pp. 1653-1660.

Figure V.3.
INDICES OF SELECTED PRIMARY COMMODITY PRICES, 1970-1999

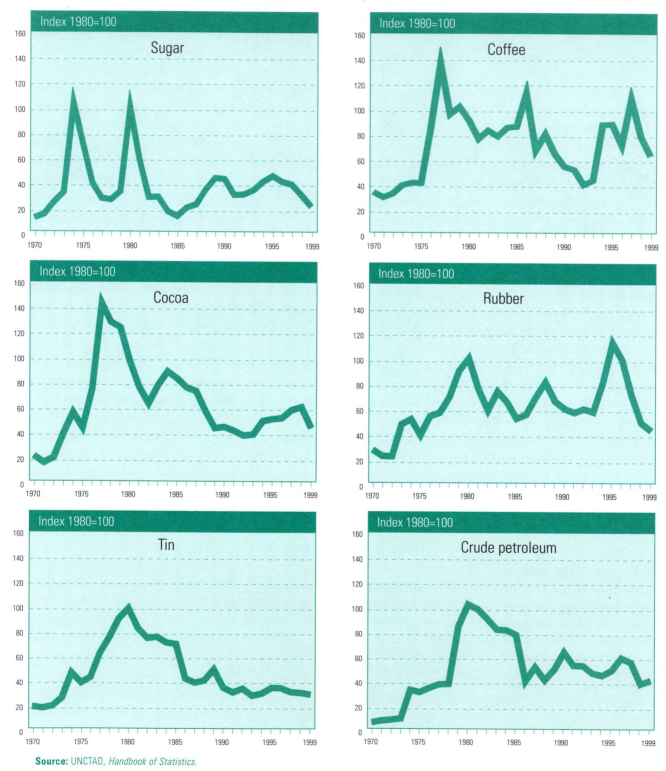

Source: UNCTAD, Handbook of Statistics.

COPING WITH COMMODITY PRICE INSTABILITY AND UNCERTAINTY

The quandary for these countries, therefore, is not just the long-run price declines engendered by relatively low-income elasticities of demand for their products. An equally difficult situation is brought about by price **uncertainty**—that is to say, price instability around the longer-run trend. Such instabilities make it difficult for these countries, already operating at extremely low resource levels, to count on regular export earnings and income streams, to plan their development strategies into the future, and to attract foreign investment. For example, one approximation is that more than 44 per cent of the fluctuation in aggregate output in African economies is explained by trade shocks.[46]

Indeed, there is evidence that even *favourable* commodity price shocks have the potential to exert negative effects—the Dutch disease phenomenon being a case in point. In addition, commodity booms may exert harmful effects because they are misdiagnosed as permanent when, in reality, they turn out to be temporary. Painful adjustments are the concomitant.[47]

Among the issues open to debate are the best means of tackling the problems associated with reliance on commodity exports, the true nature of the "disturbances" and the appropriate role of government in the policy interventions intended to stem the tide. One concern, for example, is the **duration** of the shock. There is evidence that terms-of-trade shocks are short-lived in about half the countries experiencing such a phenomenon. In such cases, it typically takes less than four years for half of the effect of the shock to dissipate. However, for another third, these events are long-lived (so that the shocks are permanent).[48] The policy response clearly has to be different in these two cases. For example, the shorter the expected period of the shock, the higher should be the windfall savings rate. The problem is the virtual impossibility of knowing, a priori, how long-lived a shock will be.

The commodity price issue for the most vulnerable

Primary commodity exports are generally recognized to be of particular importance to many least developed countries, though exact figures are hard to come by owing to poor statistics. While the non-least developed countries world average for the number of commodities exported was 182 in 1998, Kiribati exported only 5 that same year, Samoa 9 and Vanuatu 15.[49] In 1997-1998, over 70 per cent of Benin's and Burkina Faso's exports were cotton, 94 per cent of Burundi's exports were coffee and tea, almost 60 per cent of Mozambique's were shellfish and fruit and nuts, and over 60 per cent of Togo's were crude fertilizers and cotton. At the same time, however, over the past 30 years or so, primary commodity prices have made little sustained headway. Compared with a 1980 base of 100, the combined index of non-fuel primary commodity prices registered 95 in 1970, 54 in 1990 and 50 in 2000.[50] Not only have commodity prices failed to make any consistent advances, according to this index, but also year-to-year jumps have been tremendous on occasion. For example, between 1973 and 1974, the index jumped by 20 per cent, only to decline by 31 per cent the following year, 1974-1975.

46 M. Ayhan Kose and Raymond Riezman, "Trade shocks and macroeconomic fluctuations in Africa", *Journal of Development Economics*, vol. 65 (2001), pp. 55-80.

47 David Sapsford and Hans Singer, loc. cit.

48 Paul Cashin and Catherine Pattillo, "Terms of Trade Shocks in Africa: Are They Short-Lived or Long-Lived?", *IMF Working Paper* No. WP/00/72 (Washington, D.C., April 2000).

49 UNCTAD and Commonwealth Secretariat, *Duty and Quota Free Market Access for LDCs: An Analysis of Quad Initiatives* (London and Geneva, 2001), p. 6.

50 UNCTAD, *Monthly Commodity Price Bulletin* (various issues), table A.20.

Dependency on only a few commodities, coupled with uncertain commodity prices, exposes both the Governments of the least developed countries and their private sectors to uncertain revenues and expenditures, making planning difficult. Private exporters and traders, who operate under tight margins, may also run into serious difficulties when commodity prices gyrate. Thus, an exporter or trader who has purchased a commodity from a producer, but has not yet sold it, faces huge losses if prices collapse in the interim. Lacking other means to counter uncertainty, traders require large margins to avoid negative consequences. Commodity price uncertainty also has negative implications for commodity financing. Banks and other lending institutions will be reluctant to finance commodity trade or commodity-related projects because repayment usually hinges on future commodity prices.[51] Not surprising, therefore, is the finding that negative price shocks have had significant and negative effects on growth.[52]

Commodity agreements and the role of government

The most common approach used by developing countries to manage commodity price risk includes domestic and international commodity price stabilization schemes. The former most often involve the creation of a buffer stock that purchases commodities when prices fall below a certain threshold and sells when prices recover. Empirical work on commodity prices has found that they do revert eventually to their mean—this being a requirement for the viability of a stabilization fund or buffer stock—but only very slowly, over a period of years, not months. Hence, a commodity stabilization fund has to be very large to be effective or access to foreign borrowing needs to be ensured. It is argued that the former is unlikely because of spending pressures and the latter not feasible because of risk concerns. An additional problem with such schemes is that they tie up scarce resources that could be more fruitfully employed elsewhere in the economy. Finally, they merely redistribute the risks within the country—from producers to the Government—rather than diversify them outside the country among entities better able to bear such risk. It also appears that a significant part of the cost of price stabilization in agricultural commodities ends up being borne by the farmers themselves. Farmers in commodity stabilization systems usually receive a lower percentage of the free-on-board (f.o.b.) price than do farmers in free market systems. For instance, in the second half of the 1990s, cocoa farmers in Côte d'Ivoire and Ghana received less than 50 per cent of the f.o.b. price, compared with farmers in Indonesia, Malaysia and Nigeria, who received over 80 per cent.[53]

For all these reasons, a number of countries that once relied on such instruments have abandoned them. For example, Nigeria eliminated stabilization in the cocoa sector in 1986. Madagascar, Burundi and Uganda did likewise in the coffee sector in 1989, 1990 and 1992, respectively. Cameroon did the same for both coffee and cocoa in 1994. Alternatively, there have been some stabilization funds that have been successful. Included here are the coffee fund in Columbia, Chile's Copper Stabilization Fund and the Mineral Resources Stabilization Fund in Papua New Guinea. The latter two, however, were designed to stabilize commodity-related revenues, rather than the prices of the internationally traded commodities.[54]

[51] Panos Varangis and Don Larson, "Dealing With Commodity Price Uncertainty", *World Bank Policy Research Working Paper*, No. 1667 (Washington, D.C., October 1996).

[52] Jan Dehn, "Commodity Price Uncertainty in Developing Countries, *World Bank Policy Research Working Paper*, No. 2426 (Washington, D.C., August 2000); and "The Effects on Growth of Commodity Price Uncertainty and Shocks", *World Bank Policy Research Working Paper*, No. 2455 (Washington, D.C., September 2000).

[53] Varangis and Larson, loc. cit., p. 6.

[54] Ibid.

International measures

International commodity stabilization schemes aim at raising and/or stabilizing commodity prices via stocks and export quotas. The first two such schemes were established, under United Nations auspices, in 1954—namely, the International Sugar Agreement and the International Tin Agreement. The 1962 International Coffee Agreement, the 1972 International Cocoa Agreement and the 1979 International Natural Rubber Agreement followed. All lapsed, collapsed or were suspended.

A variety of problems with such schemes have been identified. It has, for example, been demonstrated that the benefits to producers are not equally distributed among member countries. Producers may even benefit by not joining a commodity agreement. Brazil, for instance, did not join the International Tin Agreement. Its production expanded and it captured a larger share of the world market. Similarly, Viet Nam has become a major coffee exporter despite, or because of, not having joined the International Coffee Agreement.[55] Furthermore, research has demonstrated that, when buffer stock operations are used to influence world prices, even random commodity price movements will eventually bankrupt such schemes. One such example was the dramatic failure of the International Tin Agreement in 1985, sending the price of tin down by 40 per cent in a short space of time and almost bringing down the London Metals Exchange in the process. In the same vein, it has been maintained that even moderate inflation or deflation of world commodity prices will render an agreement ineffective after a time, necessitating periodic—though often cumbersome—renegotiations of the agreement's price range.[56] An additional problem is that such schemes are designed based on existing market conditions and tend not to be sufficiently flexible in a changing world economy. Then, too, when such a Government-negotiated agreement actually does succeed in raising prices, it may be undermined by farmers' decisions to produce more, thereby swamping the resources of the operation.[57] In addition, the fact that commodity prices often move together (coffee and cocoa prices in figure V.3, for example) makes such schemes difficult and expensive to operate. Finally, there is the difficult question whether the inefficiencies introduced by tampering with the market-driven play of supply and demand on price are compensated by a benefit in risk-sharing between producers and consumers. Recent research suggests that there is scope for a net improvement in world welfare. However, in order to receive this benefit, it may be necessary to allow a buffer stock scheme to incur heavy losses—thus necessitating substantial, but unpalatable, injections of public funds.

Alternative solutions: compensatory financing and hedging

There are three sorts of instruments to deal with commodity price uncertainty. First, there are devices to reduce the variability of commodity prices. Second, there exist tools to increase the predictability of commodity prices and perhaps even commodity-related revenues. Third, there are instruments designed to keep expenditures in line with income flows. Government price support programmes and commodity agreements, as noted above, are examples of instruments used to reduce price variability. Commodity derivative markets—such as futures, options, swaps, and commodity-linked notes—are tools for

55 Takamasa Akiyama and Donald Larson, "The adding-up problem: strategies for primary commodity exports in sub-Saharan Africa", *World Bank Policy Research Paper*, No. 1245 (Washington, D.C., January 1994).

56 W. J. H. Van Groenendaal and J. W. A. Vingerhoets, "Can international commodity agreements work?", *Journal of Policy Modeling*, vol. 17, No. 3 (1995), pp. 257–278.

57 Varangis and Larson, loc. cit.

hedging, designed to make revenues more predictable. Lastly, compensatory financing schemes, such as the International Monetary Fund (IMF) Compensatory and Contingency Financing Facility (CCFF) and the EU Stabex scheme (stabilization of export earnings for agricultural commodities), tend to smooth consumption expenditures.[58]

The **Compensatory Financing Facility** (CFF) of IMF was established in 1963 to help countries cope with temporary exogenous shocks affecting their export earnings, without resorting to undue and unnecessary adjustments. Coverage was expanded in 1979 to include shortfalls in receipts from tourism and workers' remittances, and again, in 1981, to include excess cereal import costs.

Since 1989, 28 IMF members (about 16 per cent of the Fund's average membership) have made 45 purchases under the CFF, amounting to SDR 8.4 billion. About three quarters of the countries that made purchases were middle-income. There was only one least developed country in this set, though a number were low-income (Azerbaijan, Côte d'Ivoire, Ghana, Honduras, India and Pakistan).

The case for low-conditionality or relatively low conditionality financing of temporary exogenous balance-of-payments shocks through the CFF rests on three premises. First, it is assumed that the appropriate response to the temporary shock consists of timely financing rather than adjustment. Second, members must have little or no access to alternative sources of financing. Third, other Fund facilities must be deemed unsuitable for the purpose at hand. However, several doubts about these premises have been raised.

To begin with, there are several reasons why the appropriate response to a shock may not consist entirely of financing. In practice, it is difficult to distinguish between temporary and permanent shocks. While fluctuations in the prices of primary commodities were a major concern in the 1950s and ensuing decades, at least since the 1980s secular trends in these prices appear to have become more important and evidence has accumulated that commodity price shocks typically do not reverse quickly.[59] If true, this suggests that the proper response to a commodity price shock should involve adjustment as well as financing. A second concern emanates from the fact that few countries have "ideal" policies. Even in cases where good policies are being implemented, some policy response might still be required in the presence of exogenous shocks that are identifiable and transitory. Third, there may be issues of adverse selection. Availability of relatively unconditional disbursements may bias use of such a facility towards countries unprepared to pursue necessary adjustment policies. Another doubt about the CFF emerges from the fact that a growing number of middle- and upper-income developing countries have access to international capital markets during normal times. It is the low-income members with limited access to such funds that have the greatest potential need for compensatory financing. Not only may the terms that apply to the CFF not be appropriate for them, but it may be for this very reason that mostly middle-income countries have been using this facility. Moreover, since the creation of the Enhanced Structural Adjustment Facility (ESAF) in 1987, many of the low-income countries that have suffered droughts or commodity price shocks, leading to export shortfalls or cereal import excesses, have had ESAF arrangements either in place or close to approval. The question therefore arises whether the financing for shocks could not more suitably be provided through the ESAF.

[58] Varangis and Larson, loc. cit.

[59] Paul Cashin, Hong Liang and C. John McDermott, "How Persistent are Shocks to World Commodity Prices?", *IMF Working Paper*, No. WP/99/80 (Washington, D.C., June 1999). The authors found that for the majority of individual commodities, it typically took more than five years for one half of the initial price shock to reverse itself. In the same vein, Paul Cashin, C. John McDermott and Alasdair Scott, ("Booms and Slumps in World Commodity Prices", *IMF Working Paper*, No. WP/99/155 (Washington, D.C., November 1999)) found that for most commodities, price slumps lasted longer than price booms. How far prices fell in a slump was found to be slightly larger than how far they rebounded in a subsequent boom. Nor did the authors find evidence of a consistent "shape" to commodity-price cycles.

The **Compensatory and Contingency Financing Facility** (CCFF) was created in 1988 with the integration of the CFF and the new **External Contingency Mechanism** (ECM). The latter is an instrument attached to a Fund arrangement that provides additional resources in the event that certain critical external variables (such as export prices) depart from the assumptions of the programme. Whereas the CFF had been designed to address deviations in specific current-account variables from past trends, the ECM was designed to deal with departures of a broader number of current-account variables from programme assumptions. The ECM has been used infrequently and not at all since 1992. ECMs have been attached to only 11 Fund-supported arrangements, 8 of which were approved in 1991-1992. In only one case has a drawing actually been made (Bulgaria in 1992). The Fund itself acknowledges that the complexity and rigidity of the conditions governing the CCFF have made it difficult for countries to avail themselves of this instrument. To begin with, it is extremely difficult—equally so for academics, private agents and international organizations to establish a baseline forecast from which deviations can be determined.

The **Buffer Stock Financing Facility** (BSFF) was established in 1969 to provide financial assistance to members with temporary balance-of-payments needs arising from their contributions to buffer stocks established under approved international commodity agreements. No IMF member has used the BSFF since 1984, and all commodity agreements for which BSFF eligibility was approved have expired. The BSFF was eliminated in 2000, after having been dormant for 15 years.[60] Eighteen countries have made 39 purchases, during its 30-odd-year existence, for total drawings of SDR 558 million. These purchases were made under the three International Tin Agreements, under the International Sugar Agreement and under the 1979 International Natural Rubber Agreement. The last eight purchases were made by Brazil, the Dominican Republic, Côte d'Ivoire, Thailand and Zimbabwe, mostly to cover contributions made under the now lapsed 1977 International Sugar Agreement.

A serious drawback to all such schemes is that, by their very design, compensatory financing provides ex post financial assistance for adjustment to commodity price or volume shocks. Such arrangement do not therefore enable ex ante risk management. Thus, the limited success of both stabilization and compensatory financing schemes in limiting price uncertainty has led to the evolution of alternative instruments, such as commodity derivatives.

Hence, there has been a shift in emphasis towards using futures markets for risk management. There are active futures markets for each of the commodities once subject to international commodity agreements. Furthermore, a vast array of instruments of this sort exist.[61] For example, a forward contract is an agreement to purchase or sell a given commodity at a future date at a predetermined and fixed price. Futures contracts differ significantly from forward contracts. First, contract terms are generally standardized. Second, transactions are handled only by organized exchanges through a clearing house. Third, profits and losses are settled daily. Fourth, futures contracts require depositing money as collateral. Fifth, while forward contracts involve physical delivery at maturity, futures are usually closed before or at maturity. Therefore, futures separate the physical sale or purchase of commodities from hedging.

[60] IMF, "Review of the Compensatory and Contingency Financing Facility (CCFF) and Buffer Stock Financing Facility (BSFF): preliminary considerations" (EBS/99/222), 9 December 1999; and "Review of Fund Facilities: preliminary considerations", 2 March 2000.

[61] Varangis and Larson, loc. cit. The various commodity instruments are detailed in annex I of this paper.

An option on a futures contract is the right—not the obligation—to purchase or sell a specified quantity of an underlying futures contract, at a predetermined price, on or before a given date. Exchange-traded options are standardized. Over-the-counter options are offered by banks and commodity brokers and can be customized. The purchase of an option is equivalent to price insurance.

A swap contract is an agreement to exchange—or swap—a floating price for a fixed one (or vice versa) for a given quantity at specific time intervals. Swap contracts are the equivalent of a series of scheduled forward contracts lined up on a schedule, but do not involve physical deliveries. A variation on this is the commodity note. This, too, can be customized and does not necessitate physical delivery. However, such notes are shorter-term, usually from six months to a year.

In commodity-linked loans, interest and/or repayment amounts are linked to the price of a certain commodity or to an index of commodity price(s). A variation is the commodity inventory purchase agreement-linked note, in which the transaction centres on bonded warehouse receipts as security for the loan. Commodity bonds are yet another instrument. These are useful to producer Governments because of their long-term nature. However, since most are for periods exceeding five years, they are not suited to soft commodity or grain markets. Moreover, they require a fairly sophisticated distribution network to market them.

While all these instruments help to reduce uncertainty, this is not the same thing as lessening price variability. Commodity futures prices are only slightly less variable than cash prices. However, a policy of futures sales permits the individual producer, or producer Government, to eliminate the uncertainty associated with such variability over an annual time horizon. This has a variety of benefits, including increased budgetary control. While the advantages may be substantial, they are not equivalent to revenue stabilization, nor do they shift the terms of trade in favour of commodity producers.[62]

POLICY CONSIDERATIONS

Attempts to stabilize commodity prices have had a chequered history at best. Their inherent difficulty raises the question whether stabilization is worth the effort. The case for stabilization rests on three premises: the benefits for consumers, the benefits for producers, and the macroeconomic benefits. In the absence of stabilization, sharp price hikes for staple foods in low-income countries could cause severe hardships—famine even—for consumers who are not wealthy enough to afford the price increase. Such a situation would clearly have negative health and welfare implications. Moreover, there may also be adverse consequences for labour productivity. This is an argument analogous to the "efficiency wage" argument, which states that higher wages may result in higher worker productivity.[63] On the supply side, farmers also benefit from stability because they are protected from periods of abnormally low prices, which can enhance efficiency in the farm sector. Then, too, there may be macroeconomic benefits in terms of investment and growth effects. This will be especially true if, as earlier suggested, there are negative growth consequences to negative commodity price shocks.

62 For details, see Christopher L. Gilbert, "International commodity agreements: an obituary notice", *World Development*, vol. 24, No. 1 (1996), pp. 1-19.

63 David Dawe, "How far down the path to free trade? the importance of rice price stabilization in developing Asia", *Food Policy*, vol. 26, issue 2 (April 2001), pp. 163-175.

Prime among the policy concerns is the question of the extent to which there is a role for government intervention and how to assess alternative intervention strategies. Of paramount importance here is determining not only the point of the intervention (whom it is designed to help) but also the nature of the problem (whether the volatility is temporary or not). For example, there is some evidence that private agents in developing countries may be more resourceful than often believed in finding ways to smooth consumption. In contrast, Governments have frequently shown a tendency to display less foresight—for example, by overspending during temporary booms.[64]

Thus, institutional arrangements—such as stabilization funds—that establish rules for government behaviour as regards revenue acquisition from commodity exports can be useful. By the same logic, trading boards and other government devices to smooth producers' income can easily become distortional and hence welfare-reducing. From the perspective of avoiding distortions, futures and options markets are useful tools, enabling countries to "trade away" the risk associated with commodity price volatility and thereby diminishing the need for income- or consumption-smoothing policies. At the same time, however, futures markets will not reduce the vulnerability of poor consumers and farmers unless these actors participate directly in such markets themselves. This is still fairly rare in developing countries and even harder to imagine in the poorest developing countries.[65]

Policy prescriptions emanating from well-fitting, but inappropriate, models are potentially catastrophic. Thus, in some instances, the institutional underpinnings may be absent. To take another example, income from a commodity boom, instead of being assessed as a long-lived, but nonetheless temporary, windfall, may be misdiagnosed as permanent or as but the first instalment of a larger windfall to come (when prices changes are positively autocorrelated). In either case, based on an incorrect supposition, a government would feel justified in raising consumption more than current windfall income.[66]

Indeed, the need to get policies and assessments "right" highlights the importance of fundamental micro- and macroeconomic policies, such as improved efficiency, constant flexibility, and diversification in the longer run. Trade is but one tool in the development planner's arsenal. Other necessary conditions include macroeconomic discipline, improving the physical and human infrastructure, tax reform and strengthening the financial sector. All of these are critical in reducing vulnerability.

At the same time, as a counterpart, the world trading system needs an activist trade agenda to ensure future openness. Measures need to be in place to prevent the imposition of unjustified NTBs and to avoid placing issues on the World Trade Organization agenda, that are not, first and foremost, trade-related since such topics can easily evolve into "daggers aimed at the developing countries".[67]

[64] Eduardo Borensztein, and others, "The Behavior of Non-Oil Commodity Prices", *IMF Occasional Paper*, No. 112 (Washington, D.C., August 1994).

[65] For this reason, one analysis argues that futures markets for rice, a commodity of special importance to the bulk of the world's poor, are not particularly "viable". See David Dawe, loc. cit.

[66] For more on this point, see Angus Deacon, loc. cit.

[67] Jagdish Bhagwati, "After Seattle: free trade and the WTO", *International Affairs*, vol. 77, No. 1 (January 2001), pp. 15-29.

VI   THE CHALLENGE TO SMALL, LANDLOCKED TRANSITION ECONOMIES

Many of the transition countries in the Commonwealth of Independent States (CIS) as well as Mongolia are in a difficult geographical location which is not helpful to economic development: they are far from the three major markets in the world—Japan, the United States of America and Western Europe—and some are landlocked. Unlike the transition economies of Central and Eastern Europe countries, there are no rich neighbours, which, in theory, can help to pull their economies out of stagnation through trade linkages and by serving as models for learning by watching.

They also were hit by huge socio-economic shocks in the 1990s, the first decade of transition, and were affected more severely than the Central and Eastern European transition economies by many of them. In 1989 and 1990, the Council for Mutual Economic Assistance (CMEA) trading arrangements broke down as the Central and Eastern European countries sought to re-establish their trading links, this time based upon market principles, with their natural partners in Western Europe. CMEA was formally abolished in June 1991 and they suddenly became actors in the market economy without traditional market economy partners. CMEA had provided the present CIS countries and Mongolia with industrial and trade links with each other and the Russian Federation and with the Central and Eastern European economies. Whereas it was natural for the Central and Eastern European transition economies and the Baltic States to revert to their traditional trade and industrial links with Western Europe, there were no such alternative and traditional partners for the CIS member countries.

At the end of 1991, the Soviet Union itself collapsed, and the constituent republics, with the exception of the Baltic States, formed CIS. The Soviet Union's eventual collapse had been anticipated and prepared for by the Baltic States which achieved the sort of independence that they had enjoyed before 1940. However, for many of the CIS countries, independence came unexpectedly and they suddenly found themselves with the task of creating the institutions needed for existence as small States. Moreover, unlike the Baltic States, whose transit links the Russian Federation needed, many of the newly independent countries became, at a stroke, landlocked. With the collapse of the Soviet Union came the breakdown of all the transfer payments from the central Government to the different republics of the Union. These represented a net transfer to the poorer republics and poorer members of CMEA, such as Mongolia. The budgetary transfers had financed a wide range of social and economic programmes in these republics. The newly independent States were also subjected to new constraints that had not existed when they were part of a unitary State, such as having to balance imports with exports and fiscal revenue with expenditure at "appropriate" existing prices.

CIS, however, could not preserve, and even less strengthen, the links between the different countries that had existed when they formed part of the same country. In particular, in 1993, the rouble payments area was terminated. This had allowed the different CIS countries to use the Russian rouble to settle their accounts and so had facilitated the preservation of their trading links. Now the different countries had to establish their own currencies and conduct trading relations with partners that would expect payment in a transferable currency.

The most recent shock to the smaller CIS economies was the 1998 financial crisis in the Russian Federation. This resulted in a large devaluation of the rouble against the United States dollar and a reduction in demand in the Russian Federation. The fall in Russian imports affected adversely many countries in CIS. At the same time, significant depreciations against the dollar of the currencies of many (but not all) countries in the region worsened their external debt situation.

The various shocks that the CIS countries went through in the course of a decade—the sudden losses of reliable trade partners as well as fiscal and financial transfers, and the necessity of adjusting their industrial and trade structures in line with market forces—have seriously reduced the fiscal and financial strength of many CIS Governments, with consequent harm to the economic and social lives of the people. There was a resurgence of several diseases in the 1990s that had largely disappeared during the decades under the central planning system, because of post-1990 reductions in health-related expenditure. Rates of secondary school enrolment also declined in response to economic hardship and reductions in education subsidies. The countries were also struck by natural disasters, such as the unusually hard winter of 2000 in Mongolia and the summer drought of 2000 in Armenia, whose impact was exacerbated by the lack of or reductions in financial and material resources available to the relevant authorities.

The present chapter looks at the impacts of these shocks on three countries —Armenia, Kyrgyzstan and Mongolia. They share the characteristics of being small, formerly centrally planned landlocked countries. Two of them suddenly became landlocked independent countries. They did not have the oil or natural gas wealth of many of their neighbours and have been vigorously pursuing market and trade liberalization policies as part of their strategy to build modern, market-based economies. While liberalization of their economies led to improved economic performance in the second half of the 1990s, the sharp decline of government revenues forced many reductions in the provision of social services, especially health care and education, which led to a worsening of some social indicators. Their experience will, then, shed light on the time framework needed in order for liberalization policies to produce results.

Although they do not have the energy resources of some of the other countries in CIS, and are all net energy importers, the three countries have considerable mineral potential.[1] Kyrgyzstan mines and processes the fol-

[1] The information on their mineral industries is from the United States Geological Survey, International Minerals Statistics and Information: http://minerals.usgs.gov/minerals/pubs/country/.

lowing minerals—antimony, coal, gold, mercury, molybdenum, tin, tungsten and uranium. It is the third largest gold producer of CIS and the country's immediate prospects very largely depend on the gold industry. Armenia's mineral industry has attracted foreign investment and increasing production of copper, cut diamonds, gold and molybdenum would be significant for its economy. At the present time, some 40 per cent of Armenia's exports are now finished diamonds and jewellery from three firms owned respectively by Belgian, British and Israeli investors.[2] In Mongolia, the enactment of the Mineral Resources Law of 1997 which conferred equal rights to investors, regardless of their nationality, and allowed complete foreign ownership with no restrictions on the repatriation of dividends and profits, has led to a boom in exploration, and major companies have taken out licences for exploration. The output of the mineral industry is important for the economy, having contributed in 1998 about 55 per cent of the output of the industrial sector, 58 per cent of exports and 30 per cent of State budget revenues. The major export mineral products are gold, ore and concentrates of copper, fluorite and molybdenum. The industry has proved a strong defender of its interests—in 1998, it strongly opposed a government plan, backed by the International Monetary Fund (IMF), to impose a value-added tax on sales and exports of gold. The President accepted its arguments that this would have an adverse impact on the investment climate. The industry can be expected to play a major role in the overall development of the three countries although it will be some time before many investments come on line. The three countries have shown an appreciation of the industry's special needs and the opportunities for development that it presents.

The mineral industry is but one of those in which the countries have shown the need to provide an environment conducive to private enterprise and domestic and foreign investment. They did not have an industry, such as the oil industry, that would provide them with large rents which could be used to develop other industries or to cover social expenditures. Nor were they geographically located near a major market, or expecting to become part of such a market and so attract the foreign direct investment (FDI) seeking to gain access to it (as was the case for the Central and Eastern European countries that will soon enter the European Union). For their long-term growth, then, they had to rely on the free market to build up their economies. They needed to become very attractive to domestic and foreign investment and to ensure that those industries that could not operate in a competitive globalized market economy, and would otherwise have been a drain on the State budget, were closed down as soon as possible. These factors then—their geographical remoteness, the small size of their domestic markets and the absence of a huge rent-generating industry—help explain the strategy of rapid liberalization that they followed. The speed and depth of the liberalization might have surprised some observers, but not the policy makers, who appreciated the realities of the situation, nor those who understood the differences between these economies and other transition economies.

This chapter examines the forms of liberalization and economic cooperation pursued by these countries in the past decade. It assesses the impact of this cooperation on their economies. Finally, it analyses the

[2] See "Survey: investing in Central and Eastern Europe", *Financial Times*. 2 July 2001.

long-term prospects of these countries based on the size of their economies, their landlocked situation and their remoteness from world markets. It should be noted that these three factors not only limit the prospects of economic development, but also restrict options available to the countries' policy makers.

The chapter aims to focus more international attention on these countries so as to promote effective, long-term regional and global cooperation that will help them to carry out sustainable development and to achieve reintegration into the globalized world economy.

THE GEOGRAPHICAL AND ECONOMIC BACKGROUND TO TRANSITION

While Armenia, Kyrgyzstan and Mongolia each have a unique, proud history and culture, they share many economic, social and geographical characteristics. The fact that all three have small domestic populations and markets makes any attempt at widening their export bases difficult. That they are landlocked and remote from world markets makes trade links with the rest of the world more difficult because of high transport costs and the need for goods to go through a complicated transit system. Mongolia occupies a large, but thinly populated land area between China and the Russian Federation. Armenia is located in the Transcaucasus area, surrounded by four countries (Azerbaijan, Georgia, the Islamic Republic of Iran and Turkey); Kyrgyzstan, in Central Asia, is surrounded by China, Kazakhstan, Tajikistan and Uzbekistan. Armenia and Kyrgyzstan are involved in, or close to countries involved in, conflict. Armenia and Kyrgyzstan, as republics of the former Soviet Union, and Mongolia as an independent country, pursued socialist policies on education—that is to say, they tried to provide the widest possible access to all levels of education to the population—until the collapse of the Soviet Union in 1991. Largely because of those policies, educational levels and literacy rates in these countries are much higher than in countries with similar income levels in other regions in the world. Their per capita income levels (in purchasing power parity) are, however, among the lowest in the CIS countries at present, and are roughly equal to those of South Asia.[3]

The similarities among the three countries are not, however, confined only to their geographical locations and the legacy of the central planning system. They proceeded, in earnest, with deregulating and liberalizing their economies during the 1990s in order to maximize the potential benefits from reintegration within the world economy. While the implementation of deregulation and liberalization measures often constituted a precondition for receiving aid from international financial organizations, their not having a rent-generating industry like the mineral fuel industry that could provide sufficient export earnings to cover import needs, and sizeable tax revenues to cover budget needs, left them with few alternatives to accepting international assistance—with conditions—so as to cover their foreign exchange and budget exchange needs during the transition. Moreover, while sizeable fuel resources can earn foreign exchange and attract FDI, countries without such resources cannot afford to "sit and wait" for trade or investment partners to rush to develop their resources.

[3] Based on United Nations Development Programme (UNDP), *Human Development Report, 2000* (New York, Oxford University Press, 2000), Human development indicators, table 1.

The integration of the three countries into the multilateral trading system has been smoother than anticipated by many observers at the beginning of the transition. As a result of the successful implementation of liberalization and deregulation policies during the 1990s, Kyrgyzstan and Mongolia are now members of the World Trade Organization and Armenia is at an advanced stage of setting out the terms and conditions of entry. All three countries have taken measures to restructure and liberalize their economies, in the expectation that a more liberalized and open economy will enable them to be quickly integrated within the world economy. The resulting benefits should thus help them recover from the collapse of CMEA and the Soviet Union and counteract the adverse effects of having become at a stroke small and landlocked. Armenia and Mongolia have gone so far as to establish the most liberal trade regimes in the world. Because of economic and geographical factors, the "gestation period" during which these economies are put on a firm footing for long-term economic development path can easily last a decade or longer. The depth, size and duration of regional and international assistance to these countries must be strengthened to help them carry out the policies that will result in sustainable development.

The three countries have not so far been able to take full advantage of the possibility of access to the globalized world economy—with increasing shares of **market-based**, cross-border activities and more intense competition among private enterprises and even among States. The legacy of their central planning systems, together with their intrinsic geographical disadvantages, continues to hinder them, to varying degrees, from participating effectively in global markets. Their industrial and trade structures were parts of the overall economic structure of the CMEA member States, particularly the Soviet Union; and, in many instances, the existing industries were built for the sake of creating employment or "industrializing" local areas, and thus were without firm economic cost calculations. Their geographical location makes international trade more costly because of high transport costs; insufficient physical and institutional infrastructure also makes transport slow and expensive. Their not sharing a common currency and the erection of national borders after their independence are also not conducive to international trade. Moreover, their lack of experience with market-based economic development, for seven decades, also hampers their efforts to integrate their economies into the global market.

INCREASED VULNERABILITY AS A CONSEQUENCE OF TRANSITION

Macroeconomic conditions

Economic performance in the CIS countries and Mongolia was poor for much of the 1990s.[4] The average cumulative output decline from 1989 (the generally accepted starting point for the transition) among the countries in the former Soviet Union was more than 50 per cent.[5] While most of these countries recovered somewhat in the second half of the 1990s, their combined output level in 1998 was still only 60 per cent of that in 1989. This contrasts with the economic performance of some countries in Eastern Europe, such as the Czech Republic, Hungary, Poland, Slovakia and Slovenia, which have nearly or fully recovered from the initial decline of output in the early 1990s.[6]

[4] For reviews of the economic performance of the economies in transition, see Economic Commission for Europe (ECE), *Economic Survey of Europe*, 2000, *No.1* (United Nations publication, Sales No. E.00.II.E.12).

[5] Stanley Fischer and Ratna Sahay, "The Transition Economies after Ten Years", *IMF Working Paper*, No. WP/00/30 (Washington, D.C., IMF, February 2000), table 1. Output and its growth rates for the transition economies tend to be underestimated, particularly at the initial stage of transition, owing to the emergence of the non-State sector and the development of the untaxed economy, neither of which is likely to be reported in official statistics.

[6] Ibid. Poland, among all of the economies in transition, was the only country that surpassed its 1989 output level in 1998.

Among Armenia, Kyrgyzstan and Mongolia, the transition shock affected Mongolia least; its gross domestic product (GDP) in 1993, its lowest year in the decade, was about three quarters of that in 1989, which was the highest level in its history (see table VI.1). In contrast, in Armenia the cumulative output decline from its high in 1989 to its low in 1993 was 56 per cent, and in Kyrgyzstan output declined 52 per cent from its high in 1990 to its low in 1995. Such declines are unprecedented in peacetime: real GDP in Indonesia and

Table VI.1.
MACROECONOMIC INDICATORS OF ARMENIA, KYRGYZSTAN AND MONGOLIA, 1989-2000

	1989	1990	1991	1992	1993	1994	1995	1996	1997	1998	1999	2000
Armenia												
GDP at market prices (1990=100)	107.3	100	88.3	51.4	46.9	49.4	52.9	56.0	57.8	62.0	63.9	67.7
Industrial output												
Agriculture	..	100	98.0	89.5	84.3	86.9	90.4	92.2	88.1	99.5	100.6	..
Industry	..	100	96.0	38.7	42.1	46.1	47.3	47.8	48.4	47.3	49.8	..
Services	..	100	82.8	51.9	35.9	39.1	44.6	49.3	51.9	54.8	57.8	..
Debt service as proportion of GNP (percentage)	..	..	..	..	0.1	0.2	0.4	3.1	1.7	2.2	..	..
External debt stock (millions of dollars)	..	..	1	41	134	214	371	614	786	801	870	..
Kyrgyzstan												
GDP at market prices (1990=100)	93.6	100	90.9	76.5	64.1	51.2	48.4	51.9	57.0	59.0	61.1	64.6
Industrial output												
Agriculture	98.3	100	85.4	81.1	74.2	67.8	66.4	76.5	85.9	88.1	95.8	99.6
Industry	..95.0	100	90.6	66.7	49.8	31.1	28.6	29.4	35.5	36.6	36.0	38.4
Services	87.3	100	..	..	70.5	58.0	55.4	55.3	54.6	55.5	..	..
Debt service as proportion of GNP (percentage)	..	..	..	..	0.0	0.5	1.8	2.8	2.5	3.5	..	..
External debt stock (millions of dollars)	..	..	..	4	290	446	608	764	928	1 148	..	..
Mongolia												
GDP at market prices (1990=100)	102.6	100	90.8	82.1	79.7	81.5	86.6	88.7	92.3	95.5	98.4	..
Industrial output												
Agriculture	10.3	100	84.6	92.7	89.9	92.3	101.1	105.9	110.9	114.4	117.8	..
Industry	99.7	100	87.4	71.9	62.7	64.0	75.2	73.7	76.9	79.4	80.9	..
Services	105.5	100	95.6	87.9	91.5	93.6	92.3	96.8	100.1	103.9	107.9	..
Debt service as proportion of GNP (percentage)	..	..	20.2	202.8	268.4	88.3	56.8	49.3	36.6	9.4	7.6	..
External debt stock (millions of dollars)	..	..	..	350	384	461	525	532	609	739	..	..

Source: UN/DESA, based on national and international sources.

Thailand dropped by 13 and 10 per cent, respectively, in 1998 owing to the financial crisis in East Asia.[7]

Since the beginning of the transition, Armenia, Kyrgyzstan and Mongolia have deindustrialized their economic structures. The real value of their industrial output fell sharply and its share in national output decreased, while the shares of agricultural output and services increased. Because the previous central planning regime did not emphasize development of the service sector, that sector has developed rapidly with the emergence of market-based economic activities. In contrast, the industrial sector, which Soviet planners considered to be the engine of economic growth and the main source for job opportunities, has experienced a sharp decline.

The decline in industry was partly the result of changes in relative prices and of disruption and disorganization of the input-output linkages and payment systems among the former State enterprises.[8] The changes in relative prices were most pronounced for energy prices, including the price of oil, which had been priced at unrealistically low levels. For the energy-importing countries in CMEA, the collapse of the central planning system and the adjustment of energy prices caused an "oil shock" in the form of a sharp deterioration in their terms of trade. The collapse of the rouble bloc in 1993, which entailed the breakdown of the payments system among the CIS countries, disrupted their economies and reduced labour and total factor productivity, aggravating the depth and duration of their economic contractions.[9] The sharp decline of demand in the former CMEA member States reinforced a vicious international cycle of output contractions.

The decline of industrial output was 71 per cent in Kyrgyzstan, 61 per cent in Armenia and 37 per cent in Mongolia. As with GDP, output in the industrial sector recovered somewhat during the second half of the 1990s, but in 1999 it remained well below the pre-transition level in the three countries. Employment in the industrial sector declined and many former industrial workers became economically inactive or found new jobs in agriculture, retail trade, or other services (see table VI.2). In Kyrgyzstan, employment in the industrial sector shrank about 60 per cent from 1989 to 2000, even as total employment in the economy increased slightly; in Armenia, the share of industry in total employment dropped from 38 per cent in 1991 to 19 per cent in 2000, and the number of industrial workers dropped even more drastically, as total employment fell more than 20 per cent over the same period.

The agricultural sectors of the three countries have become their major source of employment, providing half of the total in Kyrgyzstan and Mongolia, and over 40 per cent in Armenia. The agricultural output of the three countries now exceeds or is close to its pre-transition level, but it did not increase as fast as the sector's employment; thus, productivity per worker is lower than before. Particularly during the first half of the 1990s, the shift in economic activity towards the agricultural sector reflected the population's need to survive in such harsh economic conditions, rather than new economic opportunities. In many instances, farmers and nomadic herdsmen had to return to traditional, more subsistence-based agricultural activities, owing to the breakdown of State-assisted production and distribution systems of foods and agricultural inputs. The systems were valuable instruments for farmers and nomads, who could exchange their products for foods and other materials. The breakdown

[7] *World Economic and Social Survey, 2000* (United Nations publication, Sales No. E.00.II.C.1), table A.4.

[8] Olivier Blanchard, "Assessment of the economic transition in Central and Eastern Europe", *American Economic Review Papers and Proceedings*, vol. 86, No. 2 (May 1996), pp. 117 – 122; and Wei Li, "A tale of two reforms", The Fuqua School of Business, Duke University (November 1994).

[9] Mark De Broeck and Vincent Koen, "The Great Contractions in Russia, the Baltics and the Other Countries of the Former Soviet Union: A View from the Supply Side", *IMF Working Paper*, No. 00/32 (Washington, D.C., IMF, March 2000).

Table VI.2.
SECTORAL EMPLOYMENT IN ARMENIA, KYRGYZSTAN AND MONGOLIA, 1989-2000

	1989	1990	1991	1992	1993	1994	1995	1996	1997	1998	1999	2000
Armenia												
Total employment (thousands)	..	..	1 671	1 578	..	..	1 476	1 436	1 372	1 337	1 298	1 283
Share (percentage)												
Agriculture	..	..	22.4	30.0	..	..	37.1	40.5	41.0	42.1	42.9	42.5
Industry	..	..	38.0	34.3	..	..	25.7	22.5	21.0	19.9	19.2	19.2
Others	..	..	39.6	35.7	..	..	37.3	37.0	38.0	38.0	37.9	38.3
Kyrgyzstan												
Total employment (thousands)	1 739	1 748	1 754	1 836	1 681	1 645	1 641	1 650	1 689	1 705	1 764	1 767
Share (percentage)												
Agriculture	33.2	32.7	35.5	38.1	39.8	41.7	46.0	45.9	47.4	48.1	52.4	52.9
Industry	27.9	27.9	26.6	22.6	21.4	19.3	16.5	14.6	13.5	12.8	11.7	11.4
Others	38.9	39.4	37.9	39.3	38.9	39.0	37.5	39.5	39.1	39.1	35.9	35.7
Mongolia												
Total employment (thousands)	764	784	796	806	773	787	795	792	788	810	830	..
Share (percentage)												
Agriculture	32.0	33.0	34.5	36.5	39.1	42.7	44.6	45.2	47.9	49.7	48.5	..
Industry	16.1	16.8	16.6	16.6	16.1	12.8	13.6	13.2	12.7	12.4	11.9	..
Others	51.9	50.2	48.9	46.9	44.8	44.5	41.8	41.6	39.4	37.9	39.6	..

Sources: UN/DESA, based on Statistical Division of the Government of Mongolia and UNDP, *Human Development Report, Mongolia, 2000: Reorienting the State* (Ulaanbaatar, Mongolia, UNDP, 2000); Asian Development Bank web site (http://www.adb.org/statistics/country.asp); and Inter-State Statistical Committee of the Commonwealth of Independent States, *Commonwealth of Independent States in 2000* (Moscow, Inter-State Statistical Committee of CIS, 2001).

[10] There is some evidence, however, that agriculture in Kyrgyzstan has shifted away from subsistence to more productive activities. See Georges Heinrich, "Fundamental Economic and Social Changes: The Case of Kyrgyzstan 1993—97", *World Institute for Development Economics Research (WIDER) Working Papers*, No. 174, February 2000.

[11] C. Csaki, "Agricultural reforms in Central and Eastern Europe and the former Soviet Union: status and perspectives", *Agricultural Economics*, vol. 22, No. 1 (January 2000), pp. 37 – 54. According to the author, the use of agricultural inputs was about 15 to 20 per cent of pre-transition levels, for the Central and Eastern European and CIS regions combined.

was caused by the fiscal retrenchment at the onset of transition and the shrinking role of the State thereafter.[10] The use of agricultural inputs declined substantially.[11] Subsistence household plots and individual farms became the dominant forms of agricultural production.

The appropriate policy for the agricultural sector, however, has to be assessed in the light of the countries' suddenly becoming independent. Previously, food security could be assured by supplies coming from other parts of the same country. If these had been imported supplies, they could have been financed by other exports, especially those of mineral fuels of which the Soviet Union had abundant supplies. However, after the dissolution of the Soviet Union, the new countries had to achieve food security by increasing their own agricultural production or by ensuring that their non-agricultural food exports provided sufficient revenue to purchase food imports. This latter policy was not an option for the mineral fuel importers in the short term—even their exports of non-fuel minerals would take some time to reach their full potential, as mentioned earlier. Thus, the three countries had to increase domestic agricultural production to achieve food security. They laid the foundations for doing so by undertaking the privatization of the agricultural sector which was itself an important factor contributing to household food security in the critical period 1991-1995. However, in the longer term, for the agricultural sector to reach its full potential, many of the constraints on marketing the product must be removed.[12] This is recognized by the international community which is giving assistance to help marketing.[13] With a liberal and encouraging climate for FDI, foreign investors can also be expected to contribute to the agricultural potential of these countries.

In the short to medium term, however, the transition to a market-based system was bound to cause difficulties. The extent of disorganization in both production and distribution in agriculture in the first half of the 1990s is suggested by the sharp decline in the consumption of fertilizers, especially in Mongolia and Armenia (see figure VI.1). Poor maintenance of roads has made transportation difficult and costly in Armenia.[14] Government institutions used to transfer food, fodder and other non-food materials from one district (or region) to another in case of an emergency. During this transition period, farmers, nomadic herdsmen and their animals are more exposed to risks from natural disasters and have suffered more damage than before. In Mongolia, the severe winter weather in 2000 killed an estimated 3 million livestock, affecting about 20 per cent of the country's population.[15]

Closely related to the economic disruption has been increased emigration from Armenia and Kyrgyzstan, prompted by limited prospects for new job opportunities, particularly for the economically skilled, who are more likely to be mobile. While detailed data on outflows of workers are lacking, net emigration to the Russian Federation, the major destination, increased sharply in the middle

[12] For a fuller description of the agricultural situation in Armenia, see Food and Agriculture Organization of the United Nations (FAO) Global Information and Early Warning System on Food and Agriculture and World Food Programme, (WFP), *Special Report FAO/WFP Crop and Food Supply Assessment Mission to Armenia*, 5 October 2000. http://www.fao.org/WAICENT/faoinfo/economic/giews/english/alertes/2000/SRARM100.htm.

[13] For instance, in 1995, the first credit line from the European Bank for Reconstruction and Development to an Armenian bank was extended to a private bank, Agrobank, to finance small businesses in the agribusiness area. It would promote the development of a modern wholesale market distribution network for fresh food products.

[14] Special Report: FAO/WFP *Crop and Food Supply Assessment Mission to Armenia* ....

[15] Asian Development Bank, "Helping Mongolia to combat effects of harsh winter", news release, No. 011/01, 14 February 2001. Available at http://www.adb.org/Documents/News/2001/nr2001011.asp.

Figure VI.1.
CONSUMPTION OF TOTAL FERTILIZERS OF ARMENIA, KYRGYZSTAN AND MONGOLIA, 1991-1998

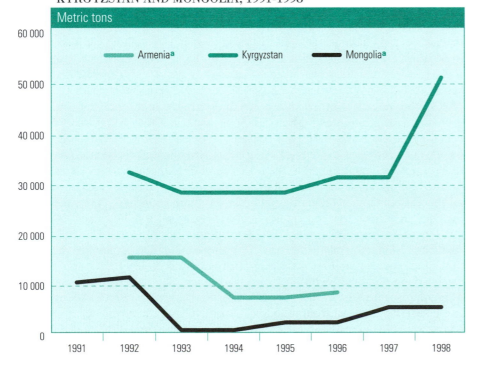

Source: Food and Agriculture Organization of the United Nations (http://apps1.fao.org/servlet, as retrieved in January 2001).

[a] Nitrogenous fertilizers consumption only.

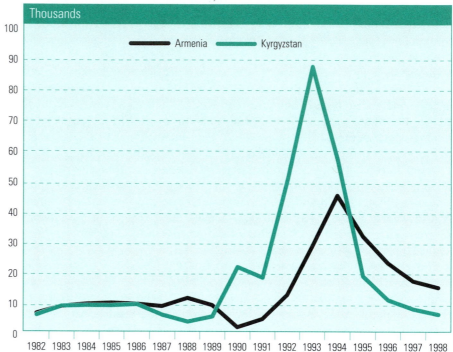

Figure VI.2.
NET EMIGRATION FROM ARMENIA AND KYRGYZSTAN
TO THE RUSSIAN FEDERATION, 1982-1998

Source: UN/DESA, based on State Committee of the Russian Federation on Statistics (Goskomstat of Russia), *The Demographic Yearbook of Russia: Statistical Handbook* (Moscow, State Committee of the Russian Federation on Statistics, 1999), table 7.2.

[16]   These reported numbers most likely underestimate the magnitude of emigration from the countries.

of the 1990s (see figure VI.2)[16]. In the short term, the large movement of skilled workers out of these countries exacerbated the drastic decline in industrial output. In the longer term, shortages of skilled workers will hinder the adaptation and efficient use of new production technologies. In Kyrgyzstan, emigrants include not only nationals, but also Russian nationals and ethnic Germans.

Most of the economies in transition began the transition process with varying degrees of monetary overhang and price controls, which generated latent or actual inflationary pressure. When price controls were removed in the early 1990s, the three countries experienced extremely high rates of inflation. Armenia had inflation as high as 5,000 per cent in 1994; Kyrgyzstan experienced inflation of over 1,200 per cent in 1993 (see table A.9). Mongolia fared better, but it suffered triple-digit inflation in two consecutive years. The inflationary pressure contributed to the contraction of output in all three countries.

The high inflation was reduced by anti-inflationary measures as part of overall macroeconomic stabilization policy in the three countries. These measures included tight monetary and credit policies, wage control policies and the introduction of treasury bills and other non-inflationary sources of fiscal deficit financing. Mongolia, one of the early reformers among the economies in transition, implemented its first stabilization programme in 1992. Because of this early action, together with the fact that it already had its own currency, Mongolia was the first of the three countries to dampen its inflationary pressure and it suffered the least from inflation. Despite having excess stocks of roubles, Kyrgyzstan did not start a stabilization programme until mid-1993, and Armenia not until late 1994/early 1995, after prolonged and severe inflation.

Export demand fell sharply as a result of the economic decline of other CMEA member States and the shift from State-managed trade to a market-based trading system.[17] Following the breakdown in CMEA trade arrangements in 1989 and 1990, the collapse of the rouble bloc in 1993 and the fall in output in their former markets, payment problems caused a drastic decline in trade among the former CMEA member States and a rapid shift towards trade with countries outside the CMEA area (see table VI.3). Of the three countries, Mongolia's trade structure changed the least, but depressed commodity prices during the second half of the 1990s hurt its exports. The loss of export markets seems to have been particularly significant for Armenia and Kyrgyzstan. These two countries' trade with other republics in the Soviet Union had been as great as their annual GDP.[18]

Imports recovered faster than exports, reflecting the more open and liberalized trade regimes in the second half of the 1990s. As a result, trade deficits have become a major concern for these countries. The trade deficits stood at 30.5 per cent of GDP in Armenia in 1998, 13.9 per cent of GDP in Kyrgyzstan in 1999 and 11.7 per cent of GDP in Mongolia in 1998.[19] These trade deficits, together with deteriorating fiscal positions, put strong pressures on their external debt positions, as discussed below.

Fiscal balances deteriorated sharply at the beginning of the transition, but later stabilized in response to fiscal consolidation efforts and modernization of the fiscal system (see figure VI.3). Fiscal deficits in the early stage of transition probably were inevitable because of the sudden loss of revenues from taxes on income and profits, due to the sharp decline in total output and, to a lesser extent, the loss of resource transfers from the central Government of the Soviet Union. While the transformation of a centrally planned economy to a market-based system implies a large reduction in the role and size of a country's Government, the fiscal authorities in most of the transition economies were unable to devise and enforce tax collection methods that could keep up

[17] United Nations Conference on Trade and Development (UNCTAD), "The integration of selected economies in transition into the international trading system, and its implications for their trade with developing countries" (UNCTAD/ITCDITSB/3 of 15 April 1998), para. 9.

[18] Official trade data for before and after the break-up of the Soviet Union do not provide clear evidence because inter-republic trade under the former Soviet Union was managed at artificially set prices, making conversion of the rouble trade values into market-based dollar prices very uncertain.

[19] Based on International Monetary Fund, "Armenia: Recent Economic Developments and Selected Issues", *IMF Staff Country Report* No. 99/128 (Washington, D.C., IMF, November 1999); Kyrgyz Republic: Selected Issues and Statistical Appendix", *IMF Staff Country Report*, No. 00/31 (Washington, D.C., IMF, October 2000); and "Mongolia: Statistical Annex", *IMF Staff Country Report*, No. 00/26 (Washington, D.C., IMF, March 2000).

Table VI.3.
INTERNATIONAL TRADE OF ARMENIA, KYRGYZSTAN AND MONGOLIA, 1991-1999

	1991		1995		1998		1999	
	Exports	Imports	Exports	Imports	Exports	Imports	Exports	Imports
Total exports and imports (millions of dollars)								
Armenia	68.0[a]	791.0[a]	271.0	856.0	220.5	902.4	232.0	811.0
Kyrgyzstan	46.0[a]	559.0[a]	409.0	522.0	514.0	842.0	454.0	600.0
Mongolia	348.0	360.9	473.3	415.3	345.2	503.3	335.7	425.6
Trade with non CIS-countries as percentage of total trade								
Armenia	..	..	37.3	39.7	79.4	69.1	75.4	76.9
Kyrgyzstan	..	..	34.2	32.4	55.1	47.6	59.7	80.1
Mongolia	32.4	34.0	85.4	49.9	88.2	70.2	87.5	67.4

Source: UN/DESA, based on Inter-State Statistical Committee of the Commonwealth of Independent States, *Commonwealth of Independent States in 2000* (Moscow, Inter-State Statistical Committee of CIS, 2001); and Asian Development Bank, Statistics and Data Systems Division (http://www.adb.org/Statistics/country.asp).

[a] Not including inter-republic trade in the USSR.

Figure VI.3.
GOVERNMENT REVENUE AND EXPENDITURE AS A PERCENTAGE OF GDP OF
ARMENIA, KYRGYZSTAN AND MONGOLIA, 1985-1999[a]

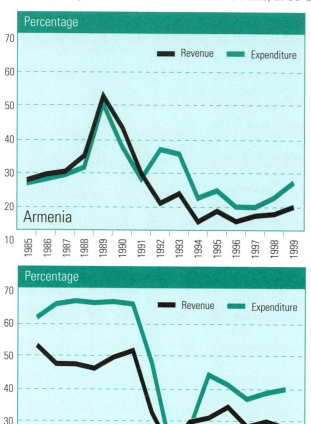

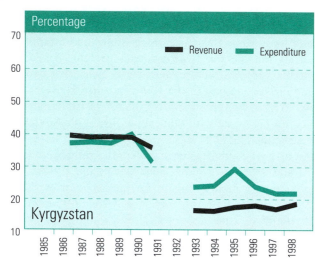

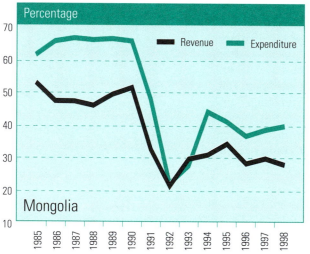

Source: UN/DESA, based on national and international sources.

a   There was a break in series in Kyrgyzstan in 1992.

20   For an international comparison, see *Human Development Report, 2000...*, Human development indicators.

21   Based on World Bank, *Statistical Handbook 1993: States of the Former USSR* (Washington, D.C., World Bank, 1993). While the same data for Mongolia are not available, the country owes 11.1 per cent of the total of the Russian Federation's external claims, the second largest share after Cuba (18.1 per cent). See Oganian N. Hishow, "Russia's external debt: infinite rescheduling?", *Communist and Post-communist Studies*, vol. 34 (2001), pp. 113—128, table 3.

with the changing nature of private economic activities, including a growing unofficial economy. At the same time, demands for fiscal expenditure remained high to maintain previous social and educational programmes, in which the pre-transition levels of attainment had been high relative to countries with similar income levels in the rest of the world.[20]

The sudden and complete loss of fiscal and financial assistance from CMEA and the central Government of the Soviet Union further worsened the fiscal position of these countries. During 1989-1991, the three years prior to its independence, about 31 per cent of the total fiscal revenue of Armenia, or 12 per cent of its GDP, was in the form of grants, presumably from the central Government of the Soviet Union; the corresponding figures were 30 per cent of revenue and 11 per cent of GDP for Kyrgyzstan.[21] Moreover, the grants of government revenue alone do not capture the total magnitude of resource transfers from the central Government of the Soviet Union. Economic assistance was often embedded in the form of barter exchanges of goods and services, with artificially set prices: petroleum produced in the Soviet Union was probably exchanged for less than its international price, for cotton or wool from Kyrgyzstan, for example. Turnover taxes, subsidies and profit rates were set arbitrarily, and sometimes used to inflate or deflate the value of products, making difficult any attempts to estimate the true value of the assistance from the central Government of the Soviet Union to each of its republics and to Mongolia.[22]

The rising external debts of Armenia, Kyrgyzstan and Mongolia during the 1990s reflected both trade and fiscal deficits. The total external debt stock increased from zero at the start of the decade to $800 million in Armenia (42 per cent of its gross national product (GNP)), to $1,150 million in Kyrgyzstan (69 per cent of its GNP) and $740 million in Mongolia (75 per cent its of GNP) in 1998 (see table VI.1).[23] In less than 10 years, the ratios of the total external debt stock to GNP of Kyrgyzstan and Mongolia had risen to exceed the average ratio among the developing and transition countries (42 per cent). Armenia's had risen to reach the average.[24] Along with their increasing external debt, annual debt service is rising in the three countries, though their ratios of debt service to GNP are still below the international average (5.7 per cent in 1998), mainly because most of their debts are in the form of publicly guaranteed long-term loans from donor countries or international financial organizations, including IMF, the World Bank, the Asian Development Bank and the European Bank for Reconstruction and Development. However, without a rapid and significant improvement in their macroeconomic performance and/or a combination of debt rescheduling and forgiveness, these countries, particularly Kyrgyzstan and Mongolia, will have difficulty servicing their debts in a few years time.[25]

Their dependence on external financing is manifested in the fiscal budgets of the three countries. During 1995-1998, the average ratio of external financing to total government revenue was 39 per cent in Armenia, 49 per cent in Kyrgyzstan and 30 per cent in Mongolia; as a proportion of GDP, the averages were 6.5 per cent, 8.2 per cent and 8.8 per cent, respectively.[26] While caution is required in comparing the situations before and after the collapse of the Soviet Union, the dependence of Armenia and Kyrgyzstan on external financing for their fiscal budgets seems to be equal to or greater than their dependence on grants from the central Government of the Soviet Union. Their increasing dependency on external financing and thus their rising debt-service requirements will put significant pressure on the cash flows of the Governments of all three countries, reducing their ability to combat increased poverty and deteriorating social conditions.

Increased vulnerability: poverty and deteriorating social conditions

The severe economic contractions and difficult fiscal conditions during the 1990s have affected every aspect of the lives of the people in the three countries. The economic contractions reduced personal incomes through the loss of jobs, wage reductions and often the non-payment of wages or other forms of compensation. The shrinking role of government institutions, particularly for

[22] For example, while the Government of Armenia under the Soviet Union was a net recipient of grants, the republic appeared to have produced more goods and services than it consumed, based on the difference between net material product (NMP) produced and NMP used. The republic, in essence, was a net creditor of financial resources. See Stuart S. Brown and Misha V. Blekindas, "Who's feeding whom?: a balance of payments approach to Soviet interrepublic relations", mimeo, 1992.

[23] Besides the traditional donor countries, the Russian Federation and Turkmenistan — energy-exporting countries among CIS — are also major creditor countries to some countries in CIS.

[24] Including all the developing and transition countries reported in the Debtor Reporting System of the World Bank. See *Global Development Finance, 2000: Analysis and Summary Tables* (Washington, D. C., World Bank, 2000).

[25] For a detailed study of the debt situation of Armenia and Kyrgyzstan, see International Monetary Fund and World Bank, "Armenia, Georgia, Kyrgyz Republic, Moldova and Tajikistan: external debt and fiscal sustainability", 7 February 2001.

[26] See Stanley Fischer, Ratna Sahay and Carlos A. Vegh, "From Transition to Market: Evidence and Growth Prospects", *IMF Working Paper*, No. WP/98/52 (Washington, D.C., IMF, April 1998).

social programmes, has harmed many aspects of people's lives, and is likely to inhibit medium- to long-term development.

In the former Soviet Union, relatively low income inequality went along with high levels of social expenditure.[27] Since the majority of workers in Armenia, Kyrgyzstan and Mongolia were employed in State-owned enterprises, almost all forms of income—including transfers as well as wages and salaries—were determined by and transmitted through State institutions. As a result, while the average income levels were not as high as those in developed countries, virtually no poverty was reported.

The economic contractions and the resulting shrinkage of the public sector sharply increased the incidence of poverty (table VI.4). The contractions greatly reduced the average income levels in the three countries and many workers lost their jobs in the "official" sector. The Gini coefficient for the distribution of monthly earnings in Kyrgyzstan increased from 0.26 in 1989 to 0.43 in 1996.[28] Armenia, which is rapidly reforming its economy, now has the highest Gini coefficient (0.59) among the economies in transition, for which the average level stands at 0.34.[29] The fall in average incomes and the widening of the income distribution have pushed many people below the poverty line.

The weakening of pension systems also has worsened the incidence of poverty. The systems were inherited from the State pension system in the Soviet Union. They became unsustainable, mainly because of the collapse of

[27] For income distribution in the pre-transition period of Eastern Europe and the Soviet Union, see Anthony B. Atkinson and John Micklewright, *Economic Transformation in Eastern Europe and the Distribution of Income* (New York, Cambridge University Press, 1992) Though the data are not available for Mongolia, income distribution in the country was most probably similar to that in the former Soviet Union.

[28] The coefficient can range from a value of zero, with a completely equal distribution of income (in other words, everyone receives the same income), to a value of 1.0, with a completely unequal distribution (in other words, one person earns the entire income of the society). A Gini coefficient of 0.43 is high by international standards. See Jane Falkingham, "Welfare in transition: trends in poverty and well-being in Central Asia", Centre for Analysis of Social Exclusion (CASE), London School of Economics, CASE paper, No. 20, February 1999.

[29] Government of Armenia, "Interim poverty reduction paper" (March 2001).

Table VI.4.

INCIDENCE OF POVERTY IN ARMENIA, KYRGYZSTAN AND MONGOLIA AS PERCENTAGE OF THE POPULATION, 1991-1999[a]

	1991	1992	1993	1994	1995	1996	1997	1998	1999	Per capita income in 1998 (United States dollars)
Armenia[b]										480
Extreme poverty	..	..	..	..	28	..	..	23	..	
Poverty	..	..	..	..	55	..	..	55	..	
Kyrgyzstan[c]										380
Food poverty	..	..	..	..	..	20	15	23	23	
Poverty	..	..	40	..	..	52	51	64	64	
Mongolia										380
Poverty (World Bank)[d]	..	..	..	..	36	..	..	36	..	
Poverty (Government of Mongolia)[e]	15	18	18	20	16	19	..	..	..	

Source: UN/DESA, based on national and international sources.

[a] Methodologies used vary across countries and over time within a country. Great caution is required when making cross-country comparisons or comparisons over time.

[b] Extreme poverty is set at the level of the value of the minimum consumption basket equal to 7,194 drams per month. Poverty, on the other hand, is set at 11,735 drams per month. The difference is that the latter takes into account the relative shares of food and non-food expenditure of an average household.

[c] Food poverty is set at the level of consumption, below which, even if all resouces were devoted to food, minimum calorific intake (2,100 kilocalories (kcal) could not be met. Poverty represents a minimum level of consumption, taking into account both food and non-food necessities.

[d] World Bank Living Standards Measurement Study survey.

[e] Household Survey, State Statistical Office, Government of Mongolia.

employment, the acceleration of inflation and the loss of tax revenues, leading to the accumulation of pension arrears.

While it is generally agreed that income inequality widened during the initial stages of economic transformation of the former command economies, there is little evidence that the continued liberalization efforts throughout the 1990s have further worsened the situation of the poor. Income distribution in Mongolia seems to have stopped deteriorating in the middle of the 1990s. However, it deteriorated in Kyrgyzstan from 1996-1997 to 1998-1999. Some researchers assert that, among four of the Central Asian countries—Kazakhstan, Kyrgyzstan, Turkmenistan and Uzbekistan—Kyrgyzstan experienced the most pronounced rise in income inequality. As the earliest reformer among this group, Kyrgyzstan vigorously undertook market reforms, which were expected to eventually result in actual or potential earnings' becoming more closely linked to each person's human capital (education and training), efforts and risk-taking. The countries that reformed less rapidly also had increasingly unequal income distributions during the same period, but the changes were less drastic than in Kyrgyzstan. [30]

Poverty, and thus vulnerability to natural or human–caused shocks, also has other facets that cannot be fully described in terms of personal income or expenditure. One is access to public services, such as those that help to provide adequate nutrition for a healthy life, free of avoidable morbidity, and education. Both "input" variables (especially government expenditure on social programmes) and "output" variables (social indicators) help to outline the non-economic aspects of poverty and vulnerability. Government expenditure on education and health declined dramatically in Armenia, Kyrgyzstan and Mongolia during the economic contractions noted earlier, both in absolute terms and as a share of GDP. The shares stabilized, but remained lower than before, in the second half of the decade (see table VI.5). The decline in education spending had noticeable effects on school enrolment ratios in the three countries, particularly at the secondary level. The secondary enrolment ratios in Kyrgyzstan and Mongolia dropped by 15 to 20 percentage points from 1991 to the mid-1990s, and in Armenia by 9 percentage points. Primary education continues to be compulsory, however, keeping the enrolment ratios at that level of education above 80 per cent (table VI.5).

Cuts in education-related subsidies, combined with increasing poverty, have made education more costly relative to household income; the cost of textbooks, school supplies and transportation increasingly have been passed on to students' families. The declining enrolment ratios at the secondary level contrast starkly, however, with increases at the tertiary level, which has seen a proliferation of private colleges and other institutions. More children from relatively affluent families now receive higher forms of education, which will enable them to earn higher incomes in the future, while children from poor families now receive even less education, making it more difficult for them to escape from poverty. There already is some evidence of a stronger relationship between the level of education and earning ability in the economies in transition. [31] The widening education gap between the rich and poor may thus impede both social mobility and economically and socially balanced development in the future.

Reductions in health spending and decreased effectiveness of their health-care systems [32] have worsened the general level of health in Armenia and

[30] See Fischer and Sahay, loc. cit., table 4, for comparisons of the speed and depth of reform among the countries in transition.

[31] Vladimir Mikhalev and Georges Heinrich, "Kyrgyzstan: A Case Study of Social Stratification", *World Institute for Development Economics Research (WIDER) Working Papers*, No. 164, September 1999.

[32] For a brief description of the Soviet era health-care system and reforms now being undertaken, see Serdar Savas and G. Gedik, "Health care reforms in Central Asia" (chap. 8), in UNDP Regional Bureau for Europe and CIS, *Central Asia 2010: Prospects for Human Development* (United Nations publication, Sales No. 99.III.B.7).

Table VI.5.

GOVERNMENT EXPENDITURE AND SOCIAL INDICATORS OF ARMENIA, KYRGYZSTAN AND MONGOLIA, 1991-1999

	1991	1992	1993	1994	1995	1996	1997	1998	1999
Public educational expenditure as percentage of GDP									
Armenia	6.6	7.3	4.5	2.0	2.6	2.0	1.7	1.8	1.9
Kyrgyzstan	..	..	4.2	6.1	6.5	5.2	4.8	4.8	3.9
Mongolia	10.8	6.9	5.8	5.8	5.9	5.7	6.1	6.7	..
Public-health expenditure as percentage of GDP									
Armenia	2.8	4.3	3.3	1.4	1.8	1.4	1.2	1.4	1.4
Kyrgyzstan	..	..	2.6	3.5	3.9	3.1	3.2	2.7	2.3
Mongolia	5.9	4.1	3.8	4.1	3.9	3.8	3.8	3.8	..
Primary enrolment ratio (percentage)									
Armenia[a][b]	72.1	71.9	67.8	61.2	82.3	85.7	86.3	85.7	81.7
Kyrgyzstan	110.7	110.5	112.1	112.7	104.1	..	..	..	..
Mongolia	87.3	75.3	74.7	81.1	88.1	88.4	..	..	..
Secondary enrolment ratio (percentage)									
Armenia[b]	85.8	84.8	81.9	78.1	76.5	77.9	78	76.8	77.4
Kyrgyzstan	98.5	94.8	89.8	88.4	78.8	..	..	..	..
Mongolia	73.8	64.1	62.6	59	59.2	56.2	..	..	..
Tuberculosis incidence (number of new cases per 100,000 population)									
Armenia	20	15.8	15.8	19.5	21.6	24	27.6	37.9	37.7
Kyrgyzstan	56.8	58.1	54.5	61.2	75.8	91.6	119.3	126.9	136.6
Mongolia	71	64.8	60.6	71.8	132.2	119.7	117.7	113	127.8
Infant mortality rate (per 1,000 live births)									
Armenia	17.9	18.5	17.1	15.1	14.2	15.5	15.4	14.7	15.4
Kyrgyzstan	29.7	31.5	31.9	29.1	28.1	25.9	28.6	26.2	..
Mongolia	62.2	59.8	57.4	46.8	44.4	40.0	39.6	35.3	37.3
Life expectancy at birth (years)									
Armenia	72.2	71.5	71.1	71.4	72.3	72.7	73.7	74.4	73.2
Kyrgyzstan	68.6	68.1	67.2	66	65.8	66.5	66.9	67.1	..
Mongolia	62.7[c]	63.6	..	..	63.8	..	65.8	66.2	..

Source: UN/DESA, based on national and international sources.

[a] Up to 1994, the primary schools included grades 1-4, but from 1995 only grades 1-3.
[b] Owing to the large number of unregistered emigrants, the number of students enrolled at school is very low, relative to the total number of school-age children estimated based on the registered population.
[c] 1990.

Kyrgyzstan, particularly during the first half of the 1990s, as evidenced by the increase in tuberculosis (see table VI.5). It is difficult to identify the causes of the deterioration, but it is generally attributed to poor sanitary conditions, infectious diseases, a lack of pharmaceuticals, lower quality of medical care and fragmented health services at the regional level. Another aspect of the weakening of the health system is a lack of good data on morbidity; but there is evidence that the incidence of tuberculosis—a disease that is partly influenced by poverty and economic disadvantage—and sexually transmitted diseases (STDs), such as syphilis and gonorrhoea, are on the rise.[33] The rising incidence of STDs is particularly worrisome because the incidence of human immunodeficiency virus/acquired immunodeficiency syndrome (HIV/AIDS) has followed the trends in STDs in some of the countries that now have major epidemics of HIV/AIDS.

The spread of infectious diseases reflects increased susceptibility of both children and adults, which is largely a consequence of the deterioration of general socio-economic conditions and the lack of funding for building and maintaining the health infrastructure, providing vaccines and other control measures.[34] Because of the increase in susceptibility, the countries' systems of disease surveillance and control, which formerly included widespread childhood vaccination, aggressive case investigation and vaccination of adults in high-risk occupations, have lost their effectiveness.[35]

REGIONAL AND INTERNATIONAL COOPERATION DURING THE 1990s

During the 1990s, the three countries strengthened cooperation with other nearby countries, to try to alleviate the difficulties and increased vulnerability brought about by the transformation of their economies. The international community, recognizing the hardships that these three countries faced and their determined efforts to liberalize their economies, has provided much external assistance, including bilateral aid from donor countries and loans from IMF, the World Bank, the European Bank for Reconstruction and Development and the Asian Development Bank. Mongolia received high and relatively steady flows of aid, amounting to over 20 per cent of its GNP during most of 1993-1998, and Kyrgyzstan received aid amounting to 13-14 per cent of its GNP in 1996-1998. Aid to Armenia, however, declined from a range of 11-15 per cent of its GNP in 1993-1995 to 6-9 per cent in 1996-1998 and to only 5 per cent in 1999 (see table VI.6). International assistance has helped to ease the countries' hardship and vulnerability by financing some of their economic and social programmes, but many aspects of the new cooperation are at an early stage and have produced only limited results.

Armenia, Kyrgyzstan and Mongolia and their neighbours, some of which have similar economic, political and social problems, have recognized the synergy that regional economic cooperation can create. Through stronger trade and investment linkages, robust growth in one country can have a positive effect on the others. The experience of the Association of Southeast Asian Nations (ASEAN) has shown the contribution that regional cooperation can make to its member countries' intraregional trade, and also to trade and FDI between them and north-east Asia, particularly Japan, the Republic of Korea and Taiwan Province of China. Such an association can facilitate the reduction of intraregional tariffs and non-tariff barriers and can create an environment in which member States are more willing to learn from each other about prioritizing, planning and implementing economic and social policies (so-called learning by watching).

[33] Infant mortality rates, the incidence of tuberculosis and other diseases in the CIS countries and Mongolia are likely to be underestimated, because of under-reporting since the transition.

[34] S. Dittmann and others, "Successful control of epidemic diphtheria in the states of the former Union of Soviet Socialist Republics: lessons learned", *Journal of Infectious Diseases*, vol. 181, supplement 1 (2000), pp. S10-S22.

[35] Inefficiency in the health-care system, together with the restricted general government budgets, has led to discussions about rationalizing services, including privatization of health-care services and payment mechanisms.

Table VI.6.
INTERNATIONAL ASSISTANCE TO ARMENIA, KYRGYZSTAN AND MONGOLIA, 1991-1999

	1991	1992	1993	1994	1995	1996	1997	1998	1999
Net official development assistance (millions of dollars)									
Armenia	..	..	55	94	150	117	149	12	94
Kyrgyzstan	..	..	94	172	283	231	238	216	267
Mongolia	..	..	126	182	206	200	247	203	219
International aid as percentage of GNP									
Armenia	0.1	2.4	11.2	14.7	11.3	7.1	8.6	5.8	4.9
Kyrgyzstan	..	0.2	2.2	5.5	8.6	12.9	14.0	13.8	..
Mongolia	..	..	24.0	27.6	21.8	18.9	27.2	20.6	..

Sources: Organisation for Economic Cooperation and Development (OECD), *Development Co-operation* (Paris, OECD, various issues); World Bank, *2000 World Development Indicators CD-ROM* (Washington, D. C., World Bank, 2000); and the National Statistical Service of Armenia.

36 The date of formation and the member States of these organizations are as follows; BSEC was established in 1992: Albania, Armenia, Azerbaijan, Bulgaria, Georgia, Greece, Republic of Moldova, Romania, Russian Federation, Turkey and Ukraine; CAEC in 1998: Kazakhstan, Kyrgyzstan, Tajikistan and Uzbekistan; ECO in 1985: Islamic Republic of Iran, Pakistan and Turkey (six former Soviet republics (Azerbaijan, Kazakhstan, Kyrgyzstan, Tajikistan, Turkmenistan and Uzbekistan) as well as Afghanistan joined in 1992); EAEU in 2000: Belarus, Kazakhstan, Kyrgyzstan, Russian Federation and Tajikistan; GUUAM in 1999: Azerbaijan, Georgia, Republic of Moldova, Ukraine and Uzbekistan.

CIS represented an early attempt to form such a regional association, but it has not been an effective vehicle to ignite economic synergy among the member States, largely because its formation was based on the former political alliance and not on market-based economics. The trade flows of its member countries have tended to be with countries outside CIS.

In the past 10 years, diverse political and economic interests among the members of CIS led to the formation of several subregional and interregional groups or to different members, applying to join existing organizations. The pre-existing or new groups include Black Sea Economic Cooperation (BSEC), the Central Asian Economic Community (CAEC), the Eurasian Economic Union (EAEU), the Economic Cooperation Organization (ECO) and the alignment of five countries: Georgia, Ukraine, Uzbekistan, Azerbaijan and the Republic of Moldova, known as GUUAM.[36] These groups have been established, inter alia, to strengthen regional cooperation in economic development and to facilitate cross-border trade. Because they are still at a very early stage of institutional development, it is difficult to forecast the results these groups eventually produce.

The viability of EAEU as an economic group is uncertain since it does not derive any obvious economic advantage from the cooperation except for its members' proximity to the Russian Federation, which is the centre of economic and political gravity in the region. BSEC and GUUAM have a more viable market-based economic rationale and thus have better prospects of producing regional synergies among their members. BSEC aims to strengthen regional cooperation in the field of economic development, including transport and communications, environmental protection, the elimination of obstacles to the expansion of trade and the creation of appropriate conditions for investment. GUUAM aims to create a free trade zone, strengthen development of Caspian oil deposits and integrate its members into European structures of cooperation. The Presidents of the five countries in GUUAM have emphasized, among other things, cooperation in building a Eurasian Transcaucasus transportation corridor (TRACECA) and other transportation projects. CAEC and ECO have not yet been very active, but the similarity of the trade structures of the Central Asian member countries in both groups would appear to limit the possibilities for increasing intra-group trade flows.

Mongolia does not belong to any of the foregoing regional groups. It is a member of the World Trade Organization and has been reorienting its trade towards several East Asian partners, especially China, Japan and the Republic of Korea; such a reorientation is geographically natural and economically more viable. These partners have traditionally preferred to participate in the multi-lateral, that is to say, World Trade Organization-based, trading system rather than in regional or bilateral systems, though they are now discussing the possi-bility of establishing regional and bilateral agreements to supplement the mul-tilateral system.

Regional conflicts in the Transcaucasus area and related political, rather than economic, considerations are major reasons why Armenia has not joined the GUUAM group. Given the currently fragile economic conditions of the GUUAM member countries, Armenia's decision not to join the group does not seem to be having any negative (or positive) economic impacts. While the lack of economic linkages to adjacent countries is not encouraging for Armenia's long-term development, its membership in the BSEC group should be helpful. Historical differences have complicated the process of regional integration in the Transcaucasus area and neighbouring countries, and will continue to be important obstacles for the foreseeable future, but strong political will and lead-ership at both national and regional levels could facilitate viable integration.

As part of their efforts to liberalize their economies, Kyrgyzstan and Mongolia have become members of the World Trade Organization and Armenia is at an advanced stage of setting out the terms and conditions of its entry, as noted earlier.[37] World Trade Organization membership will consolidate their open trade policies and is expected to help them, to some extent, re-establish regional and establish new global trade linkages in the future. World Trade Organization membership—even the act of negotiating it—is an important sig-nal of a country's intentions because it legally binds a Government to policy reforms.

In the short run, however, the remoteness of these countries from the major global markets and the small size of their economies and of the economies of most of their adjacent countries will limit the impact of trade liberalization; with a narrow trade base and limited access to the external market, the imme-diate impacts of liberalization cannot be expected to be very large. Ongoing regional conflicts, particularly some involving Armenia, and an increasing inci-dence of illegal drug trafficking in Central Asia, including Kyrgyzstan, make customs clearance at their borders slow and costly, constraining the potential benefits from their World Trade Organization accession. Kyrgyzstan's acces-sion to the World Trade Organization has posed economic problems for other members of a customs union formed by members of EAEU: Kazakhstan and the Russian Federation (non-members of the World Trade Organization) raised tariffs, at least temporarily, on imports from Kyrgyzstan, to prevent imports that have originated outside of Kyrgyzstan from evading Kazakh or Russian customs duties.

The reduction of transport costs is an issue that the three countries and the international community have recognized as being important for sustainable

37 World Trade Organization web site, http://www.wto.org. According to EBRD, *Transition Report, 2000: Employment, Skills and Transition* (London, EBRD, 2000), Armenia's acces-sion to the World Trade Organization is expected in 2001.

development. The United Nations General Assembly and United Nations organizations have emphasized the importance of the transit environment in the landlocked countries, including countries in the former Soviet Union and Mongolia, as a factor affecting their ability to enter world markets.[38] Various efforts have been undertaken to improve this environment, including efforts to introduce the Automated System for Customs Data (ASYCUDA) and the Advanced Cargo Information System (ACIS) in some countries.[39] However, there is a lack of financial resources, infrastructure, human resources and managerial development to put these systems in place, as recognized by the Assembly and other United Nations bodies.

Investing to create more efficient transit transport systems in landlocked countries should benefit consumers because they could purchase more varieties of imported goods at lower prices. However, Armenia, Kyrgyzstan and Mongolia already have chronic trade deficits and large accumulated external debts, because their exports have not grown as fast as their imports. Governments and the international community should pay due attention to the trade balance of these economies when they become more integrated into the global economy through improved transport systems.

Geography and its effect on policy choices

The economic and social shocks associated with the collapse of CMEA and the Soviet Union are not the sole reason for the hardships suffered by the transition economies in Central Asia. Some countries in Central and Eastern Europe are already recovering from these shocks, having devised new policies and institutions aimed at establishing fully fledged market economies. However, many of the smaller, less developed countries, notably Armenia, Kyrgyzstan and Mongolia, have found it difficult to develop new market-based activities that could benefit from their new access to the globalized economy. The main differences between the Eastern and Central European countries and these three countries involve geography and other initial conditions at the onset of transition. International proposals to reduce their transport costs reflect a recognition of the geographical burden that landlocked countries must shoulder.

Armenia, Kyrgyzstan and Mongolia are landlocked inside the vast Eurasian continent, do not have the large fuel resources of other CIS members, are distant from the major world markets and are surrounded by countries with similarly low per capita incomes.[40] Besides these geographical disadvantages, these countries did not have any recent history of market-based development; when CMEA and later the Soviet Union collapsed, they did not have the types of institutions needed to support or complement the development of market-based activities. Their difficult path of economic transformation during the 1990s has reflected, to a large extent, their initial conditions and geography, which "imply that different countries faced different opportunities, and these differences in prospects might account for the success and/or the speed of transition".[41] In short, their initial conditions were not conducive to achieving sustainable development in the short to medium term.

Some recent analyses of economic growth theory have found that the lower the initial per-capita income (one of the many initial conditions), the faster the

[38] General Assembly resolution 55/181 of 20 December 2000 entitled "Transit environment in the landlocked states in Central Asia and their transit developing neighbours".

[39] UNCTAD, "Other matters in the field of trade and development: (a) specific actions related to the particular needs and problems of landlocked developing countries" (TD/B/46/7), 20 September 1999.

[40] Austria and Switzerland, and of the former CMEA countries, the Czech Republic, Hungary and Slovakia, are small landlocked countries, but are adjacent to rich neighbours and part of a major world market.

[41] Joseph E. Stiglitz, "Quis custodiet ipsos custodies?: corporate governance failures in the transition", paper presented at the Annual Bank Conference on Development Economics – Europe, Paris, 21–23 June 1999, p. 3.

subsequent rate of growth[42]. According to these analyses, with other things being equal, countries with lower levels of per capita income at the onset of the transition have more opportunities to catch up with the world's most productive technologies than those with higher levels of income. They should thus experience a higher growth rate, although they might not attain in the medium term a higher per capita income. The experience of the economies in transition in the 1990s, however, shows the opposite; those with higher per capita income grew faster than those with lower income because other things were not equal. In particular, any market system must be supported by a set of institutions—laws, regulations and organizations to enforce them—that facilitate, strengthen or complement market transactions and in this case the quality of institutions varied widely across countries.[43] There were also great differences in the geographical situation of the transition economies.

Differences in geographical conditions have important implications for long-term development. First, a remote country (as measured by its distance from the nearest cluster of rich countries) is at an obvious disadvantage for trade. While there is no comprehensive explanation of how distance affects trade,[44] the geographical distance between two countries can be thought of as a proxy for differences in language, culture, consumer taste, market conditions and so forth, as well as a measure of transport cost, all of which make international marketing efforts more difficult, thus limiting trade flows. Second, high costs of international trade associated with being landlocked "represent a serious constraint on the economic development of landlocked countries".[45] Third, the newly independent countries in the former Soviet Union have established their own currencies and national legal frameworks, which add extra costs to their already high trade and transit transport costs, further inhibiting trade of goods and services and movement of people among these countries. Fourth, because of their small economic size, establishing large-scale industries in these countries is difficult. Without large external markets, increasing returns to scale in production (the characteristic of large-scale industries and continuing improvement in global transportation) may limit the extent to which a small country can develop or sustain a viable industrial structure. Finally, geography itself is a factor in the choice of economic policy, which, in turn, affects the path of development; for example, countries with large rents coming from the export of mineral resources may be able to afford a restrictive trade policy.

The disadvantage of suddenly becoming remote is clear if one compares Armenia, Kyrgyzstan and Mongolia with the Baltic countries, Estonia, Latvia and Lithuania. One of the reasons why the Baltic (and other Central and Eastern European) countries had a better economic performance than these three countries during the 1990s was their proximity to Western Europe. Partly because of this proximity, the historical and cultural traditions in the Baltic countries also are more like those in Western Europe, and these areas also had had more recent experience with a market economy than Armenia, Kyrgyzstan and Mongolia. While the three Baltic countries are small and resource-poor, they have access to the sea and to richer neighbouring countries. This access helped them to recover from the collapse of the Soviet Union and CMEA, through water-borne trade with the West.[46] The external trade of Latvia and Lithuania did not decline as sharply as that of the three landlocked countries in

[42] See, for example, Robert J. Barro and Xavier Sala-i-Martin, *Economic Growth* (Cambridge, Massachusetts, MIT Press, 1999)

[43] *World Economic and Social Survey, 2000 …*, chap. VIII.

[44] John McCallum, "National borders matter: Canada-U.S. regional trade patterns", *American Economic Review*, vol. 85, No. 3 (June 1995), pp. 615–623.

[45] UNCTAD, "Other matters in the field of trade and development "…, p. 1.

[46] Martha de Melo and others, "Circumstance and Choice: The Role of Initial Conditions and Policies in Transition Economies", *World Bank Policy Research Working Paper*, No. 1866 (Washington, D. C., World Bank, December 1997).

[47] Constantine Michalopoulos, "The Integration of Transition Economies into the World Trading System", *World Bank Policy Research Working Papers*, No. 2182 (Washington, D. C., World Bank, September 1999), table 1.

[48] Fischer and Sahay, loc. cit.

[49] High freight and insurance costs are associated with being landlocked and with distance from world markets. See John Luke Gallup, Jeffrey D. Sachs and Andrew D. Mellinger, *Geography and Economic Development*, NBER Working Paper, No. 6849 (Cambridge, Massachusetts, National Bureau of Economic Research, December 1998), sect. III.

[50] UNCTAD, "Other matters in the field of trade and development" … para. 6. See also UNCTAD, *Handbook of International Trade and Development Statistics* (United Nations publication, Sales No. E/F.95.II.D.15), table 5.3.

[51] UNCTAD, "Statistical tables" submitted to the Trade and Development Board, Meeting of Governmental Experts from Landlocked and Transit Developing Countries and Representatives of Donor Countries and Financial and Development Institutions, New York, 18–20 June 1997.

[52] For further discussion of the gravity model, see Jeffrey A. Frankel, *Regional Trading Blocs in the World Economic System* (Washington, D. C., Institute for International Economics, 1997), chap. 4. It should be noted that the same idea could be applied to bilateral FDI.

[53] Ibid., p. 71.

[54] Jeffrey A. Frankel and David Romer, "Does trade cause growth?", *American Economic Review*, vol. 89, No. 3 (June 1999), pp. 379–399.

the 1990s, and Estonia's trade was even higher in 1998 than in 1991.[47] Partly because of their geography and favourable initial conditions and effective policy implementation, the Baltic countries had better growth performance during the 1990s than other countries in the former Soviet Union.[48]

High transit transport costs hinder the integration of landlocked countries into the global economy.[49] The high costs of exporting goods and services, including high insurance payments for potential losses or damages, limit the price competitiveness of these countries; similarly, the high costs of importing goods and services make domestic prices more expensive than typical international prices. The high prices of imported materials, capital goods and services also may be reflected in the prices of exportable goods produced at home, further eroding these countries' competitive position. Freight costs were 14.7 per cent of total c.i.f. (cost, insurance and freight) import values of a number of landlocked developing countries in 1994 (the latest year for which data are available), compared with 7.2 per cent for all developing countries and 4.0 per cent for developed countries. Similarly, landlocked countries had to spend 17.7 per cent of their export earnings on freight and insurance while the developing countries as a whole spent 8.7 per cent.[50] Mongolia spent 14.7 per cent of its export earnings to cover these costs in 1994.[51] Data on Armenia and Kyrgyzstan are not available, but it is reasonable to assume that the two countries have a high ratio similar to or higher than that of Mongolia, given the poor conditions of their and their neighbours' transport infrastructure.

If the gravity model of bilateral trade is used to measure the disadvantages of being remote and landlocked, and thus of having high transit transport costs, it posits in a simple form that the volume of bilateral trade is positively related to the product of the sizes of two economies (typically measured by GDP or population), but inversely related to the distance between the two economies.[52] The model implies that, given the size of a country and its location, it should trade more with countries in the same region, because they are closer, and more with larger countries. African countries should trade more with Europe than with the United States of America, while countries in Latin America and the Caribbean should have stronger trade linkages with the United States than with Europe. Small, remote countries, such as Armenia, Kyrgyzstan and Mongolia, will not be major trading partners for most countries.

According to a typical analysis based on this theory, after allowing for the effects of other relevant variables, when the distance increases by 1 per cent, trade falls by 0.6 per cent.[53] This implies that, for example, if Armenia were located halfway between Western Europe and its actual location, the volume of trade between the two areas would be 30 per cent higher. Similar analysis suggests that being landlocked further limits bilateral trade. One estimate is that, if one bilateral trading partner is landlocked, trade is about one third less, when other variables, including the sizes of the countries and the distance between them, are held constant.[54] If Armenia had access to navigable waters, for example, its trade with Western Europe should be similar to that in the hypothetical case of reducing its distance from Western Europe by half.

The basic gravity model does not, however, encompass changes in institutional arrangements (including political and legal frameworks) over time. For example, the decline in trade among countries in the former Soviet Union is difficult to explain solely by the contractions of aggregate economic activities of these countries. One possible explanation for the drastic declines is that the trade framework under CMEA had favoured trade among CMEA member States but once the framework was dissolved and the legal and political barriers between these countries and the West were lowered, trade among the former CMEA members became relatively less attractive.

Of particular significance has been the creation of the new economic borders between the countries that were part of the former Soviet Union. Each of these countries has established its own legal and policy frameworks within its own territories and these national systems may be detrimental to increased international trade.[55] Visa requirements and other forms of border inspections, which are important at least partially to prevent smuggling and terrorist activities in some countries in Central Asia, also limit the legitimate cross-national movement of people, goods and services, and may cause hardship for people living in remote areas. National borders have surprisingly large effects on flows and prices, according to many empirical studies. For example, trade between two provinces in Canada is more than 20 times larger than trade between a province in Canada and a State in the United States, after accounting for other relevant variables.[56] The historical, linguistic and legal differences between two countries may partially account for such border effects, but some economists argue that exchange-rate volatility and other costs of international trade, including tariff and non-tariff barriers, explain a larger part of the border effect.[57]

No matter what factors account for the effect, borders have negative effects on trade flows. Strong feelings of national spirit at the initial stage of independence may not harmonize well with those of other countries, especially other former members of a unified State, thus leading to mutual isolation.[58] This consideration is less relevant for Mongolia than for Armenia and Kyrgyzstan.

A third implication of a country's geographical isolation for its long-term development is that fewer economic linkages with the rest of the world, particularly with neighbouring countries, imply fewer chances of establishing new industries in small countries (other things being equal). Once a country seeks to end its isolation, it should expect to see the development of industries that are location-specific, such as mineral extraction, tourism and agro-industry. Industrial development in Armenia, Kyrgyzstan and Mongolia seems to have evolved along these lines, notably mining industries in Mongolia and Kyrgyzstan, tourism in Kyrgyzstan and agro-industry in Armenia and Mongolia. The question, however, is what other industries can be expected to develop subsequently. Agro- or mining-processing industries based on raw materials that the countries produce can be expected to arise. However, high transport costs are not conducive to the development of those industries with a high weight-to-value content, such as unprocessed primary products. In general, high transport costs offset or limit the gains from liberalized market access and impede landlocked developing countries' effective participation in international trade. The advance of transportation and communication technology over the last 100 years has made it faster and cheaper to ship goods and deliver services, but has not eliminated the distance factor in bilateral trade flows.[59] Even though transportation has become faster, cheaper and safer, the distance between two locations still matters, partly because technological improvement in transportation has not completely eliminated the cultural and linguistic "distance" between countries. Better transport technologies have affected all modes

[55] For a discussion of how history and tradition have influenced institution-building in the economies in transition, see Pauline Jones Luong, "After the break-up: institutional design in transitional states", *Comparative Political Studies*, vol. 33, No. 5 (June 2000), pp. 563–592.

[56] McCallum, op. cit. His estimates are based on the year 1988, the dawn of the Canada-United States free trade agreement. Helliwell subsequently re-estimated the border effect between the two countries using data for 1993–1996, concluding that the factor is about 12, which is still very high (John F. Helliwell, *How Much Do National Borders Matter?* (Washington, D. C., Brookings Institution, 1998)).

[57] For example, a recent paper estimates that the factor is about 6 within Canada, while with the United States, trade rises only 25 per cent, after controlling for the sizes of the countries and for the size of the bilateral trade barrier relative to the average barrier of the two countries with all their trading partners. See James E. Anderson and Eric van Wincoop, *Gravity with Gravitas: A Solution to the Border Puzzle*, NBER Working Paper, No. 8079 (Cambridge, Massachusetts, National Bureau of Economic Research, January 2001). Maurice Obstfeld and Kenneth Rogoff, in *The Six Major Puzzles in International Macroeconomics: Is There a Common Cause?* NBER Working Paper, No. 7777 (Cambridge, Massachusetts, National Bureau of Economic Research, July 2000), on the other hand, emphasize the importance of transportation costs in explaining the magnitude of the border effect.

[58] S. Frederick Starr, "Lands of the former USSR: eight years on", Central Asia-Caucasus Institute, Johns Hopkins University (http://www.sais-jhu.edu/caci/Publications/land%20%ofFSU.htm).

[59] Frankel, op. cit.

60 William R. Block, "An unpopular essay on transportation", *Journal of Transport Geography*, vol. 9 (2001), pp. 5-6.

61 Charles Kenny, "Why aren't countries rich?: weak states and bad neighourhoods", *Journal of Development Studies*, vol. 35, No. 5 (June 1999), pp. 26–47.

62 For implications of such policy mismanagement for Central Asian countries, see Richard Auty, "Does Kazakstan oil wealth help or hinder the transition?", Harvard Institute for International Development, Development Discussion Paper, No. 615 (December 1997); and R. M. Auty, "Transition reform in the mineral-rich Caspian region countries", *Resources Policy*, vol. 27, No. 1 (March 2001), pp. 25–32.

63 Furthermore, in the first three years of the World Trade Organization (1995–1997), non-World Trade Organization and non-market economies were more likely to be subjected to anti-dumping actions. See Richard Pomfret, "Regional trade arrangements and economies in transition: the Central Asian countries", School of Economics, Adelaide University, Working Paper 00-9 (December 2000).

64 De Melo and others, loc. cit., p. 33.

65 For related theoretical discussion, see Gallup and others, loc. cit., pp. 27–30.

of transportation—air, ground and water—for both short and long distances, so that the transport costs of landlocked countries have remained high relative to those of other countries.[60]

Just as the size of a country limits the types of industries that can operate profitably there, so does its geographical conditions as a whole limit the spectrum of policy options.[61] One aspect of the relationship between geography and the choice of economic policy is the availability of mineral rents. Countries with large mineral rents face less stringent foreign exchange constraints, but they often form over-optimistic expectations about future returns from mineral extraction, leading to a less disciplined fiscal stance.[62] A striking difference between the policies of Armenia, Kyrgyzstan and Mongolia, on the one hand, and those of some CIS countries with relatively abundant mineral fuel resources, on the other, is in their degree of liberalization of the external sector. As noted above, Mongolia and Kyrgyzstan are now members of the World Trade Organization and Armenia is at an advanced stage of setting out the terms and condition of entry; although some other CIS countries have established working parties with the World Trade Organization to prepare for possible accession, they still lag behind Armenia in this respect.

Armenia, Kyrgyzstan and Mongolia, with few economically exploitable mineral fuel resources (as of now at least) and small domestic economies, had very limited options for sustainable development without ready access to external markets and financing. Their decision to join the World Trade Organization, therefore, is a sound policy choice. It enables them to benefit from the most-favoured-nation clause guaranteed under its rules, with the lower tariff rates of the Generalized System of Preferences, and affords them access to official multilateral funding, which often is conditional upon the implementation of new policies for structural reform and liberalization.[63] It has been suggested that "Mongolia and the Kyrgyz Republic, for example, reformed more rapidly than would have been expected given their initial conditions";[64] but this type of assertion, based on cross-country regressions, does not pay due consideration to the role that geographical conditions play in policy choices.[65] As argued earlier, liberalization was the correct strategy for the countries to pursue, and this has been recognized by those who have provided external financing, including IMF, the World Bank, and the regional development banks.

CONCLUDING REMARKS: IS LIBERALIZATION A BLESSING OR A CURSE?

As a result of the sharp contraction of economic activity during the first half of the 1990s, Armenia, Kyrgyzstan and Mongolia are facing increased uncertainty, and are more vulnerable to economic shocks and natural disasters. Severely restricted government resources do not permit the authorities to shield the population from adverse impacts. Yet these countries have not yet reached a stage where they can expect much acceleration of economic activity or social improvement in the near future, even though their economic performance has stabilized and even improved somewhat since the mid-1990s. Among the three countries, Mongolia was affected least by the collapse of the centrally planned economic system, and its overall macroeconomic performance has fared the best. Even so, some people in Mongolia are more exposed to risk than they were before the transition, as their recent experience with drought and winter storms demonstrated.[66] The countries are vigorously rebuilding their economies and societies, but remaining weaknesses in the current system, particularly in the legal and financial spheres, hinder their full integration into the global economy.

At the same time as they strive to maximize the potential benefits from increased market-based activities and greater integration into the global economy, it is a major responsibility of the Governments to rebuild the countries' economic and social systems so as to limit economic damage during the transformation to market-oriented economies. The Government, with participation of local communities and civil society, is the primary national institution that can consider, prioritize, plan and implement the realignment of a country's economic structures, based on local needs, conditions and social values, including justice. The international community and neighbouring countries can play a catalytic role in assisting these countries to rebuild their economies.

Liberalization of their economies and increased global flows of goods and services can benefit consumers in these countries, through wider access to higher-quality imported goods; but many of their existing industries have already lost domestic and external markets because of the collapse of CMEA and the Soviet Union. Underdevelopment of the financial sector, which was neglected under the socialist system, hinders both the mobilization of funds to finance domestic investment and the efficient allocation of resources among sectors and subnational regions.[67] To ease the constraints on their economies, the countries have undertaken much deregulation and market liberalization, which caused hardships for many of their citizens. Globalization of the world economy, particularly increased access to markets in other countries and to private external finance, is potentially beneficial to these countries (and other newly independent countries in the former Soviet Union). In fact, inflows of FDI increased sharply in the late 1990s; in 1998, the year for which the latest data are available, the share of FDI in gross fixed capital formation was 71 per cent in Armenia and 50 per cent in Kyrgyzstan (though investment levels in the two countries have been depressed).[68] In Mongolia, the share was only 7 per cent, but the average annual FDI inflow for the period of 1997–1999 was 5 times greater than the average of 1992–1993. In certain industries, FDI is playing an important role in rejuvenating production activities. For example, Canadian investment in gold mining industries in Kyrgyzstan and Mongolia led to sharp increase in gold outputs, now making gold exports the leading source of foreign exchange earnings for the two countries. Outside the mining sector, the impact of external financing has still been limited, however. Potential investors in areas often use current macroeconomic fundamentals and the perceived "potential" of a country as the litmus test for new private investments, and have not yet found these countries attractive. However, as the investment they are attracting is long-term FDI, and not speculative short-term flows, the Asian crisis did little damage to them. Moreover, the major part of their external financing has come from official sources.[69]

Overall, it is fair to say that the three countries have completed or are nearing completion of the first stage of transforming their economies—they have attained political and macroeconomic stability and laid an institutional founda-

[66] For more information, see the web site of UNDP in Mongolia at http://www.un-mongolia.mn.

[67] Daniel Gros and Marc Suhrcke, "Ten years after: what is special about transition countries?", European Bank for Reconstruction and Development Working Paper, No. 56 (August 2000).

[68] UNCTAD, World Investment Report 2000: Cross-border Mergers and Acquisitions and Development (United Nations publication, Sales No. E.00.II.D.20).

[69] There are a few cases in which foreign investors are playing a major role in reinvigorating investment and industrial output. For example, FDI in the gold mining industry in Kyrgyzstan and Mongolia by Canadian companies increased gold production in the second half of the 1990s, now making gold exports the leading source of foreign exchange earnings.

tion on which market prices can efficiently determine the allocation of resources. Price indicators have stabilized and so has output, albeit at a rather low level. As is evident in the successful accession of Kyrgyzstan and Mongolia to the World Trade Organization and the advanced state of Armenia's progress towards that goal, the majority of their economic activities are now free from unnecessary government control; private motivation and coordination through market mechanisms can now replace the former role of central planning. The achievements of the three countries during the past 10 years have exceeded most observers' expectations at the beginning of their transition. Their efforts deserve recognition, as does the hardship suffered by their people during the difficult first stage of transition.

From the beginning of the transition, the international community, particularly the Bretton Woods institutions, recognized that the rapid creation of macroeconomic stability and an environment conducive to private activities would be the key to successful transformation, as some Central and Eastern European countries have demonstrated. However, the international community underestimated the difficulties of transforming an economy from a centrally planned to a market system. These difficulties were rooted in the lack of experience with large and sudden transformations. Many ideas implemented during the transition had to be borrowed from other experiences, which might not have been readily transferable.[70] The sudden transformation of the economies to a market-based system also disrupted many public services. The market mechanism has proved to be inadequate in providing a socially optimal level of these services even in developed countries. The deterioration in education and health services, in particular, is now feared to be having long-term negative impacts on the countries' growth. During the first stage of transition, the international community learned that the legacy of the central planning system would be tenacious and that local conditions—including geographical and other initial conditions—had a strong influence on the process of transformation; the outcomes in different countries have varied a great deal.[71] In a sense, it was naive to assume that well-functioning markets would emerge as soon as the central planning system broke down.

What, then, should be the main elements of the second stage of the transformation? A likely answer is to create market-supporting or complementing institutions, including some to enforce or implement laws and regulations enacted during the first stage, in a sequence that will help markets to function effectively. And how can the international community best assist these and other countries with economies in transition to pass through that stage? A likely answer to this question is: by providing goods and services that markets often fail to offer.[72] In some ways, these are more daunting tasks than simply removing State controls and regulations. The new laws and regulations that were enacted during the early 1990s must be effectively enforced, and new rules must be introduced to make contracts binding and enforceable, particularly those in the area of competition policies, and property rights and those involving the financial industry. At the same time, public institutions must be transformed so as to create appropriate incentives (rather than impose output goals) for private activities, through regulation and monitoring.

The Governments also need to build institutional capacity to complement market activities. These cannot be expected to provide the socially optimal lev-

[70] Marie Lavigne, "Ten years of transition: a review article", *Communist and Post-Communist Studies*, vol. 33 (2000), pp. 475 – 483.

[71] Fischer and Sahay, loc. cit., p. 20.

[72] Keith Griffin, "The role of the state in transition" (chap. 4), in *Central Asia 2010* ...

els of all goods and services, especially those with public-goods characteristics. Such institution-building includes the establishment of tax codes and tax collection authorities, which should fairly and equitably levy taxes based on market transactions. The areas for government action include the provision of health care and education; the design, management and provision of social safety nets—including pensions and unemployment insurance; and environmental management. Not coincidentally, these areas experienced the steepest declines during the 1990s and, as a result, many people are now more vulnerable to poor health and other consequences of reduced income or natural disasters. At present, inefficiency in the health-care system, together with the restricted general government budgets, has led to discussions about rationalizing services, including privatization of health-care services and the institution of a payment mechanism. However, due consideration should be given to carefully balancing the need for fiscal consolidation with the need to control disease and to maintain a viable health-care system extending to all citizens.

Beyond institution-building and enforcing laws and regulations, however, questions remain about the most appropriate role for Governments during the next stage. Should the Government be actively involved in industrial policy, for example, or should the allocation of resources among different industries be left to markets, which in theory should eventually establish an economically efficient mix of businesses? While criticizing "over-industrialization" in the past, no one has convincingly proposed a way to reabsorb the large numbers of workers who left the manufacturing sector during the 1990s and are now economically inactive or employed, although not very productively, in other sectors. The post-war European experience in restructuring industry suggests a useful role for active involvement of the State, but current thinking stops most development advisers far short of recommending that role to the Governments of the countries in transition. On the other hand, the world has changed greatly since the end of the cold war, and globalization of the world economy may have made the idea of active industrial policy obsolete. In these circumstances, the best policy is the one the countries are pursuing—to rely on the market to determine how industries are structured and what type of workers and how many of them are employed in each particular industry. This is especially the case as many of the industries that operated previously had been set up without consideration of market forces or of transport costs. New industries should only be market-based and competitive on world markets, and external official assistance, therefore, must aim at assisting these countries in building their capacity both to facilitate and to complement market activities so as to attract domestic and foreign investment. Such assistance should certainly not attempt to revive industries that could not survive in the new competitive global environment.

The international community, together with each country, must devise tailor-made aid programmes that suit the country's local conditions and needs, without worsening its external debt situation. Armenia, Kyrgyzstan and Mongolia have proceeded very far in liberalizing and stabilizing their economies. With the legacy of the central planning system, with small domestic markets and with their situation of having become suddenly landlocked, the three countries have many obstacles to clear before embarking on a more sustained economic growth path. Their endeavours should continue in the foreseeable future. To sustain their determined efforts to allow their economies to develop, the international community needs a long-term strategy to assist them. For example, at present, the fact that the external debt situations of Kyrgyzstan and Mongolia are deteriorating rapidly will mean that their debt-payments situations will be difficult in a few years time. Furthermore, all three countries will face, to varying degrees, a tight liquidity constraint (high ratio of debt-service to export earnings), which limits the Governments' ability to consolidate their fiscal structures and rebuild the social safety nets that existed before the transition. Bilateral donors and international financial institutions can help by devising debt-relief programmes, perhaps comprising a combination of debt-payment rescheduling and forgiveness with increases in the grant element of concessional loans.

VII VULNERABILITY TO NATURAL DISASTERS

The number of people affected by natural disasters in the world appears to have increased considerably over the past few decades. There is also evidence that the costs of natural disasters have accelerated in recent years. The fact that rapid demographic and economic growth patterns have disturbed the balance between ecosystems has, in turn, increased the frequency or severity of some natural disasters, such as floods and droughts. It is also generally agreed that poverty and disaster vulnerability are closely intertwined because low income tends to force poor people to behave in ways that expose them to greater risk.

Vulnerability to natural disasters is the result of a complex range of variables that include not only the location of human settlements and the magnitude of the disaster itself, but also the socio-economic, institutional, demographic and environmental characteristics of the disaster area, as well as the quality of its basic infrastructure. Recurrent natural disasters may have adverse impacts on economic growth because they can disrupt investment patterns, create obstacles for integration into an increasingly globalized world economy and limit capital accumulation in the long run. Poorer developing countries prone to natural hazards are particularly vulnerable because they are often forced to divert scarce resources from socio-economic development into disaster relief activities.

The present chapter shows that floods were by far the most damaging type of natural disasters during the 1990s, in terms of both human impacts and socio-economic losses. Vulnerability to flooding disasters around the world is almost always differentiated by the socio-economic conditions of different income groups in the disaster area. In general, the poorer the income group (or the country), the more vulnerable it is likely to be to the adverse impacts of floods. Although structural engineering approaches to flood control are widely used around the world, this chapter argues that innovative tools to mitigate the impacts of natural disasters, such as floods, can be particularly effective in poor developing countries.

NATURAL DISASTERS AND DEVELOPMENT

The interaction of human development and natural disasters has gone through continuous but distinct phases, from human adjustment to natural phenomena in primitive times to increasing human control over nature during the modern age. However, rapid economic and population growth during the twentieth century had adverse environmental consequences which, in turn, contributed

1 The modern concept of sustainable development was broadly defined by the report of the World Commission on Environment and Development, *Our Common Future* (Oxford, Oxford University Press, 1987), as development that "meets the needs of the present without compromising the ability of future generations to meet their own needs". An internationally agreed programme of action on sustainable development is contained in *Agenda 21: Earth Summit—The United Nations Programme of Action from Rio* (United Nations publication, Sales No. E.93.I.11).

2 There are, of course, several well-known differences regarding economic, environmental and social dimensions of sustainable development, ranging from disagreements over poverty reduction to various perspectives on the concept of intergenerational equity. See, for example, S. Anand and A. Sen, "Human development and economic sustainability", *World Development*, vol. 28, No. 12 (December 2000), pp. 2029-2049; and W. K. Jaeger, "Is sustainability optimal? Examining the differences between economists and environmentalists", *Ecological Economics*, No. 15, (1995), pp. 43-57.

3 This is in line with the "ideal" accountant's concept of income, that is to say, the largest amount that can be currently consumed without reducing prospects for future consumption. See R. Repetto, ed., *The Global Possible: Resources Development and the New Century* (New Haven, Connecticut, Yale University Press, 1985).

4 Although a given output level can be produced by different combinations of inputs, it can be argued that human (as opposed to natural and physical) capital is the most important factor in recovery to disasters. As G. Horwich ("Economic lessons of the Kobe Earthquake", *Economic Development and Cultural Change*, vol. 48, No. 3 (April 2000), pp. 521-542) notes, "destroy any amount of physical capital, but leave behind a critical number of knowledgeable human beings … and the physical capital will re-emerge almost spontaneously".

5 Recent empirical evidence of this link is provided by J. Pretty and H. Ward, "Social capital and the environment", *World Development*, vol. 29, No. 2 (February 2001), pp. 209-227. According to them, the term social capital "captures the idea that social bonds and social norms are an important part of sustainable livelihoods".

6 Social vulnerability to natural disasters can in fact be disaggregated into individual and collective vulnerability. The former is determined primarily by diversity of income sources, access to resources and social status, whereas collective vulnerability (be it that of a community, a region or a country) is mainly determined by institutional market structures, level of development and quality of infrastructure. See W. Neil Adger, "Social vulnerability to climate change and extremes in coastal Vietnam", *World Development*, vol. 27, No. 2 (February 1999), pp. 249-269.

7 *World Economic Survey 1991* (United Nations publication, Sales No. E.91.II.C.1), Chap. I, Sect. entitled "Natural and man-made disasters".

to exacerbating the negative impacts of natural disasters. Rapid economic and population growth has also led to the concentration of more people, capital and infrastructure in disaster-prone areas, which has increased the potential costs of damage caused by natural disasters. In addition, it is now generally agreed that poverty, disaster vulnerability and environmental degradation are closely intertwined. This interaction of economic growth, and social and environmental impacts has placed the analysis of natural disasters in a broader sustainable development context. While a universally acceptable practical definition of sustainable development has proved elusive so far,[1] the concept has evolved to encompass three interacting dimensions: economic, social and environmental.[2] Natural disasters can clearly threaten all three dimensions of sustainable development.

The economic approach to sustainability is based on preserving the asset base that yields the maximum amount that an individual or community can consume over a period of time and still be better off at the end of the period than at the beginning.[3] Loss of natural capital—that is to say, natural resources and the assimilative capacity of the natural environment—can play a significant role in limiting development because it can disrupt investment patterns and have adverse impacts on economic growth. Moreover, post-disaster relief places financial and administrative burdens on Governments and can divert scarce resources from projected development activities. In addition, natural disasters sometimes result in the loss of critical levels of human capital and may lead to social and political instability which could, in turn, affect economic recovery.[4] Disasters are also a development problem in that they tend to have greater adverse impacts in poorer countries because their negative impacts on long-term development prospects are considerably greater. Lack of capital or wealth accumulation over the long run tends to undermine sustainable development because economic growth requires increasing both physical and human capital. Recurrent floods and windstorms, for example, not only destroy national wealth, but also hinder efforts to accumulate physical and human capital.

The social approach to sustainable development assumes, inter alia, that vulnerability to natural disasters is a function of human behaviour. The interaction of social capital formation and improvements in natural capital (and thus a reduction in disaster vulnerability) plays a central role in this dimension of sustainable development.[5] The resilience of socio-economic organization may thus be improved through disaster preparedness and mitigation efforts, through adaptation to anticipated risks and, ultimately, through economic development and improved living standards that enhance capacity to cope with disasters. Disaster vulnerability and poverty are mutually reinforcing because low income, poor housing and public services, and lack of social security and insurance cover, among their other effects, force the poor to behave in ways that expose them to greater risk.[6] This vital link between poverty and disaster vulnerability was clearly exposed 10 years ago in *World Economic Survey, 1991*, which, inter alia, stressed that "the victims (of natural disasters) are overwhelmingly the poor."[7]

While the environmental dimension of sustainable development is often associated with the overexploitation of natural resources or with environmental degradation, its temporal dimension also emphasizes the concept of intergenerational equity.[8] Broadly speaking, the main priority is to preserve the resilience and dynamic ability of ecosystems to adapt to change caused by human actions. Given that the occurrence or increased intensity of many types of natural disasters can be influenced by human activities, there is a clear link with environmental sustainability. For example, while overgrazing and deforestation may increase the risk of flooding, excessive carbon dioxide (CO_2) emissions arising from the burning of fossil fuels are likely to contribute to global warming, and thus sea-level rise and coastal flooding. Failure to limit environmental degradation resulting from human intervention can thus increase the vulnerability to risks posed by natural hazards.

FLOODING DISASTERS

Although it is not always possible to differentiate purely natural disasters from partly human-induced ones, the following major categories of natural disasters are generally used: (a) avalanches and landslides; (b) droughts; (c) earthquakes; (d) floods; (e) forest and scrub fires; (f) hurricanes, typhoons, cyclones and other windstorms; (g) volcano eruptions; and (h) other disasters, such as epidemics, insect infestations and cold waves.[9] The number of people affected by natural disasters in the world has increased considerably over the past three decades. It rose from 758 million during the 1970s to 1.3 billion during the 1980s and to almost 1.9 billion between 1990 and 1999.[10] There is also evidence that the costs of natural disasters are increasing. While real annual economic losses (in 1998 prices) averaged US$ 9.5 billion in the 1970s and US$ 15.1 billion in the 1980s, such losses averaged an estimated US$ 76 billion per year between 1990 and 1998.[11] It is worth noting, however, that since monitoring has increased and improved over time, recent disasters are likely to involve higher estimates of damage and of number of people affected.

One single category of natural disaster was particularly damaging to human settlements around the world during the 1990s. As table VII.1 shows, among people affected by all types of natural disasters during the last decade, more

Table VII.1.
NUMBER OF PEOPLE AFFECTED BY NATURAL
DISASTERS IN THE WORLD, 1990-1999

Category of natural disaster	Number of people affected[a] (millions)	Proportion of total number of people affected by natural disasters (percentage)
Droughts	185.5	9.9
Earthquakes	11.7	0.6
Floods	1 418.2	75.5
Landslides	0.5	0.0
Volcanoes	1.5	0.1
Wildfires	3.3	0.2
Windstorms	238.5	12.7
Other[b]	20.1	1.1
Total[c]	1 879.2	100.0

[8] Generally speaking, the concept of intergenerational equity assumes that the current generation owns the natural environment in common with past and present generations. This concept is thus based upon the utilitarian principle of maximizing the sum of total welfare of different generations, which allows the welfare of one generation to be traded off against that of a future one. For example, "if the benefit to us from economic activities which continue to emit greenhouse gases at the present rates outweighs the harm done to future generations from global warming, then the criterion would recommend no change in our activities" (S. Anand and A. Sen, loc. cit., pp. 2033-2034). Since the full environmental impacts of current economic decisions, such as the generation of nuclear waste and emissions of greenhouse gases, will not be felt for many decades or centuries, discount rates are usually employed to compare present and future costs and benefits. It is now argued, however, that the methods considered reasonable for measuring gains and losses for one or two generations into the future may not be appropriate when applied to a longer time span. For an interesting review of long-run alternatives involving simultaneous consideration of valuation, discounting and political acceptability, see P.R. Portney and J.P. Weyant, eds. *Discounting and Intergenerational Equity*, (Washington, D.C., Resources for the Future (RFF), 1999).

[9] As defined by the OFDA/CRED International Disaster Database—electronically available at http://www.cred.be/emdat/intro.html—managed by the Centre for Research on the Epidemiology of Disasters (CRED) of the Université Catholique de Louvain, Brussels, Belgium. OFDA is the Office of United States Foreign Disaster Assistance. A disaster is entered in the database if at least one of several criteria, such as at least 10 people reported killed or 100 reported affected, is met. Although there is no standard definition of loose categories, such as "internally displaced people" and "people affected by disasters", CRED takes care to update the data on a daily basis, check them at three-month intervals and revise them at the end of each calendar year.

[10] See OFDA/CRED International Disaster Database. Many disaster victims were affected by more than one disaster during those decades.

[11] See C. Benson and E. J. Clay, "Developing countries and the economic impacts of natural disasters", in *Managing Disaster Risk in Emerging Economies*, A. Kreimer and M. Arnold, eds. (Washington, D.C., World Bank, 2000) pp. 11-21.

Source: UN/DESA, based on data of the OFDA/CRED International Disaster Database, Université Catholique de Louvain.

[a] Including people affected more than once.
[b] Including epidemics but not the acquired immunodeficiency syndrome (AIDS) pandemic.
[c] Totals may differ from the sums of columns because of rounding.

than 75 per cent were impacted by floods. Similarly, floods are responsible for the largest share of economic damage—as measured by annual average estimated damage in current United States dollars—caused by all natural disasters. During the 1990s, over one third of the total estimated cost of natural disasters was the result of floods[12] (see figure VII.1).

The most flood-prone geographical areas

Human activity tends to concentrate in flood-prone areas either along river basins or on coasts because they are often the most suitable locations for both human settlements and economic activities. Many flooding disasters are thus exacerbated by inappropriate location of human settlements on flood plains. Nonetheless, periodic floods often take place in the same river basins and urban areas around the world during their respective rainy or monsoon seasons, as shown in the case study of Bangladesh given below. Similarly, many serious floods are caused by hurricanes, typhoons, cyclones and other windstorms in their respective seasons. Much of the devastation caused by hurricane Mitch in Central America in 1998 resulted from a combination of torrential rains and storm surges, which led to serious floods and mud slides both in coastal areas and inland.[13] River floods and windstorm-related coastal floods may sometimes occur at the same time or follow one another closely with catastrophic effects. In the case of the flooding disaster that disrupted the lives of 650,000 people in southern and central Mozambique in February 2000, for

[12] As shown in the *World Disasters Report, 1999* (Geneva, International Federation of Red Cross and Red Crescent Societies, 1999), damage to infrastructure will invariably result in a higher damage estimate than suffering of individual disaster victims. As a result, natural disasters, such as floods and windstorms, are often estimated to cause much larger financial loss than other disasters, such as droughts and epidemics, whose direct damage to infrastructure is much smaller. See box VII.1 on the economic impacts of drought in Africa.

[13] See *Central America: Hurricane/Tropical Storm Mitch, Situation Report No. 15* (Geneva, Office for the Coordination of Humanitarian Affairs of the United Nations Secretariat, 23 November 1998); and *World Disasters Report, 1999*.

Figure VII.1.
SHARE OF TOTAL DAMAGE CAUSED BY DIFFERENT CATEGORIES OF NATURAL DISASTERS DURING THE 1990s

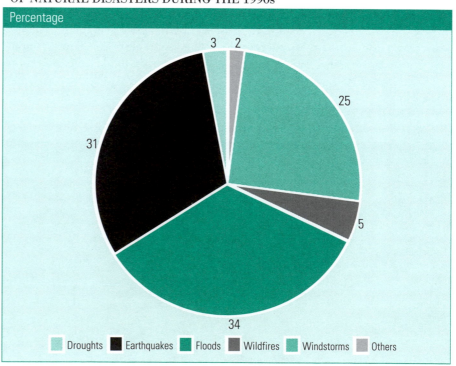

Percentage

3 2
25
5
34
31

Droughts   Earthquakes   Floods   Wildfires   Windstorms   Others

Source: UN/DESA, based on data of the OFDA/CRED International Disaster Database, Université Catholique de Louvain.

example, the impact of the original river floods was exacerbated by down-pours caused by cyclone Eline.[14]

Rising sea-levels associated with global warming can also have geographical repercussions in that they are likely to make many coastal settlements and small islands particularly vulnerable to storm surges and flooding (see box VII.2). Small islands and low-lying coastal areas are, in any case, vulnerable to tidal waves, which are often caused by other natural disasters, such as earthquakes or volcano eruptions. The devastating tidal wave on the north-west coast of Papua New Guinea in 1998—estimated to have killed over 2,000 people and to have left over 9,000 people homeless—had been originally caused by a submarine earthquake whose seismic activity did not damage the island directly.[15]

Low-lying coastlines can also be highly vulnerable to other periodic climatic phenomena, such as El Niño/Southern Oscillation (ENSO), particularly in the Pacific basin. Generally speaking, El Niño refers to abnormally warm sea temperatures in the eastern equatorial Pacific Ocean, whereas the Southern Oscillation involves an oscillating pressure pattern in the western equatorial Pacific Ocean. In fact, it is now known that ENSO has a warm phase (El Niño) that is usually followed by a cold one, generally referred to as La Niña. There is some evidence that these two different phases of ENSO are responsible for massive floods and other natural disasters not only in eastern and western Pacific countries, but also in other countries in the Atlantic and Indian Oceans, including countries as far away as eastern Africa.[16] The increasing geographical spread of the impacts of such climatic events is highlighted by the fact that it was an Atlantic Ocean rather than Pacific Ocean country that experienced Latin America's worst ENSO-related natural disaster: the heavy rainfalls, floods and mud slides estimated to have killed 30,000 people and displaced another 100,000 in a Venezuelan coastal State in December 1999.[17]

Socio-economic vulnerability to floods

Vulnerability to natural disasters is associated with a complex range of variables that include not only the location of human settlements and the magnitude of the disaster, but also the socio-economic, institutional, demographic and environmental characteristics of the disaster area, as well as the quality of its basic infrastructure. Vulnerability to natural disasters is almost always differentiated by the socio-economic conditions of different income groups in the disaster area. According to the *World Disasters Report, 1999*, increasing evidence of disparities in vulnerability between lower- and higher-income groups has been accumulated throughout the world ever since torrential rains and heavy floods struck urban areas of Rio de Janeiro, Brazil, in 1988.[18] Although the floods affected contiguous rich and poor neighbourhoods, their devastating impacts were experienced only in the latter. It is invariably poverty, not choice, that forces growing numbers of low-income groups to live in poorly-built dwellings in the least valued plots of land—such as unstable hillsides and marshes—which tend to be most vulnerable to floods.

Poverty can also encourage people to engage in environmentally unsustainable development practices that further increase their vulnerability. Massive logging operations and exploitation of wetlands, for example, reduce the soil's

[14] See *Mozambique Floods: Updated International Appeal of the Government of Mozambique for Emergency Relief and Rehabilitation in collaboration with the United Nations Agencies* (Geneva, Office for the Coordination of Humanitarian Affairs of the United Nations Secretariat, 22 March 2000).

[15] See *Papua New Guinea: Tsunami, Situation Report No. 9* (Geneva, Office for the Coordination of Humanitarian Affairs of the United Nations Secretariat, 7 August 1998).

[16] United Nations Environment Programme/National Center for Atmospheric Research/United Nations University/World Meteorological Organization/International Strategy for Disaster Reduction (UNEP/NCAR/UNU/WMO/ISDR), *Lessons Learned from the 1997-98 El Niño: Once Burned, Twice Shy?* (Tokyo, United Nations University, October 2000). It is interesting to note that the highest annual numbers of people affected by floods in the world during the 1990s were recorded in El Niño years: 1991 and 1998 (see table VII.2).

[17] See *Venezuela Floods: New Assessments on the Magnitude of the Disaster, Situation Report No. 7* (Geneva, Office for the Coordination of Humanitarian Affairs of the United Nations Secretariat, 12 January 2000); and *World Disasters Report 2000* (Geneva, International Federation of Red Cross and Red Crescent Societies, 2000). According to the latter, La Niña originally caused these floods.

[18] See *World Disasters Report, 1999* ... For a detailed analysis of the interaction of poverty and disaster vulnerability in Central America, see also G. Martine and G. M. Guzman, *Population, Poverty and Vulnerability: Mitigating the Effects of Natural Disasters* (Rome, Food and Agriculture Organization of the United Nations, December 1999), electronically available at http://www.fao.org/sd/Wpdirect/Wpan0042.htm.

Box VII.1

THE ECONOMIC IMPACTS OF DROUGHT IN AFRICA: KUZNETS REVISITED?

a   United Nations, *Treaty Series,* vol. 1954, No. 33480.

b   See "Combating desertification in Africa", secretariat of the Convention to Combat Desertification, *Fact Sheet 11,* available electronically at http://www.unccd.int/main.php.

c   Recent research on the long-term impacts in northern Nigeria of the great Sahelian droughts of the 1970s and 1980s questions the assumption that the conversion of natural woodland into farmland—including the use of more intensive cultivation practices and higher livestock densities—invariably results in a "land degradation crisis". Together with other drought adaptation strategies, such expansion of farmland may sometimes be considered sustainable coping strategies and thus new approaches to drought mitigation. See M.J. Mortimore and W.M. Adams, "Farmer adaptation, change and 'crisis' in the Sahel", *Global Environmental Change,* vol. 11, No. 1 (April 2001), pp. 49-57; and S. Batterbury and A. Warren, "The African Sahel 25 years after the great drought: assessing progress and moving towards new agendas and approaches", *Global Environmental Change,* vol. 11, No. 1 (April 2001), pp. 1-8.

d   The analysis here is based on C. Benson and E. Clay, "The impact of drought on Sub-Saharan African economies", *World Bank Technical Paper, No. 401* (Washington, D. C., World Bank, 1998).

e   However, adverse impacts of drought on staple food production in many poor countries may not be properly reflected in GDP figures, partly because the latter tend to underestimate small-scale and subsistence agricultural output. For example, according to UN/DESA calculations, based upon Food and Agriculture Organization of the United Nations (FAO) data, total cereal production in Mauritania fell from 88,000 tons in 1970 to less than 30,000 tons after the great Sahel drought in 1973. In fact, it took almost 15 years for total Mauritanian cereal production to return to pre-drought levels. Nonetheless, the country's GDP fell only slightly during the great drought and actually rose significantly during the decade, from US$ 733 million in 1970 to US$ 836 million in 1979 (in 1995 constant prices).

f   See C. Benson and E. Clay, loc. cit., p. 23.

g   Ibid.

h   S. Kuznets, "Economic growth and income inequality", *American Economic Review,* vol. 45, No. 1 (1955), pp. 1-28.

Over the past 30 years, Africa has recurrently experienced some of the world's most devastating droughts in terms of both human suffering and relative economic damage. According to the secretariat of the United Nations Convention to Combat Desertification in those Countries Experiencing Serious Drought and/or Desertification, particularly in Africa,[a] drought and desertification have their greatest adverse impacts in Africa, two-thirds of which has become desert or drylands.[b] The continent contains extensive agricultural drylands, almost three quarters of which are already degraded to some degree. Land degradation is caused by both climate variability and unsustainable human activities. The most commonly cited forms of unsustainable land use are overgrazing, over-cultivation and deforestation,[c] as well as poor irrigation practices and inadequate drainage which lead to salinization of croplands. While land degradation can also be caused by drought, the latter is a natural meteorological phenomenon that occurs when rainfall is significantly below normal recorded levels for a long period of time.

Although the human and agricultural impacts of drought in Africa have been extensively studied, little research has been conducted on its non-agricultural and macroeconomic impacts. A recent study on the impact of drought in sub-Saharan African economies, however, has shed some new light on overall macroeconomic impacts in economies with different degrees of diversification.[d] This study shows that in Africa's least developed economies, the economic impact of drought is largely experienced through its effects on the agricultural sector. Provided that targeted agricultural support is available in the aftermath of the drought, economic recovery can take place relatively fast and the return of good rainfalls can restore gross domestic product (GDP) to pre-drought levels almost immediately.[e]

On the other hand, in African developing countries with more diversified economies, the impacts of drought are spread more widely through the economy, reflecting greater overall integration and stronger intersectoral linkages than in the least developed economies. As in the latter economies, the agricultural sector in more diversified economies may recover fairly rapidly after the drought. However, this agricultural recovery is often insufficient to offset a much slower recovery of the manufacturing sector, given the relative importance of the latter in the sectoral structure of GDP. For example, largely as a result of the devastating 1991-1992 drought in southern Africa, manufacturing output fell by almost 10 per cent in Zimbabwe in 1992 and remained well below its pre-drought level in 1993. As a result, despite a strong recovery of the country's agricultural sector in 1993, Zimbabwe's GDP failed to reach its pre-drought level in that year. The slower recovery of the Zimbabwean manufacturing sector was caused by a series of factors ranging from reduced hydroelectric output to shortages of agricultural inputs to the important agro-processing sector.[f]

These findings suggest that the economic impacts of drought increase during the earlier stages of development, reach a peak and then fall as an economy becomes more developed and thus better prepared to absorb those impacts, as opposed to the conventional assumption of a continuously declining impact as economies develop. It is actually argued, in other words, that there is an "inverted U-shaped relationship between the macroeconomic impact of drought and the overall stage of development of a country",[g] based on Kuznets' seminal hypothesis of an inverted U-shaped relationship between growth and inequality.[h] This also helps to explain why, as a result of the 1991-1992 drought in southern Africa, less diversified economies such as Malawi and Zambia restored GDP to indices well above pre-drought levels by 1993 (basically because of strong agricultural recovery), whereas intermediate economies such as Zimbabwe failed to do so, in spite of an equally fast recovery of its agricultural sector. These findings also imply that Africa-wide strategies to mitigate the economic impacts of droughts are likely to be less effective than calibrated policies that take into account differences in economic structure among African countries.

ability to absorb heavy rainfall, making erosion and flooding more likely. In addition, significant increase in population densities in many developing countries forces greater numbers of poor people to live in high-risk areas. This spatial distribution of vulnerability is thus a critical determinant of risk in natural disasters. It can be argued that "spatial poverty traps" arise when households living in areas containing poorer-quality physical capital (or "geographical capital") see the fall of their standard of living over time, which contributes to a further deterioration of the quality of physical capital in these areas.[19]

At the national level, vulnerability to natural disasters such as floods can be associated with the level of development of a particular country, including the size and structure of its economy.[20] In principle, larger economies are better equipped to absorb the impacts of natural disasters. Nonetheless, poorer developing countries (both large and small) tend to be more vulnerable to natural hazards in view of their limited capacity to take measures to mitigate or respond to such hazards. It is no surprise, therefore, that a disproportionately high share of both casualties and direct economic loss from natural disasters are found in poorer countries. For example, more than 95 per cent of the estimated 105,000 deaths caused by all disasters in 1999 occurred in developing countries.[21] Similarly, over half of the US$ 65 billion in economic losses caused by all natural disasters in 1998 was incurred by developing countries.[22] Moreover, at least 40 per cent of those losses were attributed to a single event in a developing country: the devastating flooding of the Yangtze River in China (see box VII.3).

According to some estimates, the average annual direct economic loss caused by all natural disasters between 1987 and 1997 (US$ 70 billion) was more or less equally split between developed and developing countries.[23] This is somewhat surprising, given the relative concentration of capital assets in the former and the fact that the financial value attached to basic infrastructure in most industrialized countries is usually many times higher than that of equivalent structures in developing countries. In addition, some estimates of damage

[19] J. Jalan and M. Ravallion, Spatial Poverty Traps?, *World Bank Working Paper, No. 1862* (Washington, D.C., World Bank, December 1997).

[20] See R. Zapata Marti, "Natural disasters and development", paper presented to the Annual World Bank Conference on Development Economics, Paris, 26-28 June 2000; and C. Benson and E. J. Clay, loc. cit.

[21] Including purely human-made disasters, such as industrial and transport accidents. See A. Kreimer and M. Arnold, op. cit.

[22] See P.K. Freeman, "Infrastructure, natural disasters and poverty", in A. Kreimer and M. Arnold, op. cit., pp. 55-61.

[23] Ibid.

Table VII.2.
NUMBER OF PEOPLE AFFECTED BY FLOODS IN THE WORLD, 1990-1999

Year	Number of people affected by floods[a] (millions)	Proportion of total number of people affected by all natural disasters (percentage)
1990	66.7	61.0
1991	278.1	84.2
1992	13.0	19.2
1993	154.1	83.1
1994	120.5	66.7
1995	193.7	72.4
1996	147.2	85.9
1997	12.2	41.3
1998	289.1	87.4
1999	143.6	69.6

Source: UN/DESA, based on data of the OFDA/CRED International Disaster Database, Université Catholique de Louvain.

[a] Including people affected more than once.

Box VII.2

VULNERABILITY OF SMALL ISLAND DEVELOPING STATES TO SEA-LEVEL RISE AND COASTAL FLOODING

[a] The Third Assessment Report of IPCC consists of three volumes: vol. I, "Climate Change 2001: The Scientific Basis"; vol. II, "Climate Change 2001: Impacts, Adaptation and Vulnerability"; and vol. III, "Climate Change 2001: Mitigation". All three draft volumes have been accepted by the IPCC member States and are due to be published soon. Their summaries are available at http://www.ipcc.ch/.

[b] See, for example, T. M. Ali Khan and others, "Recent sea level and sea surface temperature trends along the Bangladesh coast in relation to the frequency of intense cyclones", *Marine Geodesy*, vol. 23, No. 2 (April 2000), pp. 106-116. According to this study, 21 per cent of the population of Bangladesh (about 27 million people) living in the low coastal belt are extremely vulnerable to any significant increase in sea level. See also World Bank (*Bangladesh: Climate Change and Sustainable Development*, report No. 21104-BD (Washington, D. C., World Bank, 19 December 2000), which notes that "the sea level along the Bangladesh coast is rising at about 3 millimetres a year, and the sea surface temperature is showing a rising trend" (p. xi).

[c] See M. Sharma and others, "Reducing vulnerability to environmental variability", background paper for the Bank's environmental strategy (Washington, D. C., World Bank, n.d.), p. 8.

There is increasing scientific evidence that human activity has begun to change the average temperature on the Earth's surface. According to the authoritative United Nations Intergovernmental Panel on Climate Change (IPCC), this process of "global warming" has been caused by several factors associated with the intensification of economic activities, including the emissions of "greenhouse gases", such as carbon dioxide (CO_2) produced by burning fossil fuels and forests. According to the forthcoming Third Assessment Report of IPCC,[a] it is expected that the globally averaged surface air temperature will have warmed 1.4 to 5.8 degrees Celsius by 2100 relative to 1990. One of the main consequences of global warming will be sea-level rise: according to IPCC, it is projected that globally averaged sea level will have risen between 9 and almost 90 centimetres (cm) by 2100. In addition, global warming is also expected to increase climate variability and to provoke changes in the frequency and intensity of extreme climate events, such as tropical windstorms and associated storm surges and coastal flooding.

Although significant rises in sea level would cause serious problems to densely populated low-lying countries such as Bangladesh,[b] they are also of particular concern to small island developing States. According to IPCC, because of their high degree of environmental vulnerability, small islands are likely to be among the countries most seriously affected by climate change. Furthermore, IPCC concludes that the impact of climate change and more extreme weather would fall disproportionately on the poor who have the least capacity to adapt. The likely impacts of sea-level rise and coastal flooding on small island States would include increased coastal erosion, loss of land and property, dislocation of people, increased risk from storm surges, saltwater intrusion into scarce freshwater resources and high resource costs associated with the attempt to respond and adapt to these changes.

Adverse impacts on coastal ecosystems, such as bleaching of coral reefs and deterioration of mangroves, are also expected to threaten fisheries and thus those who rely on coastal fisheries for their income and for a staple source of food. It is also foreseen with a high degree of confidence that their limited arable land and soil salinization will make agriculture in small island States, both for domestic food production and for cash crop exports, highly vulnerable to sea-level rise and climate change. In addition, climate change is also expected to severely disrupt tourism activities, which are an important source of income and foreign exchange for many islands.

In worst-case scenarios, the very existence of some small island developing States could be threatened. According to a Pacific island climate change study recently carried out by the World Bank,[c] a sea-level rise of 20-40 cm, together with storm surges, could inundate over half of the capital of Kiribati and cause shoreline retreats of up to 320 metres (m) in Fiji's main island (Viti Levu), where losses from associated coral reef bleaching could amount to US$ 11-US$ 27 million a year. Under the sea-level rise scenarios selected for the study, Viti Levu could be experiencing overall annual economic losses of US$ 49 to US$ 120 million (in 1998 prices), equivalent to between 4 and 11 per cent of Fiji's GDP.

caused by natural disasters include only insured assets, which in most developing countries represent only a small proportion of losses. It should also be emphasized that, given the disparity in per capita gross domestic product (GDP) between developed and developing countries, the damage caused by natural disasters as a proportion of GDP tends to be much higher in the latter group of countries.

The economic damage caused by natural disasters can be divided into direct and indirect costs, and secondary macroeconomic effects.[24] Direct costs are defined as damage to fixed assets, including infrastructure and residential, commercial and industrial buildings, as well as inventories of finished and intermediate goods, raw materials and crops destroyed or damaged by the natural disaster. Indirect costs relate to damage to flows of goods that will not be produced and services that will not be provided as a result of the disaster. The latter also include additional costs arising from the use of more expensive inputs owing to the destruction of or damage to cheaper usual sources of supply, and from more expensive distribution channels for the provision of goods and services. Secondary effects refer to the short- and long-term impacts of natural disasters on overall economic performance, as measured by the most significant macroeconomic variables. Examples of such macroeconomic effects include a decline in tax revenues or increase in government expenditure to cover emergency or reconstruction measures, and a deterioration in the trade balance due to a disaster. Not only are secondary effects felt during the current fiscal year but they may spill over a number of years.

While the estimation of direct impacts can be relatively straightforward, it is often difficult to estimate indirect costs accurately because the complexity of indirect impacts, particularly over the medium run, can lead to (a) inaccurate estimation of the "exact share" of a specific disaster, (b) double-counting and (c) inadequate consideration of their "knock-on effects".[25] For example, while the costs of disruption in the provision of basic services, such as water and energy, are often underestimated, indirect costs can also be partially offset by positive knock-on effects, such as increased economic activity associated with reconstruction and rehabilitation, which tend to be ignored in estimations of indirect costs. The estimation of secondary effects is equally, if not more, complicated, not only because they require an estimation of indirect costs, but also because of the complexities of evaluating both their spillover macroeconomic repercussions over a number of years and their exact impacts on specific macroeconomic variables.[26] Given the difficulties of evaluating both indirect costs and secondary effects, most estimations of the economic damage of natural disasters are based only on direct costs and, as a result, such evaluations tend to be underestimates.

THE IMPACTS OF FLOODS IN BANGLADESH

In some ways, Bangladesh can be considered the world's most flood-prone developing country, even when compared with vulnerable small island developing States, which are threatened by frequent coastal floods and storm surges. While China was home to the overwhelming majority of people struck by floods in almost every single year during the 1990s, in relative terms Bangladesh was worse off in 5 of those 10 years (see figure VII.2). This was

[24] See R. Zapata Marti, "Methodological approaches: the ECLAC methodology", paper presented to a workshop on Assessment of Economic Impact of Natural and Man-made Disasters, Université Catholique de Louvain, Brussels, Belgium, 29 and 30 September 1997.

[25] See C. Benson and E.J. Clay, loc. cit. R. Zapata Marti (loc. cit.) notes that in the ECLAC methodology, indirect costs are estimated by surveys undertaken with the main productive sector organizations and enterprises at the beginning of the disaster.

[26] According to R. Zapata Marti (loc. cit.), the estimation of secondary macroeconomic effects is based upon "a comparison between the economic performance anticipated by public and private sector organizations ... and a modified projected performance estimated after the direct and indirect damages are assessed and valued".

Figure VII.2.
SHARE OF NATIONAL POPULATION AFFECTED BY
FLOODS IN SELECTED COUNTRIES, 1990-1999

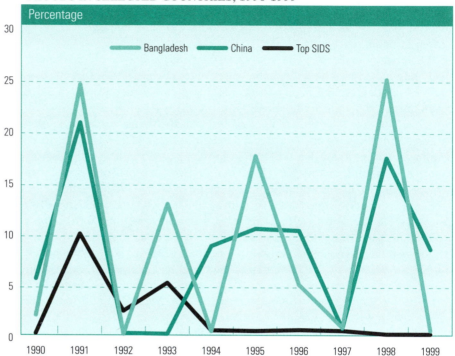

Source: UN/DESA, based on its world population statistics (see *World Population Prospects: The 2000 Revision,* vol. I (United Nations publication, forthcoming); and on floods data compiled by the OFDA/CRED International Disaster Database, Université Catholique de Louvain.

Note: Top SIDS refers to the small island developing State with the highest share of its national population affected by floods in any single year. Different SIDS are thus used for different years.

clearly illustrated in 1998, during which both countries suffered from particularly severe floods, and which recorded the highest annual number of flood victims in the world during the decade (see table VII.2). In that year, although China had less than 22 per cent of the world's population, more than 77 per cent of the 290 million people affected by floods in the world resided in China, making up 18 per cent of the country's population. By comparison, while Bangladesh flood victims accounted for less than 11 per cent of the total world population affected by floods in 1998, they represented almost 25 per cent of the population of Bangladesh (see figures VII.2 and VII.3). Primarily because of the devastating impacts of recurrent floods in the country—together with the fact that floods are by far the most damaging category of natural disasters in the world—Bangladesh can also be considered one the world's most disaster-prone developing countries (see figures VII.4 and VII.5).

The most damaging flood in the history of Bangladesh

Annual flooding during the monsoon season—when one third of the country is usually flooded—is a fact of life in Bangladesh. Lying at the confluence of two major regional rivers (the Brahmaputra and the Ganges) flowing into the Bay of Bengal, Bangladesh has the largest system of deltas and flat lands in the world (see map).[27] Among the four types of floods that occur in the country, monsoon floods from major rivers cause by far the most extensive damage.[28] Nonetheless, "normal floods" (*barsha*) resulting from monsoon rains,

[27] The Brahmaputra, locally known as the Jamuna River, flows into the Ganges (known locally as the Padma River) which, in turn, flows into a third major river (Meghna) before it reaches the Bay of Bengal.

[28] The other three types of floods are: (a) local floods from heavy rainfall; (b) flash floods due to Himalayan snow melt; and (c) coastal flooding caused by high tides, storm surges and tidal waves, often associated with tropical cyclones. See L. R. P. Reavill and T. G. Rahman, "A system-science-based analysis of the factors that influence and aggravate the effects of flooding in Bangladesh", *Technological Forecasting and Social Change,* vol. 49 (1995), pp. 89-101.

Figure VII.3.

FLOOD VICTIMS IN THE TOP THREE FLOOD-PRONE COUNTRIES IN 1998
AS A SHARE OF THE TOTAL WORLD POPULATION AFFECTED BY FLOODS

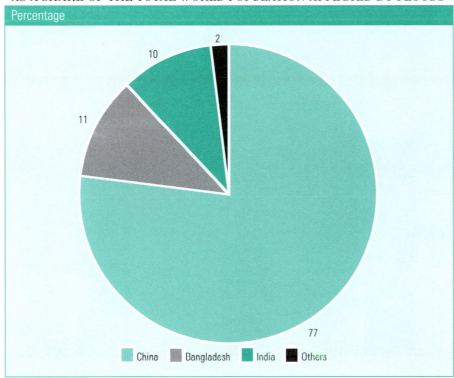

Percentage

China   Bangladesh   India   Others

Source: UN/DESA, based on data of the OFDA/CRED International Disaster Database, Université Catholique de Louvain.

Figure VII.4.

SHARE OF POPULATION AFFECTED BY NATURAL DISASTERS
IN DEVELOPING COUNTRIES, 1980-1999

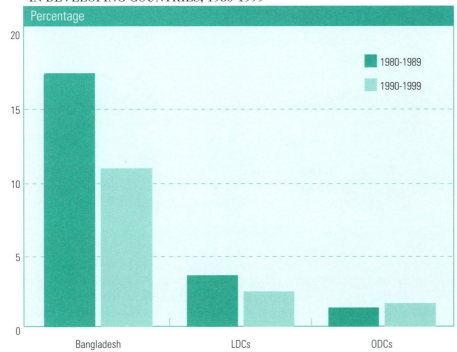

Percentage

1980-1989
1990-1999

Bangladesh   LDCs   ODCs

Source: UN/DESA.

Note: Average of annual shares for each country or group of countries during each decade. LDCs refer to the 49 least developed countries (including Bangladesh) officially recognized by the United Nations; ODCs refer to (79) other developing countries.

Figure VII.5.

ECONOMIC COST OF NATURAL DISASTERS, 1980-1998

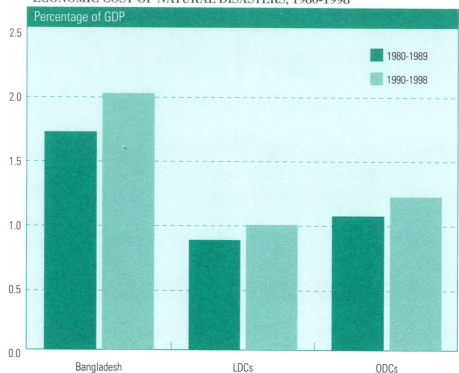

Percentage of GDP

1980-1989
1990-1998

Bangladesh   LDCs   ODCs

Source: UN/DESA.

Note: Average of annual shares for each country or group of countries during each decade. LDCs refer to the 49 least developed countries (including Bangladesh) officially recognized by the United Nations; ODCs refer to (79) other developing countries.

within certain limits of timing, duration and magnitude, are generally considered socio-economically beneficial in that they provide vital moisture and fertile silt for croplands.[29] Two of the three types of rice grown in the country (*aman* and *aus*) cannot survive without floodwaters. In addition, fish caught during the flood season constitute a vital source of protein in the diet of Bangladeshis. It is the abnormal floods (*bonna*) occurring every few years that cause the widespread damage that it is often beyond the country's ability to cope with. These floods invariably become a devastating human catastrophe because the country's large population (almost 130 million people) is crowded into a generally deltaic flat area of less than 145,000 square kilometres (km²). With almost 1,000 people/km², Bangladesh is the State Member of the United Nations with the second highest population density.

The 1998 floods were the worst in the history of Bangladesh. They were basically caused by a simultaneous rise of the country's three major rivers (Jamuna, Meghna and Padma) that until then had crested at different times. The floods lasted an unprecedented 11 weeks, between July and September. Their long duration was due to two major factors that contributed to slowing down the outflow of floodwaters into the sea: a rise of the tide in the Bay of Bengal; and the thousands of small mud embankments that had been built over the years to provide water for irrigation or as a protection against coastal flooding. The floods affected two thirds of the country, including 52 of its 64 districts, and disrupted the lives of over 30 million people.[30] They caused substantial damage to infrastructure, including almost 900,000 houses, 1,800 schools and 6,500

[29] For a detailed discussion of the positive and negative impacts of floods in Bangladesh, see B. K. Paul, "Flood research in Bangladesh in retrospect and prospect: a review", *Geoforum*, vol. 28, No. 2 (1997), pp. 121-131; and B. K. Paul, "Farmers' response to the flood action plan (FAP) of Bangladesh: an empirical study", *World Development*, vol. 23, No. 2 (February 1995), pp. 299-309.

[30] See *Bangladesh Floods, Situation Report No .9* (Geneva, Office for the Coordination of Humanitarian Affairs of the United Nations Secretariat, 18 September 1998); and *United Nations Flash Appeal in Support of the Government of Bangladesh for Relief to the Victims of the Floods in Bangladesh* (Geneva, Office for the Coordination of Humanitarian Affairs of the United Nations Secretariat, September 1998) (OCHA/GVA - 98/0281).

bridges. In addition, 4,500 km of embankments and 16,000 km of roads were severely damaged. The road between the capital (Dhaka) and Chittagong, the country's second largest city and major port, was blocked for months.

Greater Dhaka's 11 million inhabitants were seriously affected and the city's drinking water, sewage and drainage systems were severely disrupted. As a result, diseases caused by polluted water and contaminated food, such as diarrhoea and hepatitis, spread rapidly through many poor areas of the capital. This flooding disaster once again highlighted that most poor households in Bangladesh are highly vulnerable to natural disasters.[31] Empirical evidence that the socio-economic impacts of floods fall disproportionately on the poor had in fact begun to be produced after the second most severe flood in the history of Bangladesh, in 1988. For example, while 26 per cent of the assets of a low-cost house were lost in the 1988 floods, the proportion was only 7 per cent for the highest-cost houses.[32] Thus, not only are poorer groups invariably more vulnerable but they also tend to suffer greater relative losses. While it can be argued that under certain isolated conditions, some poor farmers are not necessarily vulnerable to fluctuation in their income, there is plenty of evidence to show that almost all poor households in Bangladesh are vulnerable to floods because of their frequency and magnitude.[33]

The 1998 floods had an immediate adverse impact on agriculture and on the rural economy as a whole.[34] They caused the destruction of an estimated US$ 300 million worth of rice crops, which normally make up over two thirds of the country's agricultural production. Although average seasonal daily wage rates for most rural activities actually increased during the floods fiscal year—that is to say, from July 1998 to June 1999—rural employment was particularly hard hit by the floods (see table VII.3).[35] Self-employment activities were also seriously affected, in particular those related to traditional work and small businesses. It is estimated that the average rural household income derived from self-employment activities declined by 10-18 per cent during the floods fiscal year.[36] The agricultural sector, however, recovered fairly rapidly, mainly for three reasons: (a) many farmers had anticipated flood risks by adopting several traditional adjustment techniques; (b) increased aid was targeted at the quick rehabilitation of the sector; and (c) increased sedimentation arising from the extensive flooding contributed to improved soil quality and a bumper harvest the following winter. Although Bangladesh's GDP growth rate dropped slightly in the floods fiscal year, it was still an impressive 4.88 per cent, primarily owing to the performance of the agricultural sector (see table VII.4).

The negative economic impacts of the 1998 floods appear to have been more severe in non-agricultural sectors, particularly manufacturing. There is, for example, microeconomic evidence that small- and medium-scale manufacturing enterprises in the Dhaka area were severely affected by the floods, primarily because of their long duration. According to an extensive survey of damage caused to small- and medium-sized manufacturing firms, carried out immediately after the floods, average production loss represented 1.5 months of production, and total losses—including fixed capital and inventory losses—were estimated at Bangladesh taka (Tk) 480,000 per enterprise, or almost Tk 2.9 billion (approximately US$ 62 million) in the Dhaka area alone.[37]

There is also evidence that the garment sector—probably the most "globalized" industrial sector in Bangladesh—was adversely affected by the disruption

[31] See B. Sen, Poverty in Bangladesh: A Review, electronically available at http://www.bids-bd.org/poverty.htm.

[32] See K. M. Nabiul Islam, "Linkages and flood impacts at the macro level: a case study of Bangladesh", BIDS Research Report, No. 46 (Dhaka, Bangladesh Institute of Development Studies, August 1996). Nabiul Islam also found out that the lower the costs of construction, the higher the structural damages to house values (28 as against 5 per cent for the two contrasting house types).

[33] See H. Zaman, "Assessing the impact of micro-credit on poverty and vulnerability in Bangladesh", World Bank Policy Research Working Paper, No. 2145, (Washington, D.C., World Bank, July 1999). Some poor subsistence farmers in remote areas of the country may not necessarily be vulnerable (in terms of experiencing large income fluctuations) because they can be insulated from national and international shocks.

[34] See United Nations Flash Appeal in Support of the Government of Bangladesh for Relief to the Victims of the Floods in Bangladesh ...; and S. Zohir, "Recent changes in the rural economy: findings from BIDS study villages" (summary of paper prepared for a workshop on the review of the Bangladesh economy 2000, Dhaka, 6 June 2000, electronically available at http://www.bids-bd.org/review_of_bangladesh_economy.htm, which provides preliminary results of field surveys carried out in 91 villages in 13 regions of the country since early 1998 and thus before and after the floods).

[35] A basic competitive model of the labour market would actually point towards a lower real wage rate when an aggregate shock, such as a severe flood, has reduced demand for labour. According to M. Ravallion ("Famines and economics", World Bank Policy Research Working Paper, No. 1693 (Washington, D.C., World Bank, December 1996), one possible explanation for such "wage stickiness downward" is tacit collusion on the supply side at the village level. For a path-breaking analysis and empirical evidence of a dramatic fall in agricultural real wage rates in terms of rice, following the 1974 floods and famine in Bangladesh, see A. Sen, Poverty and Famines (Oxford, Clarendon Press, 1987).

[36] See S. Zohir, loc. cit.

[37] See F. Cookson, "Pragmatic solutions for post-flood rehabilitation in Bangladesh" (College Park, Maryland, University of Maryland, 1998), mimeo. The firms covered in the survey reflect the overall structure of the manufacturing sector of Bangladesh with a heavy concentration in agro-processing and textiles. The cost in United States dollars is derived from the average 1998 exchange rate (US$ 1 = Tk 46.91) calculated by the Economist Intelligence Unit, Bangladesh Country Report (London, EIU, April 2001).

Table VII.3.

BANGLADESH: RURAL WAGES AND EMPLOYMENT[a]

Average seasonal daily rates in rural activities (Bangladesh taka)	1997-1998	1998-1999
Crop cultivation	46.2	49.8
Earth work	55.2	52.8
Brick-making	65.4	70.0
Mechanized transport work	113.2	128.6
Non-agricultural activities	61.6	65.4
Loss of labour days in rural activities in 1998-1999 (compared with 1997-1998)	Male	Female
Own farm	24	17
Wage labour	3	5
Self-employment	10	7
Total	37	29

Source: S. Zohir, "Recent changes in the rural economy: findings from BIDS study villages" (summary of a paper prepared for a workshop on the review of the Bangladesh economy 2000, Dhaka, 6 June 2000). Available at http://www.bids-bd.org/review_of_bangladesh_economy.htm.

[a] Based on field surveys in 91 rural villages.

[38] For an economic analysis of the Chittagong EPZ, the first built in the country (in the early 1980s), see A. Dowla, "Export processing zones in Bangladesh: The economic impact", *Asian Survey*, vol. 37, No. 6 (June 1997), pp. 561-574. A second EPZ was opened in Dhaka in 1993 and at least two others are being developed in other cities.

[39] Economist Intelligence Unit, *Bangladesh Country Profile, 2000* (London, EIU, 2000).

[40] However, following a 6 per cent devaluation of the taka in August 2000, there was a significant rise in both the volume and earnings of ready-made garment exports during the first seven months (July 2000 -January 2001) of the current fiscal year: total earnings during this period were 17 per cent above those of the same period in the previous fiscal year. It is worth noting, however, that ready-made garment exports are highly dependent on import of inputs: in 1998/99, for example, the cost of imported fabric and other intermediate goods represented over 62 per cent of the total export earnings for the sector in the same fiscal year (See *Bangladesh Country Report ...*, and *Bangladesh Country Profile, 2000 ...*).

[41] The European Union (EU) imposes no quotas on textiles and clothing imports from the 49 least developed countries, which, together with several other developing countries, also benefit from zero tariffs on textiles and clothing exports to EU.

in transport network leading to the country's major port, Chittagong. The Chittagong export-processing zone (EPZ), which is dominated by garment manufacturing firms, was in fact seriously affected by the floods directly.[38] The disruption caused by the floods contributed to slowing down the impressive growth of the sector: while national annual output of ready-made garments had risen steadily from 47.2 million dozen units (mdu) in 1994/95 to 65.6 mdu in 1997/98, it actually fell slightly to 64.7 mdu during the floods fiscal year.[39] The slow-down of the sector was, associated however, not only with flood-related disruptions, but also with several other factors, including the appreciation of the taka in relation to the currencies of competing garments manufacturers from other Asian countries. This slow-down was, in turn, partly responsible for the significant fall of overall manufacturing growth, from 8.5 per cent in 1997/98 to only 3.2 per cent in the floods fiscal year and 4.2 per cent in 1999/00[40] (see table VII.4).

It can be argued that Bangladesh's garment sector is at a crossroads in respect of facing the challenges of globalization. The country's garment industry has so far benefited from various preferential agreements, such as the Generalized System of Preferences (GSP), with regard to exporting ready-made garments to the European Union (EU) and the United States of America. However, the maintenance of current export levels (and prices) is threatened not only by the phasing out of the Multi-Fibre Arrangement, under the Uruguay Round of multilateral trade negotiations, but also by recent changes in the trade regimes of the two main destinations for Bangladesh's ready-made garments. That EU, for example, has recently waived the quotas on certain categories of clothing from China and Sri Lanka, is likely to impact adversely on Bangladesh's garment exports.[41] Similarly, the recently introduced United States Trade and Development Act 2000 excludes Bangladesh and other 14 least developed countries from the duty- and quota-free access to the United States market granted to other 33 least developed countries. It is estimated that

Table VII.4.
GROWTH RATE OF GDP IN BANGLADESH, BY SECTOR, 1990-2000[a]

Percentage						
Sector	Average 1990/01-1994/95	1995/96	1996/97	1997/98	1998/99[b]	1999/00[c]
Agriculture	1.55	3.10	6.00	3.19	4.77	6.43
Crops and Horticulture	-0.43	1.74	6.44	1.05	3.16	6.13
Animal farming	2.38	2.51	2.58	2.64	2.69	2.74
Forestry	2.82	3.46	4.03	4.51	5.16	5.16
Fisheries	7.86	7.39	7.60	8.98	9.96	9.50
Industry	7.47	6.98	5.80	8.32	4.92	5.55
Manufacturing	8.20	6.41	5.05	8.54	3.19	4.25
Construction	6.27	8.50	8.64	9.48	8.92	8.00
Services	4.63	4.29	4.91	4.77	4.90	4.97
GDP	4.39	4.62	5.39	5.23	4.88	5.47

Source: M.K. Mujeri, "Macroeconomic developments", summary of paper prepared for a workshop on the review of the Bangladesh economy 2000, Dhaka, 6 June 2000, electronically available at http://www.bids-bd.org/review_of_bangladesh_economy.htm), based on official figures released by the Bangladesh Bureau of Statistics.

[a] Constant 1995/96 prices; fiscal year ending on 30 June.
[b] Floods fiscal year.
[c] Provisional figures.

in order to offset the consequent tariff disadvantages and maintain their competitiveness in the North American market, Bangladesh's garment exporters will need to reduce costs by 15 to 20 per cent.[42]

Bangladesh's ready-made garment sector can thus survive intense competition from other countries only if it takes effective steps to overcome internal constraints, including unreliable infrastructure. Among the main measures proposed for the industry is the reduction of lead time for delivery, as it is generally agreed that there is a need for the industry to establish better backward linkages and more reliable delivery of inputs from other parts of both the country and the world.[43] This would clearly require significant improvements in both the port facilities of Chittagong and the national road network, including effective measures to deal with the adverse impacts of recurrent floods. Given the overwhelming importance of the garment industry to Bangladesh's exports (see figure VII.6), and the competitive challenges it faces, the adverse impacts of recurrent flooding disasters may not only discourage new foreign direct investment (FDI) into the country but also exacerbate the impacts of reduced competitiveness in world markets. Recurrent natural disasters can therefore become a further obstacle to the country's efforts to benefit from current processes of globalization.

Structural versus non-structural approaches to flooding disasters

The conventional approach to flood control is primarily based on large-scale engineering projects, such as embankments and dams, to protect particularly vulnerable areas. This emphasis on structural measures has been widely criticized in Bangladesh not only in terms of those measures' engineering feasibility, but also because of the economic, social and environmental complexities, not to mention the relatively high financial costs, involved in building large embankments to prevent flooding. As a result, increasing attention has been turned to non-structural measures more suitable to poor countries subject to frequent floods, such as Bangladesh.[44]

[42] There is evidence that some major buyers of Bangladesh ready-made garments in the United States have withdrawn from dealing with the country's exporters, and concentrated on cheaper apparel exports from countries enjoying better preferential treatment (see *Bangladesh Country Report ...*, and *Bangladesh Country Profile, 2000...*).

[43] Other measures include upgrading labour skills and technology to produce better quality products at competitive prices, and diversification into new and higher-valued products and into new markets. See S.C. Zohir, "RMG: flourish or perish? external competitiveness beyond 2004", summary of paper prepared for a workshop on the review of the Bangladesh economy, 2000, Dhaka, 6 June 2000, electronically available at http://www.bids-bd.org/review_of_bangladesh_economy.htm.

[44] Bangladesh is one of the poorest countries in the world. According to the World Bank (*World Development Report 2000/2001 Attacking Poverty* (New York, Oxford University Press, 2001), selected world development indicators, table 1) annual per capita income (GNP) was only US$ 370 in 1999; over 35 per cent of the population was below the national poverty line in 1996; and 56 per cent of children under age 5 suffered from malnutrition in the 1990s. Bangladesh's low level of development is also associated with the facts that life expectancy at birth is only 58.9 years of age and that only barely 40 per cent of its adult population is literate (see United Nations Development Programme, *Human Development Report 2001* (New York, Oxford University Press, 2001), Human development indicators, table 1.

Figure VII.6.
EXPORTS OF BANGLADESH, 1998/99a

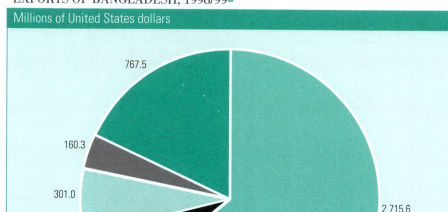

Millions of United States dollars

767.5

160.3

301.0

2 715.6

306.2

Garmentsb   Fisheries   Jute goodsc   Leather   Other

Source: Economist Intelligence Unit, *Bangladesh Country Report* (London, EIU, April 2001).

a   Covering fiscal year ending on 30 June 1999.
b   Including knitwear.
c   Including raw jute.

45   These had been the most damaging floods in the country's history before the 1998 floods and affected roughly the same number of people as the 1998 floods. In fact, according to the above-mentioned OFDA/CRED International Disaster Database, the 1988 floods were responsible for more than twice the number of deaths (2,300) than the 1998 floods, although the latter had flooded a much larger area of the country and caused greater economic damage.

46   See "Flood control in Bangladesh: a plan for action", *World Bank Technical Paper*, No. 119 (Washington, D.C., World Bank, 1990). FAP was formally launched at a donors' conference held in London in December 1989.

47   Bangladesh has invariably been dependent on foreign aid for development projects. The share of development projects scheduled to be funded from domestic sources peaked at 49 per cent of the Government's annual capital expenditure programme (the Annual Development Plan) in fiscal year 1996/97. As a result of the 1998 floods, the proportion fell to 31 per cent in 1998/99, which raised the country's dependence on foreign aid (see *Bangladesh Country Profile, 2000...*).

Structural approaches to flood control: the Flood Action Plan

In response to the devastating impacts of the 1988 flooding disaster,[45] the Government of Bangladesh, in cooperation with several bilateral donors and international agencies, decided to channel various flood control proposals into a comprehensive national strategy. This initiative led to the formulation of a massive Flood Action Plan (FAP), under the overall management of the World Bank.[46] The formulation stage of FAP entailed 26 comprehensive studies to be funded by bilateral and multilateral agencies, at an estimated cost of US$ 150 million. These studies were aimed at the implementation of systematic measures to control or significantly reduce the adverse impacts of future floods, with an emphasis on structural engineering solutions. This "structural approach" included large-scale river canalization and the construction of at least 3,500 km of embankments along major rivers, at an estimated cost of US$ 10 billion-15 billion, over a 20-year period.

The main anticipated economic benefit of FAP would be the protection of residential, commercial and industrial infrastructure, as well as transport and communication networks. This was, in turn, expected to have positive impacts on industrial output and exports. In addition, the implementation of the Plan would result in a substantial annual inflow of foreign aid and investment over a 20-year period—given that it would be mostly funded by foreign donors[47]— and in the generation of employment, particularly in the construction sector. Higher wage incomes arising from such additional employment would also help to reduce disaster vulnerability, as households would have more reserves to cope with flooding disasters. Other positive socio-economic impacts of the Plan included an expected reduction in the health costs and lost labour days associated with floods and ensuing diseases.

FAP was also expected to have positive economic effects on agriculture, both by reducing crop and material damage from the destructive impacts of abnormal floods, and by allowing farmers to intensify wet season farming and to improve cropping patterns because of the reduced risk, and thus increase productivity. More productive cropping practices would be primarily based on the greater use of higher-yield rice varieties—which were not as flood-resistant as a popular lower-yield variety. The enclosed embankments, or "flood control compartments", would allow the control of flood levels through a system of "drainage regulators" designed to simulate normal flood levels and ensure more reliable agricultural output.[48] In addition, embankments were expected to slow down damaging processes of erosion and destruction of fertile land on river banks which exacerbated geographical aspects of poverty and forced considerable numbers of peasants either to look for other available farmland or to migrate to urban areas.[49]

FAP's emphasis on a large-scale structural approach to flood management has been criticized for several reasons. First of all, the effectiveness of many large structural flood control projects in Bangladesh can obviously be undermined by continuous erosion of river banks and embankments, and above all by the constant shifting of river courses. A segment of the Jamuna River is locally known as the "dancing river" because of its gradual course shifts.[50] River straightening and canalization tend to cause higher peak flows and increase the possibility of more frequent flooding. Embankments may also divert floods to—and exacerbate their impacts in—unprotected areas.[51] In addition, increased accumulation of sediment and silt that cannot be deposited on flood plains (because of the embankments) cause river beds to rise, and thus may lead to more frequent floods and even the topping of embankments during abnormal floods.[52] When a high embankment is breached, flooding and its resulting damages are proportionately more severe, as exemplified by the collapse of an embankment on the river Meghna during the 1988 flood, which resulted in the total destruction of crops and infrastructure. There have been many cases of embankment failure in Bangladesh, the main causes of which are: (a) erosion and river shifts; (b) poor construction and inadequate maintenance; and (c) deliberate breaching by people adversely affected by them.[53]

One of the main negative economic impacts of embankments is that they tend to block or reduce the accumulation of fertile silt on croplands and reduce agricultural productivity. Other adverse impacts include a significant reduction in fish catch on flood plains and the spread of weeds and pests due to a disruption of the natural regulative mechanisms associated with alternating floods and dry spells on flood plains. The fact that flood control also encourages farmers to reduce the diversity of crops and crop varieties increases the danger of blights, plagues and pests.[54] In addition, embankments often lead to a decrease in livestock, especially cattle, because of the ensuing reduction in the size of grazing areas along river banks. At a broader macroeconomic level, it is often noted that operation and maintenance of flood control structures are expensive and to adequately cover this may be beyond the means of the Government of

[48] H. Rasid and A. Malik, "Flood adaptations in Bangladesh: is the compartmentalization scheme compatible with indigenous adjustments of rice cropping to flood regimes?", *Applied Geography*, vol. 15, No. 1 (July 1995).

[49] Ongoing shifts in river courses are responsible not only for erosion of river banks but also for the creation of river islands, locally known as "charlands", in which hundreds of thousands of small farmers live and grow crops. It was also argued, on the other hand, that some of the FAP embankments would threaten the existence of these river islands (see B. Imhasly, "The dancing rivers of Bangladesh", *Swiss Review of World Affairs*, No. 12 (December 1994), pp. 14-20).

[50] In the case of the Meghna River downstream, its gradual eastward drift took place in one sudden shift of 1.5 km in just 24 hours in 1966 (B. Imhasly, loc. cit.).

[51] Time-series data gathered by the Bangladesh Agricultural Research Council show that the total area flooded appears to have actually increased because of greater numbers of flood control embankments (see B. K. Paul, "Flood research in Bangladesh in retrospect and prospect: a review"..., p. 26).

[52] J.U. Chowdhury, "Flood Action Plan: one sided approach?", in J. L. Wescoat, Jr. and others, "Five Views on the Flood Action Plan for Bangladesh", *Natural Hazards Research and Applications Information Center/Institute of Behavioral Science (NHRAIC/IBS) Working Paper*, No. 77 (Boulder, Colorado, University of Colorado, March 1992).

[53] See P.M. Thompson and P. Sultana, "Operation and maintenance performance and conflicts in flood-control projects in Bangladesh", *Water Resources Development*, vol. 12, No. 3 (September 1996), pp. 311-328; and M. M. Hoque and M. Abu Bakar Siddique, "Flood control projects in Bangladesh: reasons for failure and recommendations for improvement", *Disasters*, vol. 19, No. 3 (September 1995), pp. 261-263.

[54] According to a detailed study carried out by a foreign donor agency (see Netherlands Development Cooperation, "Flood Action Plan, Bangladesh", *Evaluation Report* (The Hague, 1993), there is evidence that high-yield rice varieties favoured by many farmers under flood control schemes are less resistant to blight and pests.

BANGLADESH: MAJOR RIVERS AND TOWNS

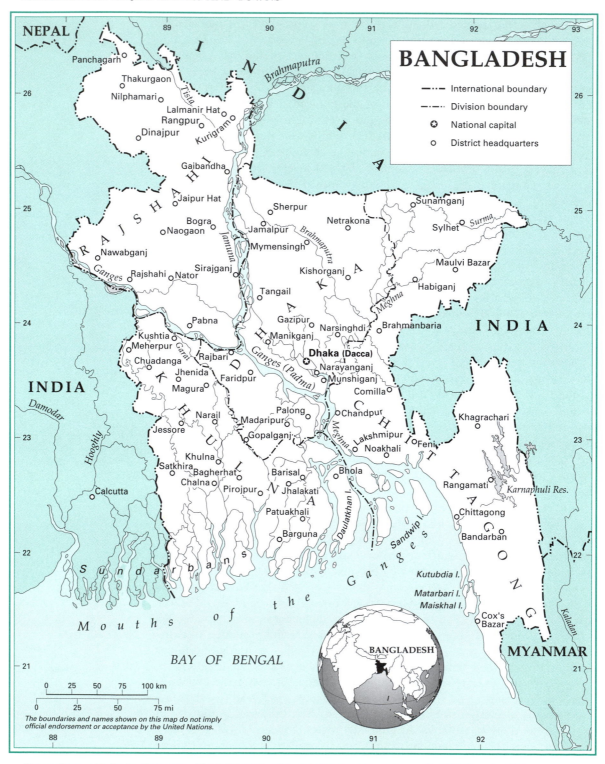

Source: Cartographic Section, Department of Public Information of the United Nations Secretariat, map no. 3711, November 1992.

Bangladesh. According to one estimate,[55] adequate annual maintenance of the FAP waterworks would require 5 per cent of the initial investment. An investment of US$ 10 billion would thus incur an annual maintenance cost of US$ 500 million a year—far more than the total cost of the estimated crop damage caused by the 1998 floods—or one third of the country's estimated total foreign exchange reserves in 2000.[56]

Potential socio-economic drawbacks include the above-mentioned adverse impacts on the consumption of fish—a primary source of protein for poor Bangladeshis; on household food security; and on possible losses by specific socio-economic groups. Besides fishers, the landless, poor rural farmers and river island (charland) dwellers have sometimes been adversely affected by the construction of embankments. This has occasionally led to the deliberate breaching of embankments by some of these groups, to the disadvantage of others, which has resulted in increasing social conflicts.[57] There is also evidence that average flood losses inside flood control projects were actually greater than in unprotected flood areas, during previous floods.[58] Even different areas within a so-called flood protection compartment may each have different flood control requirements, and even slight variations in flood level can have significant adverse impacts on agricultural output of different farmers. Compartmentalization cannot always meet specific demands of small-scale farmers, given that evidence from large-scale flood control and irrigation projects in Bangladesh show that regulated water levels are likely to be influenced by the interests of local rural elites and wealthier landowners.[59] Compartmentalization schemes also tend to be incompatible with indigenous practices of rice cropping because of operation and maintenance constraints.[60]

Probable environmental impacts of embankments include interference with migration of aquatic species and reduction of biodiversity, including loss of fisheries, given that fish habitats cover up to half of the country's area during the monsoon season (as opposed to 10 per cent in the dry season). In addition, embankments can act as obstacles to the replenishment of groundwater reservoirs during annual floods. Owing to inadequate maintenance and poor drainage, many embankments have given rise to an accumulation of stagnant water, with adverse environmental and human health consequences, including the spread of mosquito- and water borne diseases. Major environmental problems associated with stagnant water behind the 30 km embankment in western Dhaka include the accumulation of urban sewage and the spread of water hyacinth.[61]

By the mid-1990s, many of FAP's major structural projects had been scaled down or dropped altogether.[62] By the end of the decade, the whole FAP, as originally envisaged, was practically abandoned, primarily because of the above-mentioned engineering, socio-economic, financial and environmental complexities. Although no comprehensive flood prevention strategy has been developed to replace FAP, some large-scale flood control projects, such as a large embankment in Dhaka, have been built. In fact, a "cordon approach" to flood control—primarily based on the construction of large embankments to cordon off selected urban areas—appears to have emerged.[63] Given that criticism of such an approach is remarkably similar to that directed at FAP projects,[64] increasing attention has been turned to alternative, non-structural measures.

55   Ibid.

56   See Bangladesh Country Report.....

57   See, for example, D. J. Parker, "Social impacts of the Bangladesh Flood Action Plan", in J. L. Wescoat, Jr. and others, op. cit.; P. M. Thompson and P. Sultana, "Distributional and social impacts of flood control in Bangladesh", *The Geographical Journal*, vol. 162, part 1, pp. 1-13; M. Leaf, "Local control versus technocracy: the Bangladesh flood response study", *Journal of International Affairs*, vol. 51, No. 1 (summer 1997), pp. 179-200; and P. M. Thompson and P. Sultana, "Operation and maintenance performance and conflicts in flood-control projects in Bangladesh"....

58   P.M. Thompson and P. Sultana, "Distributional and social impacts of flood control in Bangladesh"....

59   D.J. Parker, loc. cit.

60   See H. Rasid and A. Malik, loc. cit.

61   See I.M. Faisal, M.R. Kabir and A. Nishat, "Non-structural flood mitigation measures for Dhaka City", *Urban Water*, Vol. 1, No. 2 (June 1999), pp. 145-53; and H. Rasid and A.U. Mallik, "Living on the edge of stagnant water: an assessment of environmental impacts of construction-phase drainage congestion along Dhaka City Flood control embankment, Bangladesh", *Environmental Management*, vol. 20, No. 1 (1996), pp. 89-98.

62   B.K. Paul, "Flood research in Bangladesh in retrospect and prospect: a review" ....

63   See N. Islam, "The open approach to flood control: the way to the future in Bangladesh", *Futures*, vol. 33, Nos. 8-9 (October 2001), pp. 783-802.

64   Ibid. N. Islam, for instance, shows that such "cordons" are harmful because, among other reasons (a) they deprive floodplains of the nurturing effects of inundation, (b) they lead to a huge waste of investment and (c) they do not solve the flood problem, as illustrated by the failure of the Dhaka-Narayanganj-Demra project to protect the area supposed to be cordoned off during the 1998 floods.

[65] See ESCAP, in cooperation with the United Nations Development Programme (UNDP), *Manual and Guidelines for Comprehensive Flood Loss Prevention and Management* (ST/ESCAP/933, 1991), p. 87. Given the regional dimension of flood control strategies in international river basins, ESCAP also considers regional cooperation increasingly important to maximize their effectiveness (see ESCAP, *Regional Cooperation in the Twenty-first Century on Flood Control and Management in Asia and the Pacific* (ST/ESCAP/1948, 1999).

[66] See *Manual and Guidelines for Comprehensive Flood Loss Prevention and Management...*, p. 86. According to ESCAP, special priority should be given to land-use control policies based on both legal measures for the enforcement of zoning and fiscal incentives for the spatial distribution of economic activity away from disaster-prone areas.

[67] See B.K. Paul, "Flood research in Bangladesh in retrospect and prospect: a review"...; and M. Leaf, loc. cit.

[68] Based on data collected from a rural area after the 1988 floods, C. E. Haque and M. Q. Zaman ("Vulnerability and responses to riverine hazards in Bangladesh: a critique of flood control and mitigation approaches", in *Disasters, Development and the Environment*, A. Varley, ed. (New York, Wiley, 1994)) show that over 70 per cent of affected farmers tried to cope with their losses by selling land, livestock and other belongings, and that most villagers received some assistance from other relatives, community organizations and local government agencies.

[69] H. Zaman, op. cit.

[70] Ibid.

[71] The plants of this rice variety can grow by 15 centimetres in 24 hours to keep pace with rising flood waters and can reach heights of 5 metres to keep their top above the water level.

Alternative approaches to flood mitigation

Generally speaking, non-structural measures should complement structural ones, provided that the latter are (a) properly designed and implemented; (b) suitable to local conditions; and (c) affordable in terms of building and maintenance. According to comprehensive regional guidelines on flood management prepared by the Economic and Social Commission for Asia and the Pacific (ESCAP), structural measures, such as the construction of embankments and river channel improvements, can provide flood protection only up to the level of the expected flood. As a result, "special provision should be considered at the design stage to incorporate measures that will ensure that the effects of failure are minimized and that the associated damages and disruptions are made no worse that the pre-protection situation."[65] Given that structural flood prevention measures usually require considerable financial resources, ESCAP guidelines also stress that countries with scarce financial resources should give emphasis to "policies and measures that will steer development away from high-risk areas and diminish vulnerability of new investments."[66]

Non-structural approaches to flood mitigation also include adaptive actions taken by affected communities, either individually or collectively, and by local and national government agencies before, during and after the floods.[67] Most of the measures resorted to by affected communities are of a preventive or corrective nature in that they are intended to minimize damage caused by floods. Some of these adjustments are related to material responses at the individual level; others are related to social organization or relationships. Selling land, livestock and personal belongings; borrowing from friends, relatives or microcredit organizations; and spending previous savings are the most popular non-structural measures used by lower-income urban and rural dwellers to mitigate loss caused by floods.[68]

There is evidence that increased subsidized microcredit provision by a leading local institution (the Bangladesh Rural Advancement Committee (BRAC), for both emergency relief and supply of seeds, contributed to mitigating the impacts of the 1998 floods.[69] Most rural flood victims consider it important to maintain close ties with traditional organizations *(samaj)*—informal social groups based on kinship and the social and religious interests of their members. There is further evidence that households that belonged to traditional or other non-governmental organizations were better prepared to mitigate and cope with flood losses than non-member neighbours.[70] This leads to the conclusion that the development of local social and institutional networks can effectively lessen the impacts of natural disasters such as floods.

There are also economic measures, particularly in the small-scale agricultural sector, that can be preventive. Farmers of Bangladesh often select the most adaptive rice varieties to hedge against abnormal floods. For example, *aus* rice is generally cultivated in elevated areas since it cannot survive floodwaters, whereas flood-adaptive *aman* rice is cultivated in low-lying areas.[71] Most farmers intercrop both rice varieties as a means of minimizing risk and in order to be able to harvest at least one rice crop—albeit at the expense of forgoing higher yields. Other preventive measures include the construction of traditional storage silos and flood shelters on naturally higher ground or on artificial levees. It is actually recommended that such "public high grounds" be considerably expanded as a vital flood mitigation measure, with emergency facilities,

Box VII.3

THE 1998 FLOODING DISASTER IN CHINA

a   All estimates of damages in this box are derived from *China: Flood, Situation Report No. 10* (Geneva, Office for the Coordination of Humanitarian Affairs of the United Nations Secretariat, 22 March 1999).

b   See X. Chena and Y. Zongb, "Major impacts of sea-level rise on agriculture in the Yangtze delta area around Shanghai", *Applied Geography,* vol. 19, No. 1 (1999), pp. 69-84.

c   The analysis here is based on Zhang Shougong, "Catastrophic flood disaster in 1998 and the post factum ecological and environmental reconstruction in China", available at http://www.fas.harvard.edu/~asiactr/fs_zhang2.htm.

d   H. Rasid and others, "Structural vs non-structural flood-alleviation measures in the Yangtze delta: a pilot survey of floodplain residents' preferences", Disasters: *The Journal of Disaster Studies and Management,* vol. 20, No. 2 (1996), pp. 93-110.

e   Shougong Zhang, loc. cit.

In mid-1998, China experienced one of the worst floods in its modern history, as the central and southern parts of the country along the Yangtze River and its tributaries suffered heavy flooding for more than two months. Huge areas behind the Yangtze River embankments were inundated for almost three months and some of these embankments were deliberately breached in order to reduce flood levels in the main river course. It is estimated that approximately 180 million people were affected and that at least 18 million were made homeless.[a] The floods caused severe damage to basic infrastructure and services, including roads, bridges, irrigation and water supply systems, hospitals and schools, as well as industrial and commercial buildings. At least 23 million hectares of crops were affected and over 5 million hectares were completely lost. According to the United Nations, by March 1999, the direct economic losses were estimated to have exceeded US$ 26 billion.

The two most evident causes of the disaster were (a) excessive rainfall—which, according to Chinese meteorologists was partly associated with El Niño/La Niña—and (b) the melting of deep snow accumulated in the Qinghai-Tibet plateau in south-west China. It is also possible that sea-level rise in the Yangtze delta may have contributed to slowing down the drainage of flood waters into the East China Sea.[b] Recent research identifies other less obvious causes, such as a deterioration of the Yangtze embankment network and deforestation in the upper and middle sections of the Yangtze River basin.[c]

Since 1949, a huge effort has been made to build embankments along 33,000 kilometres (km) of the Yangtze and its tributaries. Flood detention areas and reservoirs were also established as part of this flood control strategy. Other structural flood control measures have included the construction of diversion canals and multi-purpose dams. Financial constraints, however, have prevented the upgrading of these structures to deal more adequately with abnormal floods, such as the 1998 and 1991 Yangtze floods. In recent decades, intensified soil erosion in the Yangtze basin has contributed to the silting up of many reservoirs, tributaries and the main river course itself. For example, the river bed in a 235-km section near the city of Wuhan rose by 42 centimetres (cm) between 1966 and 1986 owing to the accumulation of 200 million tons of silt. It is estimated that in other sections, the river bed has been rising by 1 metre (m) every 10 years. It is also calculated that 1.2 billion cubic metres (m^3) of reservoir capacity along the Yangtze River is lost every year. In addition, extensive land reclamation from lakes for agriculture has considerably reduced their storage capacity and thus their flood regulation role in the Yangtze basin.

A second explanation for the magnitude of the 1998 floods is the increasing destruction of vegetation upstream. It is estimated that the total forest cover in the Yangtze Basin fell from 30-40 per cent in 1949 to only 10 per cent in 1986, and that it continues to fall significantly. Part of these forest cover losses in the mountainous areas of the Yangtze basin is caused by natural factors associated with the impacts of heavy rainfall on abrupt slopes and thin soils. Most of the deforestation in the upper and middle section of the basin, however, is associated with human activities, notably the conversion of natural forest into agriculture. The population of the Yangtze basin is estimated to have doubled to 400 million during the second half of the twentieth century, most of whom continue to be engaged in agricultural activities.

Although non-structural flood control measures—such as flood plain zoning, forecasting and warning systems and flood insurance—were introduced in China during the 1980s, until the 1998 flooding disaster, the country's flood control strategy had essentially been based upon a structural approach, that is to say, the use of embankments and other hydraulic engineering facilities. It is interesting to note that a survey of flood plain residents conducted in the mid-1990s showed that non-structural measures, such as flood insurance, attracted more favourable responses (97 per cent) than any of the structural measures (64-92 per cent).[d] Despite the huge efforts made by the Chinese authorities to mitigate the impacts of the 1998 floods, it became evident that structural engineering measures alone were insufficient to deal with abnormal floods. Attention has thus turned to non-structural measures, notably the control of deforestation and the acceleration of reforestation, particularly in the middle and upper reaches of the Yangtze River basin.[e] As a result, in 1999, the Chinese Government formulated the National Ecological and Environmental Construction Plan (NEECP), primarily aimed at forest and freshwater conservation, as well as reforestation.

72 M. Leaf, loc. cit.

73 See B. Sen, *Poverty in Bangladesh: A Review ...;* I.M. Faisal, M.R. Kabir and A. Nishat, loc. cit.; and H. Zaman, op. cit.

74 R. Jackson, *Prevention and Preparedness: Mitigating the Effects of Natural Disasters* (Rome, World Food Programme, 1998).

75 See N. Islam, loc. cit.

76 See also I. Ahmed, "Governance and flood: critical reflections on the 1998 deluge", *Futures,* vol. 33, Nos. 8-9 (October 2001), pp. 803-815. I. Ahmed argues, however, that government intervention in flood mitigation should be curtailed and that the role of civil society should be strengthened.

77 See B. Sen, *Poverty in Bangladesh: A Review....*

such as a public well, a small health unit with basic medicines, sanitary facilities, radio equipment and grain storage facilities.[72]

There is evidence that many of these non-structural measures, together with prompt action by government agencies, in cooperation with non-governmental and traditional organizations, were crucial in mitigating the impacts of what turned out be the worst floods in the country's history.[73] The increased capacity of government agencies to cope with crises, demonstrated during the 1998 flood and its aftermath, points to a greater role for non-structural measures in future flood-mitigating efforts. The experience from the 1998 floods in Greater Dhaka shows not only that non-structural measures contributed significantly to flood damage reduction, but also that coordination between agencies responsible for flood protection and drainage could significantly reduce flood damage. Furthermore, swift emergency relief and rehabilitation measures can be crucial to dealing with the vulnerability to flooding disasters and their adverse impacts. In addition, it is argued that an emergency food-based "safety net" is required to maintain poor people's access to minimum acceptable levels of nutrition and to enable them to preserve assets that would have otherwise need to be sold off to ensure their subsistence.[74]

More recently, an "open approach" to flood control appears to be emerging as an alternative, more comprehensive response to recurrent floods.[75] It includes (a) dredging watercourses in order to reduce the intensity of flooding in the major rivers, (b) minimizing obstruction on flood plains, (c) strengthening the freshwater fisheries sector, (d) redirecting crop research towards flood adaptation strategies, (e) increasing the elevation of urban and rural dwellings at risk, and (f) consolidating rural settlements around permanent flood shelters. This moves the emphasis away from structural flood prevention and control strategies towards flood preparedness and mitigation. The ultimate goal of this new approach is thus to revitalize "the culture of living with floods".[76] It is also argued that there is a greater need for developing a more "people-centred" approach to disaster management and rehabilitation.[77]

CONCLUSION

A comprehensive approach to disaster management should include at least four phases: prevention, preparedness, mitigation, and recovery. Although many countries tend to be primarily concerned with the first and last phases, the greatest potential for minimizing economic losses and reducing disaster vulnerability, particularly among lower-income groups, lies with the preparedness and mitigation phases. As the impacts of natural disasters tend to fall disproportionately on the poor, specific policies are required to tackle the link between poverty and disaster vulnerability. In addition, given that improved warning systems and dissemination of information on disaster prevention have significantly reduced the number of people seriously affected in developed countries, the availability of such information to the population at risk in disaster-prone developing countries is equally, if not more vital to their disaster prevention and mitigation efforts. Once the population mostly at risk is identified in these countries, specific prevention measures should be taken to protect them, including the enforcement of appropriate building standards.

Effective policies to regulate further growth of human settlements in risky areas should also be formulated and implemented as part of a broader disaster prevention and mitigation strategy. Since the location of human settlements is partly determined by the spatial location of economic activity, the reduction of disaster vulnerability requires the implementation of appropriate economic policies, such as fiscal incentives for orientation of economic activities away from disaster-prone areas. Efforts aimed at reorienting economic activities away from risky areas may require cooperation with the private sector, given that recurrent natural disasters can play a role in determining patterns of investment and discouraging new investment in particularly disaster-prone countries.

The case of the garment industry in Bangladesh illustrates how recurrent natural disasters can become an obstacle to both economic development and efforts to benefit from ongoing processes of globalization. Marginalized developing countries can thus help to create the enabling environment suitable for an increasingly globalized world economy not only through economic and institutional measures (such as trade liberalization, improved education and the establishment of a well-defined legal system) but also through infrastructural improvements required to render them attractive for FDI and as a competitive base for international trade. Such countries should make a particular effort to ensure that infrastructural improvements are targeted at the adverse impacts of recurrent disasters.

While it is widely assumed in the international community that development itself—and the ensuing improvement in living standards—will reduce vulnerability to natural disasters, international development assistance should be more explicit about the extent to which it is aimed at combating disaster vulnerability. This is particularly important in view of the evidence that poorer developing countries prone to natural hazards are often forced to divert scarce resources from the development of infrastructure, required to render them attractive for processes of globalization, into disaster relief activities. Within the United Nations, further support should be given to the International Strategy for Disaster Reduction, which works through an inter-agency secretariat and task force comprising United Nations agencies, as well as several organizations outside the United Nations system, to support national decision makers and local communities in the formulation and implementation of long-term disaster prevention and mitigation strategies.[78] Given that floods are the most damaging type of natural disaster in terms of both human losses and socio-economic damage, international assistance should also be specifically focused on the impacts of flooding disasters, particularly on the poor in developing countries.

Nonetheless, the recent flood experiences in Bangladesh show that disaster mitigation and response are best managed at the national level. Disaster response can be particularly effective when jointly carried out by government agencies, local communities, non-governmental organizations, and business and financial institutions, including microcredit organizations. Furthermore, bearing in mind the engineering, economic, social and environmental complexities of large-scale embankments, dams and river canalization projects—together with their often prohibitive cost—greater attention should be given to non-structural measures designed to prevent, mitigate or minimize the damage caused by floods in poorer developing countries. The main lesson from the recent flooding disaster in Bangladesh is that, in the absence of expensive structural measures, many non-structural ones can go a long way towards reducing vulnerability to natural disasters and mitigating their impacts.

[78] See "Implementation of the International Strategy for Disaster Reduction: report of the Secretary-General" (A/56/68-E/2001/63), 8 May 2001.

ANNEX STATISTICAL TABLES

ANNEX
STATISTICAL TABLES

The present annex contains the main sets of data on which the analysis provided in the *World Economic and Social Survey, 2001* is based. The data are presented in greater detail than in the text and for longer time periods, and incorporate information available as of 30 April 2001.

The annex was prepared by the Development Policy Analysis Division of the Department of Economic and Social Affairs of the United Nations Secretariat. It is based on information obtained from the United Nations Statistics Division and the Population Division of the Department of Economic and Social Affairs of the United Nations Secretariat, as well as from the United Nations regional commissions, the International Monetary Fund (IMF), the World Bank, the Organisation for Economic Cooperation and Development (OECD), the United Nations Conference on Trade and Development (UNCTAD) and national and private sources. Estimates for the most recent years were made by the Development Policy Analysis Division in consultation with the regional commissions and participants in Project LINK (see directly below). Data presented in this *Survey* may differ, however, from those published by these other organizations for a series of reasons, including differences in timing, sample composition, and aggregation methods (see also section on "Data quality" below for additional sources of data discrepancies). Historical data may differ from those in previous editions of the *Survey* because of updating and changes in the availability of data for individual countries.

Forecasts are based on the results of the April 2001 forecasting exercise of the above-mentioned Project LINK, an international collaborative research group for econometric modelling, which is coordinated jointly by the Development Policy Analysis Division and the University of Toronto. LINK itself is a global model that links together the trade and financial relations of 79 country and regional economic models, which are managed by over 60 national institutions and by the Division. The primary linkages are merchandise trade and prices, as well as the interest and currency exchange rates of major countries. The models assume that the existing or officially announced macroeconomic policies as of 6 April 2001 are in effect. The LINK system uses an iterative process to generate a consistent forecast for the world economy such that international trade flows and prices, among other variables, are determined endogenously and simultaneously. The one exception is the international price of crude oil, which is derived using a satellite model of the oil sector.[a] The average price of the basket of seven crude oils of the Organization of the Petroleum Exporting Countries (OPEC) is estimated to drop by 5 per cent in 2001 and to rise by 4 per cent in 2002.

[a] Additional information on Project LINK is available at: http://www.un.org/analysis/link/index.htm.

COUNTRY CLASSIFICATION

For analytical purposes, the *World Economic and Social Survey* classifies all countries of the world into one of three categories: developed economies, economies in transition and developing countries. The composition of these groupings is specified in the tables presented below. The groupings are intended to reflect basic economic conditions in countries. Several countries (in particular economies in transition) have characteristics that could place them in more than one category but, for purposes of analysis, the groupings were made mutually exclusive. Alternative groupings of countries may be appropriate at different times and for different analytical purposes.

The nature of each of the three categories may be given in broad strokes. The **developed economies** (see table A) on average have the highest material standards of living. Their production is heavily and increasingly oriented towards the provision of a wide range of services; agriculture is typically a very small share of output and the share of manufacturing is generally declining. On average, workers in developed countries are the world's most productive, frequently using the most advanced production techniques and equipment. The developed economies are often centres for research in science and technology. Governments of developed countries are likely to offer assistance to other countries and they do not generally seek foreign assistance.

The **economies in transition** are characterized by the transformation that they began at the end of the 1980s, when they turned away from centralized administration of resource allocation as the main organizing principle of their

Table A.
DEVELOPED ECONOMIES[a]

Europe		Other countries	Major industrialized countries
European Union	Other Europe		
EU-12	Iceland	Australia	Canada
Austria	Malta	Canada	France
Belgium	Norway	Japan	Germany
Finland	Switzerland	New Zealand	Italy
Germany		United States of	Japan
Greece		America	United Kingdom of Great Britain
Ireland			and Northern Ireland
Italy			United States of America
Luxembourg			
Netherlands			
Portugal			
Spain			
Other EU			
Denmark			
Sweden			
United Kingdom of			
Great Britain and			
Northern Ireland			

[a] Countries systematically monitored by the Development Policy Analysis Division of the United Nations Secretariat

Table B.
ECONOMIES IN TRANSITION[a]

Baltic States	Central and Eastern Europe	Commonwealth of Independent States

Estonia
Latvia
Lithuania
	Central Europe
	  Czech Republic
	  Hungary
	  Poland
	  Slovakia
	  Slovenia
	
	South-Eastern Europe
	  Albania
	  Bosnia and Herzegovina
	  Bulgaria
	  Croatia
	  Romania
	  The former Yugoslav Republic
	    of Macedonia
	  Yugoslavia
		Armenia
		Azerbaijan
		Belarus
		Georgia
		Kyrgyzstan
		Republic of Moldova
		Russian Federation
		Tajikistan
		Turkmenistan
		Ukraine
		Uzbekistan

[a] Countries systematically monitored by the Development Policy Analysis Division of the United Nations Secretariat

societies towards the establishment or re-establishment of market economies. Some of these economies began this transformation while having many of the characteristics of developed economies and others had several characteristics of developing economies. However, for the purposes of the analysis in the *Survey,* their most distinguishing characteristic is their transitional nature.

The rest of the world is grouped together as the **developing economies**. This is a heterogeneous grouping, although one with certain common characteristics. Average material standards of living in developing countries are lower than in developed countries and many of these countries have deep and extensive poverty. Developing countries are usually importers rather than developers of innovations in science and technology and their application in new products and production processes. They also tend to be relatively more vulnerable to economic shocks.

Beginning with the *World Economic and Social Survey, 1997,*[b] estimates of the growth of output in developing countries have been based on the data of 95 economies, accounting for 97-98 per cent of the 1995 gross domestic product (GDP) and population of all developing countries and territories. The countries in the sample account for more than 95 per cent of the GDP and population of each of the geographical regions into which the developing countries are divided, with the exception of sub-Saharan Africa for which the countries included in the sample account for at least 90 per cent of GDP and population.

The *Survey* uses the following designations of geographical regions for developing countries: Africa, Latin America and the Caribbean, and Asia and the Pacific (comprising Western Asia, China, East Asia and South Asia, including the Pacific islands).[c] Country classification by geographical region is specified in table C below.

The *Survey* also uses a geographical sub-grouping of sub-Saharan Africa, which contains African countries south of the Sahara desert, excluding Nigeria

[b] United Nations publication, Sales No. E.97.II.C.1 and corrigenda.

[c] Names and composition of geographical areas follow those of "Standard country or area codes for statistical use" (ST/ESA/STAT/SER.M/49/Rev.3), with the exception of Western Asia, in which the *Survey* includes the Islamic Republic of Iran (owing to the large role of the petroleum sector in its economy). Also, "Eastern Europe", as used in this *Survey,* is a contraction of "Central and Eastern Europe"; thus the composition of the region designated by the term differs from that of strictly geographical groupings.

Table C.
DEVELOPING ECONOMIES BY REGION[a]

	Latin America and the Caribbean	Africa	Asia and the Pacific		
			East Asia	South Asia	Western Asia

Net fuel exporters	Bolivia
	Colombia
	Ecuador
	Mexico
	Trinidad and Tobago
	Venezuela
		Algeria
		Angola
		Cameroon
		Congo
		Egypt
		Gabon
		Libyan Arab
		  Jamahiriya[b]
		Nigeria
			Brunei Darussalam[b]
			Indonesia
			Viet Nam
					Bahrain
					Iran (Islamic
					  Republic of)
					Iraq
					Kuwait[b]
					Oman[b]
					Qatar[b]
					Saudi Arabia[b]
					Syrain Ara[b]
					  Republic
					United Arab
					  Republic[b]

Net fuel importers	Argentina
	Barbados
	Brazil
	Chile
	Costa Rica
	Cuba
	Dominican Republic
	El Salvador
	Guatemala
	Guyana
	Haiti
	Honduras
	Jamaica
	Nicaragua
	Panama
	Paraguay
	Peru
	Uruguay
		Benin
		Botswana
		Burkina Faso
		Burundi
		Central African
		  Republic
		Chad
		Côte d'Ivoire
		Democractic
		  Republic of
		  the Congo
		Ethiopia
		Ghana
		Guinea
		Kenya
		Madagascar
		Malawi
		Mali
		Mauritius
		Morocco
		Mozambique
		Namibia
		Niger
		Rwanda
		Senegal
		South Africa
		Sudan
		Togo
		Tunisia
		Uganda
		United Republic
		  of Tanzania
		Zambia
		Zimbabwe
			Hong Kong
			  SAR of China
			Malaysia
			Papua New Guinea
			Philippines
			Republic of Korea
			Singapore[b]
			Taiwan Province
			  of China[b]
			Thailand
			
			China
				Bangladesh
				India
				Myanmar
				Nepal
				Pakistan
				Sri Lanka
					Cyprus
					Israel
					Jordan
					Lebanon
					Turkey
					Yemen

a   Countries systematically monitored by the Development Policy Analysis Division of the United Nations Secretariat
b   Net-creditor country.

and South Africa. The intent of this grouping is to give a picture of the situation in the large number of smaller sub-Saharan economies by avoiding any distortion that may be introduced by including the two large countries that dominate the region in terms of GDP, population and international trade.

For analytical purposes, developing countries are classified as **fuel exporters** or **fuel importers** because the ability to export fuel or the need to import fuel has a large effect on a country's capacity to import other goods and services—and therefore on the growth of output, as growth in developing countries is often constrained by the availability of foreign exchange. Fuels, rather than energy sources more broadly, are considered because fuel prices are more directly linked to oil prices, and oil prices are particularly volatile and often have a considerable impact on countries' incomes and capacity to import.

A country is defined as a **fuel exporter** if, simultaneously: (a) its domestic production of primary commercial fuel (including oil, natural gas, coal and lignite, but excluding hydro- and nuclear electricity) exceeds domestic consumption by at least 20 per cent; (b) the value of its fuel exports amounts to at least 20 per cent of its total exports; and (c) it is not classified as a least developed country.

A sub-group of the fuel-importing developing countries identified in some tables is the **least developed countries**. The list of least developed countries is decided by the General Assembly, on the basis of recommendations by the Committee for Development Policy. The Committee proposes criteria for identifying the least developed countries and makes recommendations regarding the eligibility of individual countries. The basic criteria for inclusion require being below certain thresholds with regard to per capita GDP, an economic vulnerability index and an "augmented physical quality of life index".[d] At present, the following 49 countries are on the list:

Afghanistan, Angola, Bangladesh, Benin, Bhutan, Burkina Faso, Burundi, Cambodia, Cape Verde, Central African Republic, Chad, Comoros, Democratic Republic of the Congo, Djibouti, Equatorial Guinea, Eritrea, Ethiopia, Gambia, Guinea, Guinea-Bissau, Haiti, Kiribati, Lao People's Democratic Republic, Lesotho, Liberia, Madagascar, Malawi, Maldives, Mali, Mauritania, Mozambique, Myanmar, Nepal, Niger, Rwanda, Samoa, Sao Tome and Principe, Senegal, Sierra Leone, Solomon Islands, Somalia, Sudan, Togo, Tuvalu, Uganda, United Republic of Tanzania, Vanuatu, Yemen, Zambia.

A classification of **net-creditor** and **net-debtor** countries is used in some tables. This is based on the net foreign asset position of each country at the end of 1995, as assessed by IMF in its *World Economic Outlook,* October 1996.[e] The **net-creditor** countries are signalized by footnote indicator [b] in table C.

Another group used in this Survey comprises the **heavily indebted poor countries** (HIPC), which are considered by the World Bank and IMF for their debt-relief initiative (the Enhanced HIPC Initiative). The heavily indebted poor countries[f] are: Angola, Benin, Bolivia, Burkina Faso, Burundi, Cameroon, Central African Republic, Chad, Congo, Democratic Republic of the Congo (formerly Zaire), Côte d'Ivoire, Ethiopia, Gambia, Ghana, Guinea, Guinea-Bissau, Guyana, Honduras, Kenya, Lao People's Democratic Republic, Liberia, Madagascar, Malawi, Mali, Mauritania, Mozambique, Myanmar, Nicaragua, Niger, Rwanda, Sierra Leone, Sao Tome and Principe, Senegal, Somalia, Sudan, Togo, Uganda, United Republic of Tanzania, Viet Nam, Yemen and Zambia.

[d] See report of the Committee for Development Policy 2000 on its second session (*Official Records of the Economic and Social Council, 2000, Supplement No. 13* (E/2000/33)), chap. IV.

[e] Washington, D.C., IMF, 1996.

[f] See "Heavily Indebted Poor Countries (HIPC) Initiative: status of implementation", report jointly prepared by the staffs of the World Bank and IMF for the joint session of the Development Committee (DC) and the International Monetary and Financial Committee (IMFC) on 29 April 2001.

DATA QUALITY

Statistical information that is consistent and comparable over time and across countries is of vital importance for monitoring economic developments, discussing social issues and poverty, or assessing environmental change. The multifaceted nature of these and other related issues calls for an integrated approach to national and international economic, environmental and social data.

The 1993 revision of the System of National Accounts (SNA)[g] and the 1993 *Balance of Payments Manual*[h] (the IMF Manual) constitute a major step forward in efforts to develop an integrated and harmonized system of statistics that reflect economic and social change. The SNA embodies concepts, definitions and classifications that are interrelated at both the macro- and microlevels. Concepts in the IMF Manual have been harmonized, as closely as possible, with those of the SNA and with the IMF's methodologies pertaining to banking, government finance and money statistics. In addition, through a system of satellite accounts, which are semi-integrated with the central framework of the SNA, it is possible to establish linkages between national accounts data and other statistical data, such as social statistics, health statistics, social protection statistics and tourism statistics.

Governments are increasingly reporting their data on the basis of these standards and, where available, such data are used in the statistics in this annex. However, inconsistency of coverage, definitions and data-collection methods among reporting countries mars some of the national and international statistics that are perforce used in this *Survey* and other international publications. Another perennial problem is late, incomplete or unreported data. In such cases, adjustments and estimations are possible, and are made in selected cases. In some areas, many developed countries report not only on an annual basis, but also quarterly or even more frequently. Considerable progress has been made by some developing countries and economies in transition in publishing annual and quarterly data on a timely and regular basis, but major lacunae have developed in other cases, particularly for economies in conflict.

One widespread source of inaccuracy arises from the use of out-of-date benchmark surveys and censuses or obsolete models and assumptions about behaviour and conditions. On the other hand, when statistical administrations seek to improve their estimates by using new sources of data and updated surveys, there can be discontinuities in the series. National income estimates are especially affected, sometimes being subject to revisions on the order of 10-30 per cent.

National accounts and related indicators mainly record market transactions conducted through monetary exchange. Barter, production by households, subsistence output and informal sector activities are not always recorded; together, the omitted items can constitute a large share of total activity and their omission can lead to a considerable underestimation of national output. As the degree of underestimation varies across countries, comparisons may give faulty results. In addition, as the non-market sector is absorbed over time into the mainstream of production through increasing monetization, output growth will be overstated.

Weaknesses at the national level become major analytical handicaps when comparisons are made between countries or groupings of countries at a given time or over time. Missing, unreliable or incompatible country data necessitate estimation and substitution by international organizations if they are to retain

g Commission of the European Communities, IMF, OECD, United Nations and World Bank, *System of National Accounts, 1993* (United Nations publication, Sales No. E.94.XVII.4).

h IMF, *Balance of Payments Manual,* 5th ed. (Washington, D.C., IMF, 1993).

consistent country composition of aggregated data over time. In particular, the absence of reliable GDP estimates for many developing countries and economies in transition requires the use of estimates in preparing country aggregations for many data series, as GDP weights often underlie such aggregations.

The veracity of estimates of output and of other statistical data of developing countries is related to the stage of development of their statistical systems. In Africa in particular, there are wide divergences in the values of the economic aggregates provided by different national and international sources for many countries. In addition, data for countries in which there is civil strife or war often provide only rough orders of magnitude. Finally, in countries experiencing high rates of inflation and disequilibrium exchange rates, substantial distortions can invade national accounts data.

The extent of economic activity not captured by national statistics and its evolution over time have become a concern in some countries, particularly economies in transition. In addition, the proliferation of new modes of production, transactions and entities has rendered the previous institutional and methodological framework for statistics inadequate. A comprehensive reform of national statistical systems has thus been under way in many economies in transition. As a result, important revisions to several data series have been released and further revisions of measures of past and current performance are expected. In the meantime, the statistical information provided, especially for many of the successor States of the Union of Soviet Socialist Republics, as well as for other economies in transition, must be treated as tentative estimates subject to revision.[i]

i   See *World Economic and Social Survey, 1995* (United Nations publication, Sales No. E.95.II.C.1), statistical annex, section entitled "Data caveats and conventions".

There are also problems with other types of statistics such as those on unemployment, consumer price inflation, and the volume of exports and imports. Cross-country comparisons of unemployment must be made with caution, owing to differences in definition among countries. For this reason in particular, table A.7 employs the standardized definitions of unemployment rates, where data are available (developed economies only). In a number of cases, then, data differ substantially from national definitions.

Consumer price indices are among the oldest of the economic data series collected by Governments, but they are still surrounded by controversy, even in countries with the most advanced statistical systems. This is attributable particularly to the introduction of new goods and changes in the quality of goods and consumer behaviour that are often not captured because of, inter alia, infrequent consumer-spending surveys and revisions to the sample baskets of commodities.

There are no clear-cut solutions to many of the problems noted above. Even when there are, inadequate resources allocated to the improvement of statistical systems and reporting can perpetuate statistical shortcomings. In this light, some of the economic and social indicators presented in this *Survey* should be recognized as approximations and estimations.

DATA DEFINITIONS AND CONVENTIONS

Aggregate data are either sums or weighted averages of individual country data. Unless otherwise indicated, multi-year averages of growth rates are expressed as compound annual percentage rates of change. The convention followed is to omit the base year in a multi-year growth rate, for example, the

10-year average growth rate of a variable in the 1980s would be identified as the average annual growth rate in 1981-1990.

Output

National practices are followed in defining real GDP for each country and these national data are aggregated to create regional and global output figures. The growth of output in each group of countries is calculated from the sum of GDP of individual countries measured at 1995 prices and exchange rates. Data for GDP in 1995 in national currencies were converted into dollars (with adjustments in selected cases[i]) and extended forward and backward in time using changes in real GDP for each country. This method supplies a reasonable set of aggregate growth rates for a period of about 15 years, centred on 1995.

Alternative aggregation methodologies for calculating world output

The *World Economic and Social Survey* utilizes a weighting scheme derived from exchange-rate conversions of national data in order to aggregate rates of growth of output of individual countries into regional and global totals, as noted above. This is similar to the approach followed in some other international reports, such as those of the World Bank. However, the aggregations used by IMF in its *World Economic Outlook* and by OECD in its *Economic Outlook* rely on country weights derived from national GDP in "international dollars", as converted from local currency using purchasing power parities (PPPs). The different weights arising from these two approaches are given in table D. The question of which approach to use is controversial.

The reason advanced for using PPP weights is that, when aggregating production in two countries, a common set of prices should be used to value the same activities in both countries. This is frequently not the case when market exchange rates are used to convert local currency values of GDP. The PPP approach revalues gross expenditure in different countries using a single set of prices, in most cases some average of the prices in the countries being compared. By construction, these revalued GDP magnitudes are then related to a numeraire country, usually the United States of America, by assuming that GDP at PPP values for that country is identical with its GDP at the market exchange rate. The PPP conversion factor is then, in principle, the number of units of national currency needed to buy the goods and services that can be bought with one unit of the currency of the numeraire country.[k]

In principle as well as in practice, however, PPPs are difficult to calculate because goods and services are not always directly comparable across countries, making direct comparisons of their prices correspondingly difficult. It is particularly difficult to measure the output and prices of many services, such as health care and education.

One problem in employing PPP estimates for calculating the relative sizes of economies is that even the most recently completed set of PPP prices covers only a comparatively small group of countries. Initially, in 1985, there were PPP data for only 64 countries. Subsequent work under the auspices of the International Comparison Project (ICP) has increased this number, but it remains far lower than the number of countries for which this *Survey* needs data.

[i] When individual exchange rates seemed unrealistic, alternative exchange rates were substituted, using averages of the exchange rates in relevant years or the exchange rate of a more normal year, adjusted using relative inflation rates since that time.

[k] Since a common set of international prices is used, the translation of purchasing power values relative to any numeraire country is defined, given the built-in transitivity property.

Table D.
OUTPUT AND PER CAPITA OUTPUT IN THE BASE YEAR

	GDP (billions of dollars)		GDP per capita (dollars)	
	Exchange-rate basis 1995	PPP basis 1995	Exchange-rate basis 1995	PPP basis 1995
World	28 767	34 716	5 154	6 220
Developed economies of which:	22 425	19 061	27 124	23 056
United States of America	7 401	7 401	27 705	27 705
European Union	8 427	7 345	22 678	19 766
Japan	5 134	2 879	41 052	23 023
Economies in transition	785	2 327	1 911	5 661
Developing countries By region:	5 557	13 328	1 279	3 068
Latin America	1 689	3 037	3 593	6 461
Africa	463	1 321	671	1 914
Western Asia	735	1 253	3 363	5 730
Eastern and Southern Asia	2 669	7 717	900	2 603
China	700	3 237	584	2 700
By analytical grouping:				
Net-creditor countries	574	791	10 393	14 318
Net-debtor countries	49 83	12 537	1 162	2 924
Net fuel exporter countries	1 308	3 184	1 627	3 961
Net fuel importer countries	4 249	10 144	1 200	2 866
Memorandum items:				
Sub-Saharan Africa	128	452	315	1 114
Least developed countries	136	514	244	924

Source: UN/DESA.

However, certain regularities have been observed, on the one hand, between GDP and its major expenditure components when measured in market prices and, on the other, between GDP and its components measured in "international" prices as derived in the ICP exercises. On that basis (and using other partial data on consumer prices), a technique was devised to approximate PPP levels of GDP and its major expenditure components for countries that had not participated in ICP. The results are known as the Penn World Tables.[1]

Neither the PPP approach nor the exchange-rate approach to weighting country GDP data can be applied in a theoretically pure or fully consistent way. The data requirements for a global ICP are enormous, although coverage has grown in each round. Similarly, since a system of weights based on exchange rates presumes that those rates are determined solely by external transactions and services and that domestic economies operate under competitive and

[1] See Robert Summers and Alan Heston, "The Penn World Table (Mark 5): an expanded set of international comparisons, 1950-1988", National Bureau of Economic Research (NBER) Working Paper No. R1562, May 1991.

liberal conditions, its application has been constrained by exchange controls and price distortions in many countries. Moreover, there are a large number of non-traded goods and services in each country to which the "law of one price" does not apply. However, the global trend towards liberalization may make possible a more consistent application over time of the exchange-rate method. Even so, the methods are conceptually different and thus yield different measures of world output growth.

The differences for the periods 1981-1990 and 1991-2000 are shown in table A.1. The estimates employ the same countries and the same data for the growth rates of GDP of the individual countries in the two computations. The differences in the aggregate growth rates are purely the result of using the two different sets of weights shown in table D.

Table A.1 indicates that the world economy as a whole has grown faster when country GDPs are valued at PPP conversion factors, even though the growth rates for the main groupings of countries do not differ much when data are converted at PPP rather than at exchange rates. This is because the developing countries, in the aggregate, grew more rapidly than the rest of the world in the 1990s and the share of GDP of these countries is larger under PPP measurements than under market exchange rates. The influence of China is particularly important, given its high growth rate for nearly two decades.

International trade and finance

Trade values in table A.13 are based largely on customs data for merchandise trade converted into dollars using average annual exchange rates and are mainly drawn from IMF, *International Financial Statistics*. These data are supplemented by balance-of-payments data in certain cases. Estimates of the dollar values of trade include estimates by the regional commissions and the Development Policy Analysis Division.

As of 1 January 1993, customs offices at the borders between States members of the European Union (EU), which used to collect and check customs declarations on national exports and imports, were abolished as the single European market went into effect. A new system of data collection for intra-EU trade, called INTRASTAT, was put in place. INTRASTAT relies on information collected directly from enterprises and is linked with the system of declarations of value-added tax (VAT) relating to intra-EU trade so as to allow for quality control of the data. There nevertheless remains a discontinuity owing to the change in methodology.

Estimates of trade values and volumes for the economies in transition, particularly for earlier years, are tentative for two reasons. First, there was a switch, mainly in 1991, from intraregional trade at arbitrarily set prices in transferable roubles to trade at world market prices in convertible currency. Second, many of the data-collection systems in the region are not yet up to world standards. These shortcomings mainly affect the reliability of calculations of changes in volumes for the Commonwealth of Independent States (CIS) countries.

The unit values that are used to determine measures of the volume of exports and imports for groupings of developing countries are estimated in part from weighted averages of export prices of commodity groupings at a combination of three- and four-digit Standard International Trade Classification (SITC) levels, based on the United Nations External Trade Statistics Database (COMTRADE); the weights reflect the share of each commodity or commodity group in the value of the region's total exports or imports.

The main source of data for table A.14 is the IMF Direction of Trade Statistics database, while tables A.15 and A.16 are drawn from the more detailed trade data in COMTRADE.

Total imports and exports comprise all 10 SITC sections (0 to 9).[m] The following aggregations were used:

Total primary commodities refer to SITC sections 0 to 4:
- *Food*s comprise SITC sections 0 and 1, namely, food and live animals chiefly for food; and beverages and tobacco;
- *Agricultural raw materials* include SITC section 2 (crude materials, inedible, except fuels), except for divisions 27 and 28 (crude fertilizers and crude minerals, and metalliferous ores and metal scrap, respectively) and section 4 (animal and vegetable oils, fats and waxes);
- *Fuels* refer to SITC section 3 (mineral fuels, lubricants and related materials).

Total manufactures comprise sections 5 to 8:
- *Textiles* include divisions 65 (textile yarn, fabrics, made-up articles, not elsewhere specified or included, and related products) and 84 (articles of apparel and clothing accessories);
- *Chemicals* are SITC section 5;
- *Machinery and transport equipment* refer to SITC division 7;
- *Metals* include divisions 67 (iron and steel) and 68 (non-ferrous metals).

The IMF *Balance of Payments Statistics* is the main source of data for tables A.19 to A.22. The tables are based, therefore, on the definitions and methodologies as specified by the IMF *Balance of Payments Manual* mentioned earlier. Regional commissions, and official and private sources, as well as estimates by the Development Policy Analysis Division, were used to complement the IMF data. Whenever necessary, data reported in national currency were converted into United States dollars at the average market exchange rate in the period. The tables on current-account transactions cover the period 1993-2000 thereby avoiding several discontinuity problems owing to the political and economic transformations that took place before 1993. Current-account transactions estimates are presented for the three country groupings specified in tables A, B, and C above. Regional and subregional aggregates are sums of individual economy data. Accordingly, the current-account balance for the euro zone countries reflects the aggregation of individual country positions; it therefore does not exclude intra euro-zone transactions.

Table A.18 is, with the exception of data for OPEC in 2001, based on the International Energy Agency (IEA) *Monthly Oil Market Report*. The estimate of supply from OPEC in 2001 is based on production data for the first quarter of 2001 and information about OPEC production quotas. The country groups and regions used in this *Survey* differ from those used by IEA, and adjustments were made to take account of these differences.

[m] See *Standard International Trade Classification, Revision 2*, Statistical Papers, No. 34 (United Nations publication, Sales No. E.75.XVII.6).

LIST OF TABLES

I. GLOBAL OUTPUT AND MACROECONOMIC INDICATORS

Table A.1.
WORLD POPULATION, OUTPUT AND PER CAPITA GDP, 1980-2000

	Growth of GDP (annual percentage change)				Growth rate of population (annual percentage change)		Population (millions)		GDP per capita Exchange-rate basis (1995 dollars)	
	Exchange-rate basis (1995 dollars)		Purchasing power parity (PPP) basis							
	1981-1990	1991-2000	1981-1990	1991-2000	1981-1990	1991-2000	1980	2000	1980	2000
World	3.0	2.6	3.0	3.1	1.8	1.4	4 367	5 980	4 535	5 624
Developed economies	3.0	2.3	3.0	2.5	0.6	0.5	756	847	20 241	30 568
of which:										
United States	3.2	3.3	3.2	3.3	1.0	0.9	230	278	20 851	32 848
European Union[a]	2.3	1.9	2.4	1.9	0.3	0.3	355	375	17 639	25 391
Japan	4.1	1.4	4.1	1.4	0.6	0.3	117	127	27 462	43 283
Economies in transition[b]	1.8	-2.5	2.0	-3.2	0.7	0.0	378	409	2 616	2 128
Developing countries	2.3	4.5	3.4	5.2	2.2	1.7	3 233	4 725	1 087	1 457
by region:										
Latin America	1.1	3.1	1.3	3.1	2.1	1.7	354	512	3 675	3 826
Africa	2.0	2.3	1.9	2.2	2.6	2.5	455	751	786	726
Western Asia	-2.8	2.7	-1.5	2.8	3.3	2.3	137	238	6 718	3 777
Eastern and Southern Asia	7.0	6.5	6.9	7.1	1.9	1.5	2 287	3 224	408	1 086
Region excluding China	6.6	5.4	5.9	5.0	2.2	1.8	1 306	1 924	587	1 266
of which:										
East Asia	7.0	5.5	6.3	5.1	1.9	1.5	414	582	1 314	3 144
South Asia	5.3	5.0	5.2	5.0	2.3	1.9	892	1 342	250	452
China	9.1	10.1	9.1	10.1	1.8	1.0	981	1 300	170	801
by analytical grouping:										
Net-creditor countries	1.6	4.6	0.9	4.1	3.2	1.9	37	61	10 624	11 767
Net-debtor countries	2.4	4.5	3.6	5.3	2.1	1.7	3 196	4 642	977	1 328
Net fuel exporters	-1.1	2.8	0.7	3.1	2.5	2.0	559	866	2 372	1 810
Net fuel importers	4.0	5.1	4.6	5.9	2.1	1.6	2 674	3 859	819	1 377
Memo items:										
Sub-Saharan Africa	1.8	2.3	1.2	1.9	2.9	2.7	262	455	387	333
Least developed countries	2.2	3.0	1.9	2.8	2.6	2.4	379	619	263	269

Source: UN/DESA.

[a] Including the eastern *Länder* (States) of Germany from 1991.
[b] Including the former German Democratic Republic until 1990.

Table A.2.
DEVELOPED ECONOMIES: RATES OF GROWTH OF REAL GDP, 1992-2001

Annual percentage change[a]

	1992-2000	1992	1993	1994	1995	1996	1997	1998	1999	2000[b]	2001[c]
All developed economies	2.5	1.7	0.9	2.8	2.3	2.7	3.0	2.5	2.8	3.6	2
United States	3.6	3.0	2.7	4.0	2.7	3.6	4.4	4.4	4.2	5.0	1¾
Canada	3.2	0.8	2.3	4.7	2.8	1.7	3.9	3.6	4.5	4.7	2¾
Japan	1.1	0.9	0.4	1.0	1.6	3.5	1.8	-1.1	0.8	1.7	¾
Australia	3.8	2.3	3.7	5.2	3.8	4.1	4.0	5.3	4.7	3.7	¾
New Zealand	3.1	0.8	6.2	5.3	2.9	2.7	3.0	-0.7	4.6	4.3	2¼
EU-15	2.0	1.2	-0.4	2.7	2.3	1.6	2.4	2.8	2.4	3.3	2½
EU-12	2.0	1.5	-0.8	2.4	2.2	1.4	2.3	2.7	2.4	3.4	2¾
Austria	2.1	1.3	0.5	2.4	1.7	2.0	1.3	3.3	2.8	3.3	2½
Belgium	2.2	1.6	-1.5	3.0	2.6	1.2	3.4	2.4	2.7	4.1	2¾
Finland	3.2	-3.3	-1.1	4.0	3.8	4.0	6.3	5.3	4.2	5.7	4
France	2.0	1.5	-0.9	2.1	1.8	1.1	1.9	3.1	3.2	3.2	2¾
Germany	1.6	2.2	-1.1	2.3	1.7	0.8	1.5	2.2	1.2	3.0	2
Greece	2.4	0.4	-0.9	1.5	1.9	2.4	3.5	3.1	3.4	4.1	4¼
Ireland	7.7	3.3	2.7	5.8	9.7	7.7	10.7	8.6	9.8	10.8	8
Italy	1.6	0.8	-0.9	2.2	2.9	1.1	1.8	1.5	1.4	2.9	2½
Luxembourg	4.4	1.8	8.7	4.2	3.8	3.0	4.8	4.7	4.2	4.5	4
Netherlands	2.9	2.0	0.6	3.2	2.3	3.1	3.6	4.1	3.2	4.0	3¼
Portugal	2.4	1.9	-1.4	2.4	2.9	3.2	3.5	3.5	2.9	2.8	2
Spain	2.5	0.7	-1.2	2.3	2.7	2.4	3.5	3.8	3.7	4.1	3¼
Other EU	2.5	-0.1	1.4	4.4	2.9	2.3	3.2	2.8	2.5	3.0	2¼
Denmark	2.3	0.6	0.0	5.5	2.8	2.5	3.1	2.5	1.6	2.4	1¾
Sweden	2.0	-1.4	-2.2	3.3	3.7	1.1	2.0	2.9	4.1	3.6	2¾
United Kingdom	2.6	0.1	2.3	4.4	2.8	2.6	3.5	2.6	2.3	3.0	2¼
Other Europe											
Iceland	2.7	-3.3	0.6	4.5	0.1	5.2	5.3	5.1	4.3	3.6	2½
Malta	4.1	4.7	4.5	5.7	6.2	4.0	4.9	3.4	4.1	1.8	2
Norway	3.2	3.3	2.7	5.5	3.8	4.9	4.7	2.0	0.9	2.2	1½
Switzerland	1.2	-0.1	-0.5	0.5	0.5	0.3	1.7	2.3	1.5	3.4	2¼
Memo item: Major industrialized countries	2.5	1.9	1.1	2.8	2.2	2.8	3.0	2.3	2.7	3.6	1¾

Source: UN/DESA, based on IMF, *International Financial Statistics*.

a   Calculated as a weighted average of individual country growth rate of gross domestic product (GDP), where weights are based on GDP in 1995 prices and exchange rates. For methodology, see *World Economic and Social Survey, 2000* (United Nations publication, Sales No. E.00.II.C.1, annex, introductory text).
b   Partly estimated.
c   Forecast, partly based on Project LINK.

Table A.3.
ECONOMIES IN TRANSITION: RATES OF GROWTH OF REAL GDP, 1993-2001

Annual percentage change[a]	1993	1994	1995	1996	1997	1998	1999	2000[b]	2001[c]
Economies in transition	-6.7	-7.2	-0.6	-0.1	2.2	-0.7	3.0	6.1	3.6
Central and Eastern Europe and Baltic States	-1.9	3.6	5.5	4.1	3.7	2.6	1.3	4.0	3.5
Central and Eastern Europe	-1.2	4.0	5.7	4.1	3.5	2.5	1.4	4.0	3.5
Albania	9.7	8.3	13.3	9.0	-7.0	8.0	7.3	7.0	7.0
Bulgaria	-1.4	1.8	2.8	-10.2	-7.0	3.5	2.4	4.8	3.7
Croatia	-8.0	5.9	6.8	5.9	6.8	2.5	-0.4	3.6	2.7
Czech Republic	0.0	2.2	6.0	3.8	0.3	-2.2	-0.8	3.1	3.3
Hungary	-0.6	3.1	1.4	1.4	4.6	4.9	4.5	5.2	4.5
Poland	3.8	5.1	7.1	6.0	6.9	4.8	4.1	4.1	3.0
Romania	1.6	3.9	7.1	4.0	-6.1	-5.4	-3.2	1.6	2.6
Slovakia	-3.6	4.8	7.0	6.5	6.5	4.1	1.9	2.2	2.7
Slovenia	2.9	5.3	4.2	3.5	4.5	4.0	3		
The former Yugoslav Republic of Macedonia	-9.0	-1.9	-1.2	0.7	1.5	2.9	2.7	5.1	2.0
Yugoslavia	-30.8	2.7	6.0	5.9	7.4	2.5	-19.3	7.0	9.0
Baltic States	-14.2	-4.7	2.2	4.1	8.5	4.6	-1.7	5.0	4.8
Estonia	-9.0	-2.0	4.3	3.9	10.6	4.7	-1.1	6.4	5.5
Latvia	-14.9	0.6	-0.8	3.3	8.6	3.9	1.1	6.6	5.5
Lithuania	-16.2	-9.8	3.3	4.7	7.3	5.1	-4.2	2.9	3.7
Commonwealth of Independent States	-9.4	-13.7	-5.1	-3.5	1.0	-3.7	4.7	7.9	3.7
Armenia	-14.8	5.4	6.9	5.9	3.3	7.3	3.3	6.0	5.5
Azerbaijan	-23.1	-19.7	-11.8	1.3	5.8	10.0	7.4	11.4	8.5
Belarus	-7.6	-12.6	-10.4	2.8	11.4	8.4	3.4	6.0	2.5
Georgia	-25.4	-11.4	2.4	10.5	10.8	2.9	2.9	1.9	4.0
Kazakhstan	-9.2	-12.6	-8.2	0.5	1.7	-1.9	1.7	9.6	6.5
Kyrgyzstan	-16.0	-20.1	-5.4	-7.1	9.9	2.1	3.6	5.0	5.0
Republic of Moldova	-1.2	-31.2	-1.4	-7.8	1.3	-6.5	-4.4	1.9	4.0
Russian Federation	-8.7	-12.7	-4.1	-3.5	0.8	-4.9	5.4	8.3	3.5
Tajikistan	-11.0	-18.9	-12.5	-4.4	1.7	5.3	3.7	8.3	5.0
Turkmenistan	-10.0	-17.3	-7.2	-6.7	-11.3	5.0	16.0	17.6	16.0
Ukraine	-14.2	-23.0	-12.2	-10.0	-3.0	-1.9	-0.4	6.0	5.0
Uzbekistan	-2.3	-4.2	-0.9	1.6	2.5	4.4	4.4	4.0	1.0

Sources: UN/DESA and ECE.

[a] Calculated as a weighted average of individual country growth rates of gross domestic product (GDP), where weights are based on GDP in 1995 prices and exchange rates. For methodology, see *World Economic and Social Survey, 2000* (United Nations publication, Sales No. E.00.II.C.1 annex, introductory text).
[b] Partly estimated.
[c] Forecast, based in part on Project LINK.

Table A.4.
DEVELOPING COUNTRIES: RATES OF GROWTH OF REAL GDP, 1992-2001

Annual percentage change

	1992-2000	1992	1993	1994	1995	1996	1997	1998	1999	2000[a]	2001[b]
Developing countries[c]	4.7	4.8	5.2	5.6	5.0	5.7	5.4	1.6	3.5	5.7	4
of which:											
Latin America and the Caribbean	3.1	2.5	3.5	5.3	1.4	3.7	5.2	2.0	0.4	3.8	3
Net fuel exporter	3.0	4.0	2.2	3.6	-2.4	3.7	5.7	3.2	1.5	5.5	3
Net fuel importer	3.1	1.9	4.1	6.1	3.0	3.8	4.9	1.5	0.0	3.1	3¼
Africa	2.4	-0.1	0.1	2.3	2.8	4.8	2.9	3.0	2.7	3.1	4¼
Net fuel exporter	2.6	1.1	-0.9	0.5	3.9	4.1	3.4	3.6	4.1	4.1	4¼
Net fuel importer	2.3	-0.8	0.7	3.4	2.1	5.3	2.7	2.6	1.8	2.6	4¼
Western Asia	3.7	5.4	4.3	-0.8	4.0	4.6	5.5	4.1	0.8	5.7	2½
Net fuel exporter	3.6	5.4	3.1	-0.5	1.7	3.9	5.9	4.7	2.8	5.8	4¾
Net fuel importer	3.9	5.3	6.2	-1.3	7.5	5.8	4.9	3.3	-2.1	5.6	-½
Eastern and Southern Asia	6.5	7.4	7.6	8.4	8.1	7.3	6.0	0.5	6.3	7.3	5
Region excluding China	5.3	5.5	5.9	7.0	7.3	6.5	5.0	-2.3	5.9	6.9	4
of which:											
East Asia	5.3	6.0	6.5	7.6	7.6	6.7	5.1	-4.6	5.9	7.3	3¾
South Asia	5.3	4.2	3.9	5.2	6.3	6.0	4.8	5.3	5.9	5.8	5½
Memo items:											
Sub-Saharan Africa (excluding Nigeria and South Africa)	2.5	0.2	-1.1	2.1	3.8	5.4	4.2	3.4	2.1	2.5	3¼
Least developed countries	3.4	1.4	0.8	2.0	4.9	5.2	4.5	3.8	3.5	4.4	4½
Major developing economies											
Argentina	3.4	9.6	5.7	5.8	-2.8	5.5	8.1	3.9	-3.4	-0.5	1
Brazil	2.8	-1.1	4.1	6.2	4.2	2.9	3.5	0.2	0.8	4.2	4
Chile	6.0	10.5	6.0	5.4	9.9	7.0	7.6	3.9	-1.1	5.4	4½
China	10.2	14.2	13.5	12.6	10.5	9.6	8.8	7.8	7.1	8.0	7¼
Colombia	2.7	4.0	5.1	6.3	5.4	2.1	2.8	0.5	-4.3	2.8	3
Egypt	4.2	2.5	2.0	2.3	4.7	5.0	5.5	5.6	6.0	3.9	4½
Hong Kong SAR[d]	4.6	6.3	6.1	5.3	4.7	4.8	5.2	-5.1	3.0	12.1	3¾
India	5.5	4.0	3.9	5.4	6.7	6.4	5.3	5.6	6.4	6.0	5¾
Indonesia	3.5	6.5	6.5	7.5	8.1	8.0	4.7	-13.1	0.1	4.8	3
Iran (Islamic Republic of)	3.4	6.0	2.6	1.8	4.2	5.0	2.5	2.2	2.5	4.0	3½
Israel	4.5	6.6	3.4	6.6	7.1	4.5	2.1	2.2	2.2	5.9	2½
Korea, Republic of	6.0	5.1	5.8	8.6	8.9	7.1	5.5	-5.8	10.7	8.8	4
Malaysia	6.2	7.8	8.3	9.2	9.5	8.2	7.7	-7.5	5.6	8.5	4
Mexico	3.6	3.7	1.9	4.6	-6.2	5.5	6.8	4.8	5.2	6.9	3
Nigeria	2.7	3.0	2.3	1.3	2.5	4.3	3.6	1.8	2.5	2.8	3½
Pakistan	4.0	5.1	3.1	4.2	4.9	5.2	1.3	3.7	3.9	4.6	3¾
Peru	4.3	-0.4	4.8	12.8	8.6	2.5	6.7	-0.4	1.4	3.6	1¼
Philippines	3.2	0.0	2.1	4.4	4.8	5.5	5.2	-0.5	3.3	3.9	3
Saudi Arabia	1.6	3.0	1.6	-2.7	-0.2	4.0	3.0	1.6	0.5	4.1	2¾
Singapore	7.3	6.0	9.9	10.1	8.9	7.0	7.8	0.3	5.9	9.9	4
South Africa	1.8	-2.2	1.3	2.7	3.4	3.2	2.5	0.6	1.3	3.1	3½
Taiwan Province of China	6.0	6.8	6.3	6.5	6.1	5.6	6.8	4.6	5.4	6.0	3¾
Thailand	3.9	7.8	8.3	8.7	8.6	6.7	-1.3	-10.2	4.2	4.3	3¼
Turkey	3.6	5.0	8.1	-6.1	8.0	7.0	6.8	3.8	-5.1	5.9	-3
Venezuela	0.8	6.1	0.7	-3.0	3.1	-1.3	5.1	0.2	-6.1	3.2	3½

Source: United Nations.

[a] Partly estimated.
[b] Forecast, based in part on Project LINK.
[c] Covering countries that account for 98 per cent of the population of all developing countries.
[d] Special Administrative Region of China.

Table A.5.
DEVELOPED ECONOMIES: INVESTMENT, SAVING AND NET TRANSFERS, 1985-1999

Percentage of GDP		Gross domestic investment	Gross domestic saving	Net financial transfer
Total[a]	1985	21.6	22.0	-0.5
	1990	22.6	22.4	0.2
	1995	21.5	22.3	-0.8
	1999	21.4	21.2	0.2
Major industrialized countries[a]	1985	21.6	21.1	0.5
	1990	22.4	22.2	0.2
	1995	21.6	22.0	-0.5
	1999	21.3	20.7	0.6
European Union (EU-15)	1985	14.5	17.0	-2.5
	1990	16.3	16.3	0.0
	1995	14.8	16.0	-1.2
	1999	15.1	16.0	-0.9
Germany[b]	1985	20.0	23.0	-3.0
	1990	22.7	26.0	-3.3
	1995	22.7	23.3	-0.6
	1999	22.2	23.2	-1.0
Japan	1985	28.2	31.5	-3.4
	1990	32.3	33.0	-0.7
	1995	28.6	30.1	-1.5
	1999	26.1	27.7	-1.6
United States of America	1985	20.2	17.4	2.7
	1990	17.6	16.4	1.2
	1995	18.1	17.0	1.1
	1999	20.3	17.6	2.7

Source: OECD, *National Accounts*.

[a] National data converted to dollars for aggregation at annual average exchange rates.
[b] Prior to 1991, data referring to Western Germany only.

Table A.6.

DEVELOPING ECONOMIES: INVESTMENT, SAVING AND NET TRANSFERS, 1985-1999

Percentage of GDP

	Gross domestic investment				Gross domestic saving				Net transfer of resources			
	1985	1990	1995	1999	1985	1990	1995	1999	1985	1990	1995	1999
All developing countries **by region:**	23.4	24.9	27.9	24.3	24.4	26.0	27.2	25.8	-1.0	-1.2	0.7	-1.5
Africa	20.8	19.4	19.6	20.1	20.9	18.7	17.7	17.3	-0.1	0.7	1.9	2.8
Latin America	19.2	19.5	21.2	20.3	23.9	21.6	20.3	19.3	-4.7	-2.1	0.9	1.1
Eastern and Southern Asia (excluding China)	24.2	29.3	31.8	24.2	25.8	29.8	30.2	28.8	-1.7	-0.5	1.6	-4.7
East Asia	25.0	32.0	33.9	25.0	31.0	34.5	33.0	33.0	-6.0	-2.6	0.9	-8.0
South Asia	23.0	23.8	24.8	22.2	18.2	20.1	20.8	18.7	4.7	3.7	4.0	3.5
Western Asia	20.8	23.5	24.5	20.8	19.2	24.2	24.7	22.0	1.6	-0.8	-0.2	-1.1
by analytical grouping:												
Net-creditor countries	22.4	22.3	24.5	23.8	32.2	34.0	32.5	31.9	-9.7	-11.7	-8.0	-8.1
Net-debtor countries	23.5	25.2	28.3	24.4	23.6	25.1	26.5	25.1	-0.1	0.1	1.7	-0.8
Net fuel exporters	22.0	23.0	23.5	21.1	24.3	26.1	25.6	23.3	-2.3	-3.0	-2.0	-2.2
Net fuel importers	20.9	24.1	26.8	22.1	22.3	24.1	24.5	23.0	-1.3	0.0	2.2	-0.9
Memo items:												
Sub-Saharan Africa	16.5	16.6	18.1	17.2	13.9	12.6	14.8	10.7	2.5	4.0	3.3	6.5
Least developed countries	15.3	16.2	18.1	18.3	4.2	6.3	8.5	9.6	11.1	9.9	9.6	8.7
Selected developing countries												
Algeria	33.2	29.3	32.1	27.4	36.4	27.5	28.4	31.7	-3.2	1.8	3.7	-4.3
Argentina	17.6	14.0	17.9	18.8	23.1	19.7	17.6	17.2	-5.5	-5.7	0.4	1.7
Brazil	19.2	20.2	22.3	20.4	24.4	21.4	20.5	19.3	-5.2	-1.2	1.8	1.1
Chile	17.2	25.1	25.8	21.1	19.6	28.4	27.6	23.0	-2.4	-3.3	-1.8	-1.8
China	37.8	34.7	40.8	37.2	33.6	37.9	43.1	40.1	4.1	-3.2	-2.3	-2.9
Colombia	19.0	18.5	25.8	13.0	20.3	24.2	19.6	11.3	-1.3	-5.7	6.2	1.6
Egypt	26.7	28.8	17.2	22.8	14.5	16.1	12.2	14.4	12.1	12.7	5.0	8.4
Hong Kong SAR[a]	21.6	27.4	34.8	25.2	31.1	35.8	30.5	30.6	-9.4	-8.5	4.3	-5.4
India	24.2	25.2	26.5	22.9	21.2	22.5	23.2	20.0	2.9	2.7	3.3	3.0
Indonesia	27.6	30.7	31.9	23.7	30.3	32.3	30.6	31.6	-2.7	-1.6	1.3	-7.9
Israel	19.4	25.1	25.3	21.0	5.7	14.4	10.5	11.4	13.6	10.7	14.8	9.6
Korea, Republic of	29.7	37.7	37.2	26.8	30.3	36.5	35.7	33.6	-0.5	1.2	1.5	-6.8
Malaysia	27.5	32.4	43.6	22.3	32.5	34.5	39.7	47.3	-5.0	-2.1	3.9	-25.1
Mexico	21.2	23.1	19.8	23.2	26.3	22.0	22.5	21.9	-5.1	1.1	-2.7	1.3
Morocco	27.1	25.3	20.7	24.2	18.1	19.3	14.1	20.1	9.0	6.0	6.7	4.1
Nigeria	9.0	14.7	16.3	24.2	12.6	29.4	18.4	18.4	-3.7	-14.6	-2.1	5.8
Peru	18.4	16.5	25.1	22.0	24.9	18.4	19.4	19.7	-6.5	-1.9	5.7	2.3
Philippines	15.3	24.2	22.5	18.6	17.4	18.4	14.6	19.6	-2.1	5.8	7.8	-1.0
Singapore	42.5	36.7	34.5	32.8	40.6	43.6	50.0	51.7	1.9	-6.9	-15.6	-19.0
South Africa	15.0	11.8	18.2	15.7	23.8	17.6	19.1	18.2	-8.7	-5.8	-0.9	-2.5
Taiwan Province of China	19.1	22.9	24.7	24.9	49.2	36.7	28.8	29.3	-30.2	-13.8	-4.2	-4.4
Thailand	28.2	41.4	41.4	21.0	25.5	33.8	34.7	33.4	2.7	7.5	6.7	-12.4
Turkey	16.5	24.3	25.5	23.3	13.4	20.1	21.0	19.6	3.1	4.3	4.5	3.7
Venezuela	18.5	10.2	18.1	15.6	27.7	29.5	23.4	22.2	-9.2	-19.3	-5.3	-6.7

Source: UN/DESA, based on World Bank, *2001 World Development Indicators* (CD-ROM), and United Nations Secretariat estimates.

[a] Special Administrative Region of China.

Table A.7.

DEVELOPED ECONOMIES, CENTRAL AND EASTERN EUROPE AND THE BALTIC STATES: UNEMPLOYMENT RATES, 1992-2001

Percentage	1992	1993	1994	1995	1996	1997	1998	1999	2000[a]	2001[b]
Developed economies[c]	7.3	8.0	7.9	7.5	7.6	7.3	6.9	6.5	6.0	6¼
United States	7.5	6.9	6.1	5.6	5.4	4.9	4.5	4.2	4.0	4¾
Canada	11.3	11.2	10.4	9.5	9.7	9.1	8.3	7.6	6.8	7
Japan	2.2	2.5	2.9	3.2	3.4	3.4	4.1	4.7	4.7	5
Australia	10.8	10.9	9.7	8.5	8.5	8.5	8.0	7.2	6.6	7½
New Zealand	10.3	9.5	8.2	6.3	6.1	6.6	7.5	6.8	6.0	5¾
EU-15	8.7	10.7	11.1	10.7	10.8	10.6	9.9	9.2	8.3	7½
EU-12	8.5	10.8	11.6	11.3	11.5	11.5	10.9	10.0	9.0	8¼
Austria	3.6	4.0	3.8	3.9	4.3	4.4	4.5	4.0	3.7	3½
Belgium	7.2	8.8	10.0	9.9	9.7	9.4	9.5	8.8	7.0	7¾
Finland	11.7	16.3	16.6	15.4	14.6	12.7	11.4	10.2	10.0	9¼
France	10.4	11.7	12.3	11.7	12.4	12.3	11.8	11.2	9.5	8½
Germany[d]	4.5	7.9	8.4	8.2	8.9	9.9	9.3	8.6	8.1	7½
Greece	7.9	8.6	8.9	9.2	9.6	9.8	10.9	11.7	11.1	10
Ireland	15.4	15.6	14.3	12.3	11.7	9.9	7.5	5.6	4.2	4
Italy	8.8	10.2	11.1	11.6	11.7	11.7	11.8	11.3	10.5	9¾
Luxembourg	2.1	2.6	3.2	2.9	3.0	2.7	2.7	2.3	2.2	2
Netherlands	5.6	6.5	7.1	6.9	6.3	5.2	4.0	3.3	2.8	2¾
Portugal	4.3	5.7	6.9	7.3	7.3	6.8	5.2	4.5	4.2	4
Spain	18.4	22.7	24.2	22.9	22.2	20.8	18.8	15.9	14.1	12½
Other EU	9.4	10.3	9.5	8.6	8.3	7.2	6.4	6.2	5.5	5
Denmark	9.2	10.2	8.2	7.2	6.8	5.6	5.2	5.2	4.7	4½
Sweden	5.6	9.1	9.4	8.8	9.6	9.9	8.3	7.2	5.9	5
United Kingdom	10.0	10.5	9.6	8.7	8.2	7.0	6.3	6.1	5.5	5
Other Europe	4.1	4.7	4.4	4.1	4.3	4.2	3.4	3.1	3.0	2½
Iceland	4.3	5.3	5.4	4.9	3.8	3.9	2.7	2.1	2.3	3
Malta[e]	4.0	4.5	4.0	3.6	4.4	5.0	5.1	5.3	4.5	4½
Norway	6.0	6.1	5.5	5.0	4.9	4.1	3.3	3.2	3.5	3½
Switzerland	3.1	4.0	3.8	3.5	3.9	4.2	3.5	3.0	2.7	2¼
Memo item:										
Major industrialized countries	6.8	7.2	7.0	6.8	6.8	6.6	6.4	6.2	5.7	6

Table A.7 (continued)

	1992	1993	1994	1995	1996	1997	1998	1999	2000[a]	2001[b]
Central and Eastern Europe[f]										
Albania	..	22.0	18.0	12.9	12.3	14.9	17.6	18.2	16.9	16
Bulgaria	..	16.4	12.8	11.1	12.5	13.7	12.2	16.0	17.9	16¾
Croatia	..	16.6	17.3	17.6	15.9	17.6	18.6	20.8	22.6	20
Czech Republic	..	3.5	3.2	2.9	3.5	5.2	7.5	9.4	8.8	8¾
Hungary	..	12.1	10.9	10.4	10.5	10.4	9.1	9.6	8.9	8
Poland	..	16.4	16.0	14.9	13.2	10.3	10.4	13.1	15.0	13
Romania	..	10.4	10.9	9.5	6.6	8.8	10.3	11.5	10.5	10¾
Slovakia	..	14.4	14.8	13.1	12.8	12.5	15.6	19.2	17.9	17¾
Slovenia	..	15.5	14.2	14.5	14.4	14.8	14.6	13.0	12.0	11½
The former Yugoslav Republic of Macedonia	..	30.3	33.2	37.2	39.8	41.7	41.4	43.8	44.9	35
Yugoslavia	..	24.0	23.9	24.7	26.1	25.6	27.2	27.4	26.6	26¾
Baltic States[f]										
Estonia	..	5.0	5.1	5.0	5.6	4.6	5.1	10.3	10.1	9¾
Latvia	..	5.8	6.5	6.6	7.2	7.0	9.2	9.1	7.8	7½
Lithuania	..	3.4	4.5	7.3	6.2	6.7	6.9	10.0	11.5	10½

Source: UN/DESA, based on data of OECD ECE.

[a]   Partly estimated.
[b]   Forecast, based partly on Project LINK.
[c]   Unemployment data are standardized by OECD for comparability among countries over time, in conformity with the definitions of the International Labour Office (see OECD, *Standardized Unemployment Rates: Sources and Methods* (Paris, 1985)); national definitions and estimates are used for other countries.
[d]   Prior to January 1993, data do not include new *Länder* (States).
[e]   Not standardized.
[f]   Registered unemployment data are used for countries with economies in transition.

Table A.8.
DEVELOPED ECONOMIES: CONSUMER PRICE INFLATION, 1992-2001[a]

Annual percentage change

	1992	1993	1994	1995	1996	1997	1998	1999	2000	2001[b]
Developed economies	3.1	2.7	2.2	2.1	2.0	2.0	1.3	1.2	2.0	2
United States	3.0	3.0	2.6	2.8	2.9	2.3	1.6	2.2	3.4	3
Canada	1.5	1.8	0.2	2.2	1.6	1.6	1.0	1.7	2.7	2
Japan	1.6	1.3	0.7	-0.1	0.1	1.8	0.6	-0.3	-0.7	0
Australia	1.0	1.8	1.9	4.6	2.6	0.3	0.9	1.5	4.5	3½
New Zealand	1.0	1.4	1.7	3.8	2.6	0.9	1.3	1.4	2.7	2¾
EU-15	4.3	3.5	2.9	2.8	2.3	2.0	1.5	1.2	2.3	2
EU-12	4.5	3.9	3.0	2.7	2.3	1.8	1.3	1.1	2.3	2
Austria	4.0	3.6	3.0	2.3	1.8	1.3	0.9	0.6	2.4	2
Belgium	2.4	2.8	2.4	1.5	2.1	1.6	1.0	1.1	2.5	2
Finland	2.6	2.1	1.1	1.0	0.6	1.2	1.4	1.2	3.4	2¾
France	2.4	2.1	1.7	1.8	2.0	1.2	0.7	0.5	1.7	1¼
Germany	5.1	4.4	2.8	1.7	1.4	1.9	0.9	0.6	1.9	2
Greece	15.9	14.4	10.9	8.9	8.2	5.5	4.8	2.6	3.1	2¾
Ireland	3.1	1.4	2.4	2.5	1.7	1.4	2.4	1.6	5.6	3½
Italy	5.1	4.5	4.0	5.2	4.0	2.0	2.0	1.7	2.6	2½
Luxembourg	3.2	3.6	2.2	1.9	1.4	1.4	1.0	1.0	3.1	2½
Netherlands	3.2	2.6	2.8	1.9	2.0	2.2	2.0	2.2	2.5	4
Portugal	8.9	6.8	4.9	4.1	3.1	2.2	2.8	2.3	2.9	2½
Spain	5.9	4.6	4.7	4.7	3.6	2.0	1.8	2.3	3.4	2½
Other EU	3.3	2.0	2.4	3.1	2.1	2.6	2.7	1.5	2.6	2
Denmark	2.1	1.3	2.0	2.1	2.1	2.2	1.9	2.5	2.9	2
Sweden	2.3	4.6	2.2	2.5	0.5	0.5	-0.1	0.5	1.0	2
United Kingdom	3.7	1.6	2.5	3.4	2.4	3.1	3.4	1.6	2.9	2
Other Europe										
Iceland	4.0	4.1	1.6	1.7	2.3	1.7	1.7	3.2	5.2	4¼
Malta	1.6	4.1	4.1	4.0	2.5	3.1	2.4	2.1	2.4	3
Norway	2.3	2.3	1.4	2.5	1.3	2.6	2.3	2.3	3.1	2¼
Switzerland	4.0	3.3	0.9	1.8	0.8	0.5	0.1	0.7	1.6	2
Memo item:										
Major developed economies	3.0	2.6	2.0	2.0	1.9	2.1	1.3	1.1	1.9	1¾

Source: UN/DESA, based on data of IMF, *International Financial Statistics.*

[a] Data for country groups are weighted averages, where weights for each year are 1995 GDP in United States dollars.
[b] Forecast, partly based on Project LINK.

Table A.9.

ECONOMIES IN TRANSITION: CONSUMER PRICE INFLATION, 1993-2001

Annual percentage change									
	1993	1994	1995	1996	1997	1998	1999	2000[a]	2001[b]
Economies in transition[c]	838.3	407.6	142.2	41.2	38.9	22.0	50.6	19.4	16
Central and Eastern Europe and Baltic States[c]	149.9	44.9	25.8	25.3	67.9	16.7	11.6	12.2	9
Central and Eastern Europe[c]	146.2	44.5	25.5	25.4	70.4	17.2	12.0	12.7	9¼
Albania	85.0	21.5	8.0	12.7	33.1	20.3	-0.1	0.0	3
Bulgaria	72.9	96.2	62.1	123.1	1 082.6	22.2	0.4	10.4	8
Croatia[d]	1 516.6	97.5	2.0	3.6	3.7	5.9	4.3	6.2	5¾
Czech Republic	20.8	10.0	9.1	8.9	8.4	10.6	2.1	3.9	4¼
Hungary	22.6	19.1	28.5	23.6	18.4	14.2	10.1	9.8	8
Poland	36.9	33.2	28.1	19.8	15.1	11.7	7.4	10.1	7¼
Romania	256.2	137.1	32.2	38.8	154.9	59.3	45.9	45.6	30
Slovakia	23.1	13.4	10.0	6.1	6.1	6.7	10.5	12.0	8½
Slovenia[d]	31.7	21.0	13.5	9.9	8.4	8.1	6.3	8.9	6½
The former Yugoslav Republic of Macedonia[d]	353.1	121.0	16.9	4.1	3.8	1.1	-1.4	10.6	6
Yugoslavia	..[e]	..[e]	71.8	90.5	23.2	30.4	44.1	75.7	80
Baltic States	232.2	54.2	32.1	22.0	9.3	6.3	2.0	2.4	2½
Estonia	89.6	47.9	28.9	23.1	11.1	10.6	3.5	4.0	5
Latvia	109.1	35.7	25.0	17.7	8.5	4.7	2.4	2.6	2¾
Lithuania	410.1	72.0	39.5	24.7	8.8	5.1	0.8	1.4	½
Commonwealth of Independent States	1 321.0	662.0	227.4	52.8	17.7	25.8	79.1	24.3	21
Armenia	3 731.8	4 964.0	175.5	18.7	13.8	8.7	0.7	-0.8	3½
Azerbaijan	1 129.7	1 663.9	411.5	19.8	3.6	-0.8	-8.6	1.8	3
Belarus	1 190.9	2 219.6	709.3	52.7	63.9	73.2	293.7	168.6	100
Georgia	4 084.9	22 286.1	261.4	39.4	7.1	3.5	19.3	4.0	6
Kazakhstan	1 662.7	1 880.1	176.3	39.2	17.5	7.3	8.4	13.2	7
Kyrgyzstan	1 208.7	278.1	42.9	31.3	23.4	10.3	35.7	18.0	11
Republic of Moldova	1 751.0	486.4	29.9	23.5	11.8	7.7	39.3	31.0	20
Russian Federation	875.0	309.0	197.4	47.8	14.7	27.8	85.7	20.2	20
Tajikistan	2 884.8	350.3	682.1	422.4	85.4	43.1	27.5	24.0	30
Turkmenistan	3 128.4	2 562.1	1 105.3	714.0	83.7	16.8	23.5	7.0	11
Ukraine	4 734.9	891.2	376.7	80.2	15.9	10.6	22.7	28.2	15
Uzbekistan	1 231.8	1 550.0	76.5	56.3	73.2	17.7	29.0	28.2	30

Source: UN/DESA, based on data from ECE.

[a]　Partly estimated.
[b]　Forecast, partly based on Project LINK.
[c]　Yugoslavia is excluded in 1993 and 1994.
[d]　Retail prices.
[e]　Annual rates of hyperinflation of over 1 trillion percentage points.

Table A.10.
DEVELOPING ECONOMIES: CONSUMER PRICE INFLATION, 1992-2001[a]

Annual percentage change

	1992	1993	1994	1995	1996	1997	1998	1999	2000[b]	2001[c]
Developing countries by region:	140.8	271.1	139.7	23.2	14.1	9.7	10.7	6.5	5.8	6¾
Africa[d]	19.8	17.4	19.6	19.3	12.9	8.0	6.3	5.5	5.8	6¼
Eastern and Southern Asia	7.0	8.0	11.6	9.6	6.7	4.7	9.1	2.3	1.9	3½
Region excluding China	7.2	5.7	7.1	6.9	6.2	5.3	12.7	3.7	2.5	4¼
of which:										
East Asia	6.1	5.3	6.2	5.9	5.3	4.6	13.0	3.4	1.9	3½
South Asia	10.9	6.8	10.1	10.3	9.0	7.7	11.7	4.6	4.1	6
Western Asia	27.5	25.9	39.6	37.4	31.2	29.4	28.3	22.6	18.5	22¾
Latin America and the Caribbean	423.9	839.3	408.5	40.8	20.1	11.3	8.2	7.5	7.4	6¼
Memo items:										
Sub-Saharan Africa (excluding Democratic Republic of the Congo, Nigeria and South Africa)	25.8	24.0	32.7	22.3	20.8	11.6	8.8	9.8	10.5	10
Least developed countries	26.2	23.0	25.3	21.4	20.0	12.6	15.3	10.7	6.2	8½
Major developing economies										
Argentina	24.9	10.6	4.2	3.4	0.2	0.5	0.9	-1.2	-0.9	-¾
Brazil	951.6	1 928.0	930.0	66.0	15.8	6.9	3.2	4.9	7.0	5¾
China	6.3	14.6	24.2	16.9	8.3	2.8	-0.8	-1.4	0.4	1¼
Hong Kong SAR[e]	9.3	7.4	8.7	9.1	6.3	5.8	2.8	-4.0	-1.3	-¾
India	11.8	6.4	10.2	10.2	9.0	7.2	13.2	4.7	4.0	5¾
Indonesia	7.5	9.7	8.5	9.4	8.0	6.7	57.6	20.5	3.8	9¼
Israel	11.9	10.9	12.3	10.0	11.3	9.0	5.4	5.2	1.1	1¾
Korea, Republic of	6.2	4.8	6.2	4.5	4.9	4.4	7.5	0.8	2.3	4
Malaysia	4.8	3.5	3.7	5.3	3.5	2.7	5.3	2.8	1.5	2
Mexico	15.5	9.8	7.0	35.0	34.4	20.6	15.9	16.6	9.5	8
Saudi Arabia	-0.1	1.1	0.6	4.9	1.2	0.1	-0.4	-1.6	-0.8	4½
South Africa	13.9	9.7	9.0	8.6	7.4	8.6	6.9	5.2	5.2	5½
Taiwan Province of China	4.5	3.0	4.1	3.7	3.1	1.8	2.6	0.2	1.3	1½
Thailand	4.1	3.4	5.0	5.8	5.8	5.6	8.1	0.3	1.6	2¼
Turkey	70.1	66.1	106.3	88.1	80.3	85.7	84.6	64.9	54.9	63½

Source: UN/DESA, based on data of IMF, *International Financial Statistics.*

a   Weights used are GDP in 1995 dollars.
b   Preliminary estimate based on data for part of the year.
c   Forecast, based in part on Project LINK.
d   Excluding the Democratic Republic of the Congo.
e   Special Administrative Region of China.

Table A.11.
MAJOR DEVELOPED ECONOMIES: FINANCIAL INDICATORS, 1992-2000

	1992	1993	1994	1995	1996	1997	1998	1999	2000
Short-term interest rates[a] *(percentage)*									
Canada	6.8	3.8	5.5	5.7	3.0	4.3	5.1	4.8	5.8
France[b]	10.4	8.7	5.7	6.4	3.7	3.2	3.4	2.7	4.2
Germany	9.4	7.5	5.3	4.5	3.3	3.2	3.4	2.7	4.1
Italy	14.0	10.2	8.5	10.5	8.8	6.9	5.0	3.0	4.4
Japan	4.6	3.1	2.2	1.2	0.5	0.5	0.4	0.1	0.1
United Kingdom	9.4	5.5	4.8	6.0	5.9	6.6	7.1	5.1	5.7
United States	3.5	3.0	4.2	5.8	5.3	5.5	5.4	5.0	6.2
Long-term interest rates[c] *(percentage)*									
Canada	8.8	7.8	8.6	8.3	7.5	6.4	5.5	5.7	5.9
France	8.6	6.9	7.4	7.6	6.4	5.6	4.7	4.7	5.5
Germany	8.0	6.3	6.7	6.5	5.6	5.1	4.4	4.3	5.2
Italy	13.3	11.3	10.6	12.2	9.4	6.9	4.9	4.7	5.6
Japan	4.9	3.7	3.7	2.5	2.2	1.7	1.1	1.8	1.7
United Kingdom	9.1	7.9	8.0	8.3	8.1	7.1	5.4	4.7	4.7
United States	7.0	5.9	7.1	6.6	6.4	6.4	5.3	5.6	6.0
General government financial balances[d,e] *(percentage)*									
Canada	-8.0	-7.6	-5.6	-4.3	-1.8	0.8	0.9	2.7	3.3
France	-4.2	-6.0	-5.6	-5.6	-4.1	-3.0	-2.7	-1.6	-1.3
Germany	-2.5	-3.2	-2.5	-3.2	-3.4	-2.7	-2.1	-1.4	1.5
Italy	-9.5	-9.4	-9.1	-7.6	-6.5	-2.7	-2.8	-1.9	-0.3
Japan[f]	1.5	-1.6	-2.3	-3.6	-4.2	-3.4	-6.0	-6.7	-5.7
United Kingdom	-6.5	-8.0	-6.8	-5.8	-4.4	-2.0	0.4	1.3	4.3
United States	-5.9	-5.0	-3.6	-3.1	-2.2	-0.9	0.4	1.0	1.9

Sources: United Nations, based on IMF, *International Financial Statistics*; OECD, *Economic Outlook*; J.P. Morgan; and EUROPA (EU online), *European Economy*.

a   Money market rates.
b   From January 1999 onward, representing the three-month Euro Interbank Offered Rate (EURIBOR), which is an interbank deposit bid rate.
c   Yield on long-term government bonds.
d   Surplus (+) or deficit (-) as a percentage of nominal GNP or GDP.
e   Part of 2000 data are estimates.
f   The 1998 outlays would have risen by 5.4 percentage points of GDP if account had been taken of the assumption by the central Government of the debt of the Japan Railway Settlement Corporation and the National Forest Special Account.

Table A.12.
SELECTED COUNTRIES: REAL EFFECTIVE EXCHANGE RATES, BROAD MEASUREMENT, 1992-2000[a]

1990 = 100	1992	1993	1994	1995	1996	1997	1998	1999	2000
Developed economies									
Australia	91.0	85.6	89.8	87.6	96.3	97.9	90.1	92.6	87.1
Austria	103.8	108.1	109.8	112.7	111.1	108.0	108.9	107.4	104.3
Belgium	104.4	106.7	110.3	113.6	112.2	108.0	109.3	109.0	103.4
Canada	91.3	88.9	88.6	92.2	91.5	92.7	90.6	89.1	89.4
Denmark	102.3	104.5	104.9	108.1	108.4	106.3	109.3	110.0	105.1
Finland	83.3	74.2	79.5	85.5	84.3	82.0	81.0	78.8	73.0
France	102.0	103.7	103.2	104.1	104.1	99.5	101.5	98.5	91.6
Germany	100.9	101.4	100.3	105.5	102.4	96.6	97.7	95.3	91.4
Greece	106.3	108.2	106.7	108.4	113.6	115.3	112.0	114.9	113.2
Ireland	101.6	96.3	97.8	98.0	100.3	101.0	98.7	96.0	90.1
Italy	95.9	80.9	79.3	75.8	83.5	84.0	84.5	82.7	81.2
Japan	106.3	121.3	126.1	127.2	108.7	103.3	100.9	110.5	116.9
Netherlands	101.0	104.0	104.1	105.7	103.6	99.3	101.3	101.6	98.8
New Zealand	89.8	93.5	100.1	107.6	117.9	120.9	105.5	101.0	92.2
Norway	101.9	99.9	98.9	101.3	100.8	102.8	98.4	97.8	94.5
Portugal	111.7	108.1	104.6	104.5	105.9	105.0	105.0	105.0	101.4
Spain	95.7	83.7	79.9	83.3	83.5	80.0	80.3	78.7	76.9
Sweden	97.3	81.7	83.8	90.9	95.7	91.7	90.8	87.6	87.8
Switzerland	101.2	105.2	111.6	118.5	116.6	109.3	112.1	111.3	108.5
United Kingdom	99.9	91.7	92.6	89.7	92.4	106.4	110.6	109.0	110.5
United States	100.8	103.1	100.4	95.7	100.3	106.5	114.5	114.6	117.9
Developing economies									
Argentina	113.5	115.1	111.6	109.2	113.2	120.9	123.4	125.3	127.9
Brazil	73.1	82.4	94.4	100.7	99.0	105.3	104.2	77.4	93.6
Chile	113.8	114.0	114.0	120.5	126.8	135.4	129.2	125.4	135.2
Colombia	108.7	110.3	118.5	117.3	121.8	132.9	126.4	113.5	109.3
Ecuador	111.7	129.0	137.6	135.1	137.2	148.6	152.9	115.1	102.2
Hong Kong SAR[b]	105.8	111.2	114.0	112.5	120.8	131.1	137.6	125.4	120.2
India	78.9	75.4	77.8	75.8	74.2	81.1	78.1	77.5	82.9
Indonesia	99.3	101.3	100.0	98.5	103.3	96.6	47.8	72.6	71.0
Korea, Republic of	89.5	87.3	85.8	87.3	89.7	84.2	65.8	72.8	78.8
Kuwait	146.1	147.4	148.6	140.3	147.9	156.2	162.8	165.7	174.5
Malaysia	106.2	109.3	106.1	105.9	111.1	108.6	83.3	84.7	86.9
Mexico	107.8	116.7	112.2	79.0	89.9	102.9	102.6	112.8	126.4
Morocco	100.7	104.2	104.9	108.2	112.1	111.6	116.3	118.5	121.5
Nigeria	74.1	93.9	141.5	58.5	79.5	91.5	100.1	99.7	100.8
Pakistan	98.0	98.7	104.8	105.1	105.8	110.6	111.1	106.4	104.5
Peru	98.6	91.2	97.9	98.4	102.6	106.6	106.5	97.2	99.0
Philippines	105.7	97.4	104.3	103.5	114.8	107.9	85.8	90.4	85.2
Saudi Arabia	98.3	102.8	99.8	96.3	103.5	114.9	126.3	129.9	140.7
Singapore	105.0	105.9	108.9	110.1	115.0	117.0	113.6	109.2	109.1
South Africa	103.4	102.7	98.5	97.1	90.8	97.4	86.2	82.9	84.3
Taiwan Province of China	100.8	97.7	96.4	97.4	95.0	96.2	87.6	82.6	87.3
Thailand	98.5	100.0	99.2	96.3	99.9	93.9	82.1	85.8	86.4
Turkey	89.3	93.0	73.1	76.2	74.8	78.9	78.7	78.1	88.1
Venezuela	100.7	104.2	109.5	139.5	119.4	139.8	158.0	169.6	180.2

Source: Morgan Guaranty Trust Company, *World Financial Markets*.

[a] Indices based on a "broad" measure currency basket of 22 OECD currencies and 23 developing-economy currencies (mostly Asian and Latin American). The real effective exchange rate, which adjusts the nominal index for relative price changes, gauges the effect on international price competitiveness of the country's manufactures due to currency changes and inflation differentials. A rise in the index implies a fall in competitiveness and vice versa. The relative price changes are based on indices most closely measuring the prices of domestically produced finished manufactured goods, excluding food and energy, at the first stage of manufacturing. The weights for currency indices are derived from 1990 bilateral trade patterns of the corresponding countries.

[b] Special Administrative Region of China

II. INTERNATIONAL TRADE

Table A.13.
WORLD TRADE: CHANGES IN VALUE AND VOLUME OF EXPORTS AND IMPORTS, BY MAJOR COUNTRY GROUP, 1992-2001

Annual percentage change										
	1992	1993	1994	1995	1996	1997	1998	1999	2000[a]	2001[b]
Dollar value of exports										
World	7.1	0.1	13.5	19.4	4.3	3.5	-2.3	3.9	12.3	6
Developed economies	5.9	-2.6	12.5	18.9	2.6	2.3	0.3	2.2	7.1	6¾
of which:										
North America	6.1	4.7	11.2	14.6	6.4	9.3	-0.7	5.0	13.4	3½
Western Europe	5.4	-6.9	13.7	22.5	3.0	-1.5	1.8	-0.3	3.1	10¾
Japan	8.0	6.6	9.6	11.6	-7.3	2.5	-7.9	8.6	12.0	-5
Economies in transition	8.9	5.6	17.5	29.1	8.0	2.2	-2.1	-1.0	27.0	3
Central and Eastern Europe and Baltic States[c]	7.5	8.8	16.3	30.1	5.7	6.5	13.5	-1.2	14.0	9
CIS	10.5	1.9	19.0	27.9	10.9	-1.8	-17.0	-1.0	39.0	-4
Developing countries	10.2	6.3	15.5	19.5	7.6	6.4	-6.5	7.7	22.7	4½
Latin America and the Caribbean	6.7	9.4	16.4	20.9	10.2	10.4	-2.4	5.6	19.4	6¾
Africa	1.1	-9.6	2.7	12.5	19.7	2.5	-15.0	10.3	25.3	¾
Western Asia	7.4	-1.0	6.6	12.3	13.6	-5.7	-24.1	25.1	44.2	-4¼
Eastern and Southern Asia	12.8	10.7	16.8	21.3	5.0	4.0	-6.9	6.5	18.4	5
China	18.1	7.1	33.1	22.9	1.6	20.8	0.5	6.1	27.7	7
Memo items:										
Fuel exporters	5.2	-3.4	5.9	15.9	19.5	0.5	-9.9	14.4	33.2	3
Non-fuel exporters	12.0	9.0	18.5	21.3	4.4	6.7	-4.7	4.7	7.0	7
Dollar value of imports										
World	6.9	-1.2	13.3	19.4	4.8	2.8	-2.3	5.4	10.8	6
Developed economies	4.4	-5.8	13.4	18.0	3.6	2.6	1.9	5.2	11.3	5½
of which:										
North America	7.9	8.7	13.7	11.3	6.2	10.3	4.6	10.9	18.8	3
Western Europe	3.9	-13.1	13.0	20.7	2.3	0.0	3.8	1.4	7.0	7½
Japan	-1.6	3.6	13.9	22.0	4.0	-3.0	-17.2	11.2	14.6	1¾
Economies in transition	5.2	0.8	13.0	33.4	13.9	9.0	0.5	-8.0	13.0	10
Central and Eastern Europe and Baltic States[c]	14.0	14.1	14.1	37.0	16.5	6.7	13.0	-2.5	12.0	9
CIS	-6.7	-21.3	10.2	24.4	6.7	15.9	-19.0	-24.0	16.0	11
Developing countries	14.0	9.7	13.0	21.0	6.3	4.3	-10.2	4.4	19.0	7
Latin America and the Caribbean	22.2	11.6	18.6	11.6	9.7	16.2	5.2	-3.7	16.3	9¾
Africa	9.6	-4.9	5.8	21.2	2.0	6.0	-1.0	1.0	7.4	4½
Western Asia	11.1	6.3	-7.9	23.1	9.3	0.6	-6.4	-0.3	12.3	1¾
Eastern and Southern Asia	11.9	10.0	18.4	24.8	5.3	2.0	-20.0	7.6	20.0	6¾
China	26.3	27.9	12.2	11.6	7.6	2.5	-1.5	18.2	35.0	9
Memo items:										
Fuel exporters	16.1	-1.6	3.9	9.5	7.8	7.1	-5.7	7.3	23.1	8½
Non-fuel exporters	13.9	12.6	15.4	23.8	5.8	3.7	-12.0	2.8	17.4	6

Table A.13 (continued)	1992	1993	1994	1995	1996	1997	1998	1999	2000[a]	2001[b]
Dollar value of exports										
World	5.4	4.3	10.5	9.4	4.8	9.3	3.6	5.1	12.1	5½
Developed economies	3.9	2.5	9.5	7.3	4.2	9.2	4.0	4.4	10.8	5¼
of which:										
North America	6.8	5.3	9.0	9.1	6.2	10.9	3.7	6.4	10.6	4
Western Europe	3.5	2.8	11.4	7.6	3.8	7.7	5.4	3.9	11.0	6¾
Japan	1.5	-2.4	1.7	3.3	0.6	9.6	-3.7	2.7	11.0	1
Economies in transition	11.0	5.7	2.7	13.7	6.0	-0.9	6.9	4.0	13.0	7
Central and Eastern Europe and Baltic States[c]	8.5	8.9	0.2	16.7	4.5	0.8	15.0	7.0	20.0	10
CIS	14.2	1.9	5.8	10.0	7.9	-2.9	0.2	2.0	7.0	4
Developing countries	9.0	8.7	14.1	13.7	6.5	9.9	1.9	7.2	15.0	5½
Latin America and the Caribbean	6.3	10.3	9.2	9.9	9.3	12.8	7.8	6.6	11.6	7
Africa	0.8	-0.9	11.7	7.3	8.2	5.2	-0.9	2.1	2.5	3
Western Asia	8.0	7.3	8.1	6.0	9.0	-0.7	-1.5	0.6	9.7	-¾
Eastern and Southern Asia	10.5	10.6	14.5	16.6	5.8	9.3	0.1	10.0	17.0	6¼
China	15.7	6.8	31.0	18.9	2.4	26.3	4.1	7.4	26.0	7½
Memo items:										
Fuel exporters	6.9	2.6	5.7	9.0	15.1	4.9	1.2	7.5	17.6	5¼
Non-fuel exporters	10.0	9.1	15.0	16.5	5.9	11.3	2.9	7.1	13.4	5¾
Dollar value of imports										
World	5.9	4.9	10.5	7.8	6.1	9.0	3.0	5.3	12.5	5½
Developed economies	4.4	1.1	11.1	7.0	4.9	8.7	5.9	6.1	11.0	4½
of which:										
North America	7.9	9.6	12.0	7.2	5.6	13.3	10.3	10.4	15.6	3
Western Europe	3.4	-2.8	10.0	5.9	4.4	7.6	6.1	3.4	9.2	6
Japan	-0.4	2.9	13.6	12.5	3.5	2.7	-10.0	9.5	6.3	1½
Economies in transition	0.8	0.8	9.6	9.9	13.8	9.0	2.0	-6.0	15.0	8
Central and Eastern Europe and Baltic States[c]	12.0	14.3	13.0	11.4	17.9	7.6	10.0	5.0	15.0	9
CIS	-13.4	-21.5	1.3	6.0	2.4	13.6	-15.0	-28.0	14.0	7
Developing countries	11.3	15.3	9.5	9.7	8.5	10.2	-4.7	4.0	16.3	7¾
Latin America and the Caribbean	22.5	10.8	14.4	4.2	8.4	23.1	7.2	-3.6	9.3	10¾
Africa	-0.3	-2.1	2.0	10.8	3.8	6.3	2.0	1.5	5.7	4¼
Western Asia	9.0	12.7	-11.1	11.3	11.8	6.4	-2.6	2.3	14.5	¾
Eastern and Southern Asia	9.7	17.4	14.8	12.5	8.2	8.4	-12.7	6.9	18.6	8
China	23.1	36.4	9.1	0.1	11.4	9.4	6.0	18.6	33.4	9¾
Memo items:										
Fuel exporters	13.6	4.1	-0.2	-1.0	11.2	13.8	-0.2	-0.4	12.0	-1½
Non-fuel exporters	11.6	20.2	11.9	11.6	8.7	10.1	-6.7	10.3	9.0	4¼

Source: United Nations, based on data of United Nations Statistics Division, ECE, ECLAC and IMF.

a   Preliminary estimate.
b   Forecast, based in part on Project LINK.
c   As of 1993, transactions between the Czech Republic and Slovakia are recorded as foreign trade.

Table A.14.
DIRECTION OF TRADE: EXPORTS (F.O.B.), 1985-2000

		World[b]	Devd.	EU	US	Japan	EIT	Devg.	LAC	Africa	SSA	WA	ESA
		Bn. $						Percentage					
World[b]	1985	1 874.5	68.1	37.0	17.5	5.9	..	23.8	4.3	3.7	1.3	5.1	10.7
	1990	3 381.7	72.1	43.7	14.5	6.1	..	22.8	3.8	2.7	1.1	3.5	12.8
	1995	5 070.8	65.2	37.6	14.8	5.8	4.3	29.0	4.9	2.3	0.8	3.2	18.5
	2000	6 341.2	66.5	35.1	18.8	5.4	4.1	28.3	5.6	2.1	0.7	3.2	17.4
Developed	1985	1 266.3	72.7	42.4	16.8	3.5	..	23.0	4.5	4.1	1.2	5.1	9.3
economies	1990	2 444.4	76.4	50.3	12.4	4.2	..	19.9	3.9	2.8	1.0	3.3	9.9
(Devd.)	1995	3 427.8	70.6	45.4	12.4	3.9	3.5	24.9	5.1	2.4	0.7	3.1	14.3
	2000	3 990.8	71.0	43.1	15.5	3.3	3.9	24.3	6.3	2.1	0.5	3.3	12.6
of which:													
European Union	1985	708.2	77.8	59.2	10.0	1.2	..	16.8	2.1	5.3	1.6	5.2	4.2
(EU)	1990	1 488.4	81.8	65.9	7.0	2.1	..	13.2	1.8	3.5	1.2	3.4	4.4
	1995	2 018.3	77.4	62.4	6.7	2.1	5.3	15.7	2.5	3.0	0.9	3.5	6.8
	2000	2 240.7	77.7	60.7	9.4	1.8	6.3	14.6	2.5	2.7	0.7	3.8	5.6
United States	1985	213.1	61.4	24.3	-	10.6	..	36.6	14.6	3.5	0.9	5.2	13.4
(US)	1990	393.1	63.9	26.3	-	12.4	..	34.6	13.7	2.0	0.5	3.4	15.5
	1995	583.5	57.3	21.2	-	11.0	1.1	41.5	16.5	1.7	0.3	3.5	19.8
	2000	772.0	55.6	21.3	-	8.4	0.9	43.4	21.7	1.4	0.3	3.1	17.3
Japan	1985	177.2	58.0	13.1	37.6	-	..	39.4	4.2	2.2	0.6	6.5	26.4
	1990	287.7	58.6	20.4	31.7	-	..	40.1	3.4	1.9	0.9	3.5	31.3
	1995	443.0	47.7	15.9	27.5	-	0.5	51.7	4.2	1.7	0.7	2.2	43.7
	2000	479.7	50.6	16.3	29.7	-	0.6	48.8	4.0	1.1	0.4	2.4	41.4
Economies in	1995	205.6	50.6	41.7	3.9	1.8	35.6	13.0	1.6	1.3	0.2	3.9	6.2
transition (EIT)	2000	274.7	58.6	48.3	5.9	1.4	28.2	12.7	1.0	1.5	0.4	4.7	5.5

Destination[a]

Table A.14 (continued)

		World[b]	Devd.	EU	US	Japan	EIT	Devg.	LAC	Africa	SSA	WA	ESA
		Bn. $						Percentage					
Developing	1985	490.3	64.0	24.5	22.9	13.1	..	28.7	4.7	2.7	1.5	5.4	16.0
countries	1990	831.3	61.3	23.4	22.2	12.2	..	32.5	4.0	2.5	1.4	4.0	21.9
(Devg.)	1995	1 435.0	54.3	18.2	22.0	11.0	1.5	41.1	5.1	2.4	1.2	3.3	30.3
	2000	2 073.0	58.8	17.9	26.8	10.1	1.2	38.0	4.9	2.2	1.0	2.9	28.2
of which:													
Latin America	1985	99.3	72.1	23.4	40.5	5.1	..	22.4	12.6	2.8	0.8	2.7	4.3
and the	1990	128.0	71.9	24.5	38.9	5.6	..	24.7	16.5	1.5	0.4	2.1	4.6
Caribbean	1995	227.8	68.2	16.7	44.6	4.0	0.9	28.9	20.5	1.3	0.4	1.3	5.8
(LAC)	2000	350.3	73.2	12.5	53.3	3.0	0.8	23.1	17.4	0.9	0.2	1.0	3.8
Africa	1985	78.5	72.8	52.6	14.7	3.0	..	12.9	3.3	4.3	3.4	2.5	2.8
	1990	98.7	71.0	50.6	14.8	3.0	..	14.2	1.1	7.0	5.2	2.3	3.7
	1995	102.0	66.2	47.2	13.3	3.1	1.4	23.6	1.9	10.6	8.0	3.0	8.0
	2000	154.3	67.5	45.1	16.3	2.9	1.5	24.3	3.0	8.7	6.6	2.8	9.8
of which:													
Sub-Saharan	1985	19.4	74.8	53.3	17.2	2.7	..	18.8	2.7	9.2	6.9	1.6	5.2
Africa	1990	28.1	75.0	49.9	16.9	3.4	..	21.2	1.7	11.8	9.2	1.3	6.4
(SSA)	1995	29.9	69.7	46.6	17.7	3.7	1.7	26.6	1.2	14.0	9.9	2.2	9.2
	2000	44.2	62.8	38.5	18.0	2.5	2.8	32.9	1.8	13.3	9.9	1.8	15.9
Western Asia	1985	105.3	57.7	29.1	6.3	20.5	..	32.5	4.2	2.6	1.4	11.7	14.0
(WA)	1990	149.4	59.7	25.4	13.7	17.7	..	31.0	3.0	2.9	0.9	10.6	14.6
	1995	169.6	50.3	22.8	10.3	15.1	3.4	34.4	1.6	3.0	0.8	9.9	19.8
	2000	248.1	57.8	22.7	15.7	17.1	1.8	34.6	1.1	3.1	0.9	7.1	23.3
Eastern and	1985	207.3	59.9	12.0	26.1	17.0	..	35.9	1.7	2.2	1.2	4.5	27.6
Southern Asia	1990	455.2	56.8	16.5	21.9	14.3	..	39.1	1.5	1.7	1.0	2.8	33.1
(including China)	1995	935.6	50.4	14.5	19.6	12.8	1.3	47.1	2.3	1.6	0.7	2.7	40.6
(ESA)	2000	1 320.3	54.2	15.2	23.1	11.5	1.1	44.3	2.5	1.5	0.6	2.6	37.7

Source: UN/DESA, based on IMF, *Direction of Trade Statistics.*

a   Owing to incomplete specification of destinations in underlying data, shares of trade to destinations do not add up to 100 per cent.

b   Including economies in transition; before 1994, data for economies in transition are highly incomplete.

Table A.15.

COMPOSITION OF WORLD MERCHANDISE TRADE: EXPORTS, 1985-1999

Billions of dollars and percentage

Exporting country group	Total exports (billions of dollars)			Primary commodities											
				Total			of which:								
							Food			Agricultural raw materials			Fuels		
	1985	1990	1999	1985	1990	1999	1985	1990	1999	1985	1990	1999	1985	1990	1999
World (billions of dollars)	1 606.3	2 848.5	5 606.5	596.1	797.5	1 023.3	160.2	268.8	408.3	77.7	119.2	146.5	332.1	372.7	406.4
World (percentage share)	-	-	-	100.0	100.0	100.0	100.0	100.0	100.0	100.0	100.0	100.0	100.0	100.0	100.0
Developed economies	1 021.1	1 865.1	3 687.5	40.0	45.1	49.1	59.4	63.0	64.6	60.5	62.2	58.6	24.6	23.0	30.3
Economies in transition[a]	89.4	124.6	218.9	7.2	6.1	6.5	3.4	3.5	3.4	5.1	5.3	7.2	9.7	8.2	8.9
Developing countries	495.7	858.9	1 700.1	52.7	48.8	44.4	37.2	33.5	32.0	34.4	32.5	34.2	65.7	68.8	60.9
Africa	78.1	92.5	121.2	11.5	8.5	7.7	6.1	4.1	4.1	4.6	5.1	4.4	16.0	13.7	12.2
Latin America	107.6	154.3	312.7	12.7	11.0	11.7	16.1	14.5	13.6	8.0	7.3	10.0	11.9	9.3	9.4
Eastern and Southern Asia	210.8	459.1	1 073.2	13.7	13.4	12.5	12.9	13.1	12.4	20.3	19.0	18.3	12.7	12.3	10.6
Western Asia	99.2	153.0	193	14.8	16.0	12.5	2.2	1.9	1.9	1.4	1.1	1.5	25.1	33.6	28.7
Memo items:															
Sub-Saharan Africa	22.5	29.7	34.7	3.1	2.6	2.6	4.6	2.6	2.5	3.0	3.1	3.0	2.3	2.3	2.6
Least developed countries	24.3	58.4	27.7	2.5	2.9	1.5	2.4	2.0	1.1	2.4	3.0	1.8	2.4	3.9	1.9

Table A.15 (continued)

	Manufactures														
	Total (billions of dollars)			*of which:*											
				Textiles			Chemicals			Machinery and transport			Metals		
Exporting country group	1985	1990	1999	1985	1990	1999	1985	1990	1999	1985	1990	1999	1985	1990	1999
World (billions of dollars)	983.4	1 992.0	4 406.3	86.8	178.2	356.1	120.5	236.4	513.1	472.4	953.1	2 320.0	88.3	152.7	233.5
World (percentage share)	100.0	100.0	100.0	100.0	100.0	100.0	100.0	100.0	100.0	100.0	100.0	100.0	100.0	100.0	100.0
Developed economies	77.1	73.3	69.1	46.2	42.1	39.1	82.7	81.0	80.9	83.8	79.7	73.2	70.3	65.2	61.4
Economies in transition[a]	4.6	3.7	3.4	3.3	2.1	4.5	4.9	3.6	3.2	4.8	3.7	2.2	7.2	8.5	13.9
Developing countries	18.3	23.0	27.5	50.5	55.7	56.4	12.4	15.4	15.9	11.4	16.5	24.7	22.3	26.3	24.7
Africa	1.3	1.1	0.8	2.0	2.5	2.6	1.8	1.4	0.9	0.3	0.3	0.3	5.5	6.2	3.6
Latin America	3.4	3.3	4.2	3.2	3.4	6.4	3.7	2.9	2.8	2.6	2.6	4.1	8.5	9.4	7.3
Eastern and Southern Asia	12.5	17.3	21.1	42.3	47.3	43.4	5.0	8.2	10.2	8.0	13.2	19.6	6.9	8.7	11.7
Western Asia	1.2	1.3	1.4	3.0	2.5	3.9	1.9	2.9	2.1	0.5	0.4	0.7	1.4	2.0	2.0
Memo items:															
Sub-Saharan Africa	0.4	0.5	0.2	0.5	0.5	0.5	0.4	0.3	0.1	0.1	0.2	0.0	2.4	2.2	0.5
Least developed countries	0.7	1.6	0.3	1.6	1.6	2.0	0.6	1.6	0.1	0.6	1.6	0.0	2.3	2.6	0.3

Source: UN/DESA, based on COMTRADE.

a   Data for 1999 including trade flows between the States of the former USSR. Prior to 1992, these flows were considered internal.

Table A.16.

COMPOSITION OF WORLD MERCHANDISE TRADE: IMPORTS, 1985-1999

Billions of dollars and percentage

	Total imports (billions of dollars)			Primary commodities											
				Total			of which:								
							Food			Agricultural raw materials			Fuels		
Importing country group	1985	1990	1999	1985	1990	1999	1985	1990	1999	1985	1990	1999	1985	1990	1999
World (billions of dollars)	1 606.3	2 848.5	5 606.5	596.1	797.5	1 022.1	160.2	268.8	407.1	77.7	119.2	153.8	332.1	372.7	398.0
World (percentage share)	-	-	-	100.0	100.0	100.0	100.0	100.0	100.0	100.0	100.0	100.0	100.0	100.0	100.0
Developed economies	1 090	1 941.6	3 889.0	71.9	68.6	68.6	65.1	66.2	72.3	64.5	66.0	64.3	76.2	69.0	66.3
Economies in transition[a]	92.3	128.9	211.3	5.8	5.5	4.3	7.6	8.2	4.7	6.7	3.9	2.9	4.5	4.2	4.6
Developing countries	424.0	778.0	1 506.2	22.3	25.9	27.1	27.3	25.6	23.0	28.8	30.1	32.8	19.2	26.8	29.1
Africa	60.3	98.8	112.1	3.1	3.0	2.4	6.1	4.9	3.3	4.1	3.7	3.1	1.5	1.4	1.5
Latin America	75.1	110.7	289.7	4.3	4.4	4.8	4.4	4.7	5.2	4.2	3.9	4.7	4.4	4.5	4.8
Eastern and Southern Asia	204.3	467.3	941.5	11.0	15.2	17.1	9.2	10.9	10.4	17.2	19.8	22.2	10.7	18.3	21.4
Western Asia	84.3	101.2	162.9	4.0	3.3	2.7	7.6	5.2	4.1	3.2	2.8	2.9	2.7	2.7	1.5
Memo items:															
Sub-Saharan Africa	20.6	29.6	37.6	1.1	1.0	0.8	2.2	1.5	1.3	0.9	0.8	0.8	0.8	0.7	0.4
Least developed countries	18.6	27.4	36.6	1.4	1.0	1.0	2.1	1.6	1.2	1.3	1.7	1.1	1.8	2.7	0.8

Table A.16 (continued)															
	Manufactures														
								of which:							
	Total (billions of dollars)			Textiles			Chemicals			Machinery and transport			Metals		
Importing country group	1985	1990	1999	1985	1990	1999	1985	1990	1999	1985	1990	1999	1985	1990	1999
World (billions of dollars)	983.4	1 992.0	4 407.2	86.8	178.2	353.0	120.5	236.4	532.7	472.4	953.1	2 312.7	88.3	152.7	229.9
World (percentage share)	100.0	100.0	100.0	100.0	100.0	100.0	100.0	100.0	100.0	100.0	100.0	100.0	100.0	100.0	100.0
Developed economies	65.6	68.0	69.5	69.9	69.5	67.8	60.1	61.6	67.4	65.2	66.8	69.5	58.3	63.9	65.3
Economies in transition[a]	5.7	4.2	3.6	5.3	2.6	4.8	6.6	4.4	4.2	5.9	5.1	3.1	8.4	4.4	3.7
Developing countries	28.6	27.9	26.9	24.7	27.9	27.4	33.3	34.0	28.4	28.9	28.1	27.4	33.2	31.7	31.0
Africa	4.0	3.6	1.9	2.6	2.5	2.5	4.7	4.5	2.2	4.3	4.0	1.9	3.2	3.2	1.8
Latin America	4.9	3.8	5.3	2.3	2.1	5.2	7.3	5.9	6.0	5.6	4.0	5.5	3.4	3.4	4.0
Eastern and Southern Asia	13.7	16.9	16.8	13.5	19.8	16.5	16.2	19.4	17.1	13.5	16.9	17.2	19.5	20.0	22.2
Western Asia	6.0	3.6	2.9	6.2	3.5	3.2	5.1	4.1	3.0	5.6	3.2	2.8	7.1	5.0	3.0
Memo items:															
Sub-Saharan Africa	1.4	1.1	0.6	1.2	0.8	0.6	1.6	1.1	0.7	1.6	1.3	0.7	0.8	0.7	0.7
Least developed countries	1.2	1.0	0.6	1.3	1.2	1.0	1.3	0.9	0.7	1.4	1.1	0.6	0.9	2.2	0.5

Source: UN/DESA, based on COMTRADE.

[a] Data for 1999 including trade flows between the States of the former USSR. Prior to 1992, these flows were considered internal.

Table A.17.
INDICES OF PRICES OF PRIMARY COMMODITIES, 1990-2000

Annual percentage change[a]

		Non-fuel commodities[b]						Manufac-tured export prices[c]	Real prices of non-fuel commodities[d]	Memo item: crude petroleum[e]
	Food	Tropical beverages	Vegetable oilseeds and oils	Agricultural raw materials	Minerals and metals	Combined index Dollar	Combined index SDR			
1990	6.2	-11.4	-12.9	4.7	-9.8	-5.9	-11.2	9.9	-14.4	28.6
1991	-6.6	-8.1	8.1	-0.7	-9.5	-6.3	-7.4	0.0	-6.3	-16.4
1992	2.1	-14.0	7.5	-3.7	-3.7	-3.4	-5.7	3.0	-6.2	-1.0
1993	0.7	6.1	0.0	-6.2	-14.7	-3.5	-2.4	-5.8	2.5	-11.4
1994	10.1	75.0	24.4	15.7	12.7	18.0	13.6	2.1	15.6	-4.9
1995	5.9	1.1	10.3	15.0	20.2	9.9	4.3	11.1	-1.1	8.6
1996	6.8	-15.2	-4.2	-9.9	-12.1	-4.2	1.0	-3.6	-0.6	20.3
1997	3.5	33.3	-0.9	-10.3	0.0	0.0	5.2	-7.5	8.2	-7.9
1998	13.8	-17.3	7.1	-10.8	-16.0	-13.0	-11.8	-2.0	-11.2	-34.3
1999	18.1	-20.9	-23.3	-10.3	-1.8	-14.2	-14.4	-3.1	-11.4	42.3
2000	5.9	-13.2	-22.8	-1.0	12.0	1.9	5.2	-2.2	4.2	58.0
1998 I	-9.1	9.9	2.6	-14.6	-16.0	-8.5	-5.2	-5.0	-3.8	-35.7
II	-11.0	-27.9	9.8	-11.6	-18.0	-14.0	-11.1	-5.0	-9.5	-30.0
III	-15.6	-24.5	13.3	-8.5	-17.7	-14.8	-13.2	-2.1	-13.0	-31.6
IV	-19.2	-23.4	6.8	-7.0	-14.0	-15.3	-17.2	0.0	-15.3	-40.0
1999 I	-19.4	-29.9	-12.0	-6.5	-12.9	-16.8	-19.6	-1.0	-16.0	-17.0
II	-23.3	-20.2	-22.4	-10.2	-8.0	-17.4	-17.9	-2.1	-15.6	23.4
III	-15.8	-21.8	-30.8	-12.2	3.1	-12.4	-13.4	-3.2	-9.6	62.3
IV	-12.0	-6.6	-30.7	-11.7	11.8	-7.7	-6.5	-4.1	-3.7	112.8
2000 I	-6.9	-9.2	-24.2	-7.6	24.6	-1.9	-0.4	-3.2	1.3	135.6
II	6.1	-11.7	-20.6	-3.5	15.5	2.6	3.9	-2.2	4.9	71.5
III	10.1	-7.7	-19.0	5.3	9.2	5.3	8.8	-2.2	7.6	45.8
IV	12.8	-26.1	-25.1	3.0	2.0	1.9	9.2	-4.3	6.5	22.8

Sources: UNCTAD, *Monthly Commodity Price Bulletin*; United Nations, *Monthly Bulletin of Statistics* and *OPEC Bulletin*.

a   For quarterly data, the comparison is with the same quarter of previous year.
b   All non-fuel commodity indices are based on 1985.
c   Index of prices of manufactures exported by developed countries 1990 base year).
d   Combined index of non-fuel commodity prices in dollars deflated by manufactured export price index.
e   Composite price of the OPEC basket of seven crudes.

Table A.18.
WORLD OIL SUPPLY AND DEMAND, 1992-2001

Millions of barrels per day [a]	1992	1993	1994	1995	1996	1997	1998	1999	2000	2001[a]
World oil supply[b]										
Developed economies	16.6	16.8	17.6	18.0	18.4	18.6	18.4	18.1	18.5	18.4
Economies in transition	9.2	8.2	7.5	7.3	7.3	7.4	7.5	7.7	8.1	8.5
Developing countries	40.0	41.1	41.9	43.3	44.8	46.7	48.0	46.7	48.4	48.4
OPEC[c]	26.5	27.0	27.3	27.7	28.4	29.9	30.8	29.4	30.8	30.5
Non-OPEC developing countries[c]	13.5	14.1	14.6	15.7	16.4	16.8	17.1	17.3	17.6	17.9
Processing gains[d]	1.3	1.4	1.4	1.5	1.5	1.6	1.6	1.7	1.7	1.8
World total supply[e]	67.1	67.4	68.4	70.1	72.0	74.3	75.5	74.1	76.7	77.0
World oil demand[f]										
World total demand	67.5	67.6	68.9	69.9	71.6	73.1	73.5	74.8	75.4	76.7

Source: UN/DESA, based on International Energy Agency, *Monthly Oil Market Report,* various issues.

a   Forecast.
b   Including crude oil, condensates, natural gas liquids (NGLs), oil from non-conventional sources and other sources of supply.
c   Ecuador is included in OPEC through 1992 and in non-OPEC developing countries starting in 1993. Gabon is not included in OPEC starting in 1995.
d   Net volume gains and losses in refining process (excluding net gain/loss in the economies in transition and China) and marine transportation losses.
e   Totals may not add up because of rounding.
f   Including deliveries from refineries/primary stocks and marine bunkers, and refinery fuel and non-conventional oils.

III. INTERNATIONAL FINANCE AND FINANCIAL MARKETS

Table A.19.

WORLD BALANCE OF PAYMENTS ON CURRENT ACCOUNT, BY COUNTRY GROUP, 1993-2000

Billions of dollars

	1993	1994	1995	1996	1997	1998	1999[a]	2000[b]
Developed countries	43.3	22.7	58.2	47.6	81.4	-34.8	-197.5	-292.4
of which:								
Euro area	20.7	20.5	56.3	82.4	101.0	67.0	27.8	-6.6
Japan	131.6	130.3	111.0	65.9	94.4	120.7	106.9	116.7
United States	-82.7	-118.6	-109.5	-123.3	-140.5	-217.1	-331.5	-435.4
Developing countries[c]	-93.7	-66.7	-89.6	-72.2	-43.0	-13.2	59.1	100.9
Net fuel exporters	-50.2	-41.1	-9.7	14.4	2.4	-56.2	7.6	80.9
Net fuel importers	-43.5	-25.7	-79.9	-86.7	-45.4	43.0	51.6	20.1
Net-creditor countries	-2.6	13.3	25.9	38.2	36.8	6.8	40.5	80.2
Net-debtor countries	-91.0	-80.0	-115.4	-110.5	-79.8	-20.0	18.7	20.7
Economies in transition	-6.4	2.3	-3.0	-12.3	-24.9	-28.5	-1.0	25.0
of which:								
Central and Eastern Europe	-11.6	-2.8	-6.4	-17.0	-18.7	-19.5	-23.1	-20.2
CIS	4.8	5.2	4.2	6.1	-4.2	-6.6	24.2	46.2
World residual[d]	56.8	41.7	34.4	36.9	-13.5	76.5	139.4	166.5
of which:								
Trade residual	-77.7	-100.2	-121.2	-102.1	-120.5	-80.3	-53.0	-19.4

Source: UN/DESA, based on data of IMF and other national and international sources.

Note: Aggregates for major country groupings may not add up owing to rounding.

[a] Partially estimated.
[b] Preliminary estimate.
[c] Ninety-five economies.
[d] Unreported trade, services, income, and transfers, as well as errors and timing asymmetries in reported data.

Table A.20.
CURRENT-ACCOUNT TRANSACTIONS: DEVELOPED ECONOMIES, 1993-2000

Billions of dollars

	1993	1994	1995	1996	1997	1998	1999	2000[a]
All developed economies[b]								
Goods: exports (f.o.b.)	2 552.4	2 870.8	3 435.7	3 528.8	3 615.8	3 647.9	3 698.0	3 960.4
Goods: imports (f.o.b.)	-2 453.6	-2 777.2	-3 312.1	-3 435.2	-3 518.5	-3 619.8	-3 806.2	-4 192.2
Trade balance	98.8	93.6	123.6	93.7	97.2	28.1	-108.2	-231.8
Net services, income and current transfers	-55.5	-71.0	-65.4	-46.0	-15.8	-62.8	-89.3	-60.6
of which:								
Net investment income	11.3	7.2	11.1	21.3	30.9	10.8	-9.8	4.9
Current account balance	43.3	22.7	58.2	47.6	81.4	-34.8	-197.5	-292.4
Major industrialized countries								
Goods: exports (f.o.b.)	1 892.7	2 117.3	2 478.5	2 537.7	2 627.1	2 623.9	2 674.1	2 877.0
Goods: imports (f.o.b.)	-1 816.3	-2 049.6	-2 396.5	-2 494.2	-2 584.9	-2 628.2	-2 801.9	-3 146.7
Trade balance	76.4	67.7	82.1	43.5	42.2	-4.3	-127.7	-269.7
Net services, income and current transfers	-62.4	-71.5	-73.8	-45.7	-20.3	-50.3	-91.6	-63.4
of which:								
Net investment income	36.5	37.6	32.3	50.4	51.2	42.0	9.9	28.4
Current-account balance	14.0	-3.7	8.3	-2.2	21.9	-54.6	-219.3	-333.1
Euro area								
Goods: exports (f.o.b.)	1 160.7	1 324.0	1 653.1	1 688.2	1 668.1	1 772.9	1 748.1	1 785.4
Goods: imports (f.o.b.)	-1 085.8	-1 234.0	-1 527.3	-1 539.7	-1 514.8	-1 619.8	-1 639.6	-1 723.9
Trade balance	74.9	90.0	125.8	148.5	153.3	153.2	108.5	61.5
Net services, income and current transfers	-54.2	-69.5	-69.5	-66.1	-52.3	-86.2	-80.7	-68.1
of which:								
Net investment income	-25.3	-31.9	-32.5	-30.4	-23.5	-46.1	-43.0	-33.7
Current-account balance	20.7	20.5	56.3	82.4	101.0	67.0	27.8	-6.6
Japan								
Goods: exports (f.o.b.)	352.7	385.7	428.7	400.3	409.2	374.0	403.7	459.5
Goods: imports (f.o.b.)	-213.2	-241.5	-296.9	-316.7	-307.6	-251.7	-280.4	-343.0
Trade balance	139.4	144.2	131.8	83.6	101.6	122.4	123.3	116.6
Net services, income and current transfers	-7.8	-13.9	-20.7	-17.7	-7.2	-1.7	-16.5	0.1
of which:								
Net investment income	41.2	40.9	45.0	53.6	55.7	56.6	49.8	57.6
Current-account balance	131.6	130.3	111.0	65.9	94.4	120.7	106.9	116.7
United States								
Goods: exports (f.o.b.)	458.7	504.5	577.7	614.0	681.6	672.3	686.7	775.7
Goods: imports (f.o.b.)	-589.4	-668.6	-749.6	-803.3	-876.4	-917.2	-1 029.9	-1 222.8
Trade balance	-130.7	-164.1	-171.9	-189.4	-194.7	-244.9	-343.3	-447.1
Net services, income and current transfers	48.0	45.5	62.4	66.1	54.2	27.8	11.8	11.7
of which:								
Net investment income	27.6	21.1	25.0	23.4	11.0	-1.0	-13.1	-8.1
Current-account balance	-82.7	-118.6	-109.5	-123.3	-140.5	-217.1	-331.5	-435.4

Source: UN/DESA, based on data of IMF and national sources.

[a] Preliminary estimate.
[b] Data may not add up due to rounding.

Table A.21.
CURRENT-ACCOUNT TRANSACTIONS: ECONOMIES IN TRANSITION, 1993-2000

Billions of dollars								
	1993	1994	1995	1996	1997	1998	1999	2000[a]
Economies in transition[b]								
Goods: exports (f.o.b.)	149.8	172.4	219.0	235.1	248.2	238.4	233.1	282.1
Goods: imports (f.o.b.)	-155.1	-168.9	-220.9	-252.7	-273.2	-266.3	-233.3	-244.6
Trade balance	-5.2	3.5	-1.9	-17.6	-25.0	-27.9	-0.1	37.6
Net services, income and current transfers	-1.2	-1.2	-1.1	5.3	0.1	-0.6	-0.9	-12.6
of which:								
Net investment income	-5.7	-6.5	-7.8	-9.9	-13.8	-18.4	-14.5	-13.0
Current-account balance	-6.4	2.3	-3.0	-12.3	-24.9	-28.5	-1.0	25.0
CIS								
Goods: exports (f.o.b.)	81.9	95.4	116.1	126.8	126.9	108.2	108.2	144.3
Goods: imports (f.o.b.)	-74.4	-81.7	-99.8	-112.6	-118.3	-99.6	-73.7	-72.6
Trade balance	7.5	13.8	16.3	14.3	8.6	8.7	34.5	71.7
Net services, income and current transfers	-2.6	-8.6	-12.1	-8.2	-12.8	-15.3	-10.3	-25.4
of which:								
Net investment income	-	-1.7	-3.3	-5.9	-9.5	-13.0	-9.3	-8.6
Current-account balance	4.8	5.2	4.2	6.1	-4.2	-6.6	24.2	46.2
of which:								
Russian Federation								
Goods: exports (f.o.b.)	57.6	67.8	82.9	90.6	89.0	74.9	75.8	102.8
Goods: imports (f.o.b.)	-46.8	-50.5	-62.6	-68.1	-72.0	-58.0	-39.6	-34.7
Trade balance	10.8	17.4	20.3	22.5	17.0	16.9	36.2	68.0
Net services, income and current transfers	-3.3	-9.0	-12.9	-10.7	-15.0	-16.2	-10.9	-21.7
of which:								
Net investment income	..	-1.7	-3.1	-5.0	-8.4	-11.6	-7.8	-6.9
Current-account balance	7.5	8.4	7.4	11.8	2.0	0.7	25.3	46.3
Baltic countries								
Goods: exports (f.o.b.)	3.9	4.3	5.8	6.7	8.3	8.7	7.5	6.4
Goods: imports (f.o.b.)	-4.2	-5.1	-7.7	-9.4	-11.4	-12.4	-10.8	-8.6
Trade balance	-0.3	-0.9	-1.9	-2.7	-3.1	-3.8	-3.3	-2.2
Net services, income and current transfers	0.6	0.8	1.2	1.3	1.2	1.3	1.2	1.2
of which:								
Net investment income	-	-	-	-0.1	-0.3	-0.3	-0.4	-0.3
Current-account balance	0.4	-0.1	-0.8	-1.4	-1.9	-2.4	-2.1	-1.1

Table 21 (continued)	1993	1994	1995	1996	1997	1998	1999	2000[a]
Central and Eastern Europe[b]								
Goods: exports (f.o.b.)	64.1	72.7	97.2	101.6	113.1	121.5	117.5	131.5
Goods: imports (f.o.b.)	-76.4	-82.1	-113.5	-130.7	-143.5	-154.3	-148.8	-163.3
Trade balance	-12.4	-9.4	-16.3	-29.1	-30.4	-32.8	-31.3	-31.9
Net services, income and current transfers	0.8	6.6	9.9	12.1	11.7	13.3	8.2	11.7
of which:								
Net investment income	-5.7	-4.7	-4.5	-3.9	-4.1	-5.1	-4.8	-4.1
Current-account balance	-11.6	-2.8	-6.4	-17.0	-18.7	-19.5	-23.1	-20.2
Central Europe								
Goods: exports (f.o.b.)	47.5	55.5	76.3	80.6	91.2	99.4	97.0	107.4
Goods: imports (f.o.b.)	-56.6	-61.5	-85.3	-99.5	-110.4	-120.3	-118.5	-128.5
Trade balance	-9.1	-6.0	-8.9	-18.9	-19.2	-20.9	-21.5	-21.1
Net services, income and current transfers	-0.9	3.3	6.2	7.6	7.3	8.1	4.0	5.9
of which:								
Net investment income	-5.2	-4.2	-3.8	-3.0	-3.2	-4.1	-3.6	-3.2
Current-account balance	-10.0	-2.7	-2.8	-11.3	-11.9	-12.9	-17.6	-15.2
Southern and Eastern Europe								
Goods: exports (f.o.b.)	16.6	17.2	20.8	21.0	21.9	22.1	20.5	24.0
Goods: imports (f.o.b.)	-19.9	-20.6	-28.2	-31.2	-33.1	-34.0	-30.3	-34.9
Trade balance	-3.3	-3.4	-7.3	-10.2	-11.2	-11.9	-9.8	-10.8
Net services, income and current transfers	1.7	3.3	3.7	4.5	4.4	5.3	4.3	5.8
of which:								
Net investment income	-0.5	-0.6	-0.7	-0.9	-0.8	-1.0	-1.2	-0.9
Current-account balance	-1.6	-0.1	-3.7	-5.7	-6.8	-6.6	-5.6	-5.0

Source: UN/DESA, based on data of IMF and national sources.

[a] Preliminary estimate.
[b] It may not add up owing to rounding.

Table A.22.
CURRENT-ACCOUNT TRANSACTIONS: DEVELOPING ECONOMIES, 1993-2000

Billions of dollars

	1993	1994	1995	1996	1997	1998	1999[a]	2000[b]
Developing countries[c]								
Goods: exports (f.o.b.)	1 035.5	1 190.6	1 430.9	1 574.2	1 682.7	1 554.7	1 689.9	2 073.3
Goods: imports (f.o.b.)	-1 051.4	-1 187.5	-1 431.3	-1 548.1	-1 634.5	-1 474.5	-1 528.5	-1 859.7
Trade balance	-15.9	3.0	-0.4	26.0	48.3	80.2	161.4	213.6
Net services, income and current transfers	-77.7	-69.8	-89.2	-98.3	-91.3	-93.4	-102.3	-112.7
of which:								
Net investment income	-60.7	-66.0	-80.8	-86.9	-86.1	-95.4	-101.4	-104.4
Current-account balance	-93.7	-66.7	-89.6	-72.2	-43.0	-13.2	59.1	100.9
Net fuel exporters								
Goods: exports (f.o.b.)	275.1	294.9	346.1	412.2	436.4	372.6	449.1	609.6
Goods: imports (f.o.b.)	-246.3	-257.9	-279.1	-309.1	-346.7	-350.8	-359.2	-434.1
Trade balance	28.8	37.0	67.0	103.1	89.7	21.8	89.9	175.5
Net services, income and current transfers	-79.0	-78.0	-76.7	-88.7	-87.3	-78.0	-82.3	-94.6
of which:								
Net investment income	-20.4	-24.4	-22.7	-24.9	-22.3	-24.1	-25.6	-25.7
Current-account balance	-50.2	-41.1	-9.7	14.4	2.4	-56.2	7.6	80.9
Net fuel importers								
Goods: exports (f.o.b.)	760.4	895.7	1 084.8	1 162.0	1 246.3	1 182.1	1 240.8	1 463.7
Goods: imports (f.o.b.)	-805.2	-929.7	-1 152.2	-1 239.0	-1 287.8	-1 123.7	-1 169.3	-1 425.6
Trade balance	-44.7	-34.0	-67.4	-77.1	-41.4	58.4	71.5	38.1
Net services, income and current transfers	1.3	8.3	-12.5	-9.6	-4.0	-15.4	-19.9	-18.1
of which:								
Net investment income	-40.3	-41.6	-58.1	-61.9	-63.8	-71.3	-75.8	-78.7
Current-account balance	-43.5	-25.7	-79.9	-86.7	-45.4	43.0	51.6	20.1
Net-creditor countries								
Goods: exports (f.o.b.)	261.4	291.2	342.9	379.8	385.9	321.9	364.0	470.7
Goods: imports (f.o.b.)	-221.6	-241.0	-284.4	-297.6	-313.0	-277.9	-287.4	-351.1
Trade balance	39.9	50.2	58.5	82.2	72.9	44.0	76.6	119.6
Net services, income and current transfers	-42.5	-36.9	-32.7	-44.0	-36.1	-37.2	-36.1	-39.4
of which:								
Net investment income	12.0	9.8	13.9	14.1	17.9	16.5	16.8	21.5
Current-account balance	-2.6	13.3	25.9	38.2	36.8	6.8	40.5	80.2
Net-debtor countries								
Goods: exports (f.o.b.)	774.1	899.3	1 088.0	1 194.4	1 296.8	1 232.8	1 325.9	1 602.7
Goods: imports (f.o.b.)	-829.9	-946.5	-1 146.9	-1 250.6	-1 321.4	-1 196.6	-1 241.1	-1 508.6
Trade balance	-55.8	-47.2	-59.0	-56.2	-24.6	36.2	84.8	94.1
Net services, income and current transfers	-35.3	-32.8	-56.5	-54.3	-55.2	-56.2	-66.1	-73.3
of which:								
Net investment income	-72.6	-75.9	-94.8	-101.0	-104.0	-111.8	-118.2	-126.0
Current-account balance	-91.0	-80.0	-115.4	-110.5	-79.8	-20.0	18.7	20.7

Table 22 (continued)

	1993	1994	1995	1996	1997	1998	1999ᵃ	2000ᵇ
Totals by region:								
Latin America								
Goods: exports (f.o.b.)	166.7	193.8	235.9	262.8	292.5	287.7	304.4	365.1
Goods: imports (f.o.b.)	-175.1	-207.4	-234.3	-260.0	-308.6	-326.8	-315.3	-366.4
Trade balance	-8.4	-13.6	1.6	2.8	-16.1	-39.1	-10.9	-1.4
Net services, income and current transfers	-36.9	-37.2	-38.7	-41.2	-49.3	-50.0	-45.2	-46.7
of which:								
Net investment income	-35.8	-37.6	-41.8	-44.4	-49.1	-53.3	-53.8	-55.5
Current-account balance	-45.3	-50.8	-37.1	-38.4	-65.4	-89.1	-56.0	-48.1
Africa								
Goods: exports (f.o.b.)	91.6	95.7	111.9	123.6	126.2	106.2	116.1	145.6
Goods: imports (f.o.b.)	-89.8	-96.4	-112.7	-113.3	-119.2	-118.7	-115.2	-126.8
Trade balance	1.8	-0.7	-0.9	10.3	7.0	-12.6	0.8	18.8
Net services, income and current transfers	-7.8	-9.7	-12.2	-10.9	-11.3	-8.3	-9.2	-12.6
of which:								
Net investment income	-10.9	-10.8	-11.0	-11.8	-10.4	-9.0	-9.8	-10.4
Current-account balance	-6.0	-10.4	-13.1	-0.6	-4.2	-20.8	-8.4	6.2
Western Asia								
Goods: exports (f.o.b.)	148.0	157.3	175.7	214.3	217.1	177.4	218.5	298.6
Goods: imports (f.o.b.)	-148.3	-135.0	-159.8	-178.4	-187.5	-186.3	-185.0	-223.3
Trade balance	-0.3	22.3	15.9	35.9	29.6	-8.9	33.5	75.3
Net services, income and current transfers	-30.8	-27.4	-19.8	-31.1	-26.5	-14.3	-24.6	-27.8
of which:								
Net investment income	1.6	-3.0	0.3	0.5	1.8	2.5	0.8	1.4
Current-account balance	-31.1	-5.1	-3.9	4.8	3.1	-23.2	8.8	47.5
Eastern and Southern Asia								
Goods: exports (f.o.b.)	629.3	743.8	907.4	973.5	1 047.0	983.4	1 051.0	1 264.1
Goods: imports (f.o.b.)	-638.3	-748.8	-924.4	-996.4	-1 019.2	-842.7	-913.0	-1 143.2
Trade balance	-9.0	-5.0	-17.0	-22.9	27.8	140.7	138.0	120.9
Net services, income and current transfers	-2.2	4.5	-18.5	-15.1	-4.3	-20.9	-23.2	-25.6
of which:								
Net investment income	-15.6	-14.7	-28.3	-31.1	-28.5	-35.5	-38.5	-40.0
Current-account balance	-11.2	-0.5	-35.5	-38.1	23.5	119.9	114.7	95.3

Source: UN/DESA, based on data of IMF and other national and international sources.

ᵃ Partially estimated.
ᵇ Preliminary estimate.
ᶜ Ninety-five economies. Data may not add up owing to rounding.

Table A.23.
NET IMF LENDING TO DEVELOPING COUNTRIES: BY FACILITY, 1990-2000

Billions of dollars

	1990	1991	1992	1993	1994	1995	1996	1997	1998	1999	2000
Regular facilities	-1.4	-1.1	0.0	-0.2	-0.8	12.5	-2.6	13.0	14.1	-9.8	-6.5
Repayment terms:											
3¼-5 years (credit tranche)[a]	-1.6	0.3	1.5	-0.2	0.1	12.4	-1.4	13.6	11.2	-9.6	-5.8
3½-7 years (EAP)[b]	-0.5	-0.7	-1.5	-1.5	-1.4	-1.6	-1.3	-0.7	-0.1	0.0	0.0
4½-10 years (Extended Fund Facility)	0.7	-0.7	0.0	1.5	0.5	1.8	0.1	0.2	3.1	-0.2	-0.7
Concessional facilities	0.2	1.1	0.8	0.2	0.9	1.5	0.2	-0.1	0.2	0.1	-0.2
in order created:											
Trust Fund[c]	-0.4	-0.1	0.0	-0.1	0.0	0.0	0.0	0.0	0.0	0.0	0.0
SAF[d]	0.1	0.2	0.0	-0.1	-0.2	-0.1	-0.4	-0.3	-0.2	-0.2	-0.1
ESAF/PRGF[d]	0.5	0.9	0.7	0.4	1.1	1.6	0.5	0.2	0.4	0.2	-0.1
Additional facilities[e]	-0.8	1.2	-0.9	-0.2	-0.9	-1.6	-0.7	-0.9	-0.7	0.7	0.0
in order created:											
Compensatory financing[f]	-0.8	1.2	-0.9	-0.2	-0.9	-1.6	-0.7	-0.9	-0.7	0.7	0.0
STF[f]	-	-	-	0.0	0.0	0.0	0.0	0.0	0.0	0.0	0.0
Total	-2.0	1.2	-0.1	-0.2	-0.7	12.5	-3.1	12.0	13.7	-9.0	-6.7
Memo items:											
Selected characteristics of higher conditionality lending agreements											
Number initiated during year	12	24	17	13	26	18	20	14	15	16	18
Average length (months)	19	22	26	24	25	23	29	33	29	32	28
Total amount committed	1.3	6.4	7.1	3.0	6.6	23.2	5.2	38.4	29.5	13.0	22.1

Source: Data of IMF, *International Financial Statistics* and *IMF Survey*.

[a] Primarily standby arrangements. Includes Supplemental Reserve Facility (SRF) (created December 1997) for use when a sudden and disruptive loss of market confidence causes pressure on the capital account and on reserves, creating a large short-term financing need (higher-cost and shorter-term than regular drawings); adds to commitments under standby or extended arrangements for up to one year, with drawings in two or more tranches. Also includes emergency assistance for natural disasters and, since 1995, post-conflict situations.

[b] Enhanced Access Policy (EAP) (1981-1992) provided resources from funds borrowed by IMF from Member States on which the Fund paid a higher interest rate than the remuneration paid to countries that had a net creditor position with the Fund. Thus, users of EAP resources paid a higher interest rate than on drawings from ordinary resources, which are at below-market interest rates.

[c] Mainly using resources from IMF gold sales, the Trust Fund lent during 1977-1981 under 1-year adjustment programmes; eligibility was based on maximum per capita income criteria; loans had 10-year maturities, with repayments beginning in the sixth year; the interest rate was 0.5 per cent per year.

[d] Structural Adjustment Facility (SAF) and Enhanced Structural Adjustment Facility (ESAF) (the first financed mainly from Trust Fund reflows and the second from loans and grants) made loans to IDA-eligible countries with protracted balance-of-payments problems; funds were disbursed over 3 years (under Policy Framework Paper arrangements), with repayments beginning in 5.5 years and ending in 10 years; the interest rate was 0.5 per cent. On 22 November 1999, the facility was renamed the Poverty Reduction and Growth Facility (PRGF) and now supports policy reforms contained in Poverty Reduction Strategy Papers (PRSPs).

[e] Compensatory Financing Facility (CFF) from 1963 to 1988; Compensatory and Contingency Financing Facility (CCFF) from August 1988; CFF again from February 2000 (same terms as credit tranche).

[f] See description in table A.24 below.

Table A.24.
NET IMF LENDING TO ECONOMIES IN TRANSITION: BY FACILITY, 1990-2000

Billions of dollars											
	1990	1991	1992	1993	1994	1995	1996	1997	1998	1999	2000
Regular facilities	0.1	2.0	1.8	0.1	0.2	4.4	3.7	2.1	3.0	-3.0	-3.1
Repayment terms:											
3¼-5 years (credit tranche)	0.4	1.0	1.8	0.1	0.5	4.9	1.2	0.0	-0.8	-3.1	-3.2
3½-7 years (EAP)	-0.3	0.2	0.0	0.0	-0.3	0.0	0.0	0.0	0.0	0.0	0.0
4½-10 years (Extended Fund Facility)	..	0.8	0.1	0.0	0.0	-0.5	2.6	2.2	3.9	0.1	0.2
Concessional facilities (ESAF)	..	..	..	0.0	0.0	0.1	0.2	0.2	0.2	0.1	0.1
Additional facilities											
Compensatory financing	0.0	1.5	-0.1	0.0	-0.7	-0.6	-0.2	0.1	2.9	0.1	0.0
STF	-	-	-	2.0	2.8	0.9	0.0	0.0	-0.5	-0.8	-1.1
Total	0.1	3.5	1.7	2.1	2.3	4.8	3.7	2.4	5.6	-3.6	-4.1
Memo items:											
Selected characteristics of higher conditionality lending agreements											
Number initiated during year	3	5	6	9	8	12	12	7	6	4	5
Average length (months)	12	12	12	18	18	13	28	21	32	19	28
Total amount committed	1.6	4.9	1.5	1.6	2.1	9.2	13.2	2.1	3.4	5.6	0.3

Source: Data of IMF, *International Financial Statistics* and *IMF Survey.*

Note: The Systemic Transformation Facility (STF), created in April 1993 and closed to new drawings in December 1995, assisted economies in transition with severe balance-of-payments problems arising from discontinuance of trade arrangements under planning. For members that had not yet had a standby arrangement, drawings could be made be in two tranches in support of a written statement of policy reform intentions, the second 6-18 months after the first, assuming satisfactory progress towards an upper credit tranche. Terms were the same as for the Extended Fund Facility (EFF). See table A.23 above for description of other facilities.

Table A.25.

NET ODA FROM MAJOR SOURCES, BY TYPE, 1980-1999

Donor group or country	Growth rate of ODA[a] (1998 prices and exchange rates) 1980-1989	Growth rate of ODA[a] (1998 prices and exchange rates) 1990-1999	ODA as percentage of GNP 1999	Total ODA (millions of dollars) 1999	Percentage distribution of ODA by type, 1999 — Bilateral — Grants[b]	Bilateral — Technical cooperation	Bilateral — Loans	Multilateral — United Nations	Multilateral — IDA	Multilateral — Other
Total DAC countries	3.38	-0.43	0.24	56 378	60.1	23.1	7.0	6.5	5.0	21.4
Total EU	3.89	-0.73	0.32	26 756	64.0	22.6	-0.9	6.7	5.7	24.8
Austria	2.54	2.70	0.26	527	72.3	19.9	-7.0	5.1	0.0	29.6
Belgium	-0.94	-0.33	0.30	760	59.7	36.3	-2.2	4.9	6.1	31.6
Denmark	4.28	3.55	1.01	1 733	59.0	4.8	0.2	16.2	5.4	19.3
Finland	16.73	-4.59	0.33	416	68.8	17.3	-10.8	17.3	3.1	21.9
France[c]	6.28	-2.00	0.39	5 637	76.6	34.8	-3.5	2.1	4.0	20.7
Germany	1.79	-1.20	0.26	5 515	58.7	34.7	0.8	5.9	7.5	27.1
Ireland	0.93	12.66	0.31	245	60.8	..	..	6.9	2.9	29.8
Italy	17.74	-6.63	0.15	1 806	30.5	2.9	-5.5	8.4	16.4	50.2
Luxembourg	..	17.06	0.66	119	74.8	0.8	..	6.7	3.4	15.1
Netherlands	2.81	1.50	0.79	3 134	75.3	19.1	-6.3	7.5	7.8	15.7
Portugal	..	5.50	0.26	276	101.1	35.9	-24.1	1.8	0.0	23.2
Spain	..	11.12	0.23	1 363	47.9	8.7	12.9	3.4	4.8	31.0
Sweden	2.28	-1.16	0.70	1 630	70.1	2.9	0.2	13.6	6.4	9.6
United Kingdom	-1.98	-0.13	0.23	3 401	60.8	19.6	5.4	7.1	0.0	26.8
Australia	1.26	-0.80	0.26	982	76.0	37.6	..	6.6	7.4	11.6
Canada	2.53	-2.75	0.28	1 699	70.3	20.4	-1.4	8.0	8.0	15.0
Japan	6.21	2.03	0.35	15 323	35.7	13.9	32.6	4.8	1.0	25.9
New Zealand	-1.56	2.89	0.27	134	75.4	39.6	..	6.7	6.0	11.2
Norway	4.80	2.57	0.91	1 370	72.5	9.8	1.0	16.9	3.9	5.8
Switzerland	6.86	2.17	0.35	969	74.2	11.4	..	8.9	9.5	7.4
United States	0.54	-2.35	0.10	9 145	83.5	42.4	-8.6	6.5	8.7	9.9
Arab countries[d] of which:										
Saudi Arabia	..	..	..	185	——— -0.5 ———			——— 100.5 ———		
Kuwait	..	..	..	147	——— 100.0 ———			——— 0.0 ———		
Other developing countries:[d]										
Korea, Republic of	..	..	..	317	——— 41.3 ———			——— 58.7 ———		
Taiwan Province of China			..	..	——— .. ———			——— 100.0 ———		

Source: United Nations, based on OECD, *Development Co-operation*, 2000 report.

a   Average annual rates of growth, calculated from average levels in 1978-1979, 1988-1989 and 1998-1999.
b   Including technical cooperation.
c   Excluding flows from France to the Overseas Departments, namely, Guadeloupe, French Guiana, Martinique and Réunion.
d   Bilateral ODA includes all grants and loans; multilateral ODA includes United Nations, IDA and "other", including technical cooperation.

Table A.26.
REGIONAL DISTRIBUTION OF ODA FROM MAJOR SOURCES, 1988-1999

Millions of dollars, two-year averages

Donor group or country	All developing countries 1988-1989	All developing countries 1998-1999	of which: Latin America 1988-1989	Latin America 1998-1999	Africa 1988-1989	Africa 1998-1999	Western Asia 1988-1989	Western Asia 1998-1999	Eastern and Southern Asia[a] 1988-1989	Eastern and Southern Asia[a] 1998-1999
Total ODA[b] (net)	45 725.4	51 347.3	4 549.0	3 008.6	17 805.0	16 749.3	2 424.8	1 562.7	13 921.7	16 566.6
DAC countries, bilateral	32 434.6	36 533.0	3 564.7	4 128.0	12 061.6	10 754.9	1 982.8	854.4	9 806.4	12 099.8
Australia	664.2	740.7	1.0	0.9	59.8	43.2	66.4	1.5	504.2	596.1
Austria	181.6	317.7	8.1	27.0	58.7	56.8	38.7	20.4	22.4	92.7
Belgium	385.7	486.7	25.2	59.7	259.7	236.3	6.5	-2.0	16.7	37.0
Canada	1 582.1	1 197.2	190.3	139.8	494.1	300.2	40.4	3.8	337.8	207.8
Denmark	500.0	1 020.1	13.2	77.1	290.9	467.0	14.7	3.3	123.8	210.3
Finland	1 446.4	2 190.2	86.5	256.2	668.0	823.1	6.0	20.8	409.9	526.0
France[c]	4 325.0	4 154.6	137.6	170.9	2 580.3	2 195.8	112.6	117.5	1 001.2	963.4
Germany	3 173.4	3 384.0	411.9	432.2	1 307.3	1 089.2	319.9	195.6	593.2	1 003.6
Ireland	20.5	136.1	0.1	4.3	13.8	90.4	0.1	0.7	0.4	6.8
Italy	2 298.5	574.0	355.2	64.9	1 412.0	345.8	23.1	14.9	269.5	8.0
Japan	6 600.2	9 514.4	481.3	683.6	1 193.6	1 158.1	237.8	230.3	4 131.7	6 229.5
Luxembourg	0.0	82.7	0.0	18.0	0.0	39.3	0.0	0.9	0.0	13.2
Netherlands	1 531.7	2 147.3	280.4	367.3	555.4	583.9	40.0	56.2	477.6	250.9
New Zealand	84.9	99.8	0.4	1.7	0.8	4.6	61.5	0.1	-3.9	87.1
Norway	563.4	978.5	41.5	80.6	316.4	390.6	0.9	29.4	118.4	188.5
Portugal	74.2	191.9	0.0	1.3	36.1	146.8	0.0	0.5	0.0	34.1
Spain	211.3	833.7	114.0	350.5	57.1	220.4	6.5	8.7	14.2	93.8
Sweden	1 154.6	1 093.4	108.8	130.5	545.8	375.5	7.9	13.5	282.5	186.3
Switzerland	433.9	675.9	57.5	80.0	176.8	183.4	13.6	10.7	109.2	134.8
United Kingdom	1 446.4	2 190.2	86.5	256.2	668.0	823.1	6.0	20.8	409.9	526.0
United States	6 795.5	6 418.0	1 225.5	1 165.7	1 792.0	1 927.9	1 221.6	120.4	1 084.4	1 157.3
DAC countries, multilateral	11 749.6	14 478.5	984.1	881.8	5 549.7	5 748.0	617.4	574.9	3 761.6	4 497.7
Total DAC	44 184.2	51 011.5	4 548.8	5 009.8	17 611.3	16 502.9	2 600.2	1 429.4	13 568.0	16 597.5
Arab countries										
Bilateral[d]	1 541.2	335.8	0.2	7.0	193.7	246.4	-20.5	133.4	198.8	-30.9
Multilateral	86.1	14.5	1.6	4.0	71.7	11.0	30.8	0.9	-21.2	-4.7

Source: United Nations calculations, based on OECD, *Geographical Distribution of Financial Flows to Aid Recipients.*

a   Including Central Asian transition economies.
b   Excluding assistance provided by centrally planned and transition economies, owing to measurement difficulties. Donor total includes amounts to certain European countries and unallocated amounts and hence is larger than the sum of the amounts per region.
c   Excluding flows from France to the Overseas Departments, namely, Guadeloupe, French Guiana, Martinique and Réunion.
d   Approximately 35-40 per cent of Arab bilateral aid being geographically unallocated, depending on the year.

Table A.27.

RESOURCE COMMITMENTS OF MULTILATERAL DEVELOPMENT INSTITUTIONS, 1990-2000[a]

Millions of dollars

	1990	1991	1992	1993	1994	1995	1996	1997	1998	1999	2000
Financial institutions	34 804	39 820	39 757	39 709	40 656	43 516	44 701	45 760	57 928	42 772	37 934
African Development Bank	3 281	3 454	2 996	2 519	1 655	802	823	1 880	1 742	1 765	2 766
Asian Development Bank	4 043	4 843	5 095	5 426	3 864	5 759	5 878	9 648	6 208	5 159	6 100
Caribbean Development Bank	109	111	71	71	56	110	99	54	122	154	184
European Bank for Reconstruction and Development	..	89	1 188	2 103	2 232	2 616	2 774	2 625	2 658	2 784	2 901
Inter-American Development Bank *of which:*	4 005	5 661	6 232	6 191	5 298	7 454	6 951	6 224	10 403	9 577	5 336
Inter-American Investment Corporation	67	102	158	124	43	36	72	67	223	190	143
International Fund for Agricultural Development	323	281	331	383	364	414	447	430	443	434	409
World Bank Group	23 043	25 381	23 844	23 016	27 187	26 361	27 729	24 899	36 352	22 899	20 238
International Bank for Reconstruction and Development	15 176	17 021	15 551	15 098	16 427	15 950	15 325	15 098	24 687	13 789	10 699
International Development Association	6 300	7 160	6 310	5 345	7 282	5 973	6 490	5 345	7 325	5 691	5 861
International Finance Corporation	1 567	1 200	1 983	2 573	3 478	4 438	5 914	4 456	4 340	3 419	3 678
Operational agencies of the United Nations system	2 754	3 628	3 683	3 363	3 537	3 931	3 726	3 453	4 290	4 198	4 131
United Nations Development Programme[b]	1 042	1 134	1 027	1 031	1 036	1 014	1 231	1 529	1 764	1 632	1 458
United Nations Population Fund	211	212	164	206	278	340	285	322	326	245	171
United Nations Children's Fund	545	947	917	623	810	1 481	1 133	521	962	891	1 016
World Food Programme	956	1 335	1 575	1 503	1 413	1 096	1 077	1 081	1 238	1 430	1 486
Total commitments	37 558	43 448	43 440	43 072	44 193	47 447	48 427	49 213	62 218	46 969	42 065
Memo item:											
Commitments in units of 1990 purchasing power[c]	37 558	43 448	42 175	44 404	44 639	43 134	45 686	49 710	64 143	50 504	46 225

Source: Annual reports and information supplied by individual institutions.

[a] Loans, grants, technical assistance and equity participation, as appropriate; all data are on a calendar-year basis.

[b] Including United Nations Development Programme (UNDP)-administered funds.

[c] Total commitments deflated by the United Nations index of manufactured export prices in dollars of developed economies: 1990=100.

Table A.28.

EXTERNAL DEBT AND DEBT INDICATORS FOR ECONOMIES IN TRANSITION, 1990-1999

Billions of dollars

	1990	1991	1992	1993	1994	1995	1996	1997	1998	1999
Russian Federation/former Soviet Union[a]										
Total debt	59.3	67.8	78.7	112.4	122.3	121.7	126.6	127.7	177.7	173.9
Long-term	47.5	55.2	65.5	104.1	112.5	111.4	114.5	121.6	162.7	158.2
Concessional	0.0	0.7	0.9	0.9	1.1	1.2	1.1	1.0	1.0	0.4
Bilateral	0.0	0.7	0.9	0.9	1.1	1.2	1.1	1.0	1.0	0.4
Multilateral	0.0	0.0	0.0	0.0	0.0	0.0	0.0	0.0	0.0	0.0
Official, non-concessional	5.9	8.8	11.2	56.2	66.4	66.1	74.7	75.9	87.0	86.0
Bilateral	5.4	8.4	9.7	52.4	60.6	54.5	59.4	57.4	61.1	63.8
Multilateral	0.4	0.4	0.5	1.3	1.5	2.0	2.8	5.3	6.6	6.9
IMF credit	0.0	0.0	1.0	2.5	4.2	9.6	12.5	13.2	19.3	15.2
Private creditors	41.7	45.6	53.4	47.1	45.0	44.1	38.7	44.6	74.7	71.8
of which:										
Bonds	1.9	1.9	1.7	1.6	1.8	1.1	1.1	4.6	16.0	15.6
Commercial banks[b]	17.8	16.8	18.5	15.9	16.4	16.7	15.6	29.3	29.3	29.0
Short-term	11.8	12.6	13.1	8.3	9.9	10.4	12.1	6.1	15.0	15.7
Central and Eastern Europe										
Total debt	109.1	117.4	112.9	116.6	121.3	137.9	139.8	140.6	162.9	161.0
Long-term	90.9	101.8	99.7	103.9	109.4	120.4	121.7	116.1	137.3	137.9
Concessional	5.2	4.9	14.3	13.6	12.2	13.4	12.6	10.3	11.3	11.2
Bilateral	5.1	4.7	14.2	13.4	11.9	13.1	12.3	9.9	10.8	10.1
Multilateral	0.1	0.2	0.1	0.2	0.2	0.3	0.3	0.4	0.5	1.1
Official non-concessional	36.4	47.4	38.5	39.4	41.8	42.0	40.1	37.0	36.7	35.2
Bilateral	28.7	34.7	24.3	24.9	25.1	26.8	25.9	23.5	23.5	21.1
Multilateral	6.5	7.7	8.8	9.1	11.0	12.1	12.0	11.1	10.8	11.8
IMF credit	1.3	5.0	5.4	5.4	5.7	3.1	2.2	2.5	2.4	2.4
Private creditors	49.2	49.5	47.0	50.9	55.4	65.0	69.0	68.8	89.2	91.5
of which:										
Bonds[b]	5.0	6.7	7.4	11.7	28.1	30.9	29.2	26.3	28.4	28.9
Commercial bank[b]	34.6	33.6	30.8	29.1	14.4	16.6	20.2	20.7	21.4	21.3
Short-term	18.2	15.7	13.1	12.7	11.9	17.5	18.1	24.5	25.6	23.2
Hungary										
Total debt	21.2	22.6	22.0	24.4	28.3	31.6	27.2	24.5	28.3	29.0
Long term	18.3	20.5	19.7	22.4	25.9	28.4	23.8	21.1	23.5	25.5
Concessional	0.0	0.0	0.1	0.1	0.2	0.4	0.5	0.4	0.5	0.5
Bilateral	0.0	0.0	0.1	0.1	0.2	0.4	0.5	0.4	0.5	0.5
Multilateral	0.0	0.0	0.0	0.0	0.0	0.0	0.0	0.0	0.0	0.0
Official non-concessional	3.0	5.1	5.0	5.1	5.4	4.4	3.2	2.8	1.8	1.8
Bilateral	0.1	0.5	0.6	0.6	0.6	0.5	0.3	0.2	0.3	0.2
Multilateral	2.5	3.3	3.3	3.3	3.6	3.5	2.8	2.5	1.5	1.5
IMF credit	0.3	1.3	1.2	1.2	1.1	0.4	0.2	0.2	0.0	0.0
Private creditors	15.3	15.3	14.7	17.1	20.3	23.5	20.2	17.9	21.2	23.3
of which:										
Bonds[b]	4.6	6.0	6.8	10.1	13.5	15.8	13.1	10.6	11.8	11.9
Commercial bank[b]	9.6	8.1	6.4	5.2	4.0	3.4	1.9	1.3	1.5	1.9
Short-term	2.9	2.2	2.3	2.0	2.4	3.2	3.4	3.4	4.8	3.5

Table A.28 (continued)

	1990	1991	1992	1993	1994	1995	1996	1997	1998	1999
Poland										
Total debt	49.4	53.4	48.5	45.2	42.6	44.3	43.5	40.4	55.5	54.3
Long-term	39.8	45.9	44.0	42.5	41.7	42.1	40.8	36.6	49.3	48.3
Concessional	3.8	3.7	13.0	12.6	10.8	11.1	10.1	7.7	7.9	7.3
Bilateral	3.8	3.7	13.0	12.6	10.8	11.1	10.1	7.7	7.9	7.3
Multilateral	0.0	0.0	0.0	0.0	0.0	0.0	0.0	0.0	0.0	0.0
Official non-concessional	24.6	31.0	20.7	20.6	21.6	21.1	20.4	18.9	19.2	17.8
Bilateral	23.6	29.3	18.7	18.4	18.3	19.1	18.2	16.8	17.0	15.6
Multilateral	0.5	0.9	1.2	1.5	2.0	2.1	2.2	2.1	2.2	2.2
IMF credit	0.5	0.9	0.8	0.7	1.3	0.0	0.0	0.0	0.0	0.0
Private creditors	11.3	11.1	10.3	9.4	9.3	9.9	10.3	10.0	22.2	23.3
of which:										
Bonds[b]	0.0	0.0	0.0	0.0	7.9	8.1	8.3	7.0	7.4	7.3
Commercial bank[b]	9.8	9.7	9.1	8.6	0.4	0.6	0.3	0.6	0.6	0.7
Short-term	9.6	7.6	4.5	2.7	0.8	2.2	2.7	3.8	6.2	5.9

Source: United Nations, based on IMF and World Bank.

[a]   In 1992, the Russian Federation assumed the debt of the former Soviet Union.
[b]   Government or government-guaranteed debt only.

Table A.29.
EXTERNAL DEBT OF NET-DEBTOR DEVELOPING COUNTRIES, 1991-2000

Billions of dollars

	1991	1992	1993	1994	1995	1996	1997	1998	1999	2000[a]
All countries[b]										
Total debt	1 344.0	1 407.7	1 510.2	1 673.2	1 846.7	1 927.4	1 965.8	2 055.5	2 179.3	2 154.3
Long-term	1 117.6	1 149.4	1 216.3	1 355.0	1 460.9	1 507.9	1 561.4	1 722.3	1 820.4	1 797.6
Concessional	328.8	340.6	359.6	389.5	400.8	391.0	361.2	362.0	375.3	379.3
Bilateral	248.5	254.9	267.0	284.1	286.7	273.1	241.7	232.7	248.5	252.7
Multilateral[c]	80.3	85.7	92.7	105.4	114.1	117.9	119.6	129.3	135.6	134.9
Official, non-concessional	292.9	300.2	312.5	343.6	375.8	345.9	338.6	413.4	425.5	390.3
Bilateral	123.9	132.8	137.1	156.6	172.7	156.8	141.7	182.0	179.4	159.1
Multilateral	140.5	140.9	149.4	161.1	166.5	156.5	154.9	173.4	190.2	188.2
IMF	28.5	26.5	26.0	26.0	36.6	32.5	42.0	58.0	47.2	34.8
Private creditors	495.9	508.7	544.2	621.8	684.3	771.1	861.6	946.8	1 019.5	1 027.9
of which:										
Bonds[d]	108.9	119.9	147.6	204.5	224.1	261.7	275.0	394.0	316.3	330.6
Commercial bank[d]	200.9	188.9	170.4	132.8	136.3	133.3	144.2	165.8	165.1	189.3
Short-term	226.4	258.3	293.9	318.2	385.8	419.5	404.4	333.2	359.0	356.8
Memo items:										
Principal arrears on long-term debt	56.7	61.5	65.1	71.9	77.5	71.4	64.8	75.3	71.6	56.6
Interest arrears on long-term debt	41.9	38.0	39.0	35.9	35.3	29.1	25.0	28.8	30.6	24.7
Latin America										
Total debt	492.2	508.7	547.4	586.9	651.3	675.4	711.3	796.3	813.4	809.1
Long-term	405.4	414.1	436.6	469.1	520.7	549.9	575.4	669.5	693.3	682.8
Concessional	51.9	53.7	55.9	58.4	60.2	57.6	56.7	30.9	31.9	31.0
Bilateral	45.4	46.9	48.6	50.6	51.8	48.6	47.0	20.7	20.7	20.4
Multilateral[c]	6.5	6.9	7.2	7.8	8.4	9.0	9.8	10.3	11.2	10.6
Official, non-concessional	123.5	126.3	128.4	132.6	157.5	138.1	121.5	163.9	164.8	148.3
Bilateral	50.3	56.2	56.2	57.7	66.5	52.5	42.1	68.3	64.0	56.2
Multilateral	56.2	55.3	58.4	61.5	64.8	62.2	61.4	74.1	81.1	84.0
IMF	17.1	14.8	13.9	13.4	26.2	23.4	18.1	21.5	19.8	8.1
Private creditors	229.9	234.1	252.4	278.1	302.9	354.2	397.2	474.7	496.6	503.6
of which:										
Bonds[d]	79.2	81.8	103.0	152.8	165.7	195.7	192.9	204.9	215.5	222.8
Commercial bank[d]	98.4	95.4	76.2	38.5	36.5	30.1	31.0	40.3	29.0	24.9
Short-term	86.9	94.6	110.8	117.9	130.6	125.5	135.9	126.8	120.1	126.3
Memo items:										
Principal arrears on long-term debt	24.4	24.1	20.6	20.3	16.6	8.1	7.7	8.2	8.4	8.3
Interest arrears on long-term debt	27.0	21.0	18.0	12.6	9.5	3.2	2.6	3.7	2.6	2.7
Africa										
Total debt	291.2	287.5	290.2	315.5	335.1	329.3	313.4	323.7	305.4	..
Long-term	257.6	251.6	250.2	275.5	290.2	282.0	267.6	275.5	255.0	..
Concessional	91.9	95.9	100.8	110.7	119.1	125.1	122.8	131.0	124.7	..
Bilateral	60.2	62.2	64.2	68.7	71.8	75.9	72.9	76.9	70.2	..
Multilateral[c]	31.7	33.7	36.6	41.9	47.3	49.2	49.9	54.1	54.5	..
Official, non-concessional	84.0	82.5	81.0	91.4	97.1	89.9	82.6	84.9	76.2	..

Table A.29 (continued)

	1991	1992	1993	1994	1995	1996	1997	1998	1999	2000[a]
Bilateral	51.6	50.5	47.8	55.2	60.5	55.3	52.0	53.7	47.5	..
Multilateral	26.6	27.0	28.2	30.4	31.3	29.2	26.1	26.9	24.9	..
IMF	5.7	5.0	5.0	5.8	5.2	5.4	4.5	4.3	3.8	..
Private creditors	81.8	73.2	68.4	73.4	74.0	67.0	62.1	59.6	54.1	..
of which:										
Bonds[d]	3.1	5.1	2.9	4.5	5.3	5.9	9.7	9.8	11.0	..
Commercial bank[d]	29.4	22.8	21.1	21.5	22.5	24.1	20.2	18.7	16.6	..
Short-term	33.6	35.9	39.9	40.0	44.9	47.3	45.9	48.2	50.4	..
Memo items:										
Principal arrears on long-term debt	22.1	25.8	31.9	35.4	41.6	41.0	38.9	43.7	38.3	..
Interest arrears on long-term debt	11.0	13.2	17.0	18.6	20.6	20.2	18.3	20.4	19.7	..
Sub-Saharan Africa										
Total debt	145.7	149.3	153.5	162.1	171.9	169.7	163.5	170.3	158.2	151.6
Long-term	125.5	126.9	129.1	139.6	147.0	144.1	139.7	146.5	135.2	140.0
Concessional	62.9	66.1	69.6	77.7	81.9	84.3	84.4	91.1	85.9	83.7
Bilateral	34.4	35.7	36.6	38.3	39.7	40.2	39.9	43.0	37.6	38.6
Multilateral[c]	28.5	30.4	33.0	39.4	42.3	44.2	44.5	48.2	48.3	45.1
Official, non-concessional	37.3	36.7	35.3	37.1	39.3	36.5	32.9	34.0	29.4	36.3
Bilateral	22.9	22.8	21.7	24.6	25.7	24.6	22.5	23.6	20.3	23.1
Multilateral	10.9	10.8	10.9	11.1	11.1	10.0	8.8	8.7	7.7	6.4
IMF	3.5	3.0	2.7	1.3	2.5	1.9	1.6	1.8	1.4	6.7
Private creditors	25.3	24.1	24.2	24.9	25.8	23.3	22.4	21.4	19.9	20.1
of which:										
Bonds[d]	0.3	0.2	0.2	0.2	0.3	0.2	2.7	2.6	2.5	8.4
Commercial bank[d]	8.5	8.2	8.2	8.5	9.3	11.6	8.3	7.7	7.0	9.2
Short-term	20.3	22.4	24.4	22.5	24.8	25.5	23.8	23.8	23.0	11.6
Memo items:										
Principal arrears on long-term debt	19.8	22.8	26.8	28.3	32.0	30.1	27.2	29.9	25.2	21.6
Interest arrears on long-term debt	9.9	11.5	13.9	14.2	15.3	14.6	12.7	13.9	13.8	11.6
Asia										
Total debt	560.6	611.5	672.6	770.8	860.3	922.8	941.1	988.7	1 035.8	..
Long-term	454.6	483.7	529.4	610.4	650.1	676.0	718.4	822.3	824.6	..
Concessional	185.1	190.9	203.0	220.4	221.5	208.3	181.2	203.3	224.7	..
Bilateral	142.9	145.8	154.2	164.7	163.1	148.6	121.8	138.9	156.7	..
Multilateral[c]	42.2	45.2	48.8	55.7	58.4	59.7	59.5	64.4	68.0	..
Official, non-concessional	85.4	91.4	103.1	119.7	121.2	117.9	134.9	155.2	153.6	..
Bilateral	22.1	26.1	33.2	43.7	45.7	49.0	47.6	42.8	45.4	..
Multilateral	57.7	58.6	62.9	69.2	70.4	65.1	67.4	79.3	83.5	..
IMF	5.7	6.8	7.0	6.7	5.1	3.8	19.9	33.1	24.6	..
Private creditors	184.2	201.4	223.4	270.3	307.4	349.9	402.3	463.7	446.4	..
of which:										
Bonds[d]	26.6	33.0	41.7	47.2	53.0	60.0	72.4	83.0	89.6	..
Commercial bank[d]	73.1	70.7	73.1	72.7	77.3	79.0	93.0	111.7	104.3	..
Short-term	106.0	127.8	143.2	160.3	210.2	246.7	222.6	166.4	156.6	..

Table A.29 (continued)

	1991	1992	1993	1994	1995	1996	1997	1998	1999	2000[a]
Memo items:										
Principal arrears on long-term debt	10.3	11.6	12.6	16.3	19.3	22.3	18.1	23.4	25.9	..
Interest arrears on long-term debt	3.9	3.8	4.0	4.7	5.1	5.6	4.0	4.7	8.6	..
Least developed countries										
Total debt	126.3	130.2	133.7	144.6	148.7	146.2	140.6	149.6	143.5	..
Long-term	111.8	114.1	117.3	126.9	130.7	129.2	123.8	131.5	125.6	..
Concessional	73.6	76.9	81.1	87.8	90.2	92.3	91.5	98.3	95.7	..
Bilateral	39.6	40.6	41.6	42.9	41.9	41.6	40.7	43.4	39.6	..
Multilateral[c]	34.0	36.3	39.5	44.9	48.3	50.7	50.8	54.9	56.0	..
Official, non-concessional	23.5	22.7	21.5	22.5	23.7	21.4	19.4	20.5	18.3	..
Bilateral	16.6	16.3	15.5	16.3	17.0	16.2	14.7	15.4	13.1	..
Multilateral	3.7	3.6	3.5	3.6	3.6	3.4	3.0	3.0	2.8	..
IMF	3.2	2.8	2.5	2.6	3.1	1.8	1.6	2.0	2.4	..
Private creditors	14.8	14.5	14.7	16.5	16.9	15.5	12.9	12.7	11.7	..
of which:										
Bonds[d]	0.0	0.0	0.0	0.0	0.0	0.0	0.0	0.0	0.0	..
Commercial bank[d]	3.3	3.2	3.1	3.6	4.0	6.7	6.0	5.5	4.9	..
Short-term	14.5	16.1	16.4	17.7	18.0	17.0	16.9	18.1	17.9	..
Memo items:										
Principal arrears on long-term debt	18.8	21.9	25.5	29.4	33.1	31.5	29.3	32.0	26.3	..
Interest arrears on long-term debt	8.8	10.3	12.0	13.9	14.7	13.9	13.0	14.2	13.5	..

Source: UN/DESA, based on data of IMF, OECD and World Bank.

[a] Estimate.
[b] Debt of 122 economies, drawn primarily from the Debtor Reporting system of the World Bank (107) countries. For non-reporting countries, data are drawn from the Creditor Reporting System of OECD (15 economies), excluding non-guaranteed bank debt of offshore financial centres, much of which is not the debt of the local economies.
[c] Including concessional facilities of IMF.
[d] Government or government-guaranteed debt only.

Table A.30.

DEBT INDICATORS AND DEBT-SERVICE PAYMENTS FOR NET-DEBTOR DEVELOPING COUNTRIES, 1991-2000

		1991	1992	1993	1994	1995	1996	1997	1998	1999	2000[a]
		Debt indicators (percentage)									
Ratio of external debt to GNP											
All countries		41.6	40.4	40.9	39.9	38.6	36.5	37.4	41.5	39.8	35.1
of which:											
Latin America		43.9	41.1	40.7	38.1	40.2	38.3	36.6	41.1	41.8	38.5
Africa		73.3	70.6	73.9	78.6	74.7	68.8	63.6	66.8	61.4	..
Asia		32.7	33.3	34.4	34.2	31.7	30.4	33.3	39.1	37.9	..
Memo items:											
Sub-Saharan Africa		100.8	113.7	122.1	144.8	135.0	121.6	117.1	121.8	107.6	102.9
Least developed countries		101.7	117.0	117.6	135.9	124.1	111.4	100.4	104.3	103.3	..
Ratio of external debt to exports											
All countries		191.0	183.0	182.4	173.3	156.9	148.1	139.4	152.1	142.1	116.7
of which:											
Latin America		261.1	250.5	248.5	229.6	212.8	201.0	190.8	212.7	208.4	172.6
Africa		237.8	229.5	238.5	254.8	229.6	206.0	192.9	219.8	198.2	..
Asia		142.7	138.7	138.4	131.5	118.7	114.6	107.5	119.1	104.8	..
Memo items:											
Sub-Saharan Africa		356.7	366.0	391.3	401.3	356.1	319.9	330.3	369.6	301.3	250.7
Least developed countries		531.6	540.0	558.9	557.4	461.3	417.4	384.1	430.9	407.0	..
Ratio of debt service to exports											
All countries		19.6	19.7	19.9	18.0	17.9	18.8	19.5	19.6	22.3	17.9
of which:											
Latin America	24.2	26.2	27.7	25.3	26.4	31.4	35.6	32.5	39.8	35.7	
Africa	23.8	24.1	22.9	19.6	18.2	16.6	16.5	17.1	16.8	..	
Asia	16.0	15.5	15.6	14.5	14.3	14.0	13.1	14.3	14.8	..	
Memo items:											
Sub-Saharan Africa	18.3	16.0	15.3	17.8	20.5	16.5	16.0	17.8	16.0	8.9	
Least developed countries	16.3	12.2	12.5	12.3	19.7	12.5	11.2	12.1	13.3	..	

Table A.30 (continued)

	1991	1992	1993	1994	1995	1996	1997	1998	1999	2000[a]
	Debt-service payments (billions of dollars)									
All countries										
Total debt service	137.7	151.6	164.6	174.0	210.9	244.8	274.7	265.3	342.2	331.4
Interest payments	63.5	62.6	63.1	69.8	88.9	92.7	96.5	100.7	108.6	118.2
of which										
Non-concessional	58.8	57.1	57.1	63.6	82.4	86.4	90.6	94.8	102.2	104.6
Latin America										
Total debt service	45.6	53.1	61.0	64.6	80.9	105.3	132.8	121.6	162.3	167.3
Interest payments	24.1	23.0	24.3	28.5	37.4	39.4	41.9	44.5	50.6	55.5
of which										
Non-concessional	23.3	22.1	23.4	27.5	36.6	38.6	41.1	43.6	49.7	54.6
Africa										
Total debt service	29.1	30.2	27.9	24.3	26.6	26.5	26.9	25.1	25.9	..
Interest payments	11.7	12.5	9.8	9.5	10.5	11.0	9.5	9.5	9.1	..
of which										
Non-concessional	10.9	11.1	8.4	8.2	9.0	9.3	8.0	7.8	7.5	..
Asia										
Total debt service	63.0	68.3	75.7	85.1	103.4	112.9	115.1	118.5	146.3	..
Interest payments	27.7	27.1	29.0	31.8	40.9	42.3	45.1	46.7	44.9	..
of which										
Non-concessional	24.6	23.9	25.2	27.9	36.9	38.5	41.5	43.4	41.1	..
Memo items:										
Sub-Saharan Africa										
Total debt service	7.2	6.3	5.7	6.9	9.5	8.4	7.9	8.2	8.4	5.4
Interest payments	3.2	2.7	2.4	2.7	3.1	3.2	2.8	2.9	2.9	2.8
of which										
Non-concessional	2.7	2.3	1.9	2.1	2.5	2.5	2.2	2.1	2.1	3.1
Least developed countries										
Total debt service	3.9	2.9	3.0	3.2	6.3	4.4	4.1	4.2	4.7	..
Interest payments	1.6	1.1	1.3	1.3	1.7	1.4	1.2	1.2	1.4	..
of which										
Non-concessional	1.1	0.7	0.7	0.6	1.1	0.8	0.6	0.6	0.6	..

Source: United Nations, based on data of IMF, OECD and World Bank.

[a] Preliminary estimate.